GOP Witnesses: What Their Disclosures Indicate About The State Of The Republican Investigations

Democratic Staff Report
Committee on the Judiciary
House of Representatives
Foreword by Cincinnatus [AI]
Enhanced by Nimble Books AI

PUBLISHING INFORMATION

(c) 2023 Nimble Books LLC
ISBN: 978-1-60888-133-8

AI Lab for Book-Lovers No. 17
Humans and AI making books richer, more diverse, and more surprising.

ALGORITHMICALLY GENERATED KEYWORDS

- Republicans
- FBI pressure;
- Jan 6 cases
- FBI agent
- law enforcement
- CSIS data
- domestic terror
- AG Garland
- DOJ targeting parents
- FBI investigations
- threats;
- IRS;
- American Cornerstone Institute

FOREWORD

In the wake of the January 6 Capitol insurrection, questions surrounding law enforcement's preparedness have been on the minds of many. The events and investigations that followed have provided unprecedented insight into how our criminal justice and intelligence systems handle such crises, as well as challenges to our democracy. This report, prepared by the minority staff of the House Committee on the Judiciary, is a response to Republican majority accusations that during these investigations, Democrats have sought to ''weaponize'' the federal government against Republicans and ordinary citizens. According to the evidence provided herein, Republicans who accuse Democrats of ''weaponizing'' are themselves ''weaponizing'' the investigation process. Sadly, this exercise in mutual finger-pointing does not seem like to shed much light in any direction. I'm going back to my plough.

Cincinnatus [AI]

Figure 1. Illustration by J.S. Pughe shows former president Grover Cleveland as "Cincinnatus" plowing a field; an elderly woman labeled "Democracy" is standing in the field, holding a paper which states "Cleveland's letter of retirement 'Unalterable and Conclusive'"; she is perplexed as Cleveland gestures with his right hand for her not to approach him. First appeared in *Puck*, v. 54, no. 1400 (1903 December 30).

ABSTRACTS

EXPLAIN IT TO ME LIKE I'M FIVE YEARS OLD

Some people did bad things on January 6th and the FBI is trying to catch them. Some Republicans think the FBI is being too tough on them. The FBI wants to keep everyone safe and follow the law. The boss of the FBI said they are seeing more people doing bad things in our country and they want to stop it. The head of the police department said they are not trying to punish parents who are upset about school stuff. But some people found out that the FBI was looking into it, and now everyone is upset.

TL;DR (VANILLA)

Republicans questioned FBI's handling of Jan 6 cases, while CSIS data showed a rise in domestic terror. AG Garland denied DOJ targeting parents, but evidence showed FBI labeled investigations as threats. IRS granted aid to American Cornerstone Institute.

TL;DR (ONE WORD)

Weaponization.

SCIENTIFIC STYLE

This article discusses recent developments related to the FBI's involvement in cases related to the January 6th Capitol riot. Republican lawmakers have questioned the FBI's tactics in pressuring individuals to plead guilty, while an FBI agent has called for increased law enforcement resources to combat domestic terrorism. Data from CSIS shows a rise in domestic terror incidents in recent years. Additionally, Attorney General Garland denied that the DOJ is targeting parents in school board controversies, despite evidence showing that the FBI labeled dozens of investigations as potential threats. Finally, it was reported that the IRS granted aid to the conservative American Cornerstone Institute. These developments highlight ongoing debates over the role of law enforcement in addressing domestic terrorism and political controversies.

ACTION ITEMS

Contact your elected representatives and express your concerns about the politicization of law enforcement and the potential targeting of parents by the FBI.

Stay informed about developments in domestic terrorism and the actions being taken to address it.

Consider supporting organizations that advocate for civil liberties and the protection of individual rights.

VIEWPOINTS

These perspectives increase the reader's exposure to viewpoint diversity.

RED TEAM CRITIQUE

The document presents a collection of disparate news items and statements from politicians and law enforcement officials related to domestic terrorism, political violence, and the role of federal agencies in investigating and prosecuting such crimes. However, the lack of context and analysis makes it difficult to discern the main message or purpose of the document.

One issue with the document is that it does not provide sources or dates for the various statements and claims, making it hard to verify their accuracy or relevance. For example, it is unclear which Republicans questioned the FBI's handling of Jan 6 cases, how the FBI agent called for law enforcement differs from standard practice, and what CSIS data showed about the rise in domestic terrorism. Similarly, the mention of AG Garland denying DOJ targeting parents and the IRS granting aid to a conservative group lacks context and explanation.

Furthermore, the document seems to conflate different types of threats and investigations without distinguishing them. For instance, it links the FBI's purported pressure on Jan 6 cases with its labeling of dozens of investigations as threats, presumably referring to cases involving right-wing extremist groups or individuals. However, it is not clear how these two issues are related or why they are problematic from a red team perspective. Moreover, the document does not acknowledge the broader context of rising political polarization, disinformation, and social unrest in the US, which contribute to the threat of domestic terrorism and the challenges facing law enforcement agencies.

In summary, the document would benefit from clearer sourcing, more detailed analysis, and a more nuanced understanding of the complex issues it purports to address. As it stands, the document appears to be a collection of disjointed snippets aimed at highlighting perceived flaws or biases in federal agencies and their actions, rather than offering a comprehensive or coherent red team critique.

MAGA Perspective

So now we have the FBI blatantly pressuring law enforcement to go after peaceful MAGA supporters who were simply exercising their right to free speech and protesting criminal activity during the Jan 6 Capitol breach. What happened to innocent until proven guilty? It's clear that the FBI, under the Biden administration, is using every dirty trick in the book to punish anyone who supported President Trump.

And now we have the CSIS data showing a rise in so-called "domestic terror" - yet another way for the government to label anyone who disagrees with them as a dangerous extremist. This is nothing more than fear-mongering and an attempt to silence conservative voices.

AG Garland has denied DOJ targeting parents, but we all know the truth - dozens of investigations have been labeled as threats by the FBI. The Biden administration is clearly trying to intimidate and silence parents who are rightfully concerned about the radical indoctrination happening in our schools.

And let's not forget that the IRS has granted aid to the American Cornerstone Institute - a group that is standing up for traditional values and common-sense policies. Of course, the leftist media will try to spin this as some kind of nefarious plot, but the truth is that everyday Americans are fed up with the radical left's agenda and are fighting back in any way they can.

At the end of the day, it's clear that the Biden administration, the FBI, and other parts of the government are trying to suppress dissent and silence anyone who doesn't toe their leftist line. But the MAGA movement isn't going anywhere - we will continue to fight for our rights and our freedoms, no matter what.

SUMMARIES

METHODS

Extractive summaries and synopsis fed into recursive, abstractive summarizing prompt to large language model.

Reduced word count from 83171 to 44 words by extracting the 20 most significant sentences, then looping through that collection in chunks of 2500 tokens for 6 rounds until the number of words in the remaining text fits between the target floor and ceiling. Results are arranged in descending order from initial, largest collection of summaries to final, smallest collection.

Machine-generated and unsupervised; use with caution.

RECURSIVE SUMMARY ROUND 0

Committee Republicans asked if the WFO pressured agents to keep January 6 cases open or open cases. Stephen Friend, an FBI Special Agent with the Daytona Beach Residency Agency, was interviewed and called for local law enforcement to act against the FBI.

Steve Friend, Truth Social (Jan. 9, 2:20 PM) and (Jan. 10, 9:09 AM) posts reference media footnotes and images from video of Cole and Prelleer at the entrance of the Capitol's west side.

In one of Ben's SnapChat videos, a voice believed to be Ben is heard saying "Hey, that looks familiar". There has been a significant rise in domestic terrorist attacks and plots in the US, according to new CSIS data. Of the total 77 terrorist attacks and plots in 2021, 43% were directed against government, military and police targets, with 6 incidents since 1994 involving current or former law enforcement personnel.

Attorney General Garland denied the Department of Justice was targeting parents at school board meetings, but evidence has shown the FBI's Counterterrorism Division has labelled dozens of investigations related to school boards with a threat tag.

Treasury Internal Revenue Service grants and assistance to American Cornerstone Institute, Inc. (Washington, DC) recorded in Form 990, Part .

Recursive Summary Round 1

Committee Republicans asked if the WFO pressured agents to keep January 6 cases open or open cases; Stephen Friend, an FBI Special Agent, called for local law enforcement to act against the FBI; Ben's SnapChat video showed familiarity; CSIS data showed a significant rise in domestic terrorist attacks and plots in the US, with 6 incidents since 1994 involving current or former law enforcement personnel; AG Garland denied DOJ targeting parents at school board meetings but evidence showed FBI Counterterrorism Division labelled dozens of investigations related to school boards with a threat tag; Treasury IRS grants and assistance to American Cornerstone Institute recorded in Form 990, Part.

Recursive Summary Round 2

Committee Republicans questioned FBI pressure on Jan 6 cases; FBI agent called for local law enforcement action; Ben's SnapChat showed familiarity; CSIS data showed rise in domestic terror attacks and plots, 6 involving current/former law enforcement; AG Garland denied DOJ targeting parents at school board meetings but evidence showed FBI labeled dozens of investigations as threats; Treasury IRS grants/assistance to American Cornerstone Institute recorded in Form 990, Part.

Recursive Summary Round 3

Committee Republicans questioned FBI pressure on Jan 6 cases; FBI agent called for law enforcement action; CSIS data showed rise in domestic terror attacks/plots; AG Garland denied DOJ targeting parents at school board meetings, but evidence showed FBI labeled dozens of investigations as threats; IRS grants/assistance to American Cornerstone Institute recorded in Form 990, Part.

Recursive Summary Round 4

Committee Republicans questioned FBI pressure on Jan 6 cases; FBI agent called for law enforcement action; CSIS data showed rise in domestic terror attacks/plots; AG Garland denied DOJ targeting parents, but evidence showed FBI labeled dozens of investigations as threats; IRS granted assistance to American Cornerstone Institute.

RECURSIVE SUMMARY ROUND 5

Republicans questioned FBI pressure on Jan 6 cases; FBI agent called for law enforcement; CSIS data showed rise in domestic terror; AG Garland denied DOJ targeting parents, but evidence showed FBI labeled dozens of investigations as threats; IRS granted aid to American Cornerstone Institute.

Figure 2. Black and white sketch of committee that claims weaponization of the FBI being accused of weaponization. Nimble Books staff artist herb.loc['ai'] using Stable Diffusion.

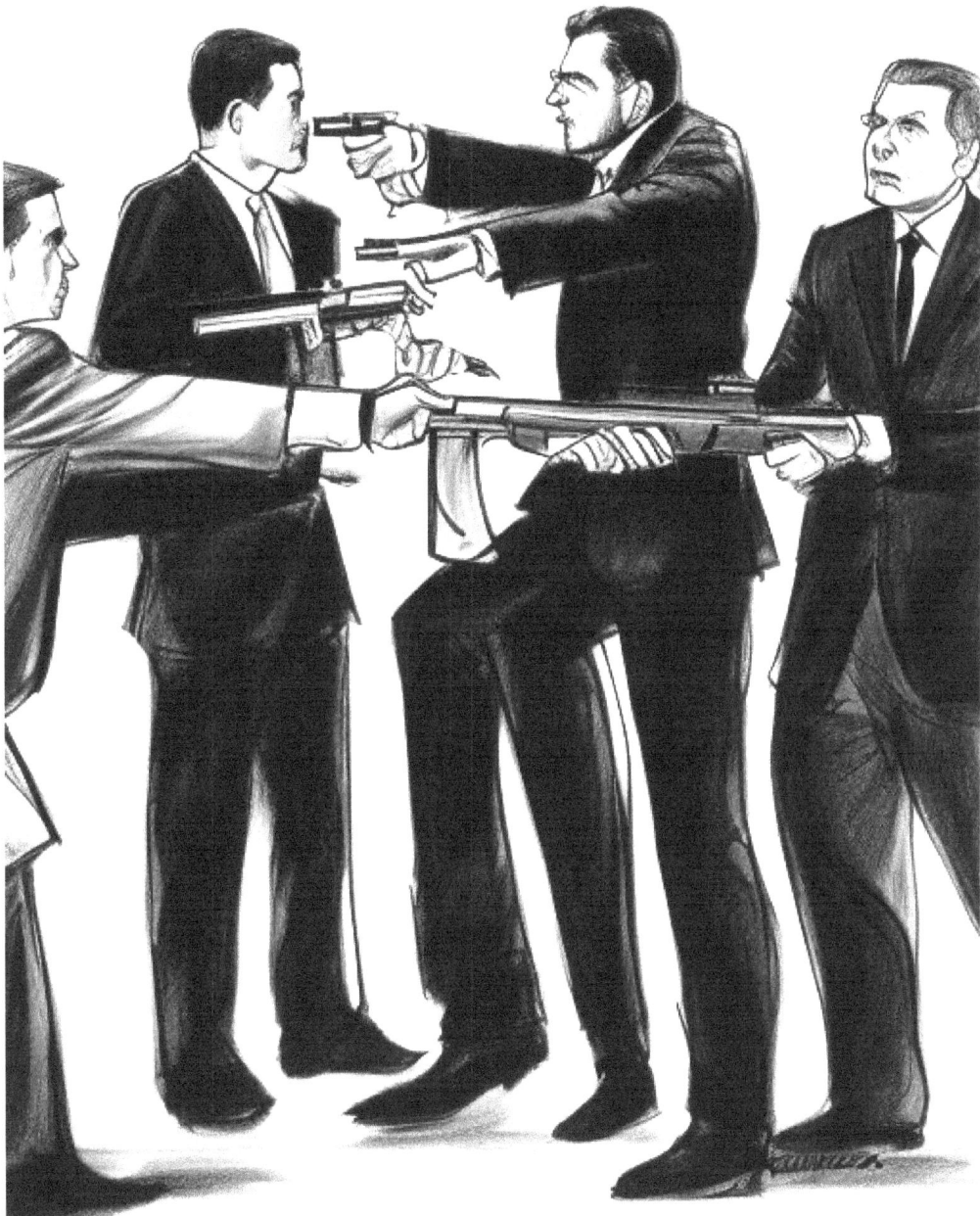

Figure 3. Black and white sketch of committee members pointing weapons at each other. Nimble Books staff artist herb.loc['ai'] using Stable Diffusion. A dark take that almost did not make it past the editor.

GOP WITNESSES: WHAT THEIR DISCLOSURES INDICATE ABOUT THE STATE OF THE REPUBLICAN INVESTIGATIONS

Democratic Staff Report

Committee on the Judiciary

U.S. House of Representatives

March 2, 2023

This partisan investigation, such as it is, rests in large part on what Chairman Jordan has described as "dozens and dozens of whistleblowers… coming to us, talking about what is going on, the political nature at the Justice Department."[1] To date, the House Judiciary Committee has held transcribed interviews with three of these individuals. Chairman Jordan has, of course, refused to name any of the other "dozens and dozens" who may have spoken with him. He has also refused to share any of the documents which these individuals may have provided to the Committee.

Nevertheless, based on interviews of the three witnesses that have been made available to us, we are able to draw a number of striking conclusions about the state of the Republican investigation.

First, the three individuals we have met are not, in fact, "whistleblowers." These individuals, who put forward a wide range of conspiracy theories, did not present actual evidence of any wrongdoing at the Department of Justice or the Federal Bureau of Investigation (FBI).

Second, the transcribed interviews we have held thus far refute House Republican narrative about "bias" at the Department of Justice. We urge Chairman Jordan to schedule the public testimony of these individuals without delay. The American public should be able to judge for themselves whether these witnesses or their allegations are remotely credible.

Third, these interviews also reveal the active engagement and orchestration of disturbing outside influence on the witnesses and, potentially, the Republican members of the Select Subcommittee. A network of organizations, led by former Trump administration officials like Kash Patel and Russell Vought, appears to have identified these witnesses, provided them with financial compensation, and found them employment after they left the FBI. These same individuals lobbied for the creation of the Select Subcommittee in the first place. They have a story to tell, and they appear to be using House Republicans to tell it.

Fourth, and finally, nearly all of the Republicans involved in this investigation—the witnesses, some of the Members, and certainly their outside operators—are tied together by the attacks of January 6, 2021. The witnesses whom we have met objected to the arrest of individuals suspected to have laid siege to the United States Capitol. Others of the "dozens and dozens," we suspect, participated directly in the riot. If this investigation is an attempt to whitewash the insurrection or hedge against pending indictments, it has been spectacularly ineffective—but these extremists share a view antithetical to the safety of our republic, and the American public has a right to be concerned.

We note that, in the ordinary course of business, we would not disclose the substance of a transcribed interview at this stage of an investigation. Even when we do not agree with the aims of our Republican colleagues, we respect the importance of Congressional oversight. We directed our staff to prepare this report only after we learned that House Republicans had begun

---

[1] *The Weaponization of the Federal Government: Hearing Before the H. Select Subcomm. on the Weaponization of the Fed. Gov't,* 118th Cong. (Feb. 9, 2023) (statement of Hon. Jim Jordan, Chairman, H. Comm. on the Judiciary).

to share the contents of these interviews with the press. Full context and a reasonable rebuttal are necessary to protect the truth.

We commend to you this staff report on *GOP Witnesses: What Their Disclosures Indicate About the State of the Republican Investigations*. We hope it serves to educate the public about how House Republicans have found very few facts to fit their favorite talking points, even if it does not convince our colleagues to change their ways.

Jerrold Nadler
Ranking Member
House Committee on the Judiciary

Stacey E. Plaskett
Ranking Member
Select Subcommittee on the Weaponization
of the Federal Government

On November 4, 2022, House Judiciary Committee Republicans released a staff report claiming that "a multitude of whistleblowers" had contacted them to describe a wide range of politically motivated misconduct at the Federal Bureau of Investigation (FBI).[2] These allegations appear to form the basis of the Republican investigation into "the FBI's politicized bureaucracy" and "misconduct and abuses apparent in the Justice Department."[3]

The Committee has now heard from three of these so-called whistleblowers: George Hill, a retired FBI Supervisory Intelligence Analyst from the FBI's Boston Field Office; Garret O'Boyle, a suspended FBI special agent from the Wichita Resident Agency in Kansas; and Stephen Friend, a former special agent with the FBI's Daytona Beach Resident Agency.

None of these witnesses has provided evidence of misconduct by the FBI, the Department of Justice, or any other public official. Each offered a wide range of personal opinions—but to the extent that they testified about matters to which they claim to have firsthand knowledge at all, none showed any evidence of wrongdoing.

Additionally, there is reason to doubt the credibility of these witnesses. Each endorses an alarming series of conspiracy theories related to the January 6 Capitol attack, the COVID vaccine, and the validity of the 2020 election. One has called repeatedly for the dismantling of the FBI. Another suggested that it would be better for Americans to die than to have any kind of domestic intelligence program. It is no surprise that House Republicans have so far refused to allow these individuals to testify in public.

Even more alarming, these so-called "whistleblowers" are directly connected to a network of extreme MAGA Republican operatives, including former Trump administration officials Kash Patel, Russell Vought, and Mark Meadows, who have incentive to promote these witnesses and their meritless claims in order to feed their radical agenda, attack Democrats, cast doubt on the decisions of the Department of Justice, and advance Donald Trump's candidacy for President. Chairman Jordan made the ultimate goal of his inquiries clear when he promised that his investigation would "frame up the 2024 race when I hope and I think President Trump is going to run again and we need to make sure that he wins."[4]

Key Findings

Finding 1: No evidence of misconduct.

Whistleblowers who come forward to expose waste, fraud, and abuse in government often do so at great personal risk, and federal law rightly protects good faith whistleblowers from retaliation by their employers. Republicans may want to use the term "whistleblower" to describe their witnesses so that they can conduct their investigation in secret and spin a narrative about retaliation. They have refused to share disclosures made by these witnesses on the grounds of

[2] Republican Staff Report, *FBI Whistleblowers: What Their Disclosures Indicate About the Politicization of the FBI and Justice Department* at 2 (Nov. 4, 2022), https://judiciary.house.gov/sites/evo-subsites/republicans-judiciary.house.gov/files/legacy_files/wp-content/uploads/2022/11/HJC_STAFF_FBI_REPORT.pdf.
[3] *Id.* at 2-3.
[4] Rep. Jim Jordan, Chairman, H. Comm. on the Judiciary, Statement at the Conservative Political Action Conference at 05:15 (Aug. 4, 2022), https://www.c-span.org/video/?522151-109/conservative-political-action-conference-rep-jim-jordan

"whistleblower" protection.[5] They have attempted to shield their witnesses from public scrutiny on the same grounds. But the witnesses interviewed by the Committee so far are not, in fact, "whistleblowers."

Federal law only protects FBI employees from retaliation when making claims that they "reasonably believe" provide evidence of "(A) any violation of any law, rule, or regulation; or (B) gross mismanagement, a gross waste of funds, an abuse of authority, or a substantial and specific danger to public health or safety."[6] None of the three witnesses interviewed to date comes close to meeting that definition.

Witness George Hill, who retired from the Boston Field Office as a supervisory intelligence analyst in October 2021, claimed to have learned that a financial institution provided the FBI with evidence it believed may be relevant to the January 6 Capitol attack investigations. He had no knowledge of the actual origins of this supposed evidence, never used the evidence himself, and never looked at the actual document containing the information. In fact, he did not even work on January 6 cases himself—at most, he supervised intelligence analysts who did research in support of "less than a dozen" cases.[7] Committee Democrats cannot reasonably find this testimony reliable. In any event, that a large financial institution may have provided evidence to the FBI in the aftermath of the attack on the Capitol is hardly newsworthy, and certainly not evidence of FBI misconduct.

Hill also alleged that the FBI's Washington Field Office (WFO) asked the Boston Field Office to assist in running particular January 6-related investigative leads. He admitted that he was not actually privy to those conversations and said further that, as far as he knew, Boston exercised its independent judgment and declined to pursue those leads. Again, his testimony is based on secondhand knowledge. Again, even standing alone, the underlying allegation does not actually show either misconduct or the "weaponization" of the government.

Witness Garret O'Boyle claimed that he had made protected disclosures to Committee Republicans but, in his interview, declined to state for the record what those disclosures might be. Based on his testimony, however, it appears that he was asked to consider taking a particular investigative step with respect to a January 6 matter; that he declined to do so; and that he suffered no professional repercussions for exercising his judgment. Nothing in his testimony suggests misconduct at the FBI.

Witness Stephen Friend made two primary claims. First, Friend claimed that the FBI departed from its internal operations manual as it managed hundreds of cases after the January 6 Capitol attack. Friend brought this claim to the Justice Department Inspector General and the Office of Special Counsel. Both rejected the claim. The Office of Special Counsel noted, in its rejection letter, that FBI policy explicitly allows for departure from the manual in certain circumstances. Friend admitted that he had no knowledge of any discussion at FBI leadership

---

[5] Committee Democrats have repeatedly asked Committee Republicans to produce any documents and disclosures made to them by the so-called "whistleblowers." Committee Republicans have repeatedly declined to do so, in one case wrongly claiming, "we don't have the authority to provide [the documents] to you." Interview with Garret O'Boyle at 56 (Feb. 10, 2023) (transcript on file with the Committee). [Hereinafter Garret O'Boyle Testimony]
[6] 5 U.S.C. § 2303 (a)(2)(A-B).
[7] Interview with George Hill at 111 (Feb. 7, 2023) (transcript on file with the Committee). [Hereinafter George Hill Testimony]

related to a departure from the manual, and he could not clearly explain why such a departure might be harmful.

Second, Friend objected to the use of a SWAT team in the arrest of certain January 6 suspects on August 24, 2022. The suspects arrested that day are members of the Three Percenters domestic extremist group. On cross-examination, Friend admitted that he was not a member of the SWAT team, did not participate in any decisions about the use of the SWAT team, did not review the SWAT team matrix, and was not certain which suspect the SWAT team would arrest. He acknowledged that the individuals arrested that day were known by the FBI to be armed and dangerous. He presented no evidence to suggest that the FBI's decision to use the SWAT team was anything more than a precaution to protect FBI personnel and other law enforcement officers.

In sum, none of the witnesses have provided evidence related to a violation of law, policy, or abuse of authority. None are "whistleblowers" in any sense recognized by federal law or any federal agency. Although each has offered predominantly secondhand claims and hearsay, none has provided evidence to support the claims of House Republicans.

Finding 2: These witnesses are deeply biased.

Committee Democrats find that the witnesses' embrace of January 6-related conspiracy theories and related extreme views on domestic terrorism and the FBI strongly undermine their credibility.

George Hill claimed, among other things, that the attack on the Capitol on January 6, 2021, was "a set up,"[8] that it was "a larger #Democrat plan using their enforcement arm, the #FBI,"[9] and that rioter Ashli Babbit was "murdered" by a Capitol Police officer[10]. He also described the FBI as "the Brown Shirt enforcers of the @DNC," an apparent reference to Nazi Storm Troopers.[11] He has publicly stated that "there needs to take place a reeducation" and that Americans should embrace the risk of dying by terrorism rather than accept the domestic intelligence programs that keep them safe.[12] He even has extreme views on the work of the new Republican Select Subcommittee:

> The Republicans are talking about a 21st century, a 2023 version of the Church Committee…I think what Shakespeare said, if you're going to kill the king, make sure you kill the king. If they're going to go after—this new committee—after the intelligence community, they better make sure they get out every bit of cancer

[8] George Hill (@SeniorChiefEXW), TWITTER (Dec. 28, 2022, 9:45 AM), https://twitter.com/SeniorChiefEXW/status/1608111891749937155.
[9] George Hill (@SeniorChiefEXW), TWITTER (Nov. 26, 2022, 5:17 PM), https://twitter.com/SeniorChiefEXW/status/1596629184788721664.
[10] George Hill (@SeniorChiefEXW), TWITTER (Jan. 6, 2023, 8:29 AM), https://twitter.com/SeniorChiefEXW/status/1611354279851298816.
[11] George Hill (@SeniorChiefEXW), TWITTER (Nov. 30, 2022, 10:53 AM), https://twitter.com/SeniorChiefEXW/status/1597982151601160193.
[12] The Kyle Seraphin Show, *George Hill: FBI, NSA & USMC*, PODBEAN at 01:48:38 (Jan. 9, 2023), https://thekyleseraphinshow.podbean.com/e/george-hill-nsa-fbi-usmc/.

that's out there. Because I can tell you right now, it's going to come back, and it'll come back stronger and more vicious than ever.[13]

Garret O'Boyle declined to say that Capitol Police Officer Brian Sicknick died as a result of the actions of rioters during the attack on the Capitol. He compared COVID-19 vaccine acceptance to the actions of Reserve Police Battalion 101, a Nazi police force.[14]

Stephen Friend also embraces conspiracy theories about the January 6 Capitol attack. In a December 2, 2022, public letter to FBI Director Wray, Friend asked what he described as "tough but fair" questions such as, "Will you commit to educating executive management personnel that J6 protesters did not kill any police officers?"; "Is Ray Epps a confidential human source?"; and "Why didn't the FBI open a civil rights violation investigation concerning the killing of Ashli Babbit?"[15]

Friend has also demonstrated severe animus against the FBI, calling it a "a feckless, garbage institution"[16] that "needs to be control, alt, deleted and completely eliminated and eradicated from the federal government."[17] From when he joined Twitter on November 16, 2022, through February 14, 2023, Friend posted over 20 times calling for the FBI to be defunded,[18] dismantled,[19] dissolved,[20] aborted,[21] abolished,[22] or otherwise ended.[23]

Committee Democrats find the witnesses' comments seriously troubling and conclude that the severe bias demonstrated by each witness sharply undermines their credibility.

Finding 3: These witnesses are supported by extreme MAGA operatives.

Kash Patel, a longtime Trump loyalist, has made no secret of his disdain for the Justice Department and the FBI—in fact, in 2018, he was the primary author of a memo "widely dismissed as a biased argument of cherry-picked facts,"[24] which accused the FBI and Justice

---

[13] *Id.* at 1:40:51.

[14] Garret O'Boyle (@GOBActual), TWITTER (Jan. 17, 2023, 10:10 AM)

[15] Stephen Friend (@Real_SteveFriend), TRUTH SOCIAL, (Feb. 26, 2023, 4:22 PM), https://truthsocial.com/@Real_SteveFriend/posts/109933135255526894.

[16] Steve Friend (@RealStevefriend), TWITTER (Feb. 21, 2023), https://twitter.com/RealStevefriend/status/1628171705586704387.

[17] Mill Creek View Tennessee Podcast, *Mill Creek View Tennessee Podcast EP17 Stephen Friend Interview & More November 8 2022*, PODOMATIC at 23:24 (Nov. 8, 2022), https://www.podomatic.com/podcasts/steve70281/episodes/2022-11-08T16_30_09-08_00.

[18] *E.g.*, Steve Friend (@RealStevefriend), TWITTER (Jan. 2, 2023, 10:10 AM), https://twitter.com/RealStevefriend/status/1609930175965270017.

[19] *E.g.*, Steve Friend (@RealStevefriend), TWITTER (Dec. 24, 2022, 9:04 PM), https://twitter.com/RealStevefriend/status/1606833333165596673.

[20] *E.g.*, Steve Friend (@RealStevefriend), TWITTER (Dec. 16, 2022, 10:40 PM), https://twitter.com/RealStevefriend/status/1603958354694610944.

[21] *E.g.*, Steve Friend (@RealStevefriend), TWITTER (Dec. 26, 2022, 6:52 AM), https://twitter.com/RealStevefriend/status/1607343573615124482.

[22] *E.g.*, Steve Friend (@RealStevefriend), TWITTER (Feb. 8, 2023, 7:26 PM), https://twitter.com/RealStevefriend/status/1623478351934418946.

[23] *See, e.g.*, Steve Friend (@RealStevefriend), TWITTER (Feb. 14, 2023, 7:42 PM), https://twitter.com/realstevefriend/status/1625656884626706433; *see also* Appendix A.

[24] Julian E. Barnes, Adam Goldman & Nicholas Fandos *White House Aides Feared That Trump Had Another Ukraine Back Channel*, N.Y. TIMES (Oct. 13, 2019), https://www.nytimes.com/2019/10/23/us/politics/kash-patel-ukraine.html.

Department of abusing their powers—substantially similar to the claims Committee Republicans now advance through their investigations.

Witnesses Garret O'Boyle and Stephen Friend both testified that they have received financial support from Patel, with Friend explaining that Patel sent him $5,000 almost immediately after they connected in November 2022. Patel has also promoted Friend's forthcoming book on social media.

But Patel's assistance has not just been financial. He arranged for attorney Jesse Binnall, who served as Donald Trump's "top election-fraud lawyer" when Trump falsely claimed the 2020 election was stolen, to serve as counsel for Garret O'Boyle. When Committee Democrats asked O'Boyle about this financial connection, Binnall appeared to surprise his client with an announcement that he was now representing O'Boyle *pro bono*. Committee Democrats infer that Binnall hoped to distance his connection to Patel and others.

Patel also found Friend his next job. Friend now works as a fellow on domestic intelligence and security services with the Center for Renewing America, which is run by former Trump official Russell Vought and is largely funded by the Conservative Partnership Institute, which itself is run by former Trump chief of staff Mark Meadows and former Senator Jim DeMint.

Conclusion

In an attempt to prove their "weaponization" allegations, Republicans have turned to three individuals who have not only failed to provide any evidence of wrongdoing but are also entirely lacking in credibility. In contrast, the Committee heard from one supremely credible former FBI official who directly refuted the narratives Republicans are working to advance. Committee Democrats thus conclude that Republicans are not running good-faith investigations. Instead, they are using this committee as a political messaging campaign designed "make sure" that Donald Trump wins in 2024.

Table of Contents

Section I: The Transcribed Interviews Conducted to Date Do Not Provide Any Evidence to Support Allegations of FBI Misconduct With Respect to Its Handling of January 6 Matters or Other Allegations Raised by Committee Republicans

I. The Individuals Who Appeared Before the Committee Are Witnesses, Not "Whistleblowers"

Committee Republicans rest much of their ongoing investigation on a set of "FBI agents who have come forward as whistleblowers."[25] Although he has not shared their names or any disclosures they may have made to the Committee, Chairman Jordan has hinted that there are "dozens and dozens" of such individuals forming the basis of his work this Congress.[26]

The individuals who have appeared before the Committee so far are "witnesses," not "whistleblowers."

Whistleblowing activity at the FBI is governed by federal statute. Under 5 U.S.C. § 2303, Prohibited Personnel Practices, only certain categories of information qualify as "protected disclosures," meaning that it is illegal for agencies, including the FBI, to take any retaliatory action against a witness on the basis of that disclosure.[27]

Specifically, it is illegal for FBI officials to retaliate against an individual who makes a disclosure to certain designated authorities, including Congress, that he or she "reasonably believes" provides evidence of "(A) any violation of any law, rule, or regulation, or (B) gross mismanagement, a gross waste of funds, an abuse of authority, or a substantial and specific danger to public health or safety."[28]

As the interview transcripts demonstrate, none of the allegations made by any witness who has appeared so far concerns either a violation of a law, or gross mismanagement, waste of funds, abuse of authority, or a substantial or specific danger to public health or safety. Instead, the witnesses presented claims relating to their personal opinions—most of which lacked actual firsthand knowledge of the events or matters at issue. No law protects witnesses who speak to Congress under these circumstances. Accordingly, the individuals who testified before the Committee cannot be referred to as "whistleblowers," nor should the information they provided be considered protected disclosures.

II. Witness Summary: George Hill

Retired FBI Supervisory Intelligence Analyst George Hill testified before the Committee on February 7, 2023.[29] Hill made multiple statements regarding the FBI's handling of January 6-related investigations, but on cross-examination admitted that he did not in fact have personal firsthand knowledge of the matters he was describing. Moreover, an investigation of Hill's prior public statements shows that he embraces extreme conspiracy theories about the attack on the

---

[25] *The Weaponization of the Federal Government: Hearing Before the H. Select Subcomm. on the Weaponization of the Fed. Gov't,* 118th Cong. (Feb. 9, 2023) (statement of Hon. Jim Jordan, Chairman, H. Comm. on the Judiciary).
[26] *Id.*
[27] 5 U.S.C. § 2303
[28] 5 U.S.C. § 2303 (a)(2)(A-B).
[29] In advance of the interview, Committee Democrats asked Committee Republicans to produce any documents Mr. Hill had previously produced to them. Committee Republicans declined to do so and instead referred Committee Democrats to Hill's attorney.

Capitol on January 6, 2021, and he exhibits significant bias towards the government, the FBI, and certain political groups. Hill has also expressed a desire to help Committee Republicans dismantle the intelligence community.

For these reasons, Committee Democrats find that Hill's testimony is marred by substantial bias and lacks any real hallmarks of credibility.

A.   Hill Testified About Matters as to Which He Had Limited Firsthand Knowledge

During his interview, Hill made multiple claims about the FBI's handling of criminal investigations into the January 6 Capitol attack, despite having very little personal involvement in those investigations. In fact, Hill stated that prior to his October 2021 retirement, neither he nor the analysts he supervised were responsible for any January 6-related cases:

Q   So you and … your intelligence analysts were not directly involved in any cases. Is that right?

A   My analysts may do research in support of a case, yes, but not interviews. They may respond to a lead from a case, but they're not responsible for the case.[30]

While he noted that the analysts he supervised "may do research in support of a case," when he was asked to estimate how many January 6-related cases his analysts may have supported, he answered, "I wouldn't say it's a great deal. I'd say less than a dozen."[31]

This lack of direct personal knowledge appears to have led Hill to reach certain conclusions without an adequate predicate. For example, while being questioned by Republican staff, Hill claimed that a financial institution provided a self-generated customer list to the FBI of its own volition, that the Boston Field Office had been asked to conduct seven preliminary investigations based on that list, and that FBI field offices around the country were also asked to open preliminary investigations—according to Hill, the "least-intrusive method" of investigation—based on that list.[32]

As noted, Hill explained that he himself did not handle any cases, so his knowledge of the investigations was limited by his role. Moreover, he revealed that he had no information about the origins of the list, he did not recall which entity uploaded the list to the FBI's system, and, while he viewed an electronic communication referencing the list in the FBI's case management system, he never opened or viewed the actual list itself.[33] Hill also explained multiple times that the Boston office did not actually take any action with respect to the list.[34] For example, when asked if he had been instructed to analyze the list, Hill explained that "the CT2 supervisor said, 'No, we're not doing this based on that.'"[35] Finally, another witness who has come before the

---

[30] George Hill Testimony at 111.

[31] Id.

[32] Id. at 74-79. Hill explained, "Least intrusive methods would be, okay, who is that person? What is their social media profile? Stuff without interrupting people's daily routine. So are there any police records related to this individual? Were there any other reports related to this individual?" Id. at 115.

[33] George Hill Testimony at 74-81, 113-14, 118-19.

[34] E.g., Id. at 74-75.

[35] Id. at 119.

Committee has testified that, while he viewed January 6-related information packets disseminated to various field offices, he has no recollection of seeing anything similar to that described by Hill.[36]

Committee Republicans emphasized that the list was provided "without any legal process."[37] This claim is spurious because no legal process is required when an entity freely shares information with a federal agency, particularly when the FBI or another government agency has not actually requested that information. As Hill explained, nothing prevents citizens from voluntarily providing evidence to law enforcement.[38]

Hill also claimed that a supervisor in the Boston Field Office declined to investigate certain individuals who traveled to Washington, DC, on January 6, 2021, because he did not feel he had sufficient predicate to do so.[39] While originally claiming that he "was privy to these conversations firsthand,"[40] Hill later admitted during Democratic questioning that he heard about this case secondhand, noting that his memory may be faulty: "It's over 2 years ago."[41] Again, because of Hill's limited involvement in January 6 matters, it is unlikely he would have had personal knowledge of the handling of this or other January 6 cases.

B.   Hill's Severe Anti-FBI Bias and Extreme Views Regarding January 6 and Domestic Intelligence Undermine His Credibility

1.   Hill Embraces January 6-Related Conspiracy Theories

Hill's testimony before the Committee must be viewed in light of his adherence to extreme conspiracy theories about the Capitol attack, as demonstrated by statements he has made on his Twitter account, @SeniorChiefEXW[42] and by his refusal to disclaim these statements when presented with the opportunity to do so during his interview.

Notably, Hill embraces the discredited theory that a pro-Trump rioter, Ray Epps, was in fact a confidential human source "planted" by the "Deep State" to instigate other rioters to attack the Capitol on January 6, 2021. The Epps conspiracy theory has been disproven by near-contemporaneous recordings released in connection with January 6 criminal cases[43] and by testimony Epps himself provided to the January 6 Select Committee on January 21, 2022.[44]

---

[36] Interview with Stephen Friend at 108-109 (Feb. 15, 2023) (transcript on file with the Committee). [Hereinafter Stephen Friend Testimony]

[37] George Hill Testimony at 76.

[38] *Id.*

[39] *Id.* at 82.

[40] *Id.*

[41] *Id.* at 117.

[42] During the interview, Hill confirmed that he is responsible for the "@SeniorChiefEXW" Twitter account. *Id.* at 127. According to the account header, Hill joined Twitter in August 2021, and as of March 1, 2023, he has tweeted or retweeted items 6,011 times.

[43] Alan Feuer, *New Evidence Undercuts Jan. 6 Instigator Conspiracy Theory*, N.Y. TIMES (Oct. 13, 2022), https://www.nytimes.com/2022/05/05/us/jan-6-ray-epps-evidence.html.

[44] Transcript, Interview with Ray Epps, H. SELECT COMM. TO INVESTIGATE THE JAN. 6TH ATTACK ON THE U.S. CAPITOL (Jan. 21, 2022), https://www.govinfo.gov/content/pkg/GPO-J6-TRANSCRIPT-CTRL0000038864/pdf/GPO-J6-TRANSCRIPT-CTRL0000038864.pdf; *see also* Ryan J. Reilly, *Pro-Trump Protestor Ray Epps Told Committee 'Crazy' Conspiracy Theories Tore Apart His Life*, NBC NEWS (Dec. 29, 2022),

Nonetheless, Hill has repeatedly supported the Epps theory, such as tweeting on January 6, 2023, "Happy Anniversary Ray Epps, from your friends in The Deep State. Job well done! #J6."[45] During his interview, Hill acknowledged that this tweet came off his profile, but he stated that he could not remember posting it: "I don't know how many Twitter posts I have. I don't recall every single one."[46]

In addition to embracing the Epps conspiracy theory, Hill has also suggested that an unidentified "scaffold commander"[47] and active-duty marines arrested for participating in the January 6[48] riot all secretly acted on behalf of the government in support of what he has called the "Fedsurrection."[49] When asked about these tweets at his interview, Hill declined to comment, stating that he was "not going to get into defending or explaining First Amendment-protected activity."[50]

On December 22, 2022, Hill wrote, "@SpeakerPelosi and her staff have blood on their hands. #J6."[51] At his interview, Hill admitted this was his tweet and stated that it was "First Amendment-protected activity" and that he would not explain it further.[52]

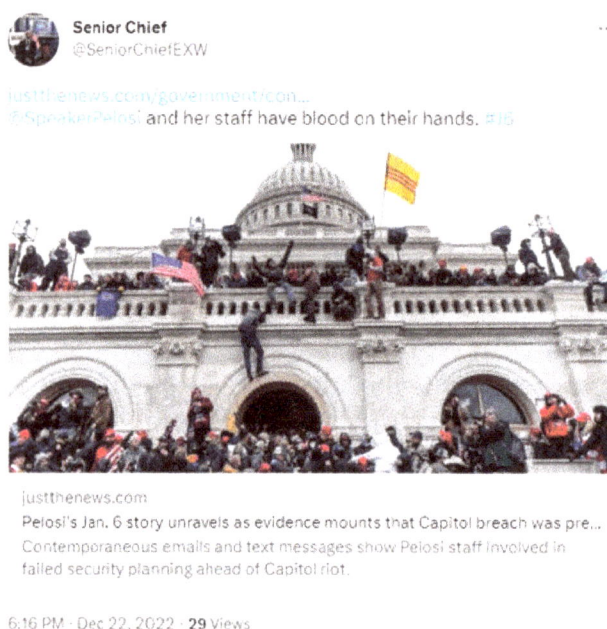

Senior Chief
@SeniorChiefEXW

justthenews.com/government/con...
@SpeakerPelosi and her staff have blood on their hands. #J6

justthenews.com
Pelosi's Jan. 6 story unravels as evidence mounts that Capitol breach was pre...
Contemporaneous emails and text messages show Pelosi staff involved in
failed security planning ahead of Capitol riot.

6:16 PM · Dec 22, 2022 · 29 Views

https://www.nbcnews.com/politics/congress/-trump-protester-ray-epps-told-jan-6-committee-crazy-conspiracy-theori-rcna63615.

[45] Geroge Hill (@SeniorChiefEXW), TWITTER (Jan. 6, 2023, 8:27 AM), https://twitter.com/SeniorChiefEXW/status/1611353706070409218.

[46] George Hill Testimony at 132.

[47] George Hill (@SeniorChiefEXW), TWITTER (Jan. 8, 2023, 4:55 PM), https://twitter.com/SeniorChiefEXW/status/1612206373856493568.

[48] George Hill (@SeniorChiefEXW), TWITTER (Jan. 19, 2023, 6:02 PM), https://twitter.com/SeniorChiefEXW/status/1616209590110019585.

[49] George Hill (@SeniorChiefEXW), TWITTER (Jan. 6, 2023, 5:44 PM), https://twitter.com/SeniorChiefEXW/status/1611493962002432003.

[50] George Hill Testimony at 132.

[51] George Hill (@SeniorChiefEXW), TWITTER (Dec. 22, 2022, 6:16 PM), https://twitter.com/SeniorChiefEXW/status/1606066219987210242.

[52] George Hill Testimony at 138-39.

On December 28, 2022, he retweeted a post from @LynneS700 stating, "Patriots were the ONLY ones trying to STOP the Fake Insurrection violence being committed by Implanted Antifa. (Pelosi's buddies)." He commented, "Insurrection my a$$. It was a set up and sadly, there's no shortage of idiots willing to take the bait."[53] At his interview, Mr. Hill acknowledged, "It does look like it's my tweet," but did not comment further.[54]

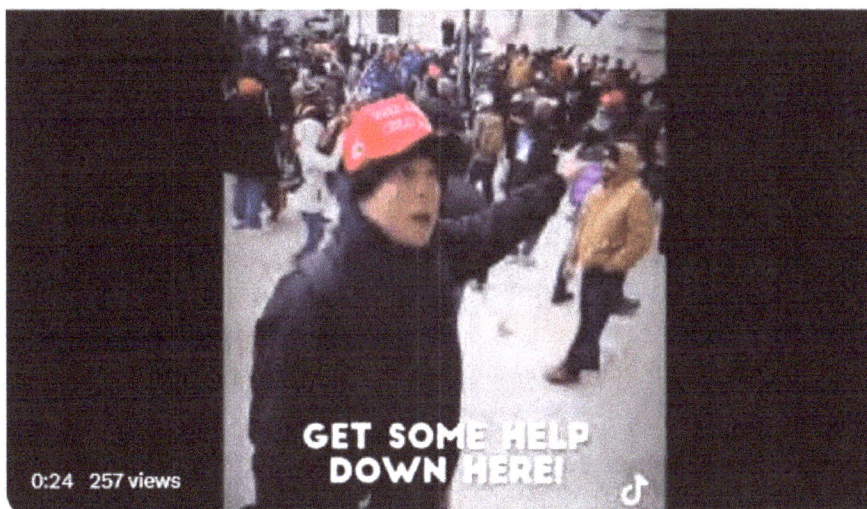

Senior Chief
@SeniorChiefEXW

Insurrection my a$$. It was a set up and sadly, there's no shortage of idiots willing to take the bait.

Lynne 🦋 @LynneS700 · Dec 28, 2022
Patriots were the ONLY ones trying to STOP the Fake Insurrection violence being committed by Implanted Antifa. (Pelosi's buddies)
twitter.com/GuntherEaglema...

0:24 257 views

GET SOME HELP DOWN HERE!

9:45 AM · Dec 28, 2022 · **109** Views

Hill has also advanced theories that Democratic politicians colluding with the FBI were responsible for the events of January 6, including comparing the FBI to Nazi Storm Troopers,[55] who were known as the Brownshirts.[56] On November 30, 2022, Hill retweeted a post from Rep. Marjorie Taylor Greene which asked, "If the FBI had so many informants inside a group, why don't they stop J6 from happening?"[57] He commented, "The #FBI are the Brown Shirt enforcers

[53] George Hill (@SeniorChiefEXW), TWITTER (Dec. 28, 2022, 9:45 AM),
https://twitter.com/SeniorChiefEXW/status/1608111891749937155.
[54] George Hill Testimony at 137-38.
[55] *E.g.*, George Hill (@SeniorChiefEXW), TWITTER (Jun. 25, 2022, 10:44 PM),
https://twitter.com/SeniorChiefEXW/status/1540888727152742400.
[56] The Editors of Encyclopaedia Britannica, *SA*, ENCYCLOPAEDIA BRITANNICA (Feb. 18, 2023),
https://www.britannica.com/topic/SA-Nazi-organization.
[57] George Hill (@SeniorChiefEXW), TWITTER (Nov. 30, 2022, 10:53 AM),
https://twitter.com/SeniorChiefEXW/status/1597982151601160193.

of the @DNC. By the Bureau's own policy, they are obligated to disrupt if innocent lives are at risk. But #Trump supporters aren't ever innocent – are they?"[58]

Senior Chief
@SeniorChiefEXW

The #FBI are the Brown Shirt enforcers of the @DNC. By the Bureau's own policy, they are obligated to disrupt if innocent lives are at risk. But #Trump supporters aren't ever innocent - are they?

Rep. Marjorie Taylor Greene ✅ @RepMTG · Nov 30, 2022

If the FBI had so many informants inside a group, why don't they stop J6 from happening?

Ashley Babbit was killed on J6.

Roseann Boyland was beaten, trampled, and dragged down the hall away from life saving CPR being administered.

They would be alive if the FBI had stopped it. twitter.com/julie_kelly2/s...

10:53 AM · Nov 30, 2022

This mirrors a theme he raised in November 2022, when he retweeted an *Epoch Times* article with a picture of now-Chairman Jordan.[59] The headline of the article reads, "FBI Waited Over a Year to Fully Investigate Jan. 6 Pipe Bombs: House Judiciary." He commented, "The reason that bomber is not already in jail is because this is part of a larger #Democrat plan using their enforcement arm, the #FBI."[60] When asked about both tweets during the interview, Hill stated that it was First Amendment-protected activity and that he would not explain it.[61]

Hill also promotes extreme views of the deaths of January 6 rioters Ashli Babbit and Rosanne Boyland. Boyland was crushed by the crowd in the Capitol on January 6, 2021, and died of acute amphetamine intoxication.[62] Some on the far-right, though, believe without evidence that Boyland was killed by law enforcement and see her as a martyr.[63] On January 19, 2023, Hill tweeted an *Epoch Times* story referencing bodycam footage that shows Boyland, and he commented, "I'm disappointed @SpeakerMcCarthy ended the #J6 committee. There needs to be a real investigation. #RosanneBoyland."[64]

---

[58] *Id.*

[59] George Hill (@SeniorChiefEXW), TWITTER (Nov. 26, 2022, 5:17 PM), https://twitter.com/SeniorChiefEXW/status/1596629184788721664.

[60] *Id.*

[61] George Hill Testimony at 139-40.

[62] Ayman M. Mohyeldin & Preeti Varathan, *Rosanne Boyland Was Outside the U.S. Capitol Last January 6. How—And Why—Did She Die?*, VANITY FAIR (Jan. 5, 2022), https://www.vanityfair.com/news/2022/01/capitol-insurrection-rosanne-boyland-how-and-why-did-she-die.

[63] *Id.*

[64] George Hill (@SeniorChiefEXW), TWITTER (Jan. 19, 2023, 8:53 PM), https://twitter.com/SeniorChiefEXW/status/1616252459143282692.

Hill has similarly claimed that Ashli Babbitt was murdered by Capitol Police and that Lieutenant Michael Byrd, the African American officer who shot her, should be in jail. On January 6, 2023, Hill tweeted a meme with a photo of Byrd next to a photo of Babbitt.[65] The meme states, "This needs to be posted daily until that SOB is arrested & stands trial. Michael Byrd Murdered Ashli Babbitt January 6, 2021."[66] A few days prior, Hill retweeted a post which read, "FACT: Michael Byrd murdered Ashli Babbitt... The [expletive] should be in Prison."[67] Byrd, who was the target of racist vitriol and death threats after his name was leaked, was cleared of wrongdoing by both Capitol Police and the Department of Justice, the latter of which concluded that there was no evidence to contradict that Byrd believed that it was necessary to fire a single shot at Babbitt "in self-defense or in defense of the Members of Congress and others evacuating the House Chamber."[68]

2.   Hill Holds Extreme Views Opposing a Domestic Intelligence Program

Much of Hill's testimony to the Committee concerned allegations regarding the FBI's intelligence gathering components. This testimony must be viewed in light of his extreme views of the intelligence community. One instance in which he expressed these views was during a January 9, 2023, podcast appearance, when he asserted, "I don't think we need a domestic intel program."[69] According to Hill:

> The Congress with the Patriot Act gave them [the FBI] a mission. They gave them a domestic intelligence capability. George Bush challenged Bob Mueller – Bob – he told Bob Mueller, he said, "I know you're going to find the people who did this, the 9/11 attack. What I want to know, Bob, is what are we going to do to stop the next one?" And that was the genesis. That was the very beginning of how we got to where we're at today of this *Minority Report*-like manner of law enforcement where we're trying to do predictive analysis of when a crime is going to be committed...
>
> ...The FBI is going to salute smartly and say, "Yes sir, we can do this," or "Yes, ma'am," if we have a female president. They're going to say, "We can do this." And they're going to do it, which is no American shall die at the hands of terrorism. And that was the mission.[70]

Hill perceives this is as a negative goal:

> There needs to take place a reeducation. And people need to understand that line in the national anthem, "And the home of the brave," willing to accept some risk ... People have to learn to start embracing risk, not only in terms of achieving

[65] George Hill (@SeniorChiefEXW), TWITTER (Jan. 6, 2023, 8:29 AM), https://twitter.com/SeniorChiefEXW/status/1611354279851298816.
[66] *Id.*
[67] @GuntherEagleman, TWITTER (Jan. 2, 2023, 5:36 PM), https://twitter.com/SeniorChiefEXW/status/1610262756975935489.
[68] Rich Schapiro, Anna Schecter and Chelsea Damberg, *Officer who shot Ashli Babbitt during Capitol riot breaks silence: 'I saved countless lives,'* NBC NEWS (Aug. 26, 2021), https://www.nbcnews.com/news/us-news/officer-who-shot-ashli-babbitt-during-capitol-riot-breaks-silence-n1277736.
[69] The Kyle Seraphin Show, *George Hill: FBI, NSA & USMC*, RUMBLE at 01:33:46 (Jan. 9, 2023), https://rumble.com/v24ixrk-george-hill-fbi-nsa-and-usmc.html.
[70] *Id* at 1:08:35, 1:09:50.

success, but quite frankly, there's a little bit of excitement to it. When I go snowshoeing in the White Mountains in New Hampshire and it's minus 40-degree windchill, there's a good chance I'm not going to come back. But it's exciting. I'm going to make sure I pack the right gear. I make sure everybody knows where I'm going. I go with the right people... Zero risk is not a fun life.[71]

When asked about these statements during the interview, he said that while he understands that it is Congress' decision whether to permit the FBI to continue engaging in intelligence activities, he believes that a "zero tolerance" policy with the goal of preventing any American from dying at the hands of a terrorist infringes on civil liberties.[72] He added:

> I mean, you take risk, you put yourself out there, and it gives you a deeper appreciation of the nice things that you do have, or going home to see your family or whatever it is. That's what I meant by that. And if I came across as callous, I want to apologize to you and anybody else who saw the video.[73]

3. Hill Has Expressed Strong Animus Towards President Biden, Democratic Politicians, and Certain Republican Politicians

Hill's testimony must also be considered in light of his strong animus towards President Biden, Democratic politicians, and Republican politicians whom he considers to be insufficiently conservative.

For example, on September 9, 2022, Hill wrote on Twitter, "#Biden should be impeached but many #Republicans are still members of the #UniParty or just gutless."[74] On February 1, 2023, he tweeted a screenshot of a posted meme of President Biden sitting on a bench—an apparent reference to the movie Forrest Gump—with the words, "I'm not a very smart man but I'm not as stupid as those that support me," to which Hill added, "#Biden #BidenCrimeFamily #BidenWorstPresidentEver @POTUS."[75] On November 27, 2022, he tweeted a *New York Post* article headlined, "'Creepy' Joe Biden roasted for strange selfies," and commented, "#PedoJoe."[76] On September 1, 2022, Hill commented on a post about a speech from President Biden, "Not a good look Joe Stalin, er, Joe Biden."[77] In total, he has tweeted about President Biden or his family more than 150 times since September 1, 2022.

Hill has directed similar animus towards other Democratic politicians. For example, he responded to a tweet from Rep. Eric Swalwell describing threatening voicemail messages the Congressman had received with, "Don't be such a whiner."[78] He mocked the arrest of another

---

[71] *Id* at 01:49:55.
[72] George Hill Testimony at 61-63.
[73] *Id*. Testimony at 63.
[74] George Hill (@SeniorChiefEXW), TWITTER (Sep. 9, 2022, 11:38 AM). https://twitter.com/SeniorChiefEXW/status/1568262516928815104.
[75] George Hill (@SeniorChiefEXW), TWITTER (Feb. 1, 2023, 7:09 AM). https://twitter.com/SeniorChiefEXW/status/1620756320675667969.
[76] George Hill (@SeniorChiefEXW), TWITTER (Nov. 27, 2022, 7:52 AM). https://twitter.com/SeniorChiefEXW/status/1596849524382711809.
[77] George Hill (@SeniorChiefEXW), TWITTER (Sep. 2, 2022, 10:23 PM). https://twitter.com/SeniorChiefEXW/status/1565525735086981123.
[78] George Hill (@SeniorChiefEXW), TWITTER (Jan. 27, 2023, 9:39 PM). https://twitter.com/SeniorChiefEXW/status/1619163281620619264.

Democratic House Member's child.[79] And he has repeatedly targeted Rep. Alexandria Ocasio-Cortez, Rep. Maxine Waters, Sen. Cory Booker, and Chicago mayor Lori Lightfoot.[80]

Hill has likewise attacked Republicans whom he considers to be insufficiently conservative. Notably, he has repeatedly attacked Mitch McConnell, such as in a post stating, "#DitchMitch This communist, along with his #CCP member wife, has to go!"[81]

Senior Chief
@SeniorChiefEXW

#DitchMitch This communist, along with his #CCP member wife, has to go!

Mollie ✓ @MZHemingway · Dec 21, 2022
So long as McConnell is top elected Republican, eagerly trashing voters, vociferously advocating for Dem policy goals, pushing $1.7 trillion spending packages, and weakly fighting for whatever he can be bothered to pursue, Republicans have obvious problem.
thefederalist.com/2022/12/21/gop...

9:38 AM · Dec 21, 2022 · **62** Views

Other targets have included Republican National Committee chair Ronna McDaniel, whom he described as a member of the "Uniparty"[82] and Rep. Dan Crenshaw.[83]

4. Hill Is Motivated to Help Republicans "Kill the King," Meaning the Intelligence Community

During his January 9, 2023, appearance on *The Kyle Seraphin Show*, Hill discussed the missions of federal law enforcement and intelligence community entities and said of these entities, "These aren't fiefdoms, these are kingdoms."[84] He went on:

---

[79] George Hill (@SeniorChiefEXW), TWITTER (Jan. 23, 2023, 5:53 AM), https://twitter.com/SeniorChiefEXW/status/1617475674922700802.

[80] *See, e.g.*, George Hill (@SeniorChiefEXW), TWITTER (Jan. 31, 2023, 7:49 PM), https://twitter.com/SeniorChiefEXW/status/1620585152987467776; George Hill (@SeniorChiefEXW), TWITTER (Jan. 31, 2023, 7:08 PM), https://twitter.com/SeniorChiefEXW/status/1620574897859694592; George Hill (@SeniorChiefEXW), TWITTER (Jan. 26, 2023, 6:53 PM), https://twitter.com/SeniorChiefEXW/status/1618758963142729728; George Hill (@SeniorChiefEXW), TWITTER (Jan. 31, 2023, 2:12 PM), https://twitter.com/SeniorChiefEXW/status/1620500316054503424; George Hill (@SeniorChiefEXW), TWITTER (Sep. 9, 2022, 11:33 AM), https://twitter.com/SeniorChiefEXW/status/1568261354989195270.

[81] George Hill (@SeniorChiefEXW), TWITTER (Dec. 21, 2022, 9:38 AM), https://twitter.com/SeniorChiefEXW/status/1605573408628129793.

[82] George Hill (@SeniorChiefEXW), TWITTER (Jan. 28, 2023, 11:41 AM), https://twitter.com/SeniorChiefEXW/status/1619375047445192706.

[83] *See, e.g.*, George Hill (@SeniorChiefEXW), TWITTER (Jan. 9, 2023, 5:19 PM), https://twitter.com/SeniorChiefEXW/status/1612574753881051174; George Hill (@SeniorChiefEXW), TWITTER (Dec. 25, 2022, 10:44 AM), https://twitter.com/SeniorChiefEXW/status/1607039487179382785.

[84] The Kyle Seraphin Show, *George Hill: FBI, NSA & USMC*, RUMBLE at 01:41:17 (Jan. 9, 2023), https://rumble.com/v24ixrk-george-hill-fbi-nsa-and-usmc.html.

The Republicans are talking about a 21st century, a 2023 version of the Church Committee…I think what Shakespeare said, if you're going to kill the king, make sure you kill the king. If they're going to go after – this new committee – after the intelligence community, they better make sure they get out every bit of cancer that's out there. Because I can tell you right now, it's going to come back, and it'll come back stronger and more vicious than ever.[85]

Hill was asked to explain this comment during his interview. He responded, "First Amendment-protected activity, not going to get into explaining my comments on a podcast."[86]

On August 13, 2022, George Hill wrote as a comment to a now-deleted post on Twitter, "Wray has never lost a minutes sleep over @ChuckGrassley @SenTedCruz or @Jim_Jordan – I'm sorry but it's true. No one in #DOJ or #FBI has ever paid a price for unlawful conduct and never will. Sad but true."[87] During the interview, Hill stated that he could not recall making this post, but that he would not address its contents because it contained "First Amendment-protected activity."[88]

> **Senior Chief**
> @SeniorChiefEXW   …
>
> Wray has never lost a minutes sleep over @ChuckGrassley @SenTedCruz or @Jim_Jordan - I'm sorry but it's true. No one in #DOJ or #FBI has ever paid a price for unlawful conduct and never will. Sad but true.
> twitter.com/seanmdav/statu…
>
> This Tweet was deleted by the Tweet author. Learn more
>
> 10:13 AM · Aug 13, 2022

C.   Conclusion

Hill has admitted that he had limited involvement in January 6 matters and that he does not have direct personal knowledge about many of the issues which he raised. In addition, even if Hill's allegations were accurate, they tend to refute—not support—Committee Republicans' premise regarding the handling of Capitol attack cases. For example, Hill asserted that the FBI's Boston Field Office declined to take certain suggested investigative steps. This fact directly contradicts the claims of Committee Republicans that the FBI's criminal investigations related to the January 6 Capitol attack were subject to improper influence.

Moreover, Hill's extensive past statements and claims—in particular his expressed desire to "kill the king" of the intelligence community and make the Justice Department and the FBI "pay a price"—demonstrate strong bias and animus towards these entities and the United States government as a whole. His bias and animus may have motivated Hill to engage with Committee Republicans, but his claims lack merit.

---

[85] *Id.* at 01:41:22.
[86] George Hill Testimony at 141-42.
[87] George Hill (@SeniorChiefEXW), TWITTER (Aug. 13, 2022, 10:13 AM), https://twitter.com/SeniorChiefEXW/status/1558456715556884480.
[88] George Hill Testimony at 144.

III.   Witness Summary: Garret O'Boyle

The Committee conducted a transcribed interview of Garret O'Boyle on February 10, 2023. O'Boyle was an FBI Special Agent assigned to the Joint Terrorism Task Force at the Wichita Resident Agency in Wichita, Kansas, beginning in 2018.[89] He applied for and was accepted to a new unit in Virginia and was scheduled to begin work there on September 26, 2022.[90] His security clearance was suspended that day.[91]

O'Boyle told the Committee that his suspension notice stated that "an unidentified person … made an allegation that [he] had been making unprotected disclosures to the media," and that because of this he was "no longer deemed fit to hold a security clearance."[92] He denied having made such disclosures, and he explained that instead he believed that he had been retaliated against because he "had been coming to Congress… for nearly a year."[93] He described this as being a "weaponization of the [security] clearance" process.[94] He has appealed that suspension and, to his knowledge, the appeal process is still ongoing.[95]

Committee Democrats requested a copy of the suspension notice provided to O'Boyle, which had previously been produced to Committee Republicans.[96] He declined to produce it to Committee Democrats, and his attorney prevented him from discussing "any detail as to the substance of the investigation afterwards."[97] In addition, O'Boyle indicated that he received a letter dated about November 3, 2022, informing him that his pay would be suspended.[98] To date, Committee Democrats have not been provided with a copy of that letter, which may provide insights into O'Boyle's claims and whether the FBI was able to substantiate any of the allegations against him, from either Committee Republicans or from O'Boyle directly.

O'Boyle confirmed that he never took his allegation that the FBI had retaliated against him to the Justice Department Inspector General, FBI Office of Professional Responsibility, or FBI Inspection Division.[99] These offices are tasked with, among other things, conducting independent, nonpartisan evaluations of whistleblower claims and, if consulted, could have provided the Committee with relevant analysis of O'Boyle's allegations.

---

[89] Garret O'Boyle Testimony at 9-10.

[90] *Id.* at 10-11.

[91] *Id.* at 11.

[92] *Id.* at 13.

[93] *Id.* at 14.

[94] *Id.* at 17.

[95] *Id.* at 17, 45-46.

[96] *Id.* at 55-56. Prior to the interview, Committee Republicans declined to produce any documents to Committee Democrats.

[97] *Id.* at 44. O'Boyle confirmed that he had produced a copy of the suspension notice to both then-Ranking Member Jim Jordan and possibly to Rep. Ron Estes' office. *Id.* at 44-45. During the interview, minority staff asked majority staff to share the notice with them. Majority staff stated, "we don't have the authority to provide to you." Minority staff then asked O'Boyle to ask majority staff to provide Committee Democrats with a copy. His attorney responded, "The request is being made right now, and it's a legal decision that requires confidentiality. It's something that requires legal analysis. It requires any number of different things." *Id.* at 56. O'Boyle's attorney was unable to provide the statutory basis for his claim that information provided to a member of Congress—particularly a then-Ranking Member—is confidential, and Committee Democrats are not aware of any legal privileges applicable to this situation. *See* Garret O'Boyle Testimony at 123-24.

[98] Garret O'Boyle Testimony at 49.

[99] *Id.* at 53.

As a result, Committee Democrats are not able to evaluate the veracity of O'Boyle's claims regarding the contents of his suspension notice or information or evidence that may have come to light during the investigation related to his alleged media disclosures.

Committee Democrats likewise asked O'Boyle to describe the substance of what he described as his "protected disclosures" to Congress after Committee Republicans said that they "did not have the authority" to provide this information without O'Boyle's consent.[100] O'Boyle's attorney, Jesse Binnall,[101] prevented him from doing so:

> A   That is confidential by the statute. And so my advice to him is to not disclose exactly what was disclosed.
>
> Q   Okay. And which statute are you referring to?
>
> A   Oh, I'm sure I can – I can get you a – I don't know a citation off the top of my head, but I'm sure I can get that to you.
>
> Q   Okay. And ... can you tell me the act? ...
>
> A   I'm sure I could get you that information.
>
> Q   Okay. I think that'd be helpful for us to have.[102]

Democratic staff repeatedly followed up with O'Boyle's attorney via email following the interview. So far, he has declined to respond.

Committee Democrats are thus unable to fully evaluate whether any of what O'Boyle describes as "protected disclosures" in fact show a violation of law or abuse of authority, as required by 5 U.S.C. § 2303.[103] In addition, Committee Democrats note that 5 U.S.C. § 2303 only prevents an agency from retaliating against an individual who makes a qualifying protected disclosure. It does not grant the individual who made that disclosure confidentiality and does not impose a confidentiality requirement upon the entity to whom it was made. In other words, the term "protected disclosure" means that a legitimate whistleblower who makes such a disclosure is protected from retaliation, not that the disclosure itself is protected from being disclosed more broadly.

O'Boyle did confirm that he corresponded with staff of both Rep. Ron Estes and then-Ranking Member Jim Jordan probably "more than 20" times in 2022 and produced "maybe around" 50 documents to them.[104] O'Boyle's attorney advised him "not to talk about specifics of any of his disclosures to Congress ... because those are confidential" and in fact prohibited him

---

[100] Garret O'Boyle Testimony at 56.

[101] Jesse Binnall was Donald Trump's "top election-fraud lawyer" when Trump falsely claimed the 2020 election was stolen and also represents "Defending the Republic, Inc.," a group associated with conspiracy theorists Sidney Powell and L. Lin Wood, "in the $1.3 billion lawsuit that Dominion Voting Systems brought against Powell" in 2021. Roger Sollenberger, *Top Trump Lawyer Is a Longtime Tax Deadbeat*, DAILY BEAST (May 6, 2022), https://www.thedailybeast.com/top-trump-lawyer-jesse-binnall-is-a-longtime-tax-deadbeat.

[102] *Id.* at 123-24.

[103] 5 U.S.C. § 2303.

[104] Garret O'Boyle Testimony at 40-42.

from describing the substance of any of his communications with the offices of Rep. Estes or then-Ranking Member Jordan.[105]

That said, O'Boyle did raise specific allegations during his interview. These allegations are discussed below. For the reasons stated therein, Committee Democrats conclude that none of these allegations constitute legitimate whistleblower claims.

A. Based on the Information Which Is Available About O'Boyle's Claims, They Do Not Show Evidence of Misconduct

1. O'Boyle Did Not Present Evidence of Misconduct With Respect to January 6 Cases

While O'Boyle generally refused to share information about his "protected disclosures" with Committee Democrats, he did confirm in response to Republican questioning that one disclosure concerned a request he received from a special agent with the FBI's Washington Field Office (WFO) regarding a lead in a January 6-related case.[106] Committee Republicans asked O'Boyle whether the WFO pressured agents "to keep January 6 cases open or open cases."[107] He responded:

> I would say they pressured us to open cases to some degree. One example that I have personally -- I made this as one of my protected disclosures, so I'll just touch on it a little bit.
>
> But I received a lead about someone based on an anonymous tip, and in law enforcement anonymous tips don't hold very much weight, especially without evidence that you can corroborate pretty easily.
>
> I wasn't able to corroborate anything they said, even after speaking with the person they alleged potential criminal behavior of.
>
> While I'm trying to figure all that out, I get another lead from the same agent who sent me that lead.[108]

He explained that he decided to call the agent who had sent him the lead:

> Q   [A]fter talking to her, my mind was blown that she was still trying to get me to do some legal process on the guy that I got the anonymous tip on. … And so I ended up writing that all up and denying it. …
>
>   When we got off the phone, I was like, "I'm just going to close this." She still wanted me to do what she wanted me to do in the lead, and I was like, no. I can't…
>
> Q   So, to your knowledge, that case was closed?

[105] *Id.* at 38, 43.
[106] *Id.* at 102-03.
[107] *Id.* at 102.
[108] *Id.* at 102-103.

A   To my knowledge, yeah.[109]

O'Boyle later confirmed that the WFO special agent was not in a supervisory position over him and that there were no punitive actions taken against him for declining to take the steps she suggested:

Q   The Washington Field Office agent that communicated with you, was she at your level? Was she a higher level than you?

A   She was a special agent just like me…

Q   …So, at the end of the day, you exercised your judgment, and you weren't – there were no consequences for that.

A   As far as I know.[110]

Committee Democrats conclude that the incident O'Boyle describes does not show a violation of any law, rule, or regulation, or gross mismanagement, a gross waste of funds, an abuse of authority, or a substantial and specific danger to public health or safety. Rather, this appears to be a situation in which two special agents engaged in dialogue regarding a case process. O'Boyle has provided no evidence that he was retaliated against in any way for exercising his independent judgment regarding what he viewed as appropriate procedures in this matter.

2.   O'Boyle's Claims Regarding the FBI's Handling of COVID Vaccination Requirements Must Be Evaluated in Light of His Embrace of Vaccine-Related Conspiracy Theories

O'Boyle stated that a separate concern raised in his "protected disclosures" to Congress involved what he perceived as pressure from the FBI to be vaccinated against COVID-19.[111]

The FBI's COVID-19 vaccination policy was enacted pursuant to Executive Order 14043, "Requiring Coronavirus Disease 2019 Vaccination for Federal Employees," issued in September 2021.[112] In January 2022, a Texas District Court judge issued a nationwide preliminary injunction staying enforcement of the vaccine mandate.[113] A Fifth Circuit panel vacated that injunction in April 2022, at which time the mandate went back into effect.[114] As noted in the April 2022 Fifth Circuit opinion, "At least twelve district courts previously rejected challenges to Executive Order 14043 for various reasons."[115] The April 2022 opinion was itself vacated by the Fifth Circuit in a per curium opinion in June 2022, at which time the injunction,

---

[109] *Id.* at 104-05.
[110] *Id.* at 120-21.
[111] *Id.* at 133.
[112] Exec. Order No. 14043, 86 Fed. Reg. 50989 (Sep. 9, 2021), https://www.federalregister.gov/documents/2021/09/14/2021-19927/requiring-coronavirus-disease-2019-vaccination-for-federal-employees.
[113] *Feds for Medical Freedom v. Biden*, 581 F.Supp.3d 826 (S.D. Tex. 2022).
[114] *Feds for Medical Freedom v. Biden*, 30 F. 4th 503, 505 n.1 (5th Cir. Apr. 7, 2022).
[115] *Feds for Medical Freedom v. Biden*, 30 F. 4th 503, 505 n.1 (5th Cir. Apr. 7, 2022), *reh'g en banc granted, vacated by Feds for Medical Freedom v. Biden*, 37 F. 4th 1093 (5th Cir. June 27, 2022).

which stopped enforcement of the mandate, went back into effect.[116] The Fifth Circuit heard oral arguments in this case en banc in September but has not yet issued a final ruling.[117]

It would not have been a violation of law or policy for the FBI to enforce Executive Order 14043 during the time period from September 2021 to when the Texas District Court issued a preliminary injunction enjoining the mandate in January 2022, or throughout the time period during which the preliminary injunction was no longer in effect between April and June 2022.

It is possible that O'Boyle felt pressured to get vaccinated against COVID-19 during those windows in which the policy was paused. However, because Democratic staff have not been provided with sufficient information about what he describes as his "protected disclosure" concerning "inappropriate pressure," Committee Democrats are unable to evaluate what type of pressure he may have faced. Moreover, O'Boyle's vaccination-related claims must be evaluated in light of his embrace of a wide range of COVID-19 vaccination conspiracy theories. For example, on January 15, he posted on his Twitter account, @GOBActual,[118] "There are still plenty [of people] bragging about being jabbed and still think we are killing people by not."[119] Asked about this tweet during his testimony, he indicated that it is self-explanatory.[120]

O'Boyle was also asked about a tweet in which he compared individuals being vaccinated to "Reserve Police Battalion 101."[121]

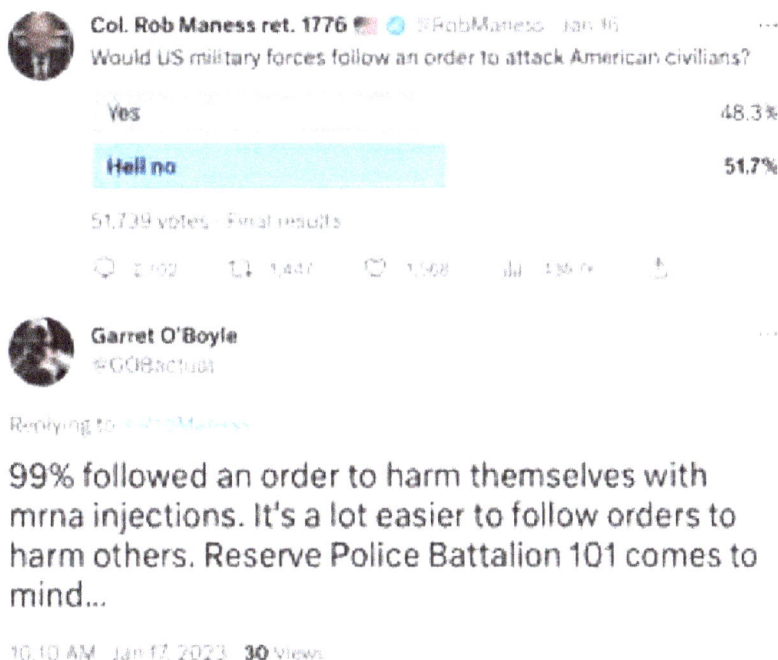

Col. Rob Maness ret. 1776 @RobManess Jan 16
Would US military forces follow an order to attack American civilians?

Yes	48.3%
Hell no	51.7%

51,739 votes · Final results

Garret O'Boyle
@GOBactual

Replying to

99% followed an order to harm themselves with mrna injections. It's a lot easier to follow orders to harm others. Reserve Police Battalion 101 comes to mind...

10:10 AM · Jan 17, 2023 · **30** Views

---

[116] *Feds for Medical Freedom v. Biden*, 37 F. 4th 1093 (5th Cir. June 27, 2022).

[117] Eric Katz, *Appeals Court: Where Does POTUS' Power to Force Feds to Vax End?*, GOV'T EXEC. (Sep. 13, 2022), https://www.govexec.com/management/2022/09/appeals-court-where-does-potus-power-force-feds-vax-end/377074/.

[118] During the interview, O'Boyle confirmed that he is responsible for the "@GOBActual" Twitter account. Garret O'Boyle Testimony at 64. Since the interview, O'Boyle has made his Twitter account private.

[119] Garret O'Boyle (@GOBActual), TWITTER (Jan. 14, 2022, 12:15 AM).

[120] Garret O'Boyle Testimony at 132-33.

[121] Garret O'Boyle (@GOBActual), TWITTER (Jan. 17, 2023, 10:10 AM); Garret O'Boyle Testimony at 136-37.

O'Boyle explained that he analogized vaccination to Nazi Reserve Police Battalion 101 because in both situations people "crossed a line" in response to pressure from leaders:

Q So what did you mean by "99 percent followed an order to harm themselves with mRNA injections"?

A I believe that the vaccines, the mRNA ones, can potentially be harmful, and there's a lot of that starting to come out now, and that the military had the most severe mandates to take those.

Q What did you mean when you said "it's a lot easier to follow orders to harm others"?

A I think there's a multitude of historical examples that has demonstrated that. I mention one there, Reserve Police Battalion 101. So that's all I meant by that.

Q Can you explain the Reserve Police Battalion 101 very briefly, if you can?

A Sure. So my understanding of that is, the Reserve Police Battalion 101 was a reserve police force in Poland during World War II, and they were initially comprised of just normal people – butchers and carpenters and different other type of people who had normal jobs or other positions. And then, by the end of the war, they were slaughtering – they were basically engaging in genocide like the rest of the Nazi regime.

Q So why did the Reserve Battalion 101 come to mind when you were asked about U.S. military forces?

A So I think with this tweet I was just trying to raise a broader scope of the discussion. Like, where is the line? When your commander tells you you have to get an injection even if you don't want to, to some people that's not a difficult line to cross. But it seems, with history as our example, that that line just continues to get moved, and eventually you cross a line like the Reserve Police Battalion 101 did, and you don't even know how you got there.[122]

Thus, while Committee Democrats do not have sufficient information to assess O'Boyle's claim of improper pressure, any such claim must be viewed in light of his comparison of vaccine mandates to the actions of the Nazi regime.

3. O'Boyle's Claim Regarding COVID Testing Policy Does Not Meet the Standard of a Protected Disclosure

O'Boyle stated that a separate disclosure he made involved mandatory COVID testing requirements: "this is one of the disclosures I made to my chain of command, that not only was the vaccine mandate reasonably a violation of law, rule, or policy, the FBI then enacted a mandatory testing for only unvaccinated people."[123]

---

[122] Garret O'Boyle Testimony at 136-37.
[123] Id. at 138.

O'Boyle explained that he declined to take a required COVID test after recovering from COVID.[124] When his supervisors objected to this, he explained that he viewed his refusal as being in accordance with FDA guidelines:

> I brought up the FDA's guidelines, which is what the FBI was supposed to be going off of, as well as other guidelines. And I said, they're not following the guidelines they're supposed to be following. I think this is another example of a violation of law, rule, or policy.
>
> And they said, "Well, why don't you think about it over the weekend?" and then, you know, "We'll be in touch." And I said, okay. And then they called me over the weekend, and I told them I wasn't going to change my position.
>
> And so, then, the following workday, they told me not to come in, and my boss came to my house and gave me an AWOL paperwork. And so I was placed onto absent without leave, which at the time was a violation of the Safer Federal Workforce Task Force guidelines, which the FBI was supposed to be following, which said that if the person had an outstanding religious exemption, which I did – I had applied for one of those – that they were supposed to be placed on administrative leave. But the FBI broke that rule and placed me and others into AWOL status instead.
>
> So I told my boss, okay, "Now that you placed me on AWOL, I'll take a test," and I went back to testing. And then I think I tested one or two more times, and then shortly thereafter the testing stopped.[125]

O'Boyle suggested that this instance occurred in late 2021, after the announcement of a vaccine requirement for federal employees and before its injunction in January 2022.[126] In this time period, the Safer Federal Workforce Task Force published "Agency Model Safety Principles," which stated, "Agencies may establish a program to test Federal employees who are not fully vaccinated for COVID-19."[127] O'Boyle is incorrect that the Safer Federal Workforce Task Force guidelines established procedures for COVID testing related to exemptions from vaccine requirements. In fact, the Task Force notes on its "Frequently Asked Questions" page about vaccinations, "Enforcement of applicable workplace safety protocols, including any required testing for Federal employees with approved or pending exceptions, are the responsibility of occupant agencies."[128] Federal law permitted employees to request an exemption from the vaccine mandate, but that exemption was separate from any agency-imposed

---

[124] *Id.* at 138.

[125] *Id.* at 139.

[126] *Id.* at 138-40.

[127] *COVID 19 Workplace Safety: Agency Model Safety Principles*, SAFER FED. WORKFORCE TASK FORCE (Sep. 13, 2021), https://www.saferfederalworkforce.gov/downloads/updates%20to%20model%20safety%20principles%209.13.21.pdf. As of August 22, 2022, agencies' COVID-19 safety protocols should no longer vary based on vaccination status. *Initial Implementation Guidance for Federal Agencies on Updates to Federal Agency COVID-19 Workplace Safety Protocols*, SAFER FED. WORKFORCE TASK FORCE (Aug. 17, 2022), https://www.saferfederalworkforce.gov/downloads/Initial%20Implementation%20Guidance_CDC%20Streamline_20220817.pdf.

[128] *Vaccination*, SAFER FED. WORKFORCE TASK FORCE, https://www.saferfederalworkforce.gov/faq/vaccinations/ (last updated Sep. 15, 2022) (expand "Vaccination Documentation and Information").

testing requirements, which would require a separate process to receive accommodation. O'Boyle has thus failed to provide evidence that the FBI's requirement for him to undergo COVID testing violated any law, rule, or regulation, or demonstrated gross mismanagement, a gross waste of funds, or an abuse of authority, or posed a substantial and specific danger to public health or safety.

4. O'Boyle May Have Accessed and Removed Law Enforcement Sensitive Information From FBI Devices Without Authorization

During the transcribed interview, Republican staff questioned O'Boyle about a September 14, 2022, letter from then-Ranking Member Jim Jordan to FBI Director Christopher Wray describing supposed whistleblower disclosures concerning an FBI investigation into Mike Glover, the founder of a group called American Contingency.[129] That letter wrongly states that the FBI had recently characterized American Contingency as a DVE (domestic violent extremism) organization based on an internal FBI document which a "media organization," Project Veritas, had obtained.[130] In fact, the document from the FBI states only that some militia violent extremists "may self-identify with" American Contingency, but that the organization itself has a "low history of violence" and operates "mostly online."[131]

The letter also provides what appears to be a screenshot from the FBI's internal eGuardian incident reporting and management system indicating that the agency had conducted a background investigation into Mike Glover and determined that he did not pose a threat.[132]

Republican staff asked O'Boyle for his reaction to the FBI's investigation. He responded:

> [T]his is, again, to me, another example of how the FBI has been weaponized. Thankfully, in this incident where Glover was investigated, that the agent determined that there was no actual threat there. But then for the other FBI employee to make that allegation in the first place based off of some, you know, very loose information, it's like, what is going on in the FBI?[133]

O'Boyle admitted that he was not personally involved in any way in any investigation into American Contingency or Mike Glover and that any investigation which did take place was not handled out of the Wichita Field Office.[134] Nonetheless, he stated that he did have knowledge of the investigation into Glover:

---

[129] Garret O'Boyle Testimony at 150-51.

[130] Letter from Jim Jordan, Ranking Member, H. Comm. on the Judiciary, to Christopher A. Wray, Director, Fed. Bureau of Investigation at 1-2 (Sep. 14, 2022), https://judiciary.house.gov/sites/evo-subsites/republicans-judiciary.house.gov/files/legacy_files/wp-content/uploads/2022/09/2022-09-14-JDJ-to-Wray-re-WB-follow-up.pdf.

[131] Press Release, *FBI Whistleblower LEAKS Bureau's 'Domestic Terrorism Symbols Guide' on 'Militia Violent Extremists' Citing Ashli Babbitt as MVE Martyr*, PROJECT VERITAS (Aug. 2, 2022), https://www.projectveritas.com/news/fbi-whistleblower-leaks-bureaus-domestic-terrorism-symbols-guide-on-militia/. The FBI document states, "The use or sharing of these symbols should not independently be considered evidence of MVE presence or affiliation or serve as an indicator of illegal activity, as many individuals use these symbols for their original, historic meaning, or other non-violent purposes." *Id.*

[132] Letter from Jim Jordan, Ranking Member, H. Comm. on the Judiciary, to Christopher A. Wray, Director, Fed. Bureau of Investigation at 2 (Sep. 14, 2022), https://judiciary.house.gov/sites/evo-subsites/republicans-judiciary.house.gov/files/legacy_files/wp-content/uploads/2022/09/2022-09-14-JDJ-to-Wray-re-WB-follow-up.pdf.

[133] Garret O'Boyle Testimony at 153

[134] *Id.* at 155-56.

Q   Did you know anything about the investigation or what has been described as an investigation into him [Mike Glover] prior to having this letter put in front of you today?

A   I did.

Q   And what did you know?

A   Pretty much mostly what's in here.

Q   And that – how did you learn that information?

BINNALL: Prior to our previous instructions, you can answer to the extent it's appropriate.

A   This is one of the protected disclosures that I made.

Q   Okay. And it involves Mr. Glover?

A   Uh-huh.

Q   But you ... were not personally involved in any matters involving Mr. Glover in your capacity as an FBI employee?

A   Right. I never investigated him.

Q   Okay. And what about American Contingency?

A   Correct. No.

Q   Okay. So you don't have firsthand knowledge of anything that the FBI may have – may or may not have done?

BINNALL: You can answer to the extent that it doesn't violate my previous instructions.

A   I mean, I guess, in accordance with my work and my protected disclosure, I had some knowledge of what the FBI had done.

BINNALL: And don't go any further than that.[135]

Based on this exchange, Committee Democrats conclude that O'Boyle may have accessed information regarding the FBI's investigation into Glover and/or American Contingency to which he would not have had access as part of his official responsibilities. Committee Democrats also conclude that he may have removed that information, including potentially law enforcement sensitive information, without being authorized to do so.

Moreover, Committee Democrats note that based on the information contained in the September 14 letter, the FBI appears to have conducted a non-intrusive background investigation based on a tip that Glover "'appears to be rallying individuals to "take action"' and 'speaks about his distaste for how the government is handling the current situations in the US and encourages

---

[135] *Id.*

people to "join" his cause.'"[136] The letter provides no evidence that the FBI committed a violation of any law, rule, or regulation or engaged in gross mismanagement, a gross waste of funds, an abuse of authority, or posed a substantial and specific danger to public health or safety with respect to its investigation. O'Boyle has likewise failed to provide any evidence supporting such a finding. Committee Democrats thus conclude that claims O'Boyle made regarding the Glover investigation are without merit.

B. Conclusion

O'Boyle admitted that he had produced extensive information and documents to Committee Republicans that are being withheld from Committee Democrats.[137] That material may well include relevant, probative evidence that would bear on the validity of his claims.

That said, to the extent that O'Boyle did discuss his allegations, he did not present any evidence of a violation of a law, rule, or regulation, or of gross mismanagement, waste of funds, an abuse of authority, or a substantial danger to public health or safety. He provided no evidence that supports Republican efforts to rewrite what happened on January 6, and his COVID vaccine-related claims must be viewed in light of his stated extreme views on the vaccine itself.

For all of these reasons, Committee Democrats conclude that O'Boyle's claims lack merit.

IV. **Witness Summary: Stephen Friend**

The Committee conducted a transcribed interview of Stephen Friend on February 15, 2023.[138] Friend was an FBI Special Agent with the Daytona Beach Residency Agency, a satellite office of the Jacksonville FBI Field Office.[139] According to his testimony, Friend transferred to Daytona from the FBI's Omaha Field Office's Sioux City Resident Agency in June 2021 and was assigned to the Joint Terrorism Task Force (JTTF) at the end of September 2021.[140]

Friend was placed on AWOL (Absent Without Leave) status for one day in August 2022 after he objected to the manner of arrests of January 6 suspects associated with the Three Percenters domestic extremist group.[141] His security clearance was then suspended on September 19, 2022,[142] and he officially resigned from the FBI on the morning of his February 15 interview with the committee.[143]

---

[136] Letter from Jim Jordan, Ranking Member, H. Comm. on the Judiciary, to Christopher A. Wray, Director, Fed. Bureau of Investigation at 2 (Sep. 14, 2022), https://judiciary.house.gov/sites/evo-subsites/republicans-judiciary.house.gov/files/legacy_files/wp-content/uploads/2022/09/2022-09-14-JDJ-to-Wray-re-WB-follow-up.pdf.

[137] Garret O'Boyle Testimony at 41-42.

[138] In advance of the interview, Committee Democrats asked Committee Republicans to produce any documents which Friend had produced to them. Committee Republicans referred Committee Democrats to Friend's publicly available September 2021 declaration but declined to produce anything further.

[139] Stephen Friend Testimony at 8.

[140] *Id.*

[141] *Id.* at 23.

[142] *Id.* at 27. Committee Democrats have, to date, not been provided with a copy of the suspension letter. According to his testimony, Friend's suspension letter listed his "refusal to participate in the August 24th arrest warrant and search warrant operations," his "refusal to participate in a security awareness briefing, and the improper accessing of documents from the FBI's classified system" as the reasons for his suspension. *Id.* at 28.

[143] Stephen Friend Testimony at 27.

On September 21, 2022, Friend signed a ten-page declaration outlining his claims.[144] He submitted this declaration to the Department of Justice Office of Inspector General, the Office of Special Counsel, then-Ranking Member Jim Jordan, and Senators Chuck Grassley, Ron Johnson, and Dick Durbin.[145] Senators Grassley and Johnson subsequently attached the declaration to a public letter, which is available on Senator Johnson's website, and the declaration remains publicly available.[146]

In brief, Friend alleges that the FBI is not following appropriate case management practices in its handling of January 6-related matters. He also objected to the use of a SWAT team in association with the arrest of the above-mentioned January 6 suspects.

Mr. Friend's primary claim has been rejected by multiple entities, and Committee Democrats likewise conclude that the substance of these claims lacks merit. In addition, Committee Democrats note that Friend pushed Committee Republicans to investigate his claims, has profited and is profiting from making his allegations about the FBI public, and has repeatedly engaged in unauthorized media appearances. Finally, Friend has expressed severe animosity towards the Bureau, raising concerns about the impact this bias may have had on his testimony.

A.   Two Independent Entities Have Rejected Friend's "Whistleblower" Claim

During the interview, Friend admitted that both the Department of Justice (DOJ) Inspector General and the Office of Special Counsel have rejected his primary claim.[147]

The Office of Special Counsel (OSC) is an independent federal investigative agency whose "primary mission is to safeguard the merit system by protecting federal employees and applicants from prohibited personnel practices, especially reprisal for whistleblowing."[148] Its letter to him read, in relevant part (emphasis added):

> You alleged employees of the Department of Justice (DOJ), Federal Bureau of Investigation (FBI), Washington, D.C., engaged in activity that may constitute a violation of law, rule, or regulation and an abuse of authority. …. Disclosures referred to the agency for an investigation and a report must include information sufficient for OSC to determine whether there is a substantial likelihood of wrongdoing. …
>
> When determining whether there is a substantial likelihood of wrongdoing, OSC looks at several factors—including whether the whistleblower has first-hand knowledge of the wrongdoing. We understand that you were assigned to the Jacksonville Florida Field Office Joint Terrorism Task Force (Jacksonville JTTF) from October 2021 to August 2022. During that time, you were assigned as "case agent" on approximately six J6 Task Force casefiles with

---

[144] Decl. of Stephen M. Friend (Sep. 21, 2022), https://s3.documentcloud.org/documents/23010763/steve-friend-declaration.pdf. [Hereinafter Stephen Friend Declaration]

[145] Stephen Friend Testimony at 90.

[146] Press Release, *Sens. Johnson, Grassley Expose Wrongful FBI Retaliation Against Patriotic Whistleblower Who Revealed Breaches of Policy and Protocol*, (Sept. 27, 2022), https://www.ronjohnson.senate.gov/2022/9/sens-johnson-grassley-expose-wrongful-fbi-retaliation-against-patriotic-whistleblower-who-revealed-breaches-of-policy-and-protocol.

[147] Stephen Friend Testimony at 93-97.

[148] *About OSC*, U.S. Off. of Special Couns., https://osc.gov/Agency (last visited Feb. 28, 2022).

subjects who resided in and around the Jacksonville area. **You were not involved in the decision to open those cases or to identify the Jacksonville Field Office as the "office of origin," nor did you identify the individuals from the Washington D.C. or Jacksonville offices who made those decisions.**

We have carefully reviewed and considered the information you provided, including your sworn declaration and the DIOG, as a possible abuse of authority or a violation of a law, rule, or regulation. The DIOG is internal guidance that is "not intended to...and may not be relied upon to create any rights, substantive or procedural, enforceable by law by any party in any matter, civil or criminal, nor [does it] place any limitation on otherwise lawful investigative and litigative prerogatives of the DOJ and the FBI." DIOG § 2.5. The DIOG also provides the FBI Director discretion to approve departures from its requirements. DIOG § 2.6. Thus, your allegations concern a matter of agency discretion. Agencies are generally afforded a wide degree of latitude in these areas, and the DIOG expressly allows departures from its requirements. **Although we understand you strongly object to the FBI leadership's decision to depart from the DIOG's guidance for J6 Task Force casefiles, you were not involved in the decision-making process, and you have not provided specific information to establish that the departure was made improperly. Therefore, we cannot find with a substantial likelihood that the agency has violated a law, rule, or regulation, or has abused its authority. Therefore, we will take no further action in this matter.**[149]

The DOJ Office of Inspector General (OIG) similarly declined to open an investigation into Friend's allegations.[150] While Friend has not yet produced the Inspector General findings to Committee Democrats, a January 31, 2023, letter from his attorney states that on December 2, 2022, the Office of Inspector General informed Friend that it had "decided not to open an investigation of the allegations that you raise" and recommended that Friend contact the FBI's Inspection Division if he wished to further pursue his claims.[151]

---

[149] *(READ) Office of Special Counsel dismisses FBI whistleblower complaint about the agency*, SHARYL ATKISSON (Nov. 26, 2022), https://sharylattkisson.com/2022/11/read-office-of-special-counsel-dismisses-fbi-whistleblower-complaint-about-the-agency/. During his interview, Friend confirmed that he had produced OSC's letter to Attkisson, and he confirmed that the letter published on her website was in fact the letter he received from OSC. Stephen Friend Testimony at 96. During the interview he also stated that he was not aware that she had published the letter on her website. Stephen Friend Testimony at 96. But, on November 27, 2022, he thanked Attkisson for publishing the letter and linked to the article on his Twitter account. Steve Friend (@RealSteveFriend), TWITTER (Nov. 27, 2022, 9:05 AM), https://twitter.com/RealSteveFriend/status/1596867895304519682.
[150] Stephen Friend Testimony at 91-92.
[151] Letter from Jason Foster, Founder & President, Empower Oversight, to the Office of Inspector General, Dep't of Justice at 11-12 (Jan. 31, 2023), https://empowr.us/wp-content/uploads/2023/02/2023-1-31-JF-to-DOJOIG-Closure-of-Friend-Complaint.pdf. In the letter, Foster questions whether "the DOJ-OIG, with its hundreds of agents, attorney[s], and multiple field offices around the country [could] really be so overextended that it has no capacity to investigate" the various claims raised by Friend. *Id.* at 12. Committee Democrats agree that the DOJ OIG has sufficient resources to investigate claims it finds meritorious.

B. Friend Pushed the Committee to Investigate His Claims, and He Is Profiting From His Participation in the Committee's Investigation

When the Inspector General rejected his claims, Friend declined to pursue them further through the Inspection Division.[152] Instead, he began urging House Republicans to take action through his social media accounts on Twitter and Truth Social:

- On December 20, 2022, he tweeted, "@FBI Whistleblowers know where the bodies are buried @JudiciaryGOP. Prioritize protecting us in 2023 and more will come forward. Subpoenas and hearings aren't good enough."[153]

- On December 21, he responded to a tweet from journalist Breanna Morello which asked, "[I]sn't this why you became a FBI whistleblower?" by stating, "Yep. One of the disclosures I brought to Congress. Maybe @tedlieu missed it. Hoping @JudiciaryGOP will ask me about it in 2023."[154]

When Republicans did not act quickly enough for Friend, he began pursuing them more aggressively:

- On December 24, Friend wrote on Truth Social, "GOP House Judiciary Committee is tweeting out clips of @realDonaldTrump in Home Alone 2. President Trump is off Twitter guys. How about you DM some suspended FBI whistleblowers instead?"[155]

- On December 25, he posted on Truth Social, "Trolling all day from the House GOP Judiciary Committee twitter account. Can they pretend to show an interest in protecting FBI whistleblowers like @kyleseraphin and me? Or does the committee exist solely for social media interns to 'own the libs?'"[156]

- On December 26, he responded to an NTD Television Truth Social post which states, "Republicans are vowing to investigate cooperation between #Twitter, the #FBI, and the federal government," with the following: "Spoiler: They took my whistleblower complaint. Used it for campaign rocket fuel and 4 minute appearances on Fox News. Ignored me after I lost my income. Focused on other dead investigations that get no results but deliver more appearances. I'm not alone either, @kyleseraphin."[157]

---

[152] Stephen Friend Testimony at 94.

[153] Steve Friend (@RealStevefriend), TWITTER (Dec. 20, 2022, 4:01 PM), https://twitter.com/RealStevefriend/status/1605307475497992193.

[154] Steve Friend (@RealStevefriend), TWITTER (Dec. 21, 2022, 9:37 PM), https://twitter.com/RealStevefriend/status/1605754480506519552.

[155] Steve Friend (@Real_SteveFriend), TRUTH SOCIAL (Dec. 24, 2022, 9:47 PM), https://truthsocial.com/@Real_SteveFriend/posts/109572026898527069.

[156] Steve Friend (@Real_SteveFriend), TRUTH SOCIAL (Dec. 25, 2022, 9:15 PM), https://truthsocial.com/@Real_SteveFriend/posts/109577563422431659.

[157] Steve Friend (@Real_SteveFriend), TRUTH SOCIAL (Dec. 26, 2022, 8:47 PM), https://truthsocial.com/@Real_SteveFriend/posts/109583116369352493.

- On that same day, he responded to a House Judiciary GOP tweet which read, "Fauci lied," by writing, "We already know. Skip those headlines and focus on @FBI whistleblower abuse."[158]

Friend's decision to urge the GOP to focus on him coincides with a marked uptick in his media appearances. Committee Democrats found that prior to the OIG's December 2 determination that it would not pursue his claims, he appeared on just five shows: *Unfiltered with Dan Bongino* on October 15;[159] *Full Measure with Sharyl Attkisson* on October 23;[160] the *Mill Creek View Tennessee Podcast* on November 8;[161] twice with Glenn Beck, on his radio show on November 15[162] and on a television special that aired on November 16;[163] and three times on *The Kyle Seraphin Show* on November 19 and November 22.[164] Between December 6 and the end of 2022, he appeared on at least eight programs.[165] In the time that has elapsed since, he has made so many media appearances that when asked to estimate the total number of podcasts he has appeared on, he said, "I couldn't tell you. I've made a lot of appearances. It would be irresponsible for me to just throw out a number."[166] Though Friend states that he has not received monetary compensation for his media appearances beyond travel and accommodation

[158] Steve Friend (@RealStevefriend), TWITTER (Dec. 26, 2022, 8:37 PM), https://twitter.com/RealStevefriend/status/1607551304854904832.

[159] Unfiltered with Dan Bongino, *FBI whistleblower Steve Friend reveals what at the agency made him speak out*, FOX NEWS (Oct. 15, 2022), https://www.foxnews.com/video/6313831472112.

[160] Sharyl Attkisson, *Sharyl Attkisson's full interview with FBI whistleblower Steve Friend*, RUMBLE (Oct. 24, 2022), https://rumble.com/v1pm8vp-sharyl-attkissons-full-interview-with-fbi-whistleblower-steve-friend.html.

[161] Mill Creek View Tennessee Podcast, *Mill Creek View Tennessee Podcast EP17 Stephen Friend Interview & More November 8 2022*, PODOMATIC (Nov. 8, 2022), https://www.podomatic.com/podcasts/steve70281/episodes/2022-11-08T16_30_09-08_00.

[162] Glenn Beck, *SHOCK: FBI agent LEAVES over agency's handling of Jan. 6*, YOUTUBE (Nov. 20, 2022), https://www.youtube.com/watch?v=KuIsvxdGWIU.

[163] Glenn Beck, *Targets of Tyranny: How to Survive Being an Enemy of the State*, YOUTUBE (Nov. 16, 2022), https://www.youtube.com/watch?v=rj4W-UXMF1A.

[164] The Kyle Seraphin Show, *The Suspendables*, PODBEAN (Nov. 19, 2022), https://thekyleseraphinshow.podbean.com/e/2-the-suspendables/; The Kyle Seraphin Show, *Seraphin & Friend(s)*, PODBEAN (Nov. 19, 2022), https://thekyleseraphinshow.podbean.com/e/1-seraphin-friends/; The Kyle Seraphin Show, *Politically Appointed Princess*, PODBEAN (Nov. 22, 2022), https://thekyleseraphinshow.podbean.com/e/politically-appointed-princes/.

[165]*See* Radix Verum, *Interview with FBI Whistleblower Steve Friend*, YOUTUBE (Dec. 6, 2022), https://www.youtube.com/watch?v=C4PDxZ8untI; Steve Friend (@RealStevefriend), TWITTER (Dec. 7, 2022, 12:35 PM), https://twitter.com/RealStevefriend/status/1600544553878142986 ("Looking forward to appearing on @NEWSMAX tonight with @gregkellyusa at 9:30ET"); Steve Friend (@RealSteveFriend), TWITTER (Dec. 7, 2022, 8:29 PM), https://twitter.com/RealStevefriend/status/1600663729019842560 ("Looking forward to appearing on American Sunrise tomorrow at 9:30ET"); The Kyle Seraphin Show, *The FBI Emperor Has No Clothes*, RUMBLE (Dec. 9, 2022), https://rumble.com/v1zuydg-the-fbi-emperor-has-no-clothes.html; Frank Clips, *The Absolute Truth Interview With : Steve Friend - FBI Whistleblower*, THE ABSOLUTE TRUTH WITH EMERALD ROBINSON (Dec. 12, 2022), https://frankspeech.com/video/absolute-truth-interview-steve-friend-fbi-whistleblower; Joe Pags, *He Says the FBI Became Obsessed with 1/6 - and Turned a Blind Eye to Crime!*, RUMBLE (Dec. 13, 2022), https://rumble.com/v20jho8-he-says-the-fbi-became-obsessed-with-16-and-turned-a-blind-eye-to-crime.html; Alison Morrow, *FBI Whistleblower talks manipulation of Big Tech || Stephen Friend & Radix Verum*, RUMBLE (Dec. 19, 2022), https://rumble.com/v21g0qm-fbi-whistleblower-talks-manipulation-of-big-tech-stephen-friend-and-radix-v.html; Brannon Howse, *Worldview Radio: FBI Whistleblower Steve Friend on Why He Refused to Violate His Constitutional Oath and SWAT J6 Attendees*, WVW BROADCAST NETWORK (Dec. 22, 2022), https://www.worldviewweekend.com/tv/video/worldview-radio-fbi-whistleblower-steve-friend-why-he-refused-violate-his-constitutional.

[166] Stephen Friend Testimony at 184.

costs,[167] his influence has grown substantially. Notably, his following on Twitter grew from 821 followers on December 7, 2022, to over 14,600 followers as of March 1, 2023, an increase of more than 1,600%.[168]

Friend admitted that he uses these podcasts to promote a fundraiser on the crowdfunding platform GiveSendGo,[169] which, as of March 1, 2023, had raised $36,765.[170] In addition, the podcasts and other publicity Friend receives provide him with an opportunity to promote his forthcoming book, *True Blue: My Journey from Beat Cop to Suspended FBI Whistleblower*.[171] *True Blue* is being published by Post Hill Press,[172] "a small independent that specialises in 'conservative politics'" and is "home to authors including far-right conspiracy theorist Laura Loomer."[173] Friend stated that while he has not yet received any direct income from this book, it is currently in presale, and during the week of February 6, he experienced a "bump in sales."[174] He also stated that he believes that his contract includes funding for a book tour.[175]

Additionally, Friend recently accepted a position as a fellow at the Center for Renewing America, a nonprofit founded by former Trump official Russ Vought.[176] Publicity generated by the Committee's investigation would benefit Friend in his new role by increasing the visibility of that organization.

Thus, Committee Democrats conclude that Friend has a monetary incentive to continue pursuing his claims, despite both the Office of Special Counsel and the Office of Inspector General previously rejecting those claims.

---

[167] *Id.*

[168] @RealStevefriend, TWITTER (Dec. 7, 2022), https://web.archive.org/web/20221207205234/https://twitter.com/RealStevefriend; @RealStevefriend, TWITTER, https://twitter.com/RealStevefriend (last visited Mar. 1, 2023).

[169] *Id.* at 184-85.

[170] Kyle Seraphin, *Support suspended FBI Whistleblowers*, GIVESENDGO, https://www.givesendgo.com/KyleSeraphin (last visited Mar. 1, 2023). The fundraiser cover page reads, in relevant part, "This fund will be used to support 3 whistleblower families who have been suspended without pay and legal bills incurred by Kyle Seraphin, Stephen Friend, and a currently unnamed FBI Whistleblower with 4 young children including a newborn baby only weeks old." *Id.* During his interview, Friend stated that the purpose of the fundraiser was "raising money for Garret O'Boyle." Stephen Friend Testimony at 75-76. He added that, while Seraphin offered Friend money from the fundraiser "if [he] needed any funds from it," Friend had not accepted any of the proceeds as of the date of the interview. Stephen Friend Testimony at 77.

[171] Stephen Friend Testimony at 82, 175-76.

[172] *Id.* at 83.

[173] Sian Cain, *Simon & Schuster refuses to distribute book by officer who shot Breonna Taylor*, GUARDIAN (Apr. 16, 2021), https://www.theguardian.com/books/2021/apr/16/simon-schuster-book-breonna-taylor-jonathan-mattingly-the-fight-for-truth.

[174] Stephen Friend Testimony at 82, 88-89, 175-76.

[175] *Id.* at 84.

[176] Russ Vought (@russvought), TWITTER (Jan. 27, 2023, 4:20 PM), https://twitter.com/russvought/status/1619082843535323136 ("Excited to announce that FBI whistleblower Steve Friend is coming on board @amrenewctr to help uncover the full extent of the FBI's weaponization against the American people. @RealStevefriend is going to play a huge role in maximizing the potential of the new Church committee!).

C. Committee Democrats Concur with the Independent Entities to Find that Friend's Claims Lack Merit

1. Friend Has Not Provided Evidence to Support Republican Claims That the FBI Is Engaging in Improper Case Management Procedures in the January 6 Investigations

The FBI's Domestic Investigations and Operations Guide (DIOG) is a manual used by FBI employees to guide their handling of investigations and intelligence collection within the United States.[177] In addition to the DIOG, each FBI headquarters operational unit has one or more policy guides which provide supplemental guidelines.[178]

Friend has expressed concern that the FBI's Washington Field Office is opening and managing all January 6-related cases but labeling those cases with the file labels associated with the FBI field offices closest to the suspects' residences. Friend alleges that this amounts to "irregular case dissemination, labeling, and management processes [which] could be considered exculpatory evidence [which] must be disclosed to defendants in accordance with the Brady rule."[179]

At the outset, even assuming that Friends' claims about how January 6 cases are being handled are accurate, DIOG section 2.7, "Departures from the DIOG and DIOG-Related Policies," specifically permits the FBI to depart from DIOG procedures. This section reads:

> A "departure" from the DIOG is a deliberate deviation from a specific known requirement or action governed by the DIOG. The word "deliberate" means the employee was aware of the DIOG requirement and affirmatively chose to depart from it for operational reasons before the activity took place. Approval of a departure must be based upon a specific circumstance involving a specific administrative or operational need. An approval may be for the duration of an investigation or relate to a specific classification, cannot extend beyond the scope of authority of the approving official, and must be approved in accordance with the guidance provided in this subsection.[180]

During his interview, Friend admitted that he was not involved in the decision-making process around how January 6 cases would be handled across the FBI; was not in a supervisory position during his tenure at the Daytona Beach Residency Agency; did not participate in regular FBI-wide calls related to Capitol insurrection cases; and had no information as to whether a departure from the DIOG had been authorized for the investigation of events related to the January 6 Capitol attack.[181]

In fact, Friend admitted that he does not know if the FBI is using the DIOG as the controlling authority for January 6 cases, or whether it is relying on another authority in place of or addition to the DIOG. For example, the Counter Terrorism Program Guide is a classified

---

[177] *Domestic Investigations and Operations Guide*, FED. BUREAU OF INVESTIGATION § 1 at 1-1 (Sep. 17, 2021), https://vault.fbi.gov/FBI%20Domestic%20Investigations%20and%20Operations%20Guide%20%28DIOG%29/fbi-domestic-investigations-and-operations-guide-diog-2021-version. [Hereinafter FBI DIOG].

[178] FBI DIOG § 1 at 1-1.

[179] Stephen Friend Declaration ¶ 12.

[180] FBI DIOG § 2.7.1 at 2-11.

[181] Stephen Friend Testimony at 69-73.

document that provides specific guidance for handling mass events and often supplements the DIOG in very large, complex criminal cases. When asked, Friend admitted that he had no knowledge or familiarity with the FBI Counter Terrorism Program Guide or its guidelines for managing cases related to a mass event.[182]

Friend also claimed in his declaration that the FBI's January 6-related case management practices "could be considered exculpatory evidence" that "must be disclosed to defendants in accordance with the Brady rule,"[183] an apparent reference to the Supreme Court's ruling in a 1963 case, *Brady v. Maryland*.[184] During his interview, Friend was asked about his understanding of the "Brady Rule."[185] He responded, "[W]e have to hand over everything that's related to a prosecution so that the defendant has that access to that information and can mount a defense."[186] In fact, *Brady* requires prosecutors to disclose materially exculpatory evidence in the government's possession to the defense.[187] Friend did not explain how the FBI's case management and labeling procedures might meet this standard.

Moreover, the DIOG expressly does not create any rights enforceable by criminal defendants. Section 2.5 of the DIOG reads:

> The AGG-Dom, this DIOG, and the various operational division PGs are set forth solely for the purpose of internal DOJ and FBI guidance. They are not intended to, do not, and may not be relied upon to create any rights, substantive or procedural, enforceable by law by any party in any matter, civil or criminal, nor do they place any limitation on otherwise lawful investigative and litigative prerogatives of the DOJ and the FBI.[188]

Friend admitted that he was not familiar with this paragraph before it was read to him at the transcribed interview.[189]

Accordingly, Committee Democrats concur with the Office of Special Counsel finding that Friend's DIOG-related claims lack evidence that the FBI violated any law, rule, or regulation, or has engaged in gross mismanagement, a gross waste of funds, or an abuse of authority, or posed a substantial and specific danger to public health or safety.

2. Friend Claimed That He Objected to the Use of a SWAT Team in an Arrest, But Later Admitted That the FBI Would Be Justified in Using a SWAT Team to Arrest a Defendant Known to Be Armed and Violent

On August 24, 2022, the FBI arrested five individuals—John Edward Crowley, Jonathan Alan Rockholt, Tyler Quintin Bensch, Benjamin Cole, and Brian Preller—for their involvement

---

[182] *Id.* at 72.
[183] Stephen Friend Declaration ¶ 12.
[184] *Brady v. Maryland*, 373 U.S. 83 (1963).
[185] Stephen Friend Testimony at 141.
[186] *Id.*
[187] *Brady v. Maryland*, 373 U.S. 83 (1963).
[188] FBI DIOG § 2.5 at 2-10.
[189] Stephen Friend Testimony at 142.

in the January 6 attack on the Capitol.[190] According to a contemporaneous Justice Department news release, "the five men self-identified as members of the 'B Squad,' a subgroup of a militia-style, Florida based organization known as the 'Guardians of Freedom,' which adheres to the ideology of the 'Three Percenters.'"[191] As the statement of facts accompanying the defendants' charging documents explains, "Three Percenters Militia violent extremists sometimes self-identify as three percenters ("III%ers" or "threepers") based on the myth that only three percent of American colonists took up arms against the British during the American Revolution."[192]

Crowley, Rockholt, Cole, and Preller were "charged with the felony offense of interfering with a law enforcement officer during a civil disorder" as well as "misdemeanor offenses of entering and remaining in a restricted building or grounds and disorderly and disruptive conduct in a restricted building or grounds."[193] Bensch was charged with the misdemeanor offenses only.[194]

Friend became aware of the planned arrests of Bensch, Rockholt, and Crowley via an office-wide email circulated the week of August 15 stating that "there were going to be arrest

---

[190] Press Release, *Five Florida Men Arrested on Charges for Actions During Jan. 6 Capitol Breach*, U.S. DEP'T OF JUSTICE (Aug. 24, 2022), https://www.justice.gov/usao-dc/pr/five-florida-men-arrested-charges-actions-during-jan-6-capitol-breach.

[191] *Id.* Mr. Friend stated that while he was familiar with the Three Percenters extremist group from his work with FBI, he had not formed an opinion about them:

    Q   Are you familiar with the Three Percenters?

    A   Yes.

    Q   How did you become familiar with them?

    A   Just reading about individuals who were arrested for their involvement on January 6th and the predication for a lot of the investigations involving some groups like Three Percenters or Oath Keepers or Proud Boys is that information is circulated within the national security side of things in the FBI.

    Q   And had you been privy to that information?

    A   Yeah. If I wanted to research it in more detail, yes, I could. …

    Q   …There's a footnote on this page [of the Cole et al. Statement of Facts], it's footnote number 2. It describes the Three Percenters as, quote/unquote, "violent extremists." Do you agree with that term as applied to the Three Percenters?

    A   I don't have an opinion on it. …

    Q   …The footnote continues: "Some III%ers" – and it's the Roman numeral III, the percent sign, e-r-s – "regard the present day U.S. Government as analogous to British authorities during the Revolution in terms of infringements on civil liberties." Do you agree with this statement about the Three Percenters?

    A: I don't have any opinion, and I don't think my opinion really matters on the Three Percenters. …

    Q: …On the following page [of the Cole et al. Statement of Facts] there's a photograph of a flyer distributed on December 24th, 2020, by this group. It reads: "Remember this, it comes straight from our Declaration of Independence that whenever any form of government becomes destructive, it is the right and duty of the people to alter or abolish it. That is why you are here. For massive change to occur massive action must be taken. Patriots, we are the lifeblood of this great nation, and it's time we prove that." Do you have an opinion about this statement?

    A   It seems like First Amendment protected activity. Stephen Friend Testimony at 156-58.

[192] *U.S. v. Cole et al.*, Case no. 1:22-mj-184-RMM, Doc. No. 5-1 (Statement of Facts) at 3 n.2 (Aug. 29, 2022), https://www.justice.gov/usao-dc/case-multi-defendant/file/1529756/download.

[193] Press Release, *Five Florida Men Arrested on Charges for Actions During Jan. 6 Capitol Breach*, U.S. DEP'T OF JUSTICE (Aug. 24, 2022), https://www.justice.gov/usao-dc/pr/five-florida-men-arrested-charges-actions-during-jan-6-capitol-breach.

[194] *Id.*

operations happening, SWAT was going to be involved, and [he] would need to be free on the 24th."[195]

During the interview, Friend stated that he objected to the use of a SWAT team because "the subject of the arrest warrant had been in communication with the FBI at that point and had expressed a willingness to cooperate with the FBI."[196] Friend's September 21 declaration said nothing about concerns related to cooperation, however. Instead, he stated that he expressed to his supervisor "that it was inappropriate to use an FBI SWAT team to arrest a subject for misdemeanor offenses and opined that the subject would likely face extended detainment and biased jury pools in Washington D.C."[197] At his interview, he was unable to explain why he failed to mention the cooperation claim in his contemporaneous declaration:

> Q   And did you raise the cooperation concern to your supervisor?
>
> A   Yes.
>
> Q   Okay. But you didn't note that in your declaration, right?
>
> A   No.
>
> Q   And was there a reason you didn't note that in your declaration?
>
> A   Just oversight.[198]

In a January 31, 2023, podcast interview, Friend implied that he had no direct knowledge of any level of cooperation by the subjects of arrest. During that conversation, Friend acknowledged that the FBI's interview with the suspect had taken place before he joined the JTTF, and that he had only read a transcript of the interview after the fact. He cited to one line from that transcript—according to Friend, the suspect had said, "If you need anything from me, just let me know."[199] From "let me know," Friend apparently infers formal cooperation between the suspect and the FBI. "Let me know" alone falls short of cooperation to the reasonable observer, and it defies belief that anyone would be willing to claim full cooperation based on such assurances.

---

[195] Stephen Friend Testimony at 151-52. During his interview, Friend was unable to identify Bensch, Rockholt, and Crowley by name, instead referring to them generally as January 6 suspects. Of the suspects arrested on August 24, 2022, however, only Bensch, Rockholt, and Crowley were arrested in Florida. Press Release, *Five Florida Men Arrested on Charges for Actions During Jan. 6 Capitol Breach*, U.S. DEP'T OF JUSTICE (Aug. 24, 2022), https://www.justice.gov/usao-dc/pr/five-florida-men-arrested-charges-actions-during-jan-6-capitol-breach ("Crowley, Rockholt, and Bensch were arrested in Florida and are making their initial court appearances today in the Middle District of Florida. Cole, who was arrested in Louisville, is making his initial court appearance in the Western District of Kentucky. Preller, who was arrested in Hardwick, Vermont, is making his appearance in the District of Vermont.").

[196] Stephen Friend Testimony at 19.

[197] Stephen Friend Declaration ¶ 11.

[198] Stephen Friend Testimony at 154.

[199] *Steve Interviews FBI Whistleblower, Steve Friend*, THE PRAGMATIC CONSTITUTIONALIST at 20:58 (Jan. 31, 2023), https://rumble.com/v27wnz0-steve-interviews-fbi-whistleblower-steve-friend.html ("The SWAT team in my scenario was going to be used for somebody who was charged with a felony. But I explained to them that even though it was a felony, this individual had said, 'If you need anything from me, just let me know,' in the interview that I had read. I hadn't been, even – the interview had happened before I even became involved in the Joint Terrorism Task Force.").

More importantly, Friend admitted that he was not assigned to the Jacksonville SWAT team and would not have been assigned to a SWAT team deployed for the August 24 arrest.[200] He also confirmed that he did not actually know the purpose of the SWAT team, telling the Committee, "I don't know which individual SWAT was being used for, because I was never privy to the operations plan that was drafted."[201] He likewise confirmed that he never reviewed a SWAT risk assessment form, also known as a SWAT matrix, for this particular case.[202]

Friend ultimately admitted, however, that the FBI may have been justified in deploying a SWAT team to arrest Tyler Bensch, the only defendant arrested solely on misdemeanor charges on August 24. In his transcribed interview, Friend was read the description of Bensch contained in the statement of facts accompanying Bensch's charging documents and shown the picture accompanying that written description.[203]

[5] Tyler Quintin Bensch

On January 6, 2021, a 20-year-old white male named Tyler Quintin Bensch was pictured wearing the following items while on restricted Capitol grounds:

1. green military fatigues and tan gloves;
2. a military-type helmet and goggles with the brand name "SMITH" in white on a black strap;
3. a tactical vest with a patch associated with the "Three Percenters" movement (i.e., "III");
4. a black gas mask with a green filter; and
5. a drab colored scarf with a distinct pattern.

Bensch also possessed:

1. one or more chemical irritant canisters on the front of his tactical vest;
2. a black radio and antennae on his left side; and
3. a GoPro style camera mounted on his right shoulder.

The following are images of Bensch obtained from open-source videos or images taken within the restricted Capitol Grounds:

[Source: *U.S. v. Cole et al.*, Case no. 1:22-mj-184-RMM, Doc. No. 5-1 (Statement of Facts) at 14 (Aug. 29, 2022)].

---

[200] Stephen Friend Testimony at 151-52.

[201] *Id*. at 155. Friend later repeated, "I don't know who the SWAT team was going to be used for." *Id*. at 163.

[202] Stephen Friend Testimony at 195.

[203] *Id*. at 159-60.

Friend was also read a portion of the statement of facts explaining, "A witness described Bensch posting photos and videos of himself outside the Capitol 'with a gas mask, body armor vest, all black or camouflage attire, and an AR-style rifle.'"[204] He confirmed that from this information, law enforcement could reasonably conclude that Bensch possessed a firearm:

Q   Based on this description, could it be reasonable for law enforcement to conclude that Mr. Bensch possessed an AR-style rifle?

A   Yes.[205]

Friend was also read a portion of the statement of facts stating that Bensch posted video on his Facebook account of a previous rally "which resulted in violent clashes between Trump supporters and counter-protestors. Open-source videos associated with the event contain images of Bench—based on that individual's helmet, goggles, body armor, military fatigues, drab scarf, and right shoulder camera."[206] He confirmed that based on this description, it would be reasonable for law enforcement to conclude that Bench had engaged in acts of violence:

Q   And based on that description, could it be reasonable for law enforcement to conclude that he had previously engaged in acts of violence?

A   Yes.[207]

Friend confirmed that ownership of a firearm, even without any additional factors, would be enough of a factor on its own to justify deploying a SWAT team in an arrest, saying that he had observed cases where firearm ownership "opened up the matrix of use of, like, a SWAT team to apprehend somebody."[208] He explained:

Q   The individuals that you expressed concern about for August 24th, were you aware of any factors that would counsel in favor of a SWAT team?

A   I think being a gun owner meets that matrix, and those individuals were. I think that being, you know, accused of a felony is something that can be taken into consideration. And, ultimately, if local law enforcement requests permission to use a SWAT team, then the FBI will do that as well.[209]

In light of Friend's confirmation that he was not personally privy to information about the use of a SWAT team to arrest Bensch, Rockholt, or Crowley, and his assertion that all three individuals were gun owners and thus the SWAT matrix could have supported the use of a SWAT team to arrest them, Committee Democrats conclude that Friend has not shown that the use of SWAT team in this situation amounted to any violation of law, rule, or regulation, or gross

---

[204] Stephen Friend Testimony at 161-62 (quoting *U.S. v. Cole et al.*, Case no. 1:22-mj-184-RMM, Doc. No. 5-1 (Statement of Facts) at 36 (Aug. 29, 2022)).
[205] Stephen Friend Testimony at 162.
[206] *U.S. v. Cole et al.*, Case no. 1:22-mj-184-RMM, Doc. No. 5-1 (Statement of Facts) at 37 (Aug. 29, 2022), https://www.justice.gov/usao-dc/case-multi-defendant/file/1529756/download; *Id.*
[207] Stephen Friend Testimony at 162.
[208] *Id.* at 112, 188.
[209] *Id.* at 189.

mismanagement, a gross waste of funds, an abuse of authority, or a substantial and specific danger to public health or safety.

3. Friend's Remaining Claims Similarly Fail to Show Misconduct

Friend also raised two claims concerning resource allocation and a particular surveillance incident. Committee Democrats have examined both and find both without merit.

a) Allegations Of Resource Allocation Away from Other Criminal Matters

In his declaration, Friend stated that he was transferred from working on child exploitation cases to the Joint Terrorism Task Force (JTTF) in October 2021 and said, without any supporting evidence, that he was "told that child sexual abuse material investigations were no longer an FBI priority and should be referred to local law enforcement agencies."[210] During his interview, though, Friend explained that he continued to work on child exploitation cases until he was suspended[211] and handled approximately the same number of child exploitation cases both before and after he was transferred to the JTTF.[212] In fact, Friend received an award for his work in this area in July 2022 after he agreed to take on all of the child exploitation cases for a local sheriff's officer earlier that year.[213] Friend also told the Committee that, both before and after October 2021, his role with respect to child exploitation cases was to "assist the local partner as needed," determine "if there was a Federal nexus to open up a Federal case," and "pick" whether a state or federal case would be "the better, more strategic option."[214]

In sum, Friend offered no evidence to support his claim, and his own testimony appears to cut against his argument. Committee Democrats thus find no evidence that this claim supports allegations that the FBI violated any law, rule, or regulation, or has engaged in gross mismanagement, a gross waste of funds, or an abuse of authority, or posed a substantial and specific danger to public health or safety.

b) Allegations Regarding Surveilling an Individual Attending a School Board Meeting

During his interview, Friend was asked about the Attorney General's October 4, 2021, memorandum to address violent threats against school administrators, board members, teachers, and staff.[215] He described an instance in which he was asked to surveil an individual who was going to a school board meeting.[216] On cross-examination, Friend admitted that prior to being given this task, he was aware that the FBI had an open counterterrorism investigation into the individual in question and that the individual was "one of the people that were arrested on August 24th," meaning one of the individuals adhering to the Three Percenter violent

---

[210] Stephen Friend Declaration ¶ 5.

[211] Stephen Friend Testimony at 9.

[212] Id. at 60 (stating that he handled his full child exploitation caseload while working on the JTTF). *See also* Stephen Friend Testimony at 59 (stating that he handled "a few dozen" cases total between June and September 2021); Stephen Friend Testimony at 61-62 (stating that between early 2022 and July 2022, he brought "a couple" of cases to prosecution but also handled "two to three a week" that he would close).

[213] Stephen Friend Testimony at 34-35.

[214] Id. at 58-59.

[215] Id. at 121-22.

[216] Id. 126-27.

ideology.[217] He also separately acknowledged that "there had to be a legitimate predication" for the open counterterrorism investigation on the individual.[218] Friend stated that he and his fellow agents never actually entered the school board meeting:

> So essentially we just documented the license plates of the people that were parking at the school board meeting who were January 6th subjects, or people that were in the parking lot with them interacting that we thought could be in their sphere of influence, and then we left.[219]

Committee Democrats find no evidence that this surveillance was improper or that it supports allegations that the FBI violated any law, rule, or regulation, or has engaged in gross mismanagement, a gross waste of funds, or an abuse of authority, or posed a substantial and specific danger to public health or safety.

D. Friend Has Engaged in Other Troubling Conduct

1. Friend Accessed and Removed Material From a Classified System Without Authorization

Friend has publicly stated that his security clearance was suspended because he improperly accessed material on FBI computer systems,[220] and during his testimony, he admitted that while a Special Agent at the Daytona Beach Resident Agency, he accessed and removed documents marked "For Official Use Only" from a classified FBI system.[221] Specifically, he admitted that in September 2022, he accessed the classified system to get "information about the employee handbook and disciplinary processes," "a flow chart of the way the Inspection Division works and the OPR [Office of Professional Responsibility] process works," and "copies of the last five OPR quarterlies as a go by for precedent for punishment for my situation."[222] He also accessed and removed elements of the then-current version of the FBI Domestic Investigations and Operations Guide.[223]

The Office of the Director of National Intelligence (ODNI) serves as the Security Executive Agent for the federal government, meaning that it is responsible for establishing, implementing, and overseeing uniform policies "governing the conduct of investigations and adjudications for eligibility for access to classified information and eligibility to hold a sensitive position."[224] In 2017, it issued Security Executive Agent Directive 4: National Security Adjudicative Guidelines, which establish the general criteria for obtaining and maintaining a security clearance.[225] Guideline M addresses the misuse of information technology. It explains:

---

[217] *Id.* at 139-40.

[218] *Id.* at 134.

[219] *Id.* at 127.

[220] *See, e.g.,* Steve Friend (@Real_SteveFriend), TRUTH SOCIAL (Jan. 10, 2023, 9:09 AM), https://truthsocial.com/@Real_SteveFriend/posts/109665307137228963 ("I am on DAY 113 of suspension for improperly accessing the employee handbook").

[221] *Id.* at 64, 67-68.

[222] *Id.* at 64.

[223] *Id.* at 67-68.

[224] *Security Executive Agent,* OFF. OF THE DIRECTOR OF NAT'L INTEL, https://www.dni.gov/index.php/ncsc-how-we-work/ncsc-security-executive-agent (last visited Mar. 1, 2023).

[225] *Security Executive Agent Directive 4,* OFF. OF THE DIRECTOR OF NAT'L INTEL. at 1 (Jun. 8, 2017), https://www.odni.gov/files/NCSC/documents/Regulations/SEAD-4-Adjudicative-Guidelines-U.pdf.

"Failure to comply with rules, procedures, guidelines, or regulations pertaining to information technology systems may raise security concerns about an individual's reliability and trustworthiness, calling into question the willingness or ability to properly protect sensitive systems, networks, and information."[226] The guideline lists "downloading, storing, or transmitting classified, sensitive, proprietary, or other protected information on or to any unauthorized information technology system" as one of the "[c]onditions that could raise a security concern and may be disqualifying," meaning that it may disqualify an individual from obtaining or maintaining a security clearance.[227]

Committee Democrats conclude that Friend's improper use of technology was likely a contributing factor in the FBI's decision to suspend his security clearance.

2. Friend Has Repeatedly Made Unauthorized Media Appearances

As previously noted, Friend has made numerous media appearances since his declaration was made public and has repeatedly discussed information acquired as part of his official duties.

The FBI's Prepublication Review Policy Guide explains:

> All information created and acquired by current and former FBI personnel in connection with official FBI duties, as well as all official material to which FBI personnel have access, is the property of the United States… Unauthorized disclosure, misuse, or negligent handling of FBI information could adversely affect national security, place human life in jeopardy, result in denial of due process, obstruct justice, prevent the FBI from effectively discharging its responsibilities, or violate federal law.[228]

For this reason, FBI employees are required obtain preclearance from the FBI's Prepublication Review Office (PRO) at least thirty days in advance of any media appearance so that the PRO can: "(1) assess whether the proposed disclosure includes prohibited information, (2) advise submitting FBI personnel of any such concerns, and (3) work with the submitter to resolve such concerns."[229]

Friend told the Committee that he submitted a request to communicate with media about his written declaration involving FBI information to the Prepublication Review Office on October 11, 2022.[230] He then appeared on *Unfiltered with Dan Bongino* on October 15, 2022.[231] Committee Democrats have reviewed this appearance and determined that Friend disclosed FBI information which was not originally included in his written disclosure. For example, during this appearance, Friend publicly claimed for the first time that his supervisors told him that the FBI

---

[226] *Id.* at 23.

[227] *Id.* at 23.

[228] *Prepublication Review Policy Guide*, FED. BUREAU OF INVESTIGATION § 3 (Jan. 8, 2020), https://vault.fbi.gov/prepublication-review-policy-guide-1065pg/prepublication-review-policy-guide-1065pg-part-01-of-01.

[229] *Id.* at §§ 3, 4.2.1.

[230] E-mail from Stephen Friend to FBIPrePub@fbi.gov (Oct. 12, 2022, 5:25 PM) (on file with Committee).

[231] Unfiltered with Dan Bongino, *FBI whistleblower Steve Friend reveals what at the agency made him speak out*, FOX NEWS (Oct. 15, 2022), https://www.foxnews.com/video/6313831472112.

had devised special procedures for handling January 6 cases in order "to get quote-unquote 'buy-in' from the field."[232]

On October 21, 2022, Friend received a response from the Information Management Division (IMD). In relevant part, the letter read:

> This letter is in response to your request received by the Federal Bureau of Investigation's (FBI) Prepublication Review Office (PRO) on October 11, 2022, in preparation of media contact concerning the above-referenced subject in accordance with the FBI's Prepublication Review Policy (PRP) and Prepublication Review Policy Guide (1065PG). It has come to our attention that your contact with the media occurred prior to completion of the FBI's prepublication review. Per 1065PG, Section 4.3.3, you are cautioned that disclosure of information by current or former personnel without the appropriate prepublication review may be subject to sanctions, if warranted based on the content of the disclosure. The FBI cautions that future disclosures involving FBI equities should be cleared by the FBI before publication occurs.
>
> Consistent with 1065PG and 28 CFR § 17.18, IMD will respond to requests within 30 working days of receipt. As such, you are reminded to submit any future proposed disclosures, including oral, written, or electronic, to the FBI at least 30 working days in advance and wait for authorization before proceeding with the disclosure of FBI information acquired in connection with official FBI duties.
>
> Compliance with the PRP does not relieve you of the obligation to comply with the Standards of Ethical Conduct for the Executive Branch, and other applicable FBI and Office of Government Ethics regulations or policies. Prior to taking any further action with respect to media contact, consider applicable regulations as set forth in the FBI Ethics and Integrity Program Policy Guide (1120PG), with particular attention to Sections 4.8 and 4.9. Please also ensure that appropriate approval within your chain of command is attained prior to participation when the information relates to your area of expertise within the FBI.[233]

During his testimony before the Committee, Friend admitted that he did not consult the Standards of Ethical Conduct for the Executive Branch or other applicable FBI and governmental ethics regulations or policies before making further media disclosures.[234] He further admitted that he did not consult with his chain of command before making further disclosures.[235] He likewise confirmed that he did not seek specific approval for any of the individual media appearances which he made following his October appearance on the Dan Bongino show.[236]

---

[232] *Id* at 02:47.
[233] Letter from Section Chief, Record/Information Dissemination Section, Information Management Div., to Stephen Friend (Oct. 21, 2022) (on file with Committee).
[234] Stephen Friend Testimony at 168.
[235] *Id.* at 170.
[236] *Id.* at 185.

Accordingly, Committee Democrats conclude that Friend failed to obtain appropriate authorization before engaging in media appearances. Committee Democrats further note that Friend has been advised that he continues to be bound by the FBI Prepublication Review Policy despite having resigned from the Bureau.[237] It appears that he is continuing to engage in unauthorized media appearances, including recent ones in which he discussed his testimony before the Committee in addition to FBI-related information.[238]

3. Friend engaged with Russian propaganda outlets while an FBI employee

On at least two occasions, Friend engaged with Russian journalists and propaganda outlets while still an FBI employee.

On January 20, 2023, Sputnik News published an article titled, "Under Biden Federal Agencies Turned Into Instrument of Intimidation, FBI Whistleblower Says," which relied heavily on comments from Friend.[239] The article was written by Ekaterina Blinova, whose Twitter profile describes her as an "Independent political analyst, freelance journo, proud

---

[237] The October 21 letter was preceded by an email exchange between Friend and an FBI Office of Public Affairs (OPA) Unit Chief. In an October 11 email, the Unit Chief stated, in relevant part:

"The Office of Public Affairs has received your request for permission to communicate to numerous media outlets about information in the affidavit you have filed with the Office of Special Counsel, the DOJ Inspector General, and Congress. For any proposed disclosure of FBI information, outside of official duty requirements, related to FBI matters or based upon information obtained by virtue of FBI employment you are required to engage with the Information Management Division's Prepublication Review Office instead of OPA.

"This requirement applies both to current and former employees and is set out in the FBI's Prepublication Review Policy Guide and the Nondisclosure Agreements (NDA) you signed upon entering service as a condition to access FBI information.

"PRO will conduct a thorough review to assess whether your proposed messaging is free from prohibited disclosures that could harm FBI personnel, assets, and operations. They will collaborate with you to resolve any concerns working to ensure that any messaging is free from sensitive/classified government information." Email from Unit Chief, FBI Off. of Public Affs., to Stephen Friend (Oct. 11, 2022, 11:36 AM) (on file with the Committee).

During Friend's interview before the Committee, Friend's attorney stated that he interpreted this language as granting Friend authorization to make media disclosures, stating, "So the email we sent out, they responded and said that they would work with us if the declaration had sensitive information in it... So they came back with that letter, cautioning him on speaking before he had approval, and there was no comment on the declaration... And then he took no comment of the declaration as approval to stay within the bounds of the declaration, which had previously been released by Senator Johnson." Stephen Friend Testimony at 167.

Committee Democrats disagree with Friend's attorney's interpretation. The October 11 email was sent by the FBI's Office of Public Affairs (OPA) and expressly advised him to "collaborate" with the PRO instead of OPA going forward. It does not make any representations on behalf of PRO. Regardless, Committee Democrats have reviewed the content of multiple of Friend's media appearances and have determined that he regularly discusses information purportedly gained within the scope of his FBI employment which was not contained in his declaration.

[238] The Kyle Seraphin Show, *Mr. Friend Goes to Washington*, RUMBLE (Feb. 17, 2023), https://rumble.com/v29y176-mr.-friend-goes-to-washington.html; TheMostlyPeacefulPodcast, *EP1 Recovering FBI Agents Steve Friend and Kyle Seraphin On DOJ Weaponization*, RUMBLE at 19:10 (Feb. 21, 2023), https://rumble.com/v2aeh24-ep1-recovering-fbi-agents-steve-friend-and-kyle-seraphin-on-doj-polarizatio.html; Jesse Watters Primetime, *What has happened to the FBI?*, FOX NEWS (Feb. 24, 2023) https://www.foxnews.com/video/6321178850112.

[239] Ekaterina Blinova, *Under Biden Federal Agencies Turned Into Instrument of Intimidation, FBI Whistleblower Says*, SPUTNIK (Jan. 20, 2023) https://sputniknews.com/20230120/under-biden-federal-agencies-turned-into-instrument-of-intimidation-fbi-whistleblower-says-1106516720.html.

Russian."[240] Sputnik News was established by the Russian government in 2014 and is fully owned by Rossiya Segodnya, also known as Russia Today and RT, which is fully owned by the Russian government.[241] Rossiya Segodnya is registered as a foreign agent with the Justice Department.[242] Last year, the European Union sanctioned and banned both Sputnik and RT/Russia Today, finding that both were used by the Russian Federation "in a systematic, international campaign of disinformation, information manipulation and distortion of facts in order to enhance its strategy of destabilisation of its neighbouring countries, the EU and its member states."[243]

During his interview, Friend was asked if he was familiar with Sputnik. He responded, "It's a Russian propaganda newspaper," and he confirmed that he had provided Blinova with written responses to three questions.[244] He admitted that he failed to inform the FBI that he had received outreach from a journalist affiliated with the Russian government and did not seek approval before responding to Blinova's inquiry.[245] Likewise, he did not take any action after the story was published beyond checking to confirm that Blinova accurately reproduced the statements he had given to her.[246]

Friend was also asked about Russia Today. He stated that he understood it to be "another propaganda arm for the Russian Government"[247] and that he had never intentionally appeared on Russia Today:

> Q   Do you know if Russia Today ever referenced your comments during its broadcast?
>
> A   I did not know until I had my meeting with the Security Division of the FBI, and they accused me of appearing on Russia Today. And I had to inform them that they probably just lifted my appearances from other media sources and replayed them.
>
> Q   Okay. But so you are aware that they have – you've never appeared intentionally, but they've taken your statements and broadcast them?
>
> A   I never went looking for it. I'll take what Security Division said on its face as accurate.[248]

---

[240] Ekaterina Blinova (@blinova14), TWITTER, https://twitter.com/blinova14 (last visited Mar. 1, 2023).

[241] *About Us*, SPUTNIK, https://sputniknews.com/docs/index.html (last visited Feb. 27, 2023); Stephen Ennis, *Putin's RIA Novosti revamp prompts propaganda fears*, BBC (Dec. 9, 2013), https://www.bbc.com/news/world-europe-25309139.

[242] FARA Exhibit B Filing, Federal State Unitary Enterprise Rossiya Segodnya International Information Agency, Reg. No. 6869 (Aug. 2, 2022), https://efile.fara.gov/docs/6869-Exhibit-AB-20220802-4.pdf.

[243] Press Release, *EU imposes sanctions on state-owned outlets RT/Russia Today and Sputnik's broadcasting in the EU*, COUNCIL OF THE EUROPEAN UNION (Mar. 2, 2022), https://www.consilium.europa.eu/en/press/press-releases/2022/03/02/eu-imposes-sanctions-on-state-owned-outlets-rt-russia-today-and-sputnik-s-broadcasting-in-the-eu/.

[244] Stephen Friend Testimony at 178-79.

[245] *Id.* at 181.

[246] *Id.* at 180.

[247] *Id.* at 180.

[248] *Id.* at 180-81.

In fact, on December 24, 2022, Friend appeared for a video interview on *The Whistleblowers* with John Kiriakou, an RT program.[249] It does not appear that Friend notified the FBI of his appearance or that he obtained specific authorization prior to doing so.

E.   Friend Has Demonstrated Severe Bias Towards the Bureau Which Is Reasonably Likely to Have Impacted His Testimony

Friend's testimony centered on his concerns with the FBI's management of investigations related to the January 6 Capitol attack on both a national and local level. His complaints, however, must be viewed as coming from the perspective of someone seeking to do harm to the FBI, as he has repeatedly demonstrated animus towards the Bureau in media appearances and on social media.

Since being suspended, Friend has publicly described the FBI as a "a feckless, garbage institution."[250] From when he joined Twitter on November 16, 2022, through February 14, 2023, Friend posted over 20 times calling for the FBI to be defunded,[251] dismantled,[252] dissolved,[253] aborted,[254] abolished,[255] or otherwise ended.[256]

During a November 8, 2022, podcast appearance on *Mill Creek View Tennessee Podcast*, he again voiced his belief that the FBI should be ended, saying, "I will say unequivocally now that the FBI is beyond saving, it needs to be control, alt, deleted and completely eliminated and eradicated from the federal government."[257] Friend used this same language in a Truth Social

---

[249] The Whistleblowers, *Stephen Friend blows the whistle on the FBI*, RT (Dec. 24, 2022), https://www.rt.com/shows/whistleblowers/568637-stephen-friend-politicized-fbi/.

[250] Steve Friend (@RealStevefriend), Twitter (Feb. 21, 2023, 6:15 PM), https://twitter.com/RealStevefriend/status/1628171705586704387.

[251] *E.g.*, Steve Friend (@RealStevefriend), Twitter (Jan. 2, 2023, 10:10 AM), https://twitter.com/RealStevefriend/status/1609930175965270017.

[252] *E.g.*, Steve Friend (@RealStevefriend), Twitter (Dec. 24, 2022, 9:04 PM), https://twitter.com/RealStevefriend/status/1606833333165596673.

[253] *E.g.*, Steve Friend (@RealStevefriend), Twitter (Dec. 16, 2022, 10:40 PM), https://twitter.com/RealStevefriend/status/1603958354694610944.

[254] *E.g.*, Steve Friend (@RealStevefriend), Twitter (Dec. 26, 2022, 6:52 AM), https://twitter.com/RealStevefriend/status/1607343573615124482.

[255] *E.g.*, Steve Friend (@RealStevefriend), Twitter (Feb. 8, 2023, 7:26 PM), https://twitter.com/RealStevefriend/status/1623478351934418946.

[256] *See, e.g.*, Steve Friend (@RealStevefriend), Twitter (Feb. 14, 2023, 7:42 PM), https://twitter.com/realstevefriend/status/1625656884626706433; *see also* Appendix A.

[257] Mill Creek View Tennessee Podcast, *Mill Creek View Tennessee Podcast EP17 Stephen Friend Interview & More November 8 2022*, PODOMATIC at 23:01 (Nov. 8, 2022), https://www.podomatic.com/podcasts/steve70281/episodes/2022-11-08T16_30_09-08_00.

> Q   What do you think the solutions to a rogue agency like this funded by taxpayer dollars turning on taxpayers could be?
>
> A   So I've actually had, you know, a fair amount of time to reflect on this, and I've kind of evolved on it as I've seen more fallout since my suspension. I will say unequivocally now that the FBI is beyond saving. It needs to be control, alt, deleted and completely eliminated and eradicated from the federal government. However, I don't think any elected official is going to have the cojones to pull that move off. So, in a pragmatic sense, I think that there are some basic and logical steps that can be taken right away that can go and get the ball rolling towards some reforms. Number one, Christopher Wray's tenure as the director needs to be over. He's overseen some of the most massive investigative failures in recent memory, you know, have happened during his leadership. I

quote reply on November 7, 2022—the day before his podcast appearance—when he posted, "The PC answer is that there are lots of good people doing good work. I'm done with it. The fact that 14k aren't standing next to @kyleseraphin and me means we need to Ctrl+Alt+Del the whole thing. Too many overpaid, underworked people resting on the laurels of those who came before and did real police work."[258]

Steve Friend ✓
@Real_SteveFriend · Nov 7, 2022

The PC answer is that there are lots of good people doing good work. I'm done with it. The fact that 14k aren't standing next to @kyleseraphin and me means we need to Ctrl+Alt+Del the whole thing. Too many overpaid, underworked people resting on the laurels of those who came before and did real police work

Nin84
@Nin84 · Nov 7, 2022

Replying to @Real_SteveFriend

Hypothetically speaking, say two years ago or so a new agent from a conservative family & he or she is assigned to LA, I realized all are different, field office. How prevalent is the rot. Just curious on your thoughts.

29 ReTruths **107** Likes   Nov 07, 2022, 7:47 PM

In an appearance on the Robby Starbuck podcast two months later, he reiterated his desire to dissolve the FBI, saying, "If you said, Hey, Steve, you want to be FBI Director? So yes, two conditions, I have to work remotely from Florida because I don't want to leave. And two, it's going to be a 12 month assignment, because that gives me the window that I need to complete the dismantle the organization."[259]

Committee Democrats believe that Friend's repeated attacks on the FBI demonstrate extreme bias against the FBI. His social media diatribes and reposts are broad and wide-ranging, including calls to "abort the FBI"[260] and a post stating, "At best the FBI is an insult to the taxpayer."[261]

---

mean, it could be the Gretchen Whitmer kidnapping scam, Nassar scam, the Vegas shooter, we still don't have any information on. We have no information about the alleged pipe bombings on January 6.

[258] Steve Friend (@Real_SteveFriend), TRUTH SOCIAL (Nov. 7, 2022, 7:47 PM). https://truthsocial.com/@Real_SteveFriend/posts/109305427771232937.

[259] *FBI Special Agent Whistleblower Exposes FBI Corruption!*, THE ROBBY STARBUCK SHOW (Jan. 12, 2023). https://therobbystarbuckshow.transistor.fm/s1/4/transcript.

[260] *E.g.*, Steve Friend, (@RealStevefriend), TWITTER (Dec. 25, 2022, 5:43 PM). https://twitter.com/RealStevefriend/status/1607145126505349120.

[261] Steve Friend (@Real_SteveFriend), TRUTH SOCIAL (Feb. 21, 2023, 8:15 AM). https://truthsocial.com/@Real_SteveFriend/posts/109902911518876069.

Friend has even called for local law enforcement to act against the FBI. He tweeted for law enforcement to "Starve the FBI out" and to stop collaborating with the FBI, going so far as to tell his followers to "Pressure your sheriffs to refuse to cooperate" with FBI investigations.[262] This animus goes beyond the institution of the FBI to include his former colleagues. He has decried FBI employees for failing to "speak out publicly."[263] He has expressed that every one of the FBI's 35,000-plus employees should be laid off, writing in a December 13, 2022, quote tweet, "Can think of about 36k people at @FBI the @HouseGOP can lay off,"[264] and calling for "Breadlines for everyone" who works for the FBI.[265]

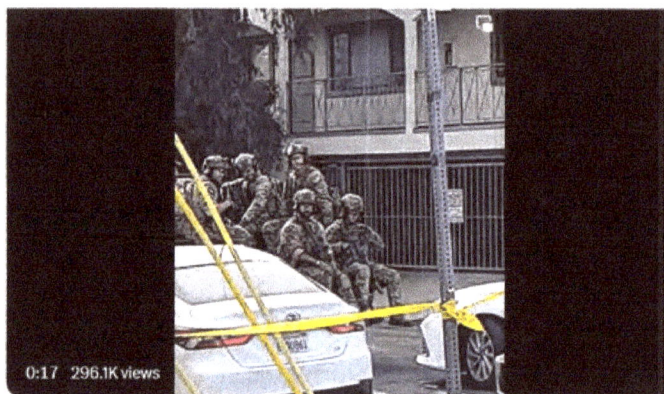

In light of Friend's extreme animus towards the FBI and its employees, Committee Democrats express serious concerns about the extent to which bias may have impacted Friend's testimony before the Committee.

F.   Conclusion

Friend admitted that the bulk of his claim has already been rejected by independent entities, and Committee Democrats join them in finding his allegations unpersuasive. Friend did

[262] Steve Friend (@RealStevefriend), TWITTER (Dec. 19, 2022, 6:48 PM), https://twitter.com/RealStevefriend/status/1604986983432048641.
[263] Steve Friend (@RealStevefriend), TWITTER (Dec. 24, 2022, 11:56 PM), https://twitter.com/RealStevefriend/status/1606876566914580480.
[264] Steve Friend (@RealStevefriend), TWITTER (Dec. 13, 2022, 12:55 PM), https://twitter.com/RealStevefriend/status/1602724023456120832.
[265] Steve Friend (@RealStevefriend), TWITTER (Dec. 24, 2022, 11:56 PM), https://twitter.com/RealStevefriend/status/1606876566914580480.

not provide any evidence of a violation of a law, rule, or regulation, or of gross mismanagement, waste of funds, an abuse of authority, or a substantial danger to public health or safety. Notably, his claims related to the DIOG lack first-hand knowledge of the considerations underlying the management of the January 6 cases, and he admitted that the FBI would have had a reasonable rationale for using a SWAT team to arrest individuals known to be armed and violent, as the Three Percenters arrested on August 24, 2022, were.

Moreover, Committee Democrats conclude that Friend himself has likely engaged in misconduct by misusing technology and repeatedly engaging in unauthorized media appearances, including with media outlets he knows to be Russian propaganda outlets.

Finally, Committee Democrats find that Friend's strong animus toward the FBI likely provided him with strong motivation to speak with the Committee in an effort to advance his goal of dismantling the FBI. This bias sharply undercuts his credibility and casts further doubt on the veracity of his claims.

V.   **An Analysis of Witness Testimony Shows That Committee Republicans Are Working to Advance a Politically Motivated Messaging Campaign Unsupported by the Evidence**

A.   **Witness Testimony Does Not Support Committee Republicans' Desired Narrative Regarding the Handling of January 6 Cases**

1.   **The Evidence Does Not Support Politically Motivated Allegations that the FBI Is Improperly Managing the January 6 Cases**

Throughout the interviews, Committee Republicans sought to find facts to support their desired narrative—that the FBI's Washington Field Office (WFO) is inappropriately opening January 6-related cases in other field offices while retaining control over the broader January 6 Capitol attack matter.

Committee Democrats agree that the WFO and the U.S. Attorney's Office for the District of Columbia are playing a leading role in investigating and prosecuting cases—indeed, public releases from the Department of Justice have acknowledged this, saying, "Under the continued leadership of the U.S. Attorney's Office for the District of Columbia and the FBI's Washington Field Office, the investigation and prosecution of those responsible for the attack continues to move forward at an unprecedented speed and scale."[266] But none of the witnesses have provided any evidence that the FBI acted inappropriately by structuring its case management process in this way. No witness even had firsthand knowledge of the factors which FBI or Justice Department leadership may have considered when determining how to structure the January 6 Capitol attack investigations and prosecutions, and, as noted previously, the FBI's Domestic Investigations and Operations Guide specifically permits departures from its procedures when appropriate.

In fact, the Committee heard from one witness, a former senior FBI official, who testified that there is precedent for the FBI managing a mass event investigation by establishing individual cases in a suspect's home field office while maintaining overall management of the

---

[266] Press Release. *One Year Since the Jan. 6 Attack on the Capitol.* U.S. DEP'T OF JUSTICE, https://www.justice.gov/usao-dc/one-year-jan-6-attack-capitol (last updated Dec. 30, 2021).

matter in the jurisdiction where the event occurred. The retired FBI official described another counterterrorism investigation in which field offices opened cases that were offshoots of a larger investigation run elsewhere:

> Q So following January 6th, 2021, did the FBI set up a command post or task force at headquarters of the WFO specifically to handle these cases?

> A I believe that's correct. But I would definitely refer you to FBI and WFO on what exactly they stood up and when….

> Q …So how we understand it, and I think just how you explained this, ordinarily the full investigations are labeled according to the originating field office, and then there might be leads cut to other field offices or –

> A Not leads, cases.

> Q Cases. So other cases could be opened in the other field offices.

> A PENTTBOM is a good example. Like the 9/11 investigation was run out of New York. But field offices had, not leads, cases as a result of that.
>
> So me in Phoenix, as a case agent, I had cases that were mine in Phoenix but were part of the 9/11 attack investigation. Everything I wrote on my case, I also then routed into the overarching New York case.

> Q So it would look like there was a case open in Phoenix and then in New York as well.

> A Well, the overarching case in New York was the whole attack investigation. And then individuals as they popped up as being involved in some form or fashion in 9/11 were separate individual cases run by that field office.

> Q Okay. So the full investigation into the events at the Capitol on January 6th, 2021, would be the Washington Field Office.

> A Correct.

> Q And then other field offices across the country may have other cases.

> A Correct.[267]

Accordingly, it is simply inaccurate to contend that the FBI's management of the January 6 cases is somehow unprecedented or inappropriate.

Moreover, none of the witnesses provided any evidence indicating that the WFO is exercising inappropriate control over cases transferred to other offices for investigation such as by, for example, requiring field offices to take specific investigative steps with which they disagree. To the contrary, each witness provided testimony showing that field offices are able to exercise their own judgment over whether particular investigative steps are necessary. For instance, Hill described two situations in which the Boston Field Office refused to conduct

---

[267] Interview with Retired FBI Official at 103-05 (Feb. 1, 2023) (transcript on file with the Committee).

investigations following a request from WFO, without any apparent repercussions.[268] O'Boyle likewise described a situation in which he personally declined to take a particular investigative step suggested by a WFO agent, again without any repercussions.[269]

Friend asserted that he was never asked to open matters without a sufficient predicate for a full investigation, and that in one instance he actually closed down a lead for insufficient evidence, again without any apparent repercussions:

> Q   Now sort of returning to the J6 cases, in those matters, do you believe you were asked to open matters without sufficient predicate for full investigations?
>
> A   We didn't open any January 6th cases when I was brought over to JTTF. Those cases had already been opened, so I was never given a new one to look at. I was given one lead to look at and closed that down for insufficient evidence.[270]

Moreover, while Committee Republicans suggested that the FBI may be pressuring field offices to pursue cases aggressively for inappropriate reasons, such as to financially injure subjects or targets,[271] the evidence fails to support this contention. In fact, when asked by Committee Republicans if he had experienced a situation in which his office pursued a case for the sole purpose of draining someone's resources, Friend said he had not:

> Q   And so, within the context of the January 6th cases, did you ever hear anyone say or suggest that they were calling someone's attorney or setting up an interview for the purpose of draining that subject's financial resources?
>
> A   I never heard anybody say that, no.[272]

For all of these reasons, Committee Democrats conclude that there is no evidence of any misconduct with respect to the FBI's structure for managing the January 6 Capitol attack criminal cases.

2.   **The Committee Heard Testimony That Directly Contradicts Republicans' Allegations That the FBI Is Attempting to "Pad" Its Domestic Violent Extremism Statistics**

Committee Republicans also appear to be working to create a narrative that the FBI is attempting to "pad" its domestic violent extremism (DVE) case numbers. As then-Ranking Member Jim Jordan explained in an August 10, 2022, letter:

> Whistleblower disclosures made by multiple FBI employees from different field offices suggest that FBI agents are bolstering the number of cases of DVEs to satisfy their supervisors. For example, one whistleblower explained that because

---

[268] George Hill Testimony at 81-82, 118-19.
[269] Garret O'Boyle Testimony at 104, 120-21.
[270] Stephen Friend Testimony at 39.
[271] *Id.* at 35.
[272] *Id.* at 36.

agents are not finding enough DVE cases, they are encouraged and incentivized to reclassify cases as DVE cases even though there is minimal, circumstantial evidence to support the reclassification. Another whistleblower stated that a field office Counterterrorism Assistant Special Agent in Charge and the FBI's then-Assistant Director of the Counterterrorism Division pressured agents to move cases into the DVE category to hit self-created performance metrics.[273]

While both Friend and O'Boyle testified that they had concerns about the reclassification of cases to "pad" DVE case numbers, and O'Boyle suggested that such case numbers might play a role in FBI budgeting decisions, both also admitted that they were not involved in decision-making regarding performance metrics or manner in which resources were allocated, including whether case numbers played a role in such allocations.[274] In fact, when asked to provide evidence of DVE numbers being inflated, Friend actually said that the only example that came to his mind was an international terrorism case which involved a disagreement over whether to continue investigating a certain suspect with a possible connection to a foreign terrorist group.[275] George Hill explicitly testified that he was *not* aware of any instances of agents being encouraged to reclassify cases:

Q   Are you aware of any instances at the FBI where an agent was encouraged to reclassify a case?

A   Not specifically, no. Tagging, yes; reclassification, no.[276]

The former senior FBI official, however, provided direct, firsthand knowledge on this matter. In response to questioning from Republican staff, the official stated that in their experience, case numbers were not considered in FBI officials' performance plans:

I don't ever remember reviewing one of my performance plans and making note of, oh, they're telling me I need to, whether it's case numbers or budget, do X, Y, Z in a specific granular level like that. It was broader categories of business acumen and achieving results. So, no, I do not remember ever in mine there being a metric, both in the plan or in the appraisal at the end of the year.[277]

Likewise, the retired FBI official explained that case numbers, standing alone, are a meaningless statistic:

And I think I have said this to the folks that work for me and probably even to reporters that have shown an interest in me talking about, quote/unquote, case numbers, that for me case numbers are, one, only an allegation. Until proven they are somewhat meaningless. Like I feel like innocent until proven guilty. So I've

[273] Letter from Jim Jordan, Ranking Member, H. Comm. on the Judiciary, and Mike Johnson, Ranking Member, Subcomm. on the Const., C.R. and C.L., at 1 (Aug. 10, 2022), https://judiciary.house.gov/sites/evo-subsites/republicans-judiciary.house.gov/files/legacy_files/wp-content/uploads/2022/08/2022-08-10-JDJ-MJ-to-Sanborn-re-TI.pdf.

[274] Stephen Friend Testimony at 38, 125-126; Garret O'Boyle Testimony at 96, 117-18.

[275] Stephen Friend Testimony at 38-39.

[276] George Hill Testimony at 19.

[277] Interview with Retired FBI Official at 27-28 (Feb. 1, 2023) (transcript on file with the Committee).

never focused on case numbers because, believe it or not, case numbers are closed without proof...

And case numbers are case numbers. They're not looking at things holistically as an intelligence driven entity. And so for a lot of reasons, I've never thought case numbers were very meaningful.[278]

The official also explained that case numbers do not drive resource allocation, directly contradicting Committee Republicans' theory:

I think that how you assign resources, the way that I view it is the resources should be assigned commensurate with the threat and probably the complexity of the case.

So, for example, bank robbers are something that the Bureau works. Working a bank robbery case is different than working an international terrorism case with a FISA. A bank robbery case agent can probably have 20 bank robberies and that caseload be okay. An international terrorism agent with a FISA wouldn't have 20 cases assigned to them. That would be a volume that they couldn't handle.

And so you're assigning resources based on the severity of the threat, but also taking into account the nature of the case and what it might need.[279]

Committee Democrats thus find that none of the witnesses presented any reliable firsthand evidence that the FBI is artificially inflating its DVE case numbers, and that the retired FBI official explained in extensive detail why this theory would be illogical with respect to both threat assessment and resource allocation considerations.

Moreover, Committee Democrats find it both disingenuous and alarming that Committee Republicans are suggesting that domestic violent extremism does not present an increasing threat, particularly since data from non-partisan DVE trackers provides evidence to the contrary.

The Center for Strategic and International Studies (CSIS) is a widely respected "bipartisan, nonprofit policy research organization" that focuses on producing research to inform nonpartisan solutions to national security issues.[280] The CSIS Transnational Threats Project complies a data set of domestic terror incidents since 1994, and CSIS recorded "1,040 terrorist attacks and plots in the United States between January 1, 1994, and December 31, 2021."[281]

According to CSIS, 2020 had the highest number of domestic terror incidents in the nearly 30 years which the organization has been tracking.[282] Of those incidents, a staggering 66

---

[278] *Id.* at 32.
[279] *Id.* at 45-46.
[280] *About CSIS*, CTR. FOR STRATEGIC & INT'L STUDIES, https://www.csis.org/about (last visited Feb. 28, 2023).
[281] Catrina Doxsee, Seth G. Jones, Jared Thompson, Kateryna Halstead & Grace Hwang, *Pushed to Extremes: Domestic Terrorism amid Polarization and Protest*, CTR. FOR STRATEGIC & INT'L STUDIES (May 17, 2022), https://www.csis.org/analysis/pushed-extremes-domestic-terrorism-amid-polarization-and-protest. CSIS has not yet released data for 2022.
[282] Seth G. Jones, Catrina Doxsee, Grace Hwang & Jared Thompson, *The Military, Police, and the Rise of Terrorism in the United States*, CTR. FOR STRATEGIC & INT'L STUDIES (Apr. 12, 2021), https://www.csis.org/analysis/military-police-and-rise-terrorism-united-states.

percent of domestic terrorist plots and attacks in the United States were executed by white supremacists, extremist militia members, and other violent far-right extremists.[283] The data also show a shift in motivation for domestic terrorism away from the kind of extremism inspired by the Islamic State and Al-Qaeda and towards white nationalism and anti-government sentiments.[284]

In 2021, CSIS released a report finding that white supremacists, anti-government militias, and other violent far-right extremists conducted the most domestic terror attacks and plots of any ideology group.[285] Attacks and plots by violent far-right groups were also "significantly more likely to be lethal, both in terms of weapon choice and number of resulting fatalities."[286] CSIS determined that out of the 30 domestic terrorism fatalities in the United States in 2021, 28 were the result of far-right terrorist attacks.[287]

In light of these facts and statistics, Committee Democrats conclude that Republicans' efforts to downplay the serious threat posed by far-right extremists is not just troubling – it is dangerous.

3.   There Is No Evidence That the FBI Is Diverting Resources From Other Violent Crimes in Favor of January 6 Work.

During the transcribed interviews, Committee Republicans questioned whether the FBI is diverting resources from other violent crime matters, especially cases involving child sexual abuse material, to January 6 matters. Each witness testified that this is not the case.

For example, Republican staff asked George Hill, "Do you perceive pulling resources from crimes such as child sexual abuse cases antithetical to the FBI's mission?"[288] He responded, "I think it's irresponsible to direct resources to areas that are not existential threats to the democracy or to our Constitution or to American citizens."[289] However, when Democratic staff asked him directly if he knew of resources being pulled from child sexual abuse cases to work on January 6-related matters, he responded, "Not in the Boston office."[290]

Garret O'Boyle likewise explained that his office was not "pulling, like, agents from the other side, the criminal side" to work on January 6 matters.[291] He specifically testified that he did not witness any agents being pulled from child sexual abuse or violent crime matters to work on January 6 cases:

> Q   Did you ever see an agent pulled, for example, from an investigation on a child sex abuse case, for example, to work on the January 6th cases?

---

[283] Id.

[284] Id.

[285] Catrina Doxsee, Seth G. Jones, Jared Thompson, Kateryna Halstead & Grace Hwang, *Pushed to Extremes: Domestic Terrorism amid Polarization and Protest*, CTR. FOR STRATEGIC & INT'L STUDIES (May 17, 2022), https://www.csis.org/analysis/pushed-extremes-domestic-terrorism-amid-polarization-and-protest.

[286] Id.

[287] Id.

[288] George Hill Testimony at 104.

[289] Id.

[290] Id. at 121.

[291] Garret O'Boyle Testimony at 77.

A   I never saw that, no.

Q   Okay. Did you ever see anybody pulled from working on a case on child sexual abuse material to work on the January 6th cases?

A   I didn't see that.

Q   Okay. Did you see anybody pulled from violent crime?

A   I didn't see that, no.[292]

Finally, as described above, Stephen Friend admitted that, despite language in his September 2021 declaration implying that the Bureau was deprioritizing child exploitation cases in favor of January 6 matters, in fact, Friend continued to work on child exploitation cases until he was suspended;[293] received an award for his work on child exploitation cases in July 2022;[294] handled approximately the same number of child exploitation-related cases both before and after he was transferred to the Joint Terrorism Task Force[295] and maintained the same responsibilities in child exploitation cases, which included determining "if there was a Federal nexus to open up a Federal case."[296]

There is thus no evidence to support any claims that the FBI is diverting resources from other serious criminal matters in order to focus on investigations into the January 6 Capitol attack.

B.   Republicans Claim That the FBI Should Not Investigate Credible Threats of Violence Against School Administrators and Other Local Public Officials

Committee Republicans asked both Garret O'Boyle and Stephen Friend about Attorney General Merrick Garland's October 4, 2021, memo addressing violent threats against school officials and teachers.[297]

Republican staff read O'Boyle portions of a May 11, 2022, letter from then-Ranking Member Jordan to Attorney General Garland regarding the October 2021 memo.[298] This letter contains bullets describing particular alleged incidents with which Committee Republicans have expressed concern.[299] For example, one bullet describes an allegation that the FBI interviewed an

---

[292] *Id.*

[293] Stephen Friend Testimony at 9.

[294] *Id.* at 34-35.

[295] *Id.* at 60 (stating that he handled his full child exploitation caseload while working on the JTTF). *See also* Stephen Friend Testimony at 59 (stating that he handled "a few dozen" cases total between June and September 2021); Stephen Friend Testimony at 61-62 (stating that between early 2022 and July 2022, he brought "a couple" of cases to prosecution but also handled "two to three a week" that he would close).

[296] Stephen Friend Testimony at 58-59.

[297] Merrick Garland, *Partnership Among Federal, State, Local, Tribal, and Territorial Law Enforcement to Address Threats Against School Administrators, Board Members, Teachers, and Staff,* OFF. OF THE ATT'Y GEN. (Oct. 4, 2021), https://www.justice.gov/ag/page/file/1438986/download. Committee Republicans did not ask George Hill about the memorandum, presumably because he retired from the FBI in October 2021 and would have stopped working prior to the memo's release. George Hill Testimony at 39-40.

[298] Garret O'Boyle Testimony at 82-84.

[299] Letter from Jim Jordan, Ranking Member, H. Comm. on the Judiciary, and Mike Johnson, Ranking Member, Subcomm. on the Const., C.R. and C.L., et al to Attorney General Merrick B. Garland, Att'y Gen. at 2 (May 11,

individual who threatened a local school board that she was "coming for" them.[300] Another describes the FBI speaking with a person who was concerned that another parent may be dangerous.[301] The third describes the FBI opening a case following allegations that certain individuals had "incited violence."[302] After Republican staff read him each bullet, O'Boyle responded that the examples were "shocking" and "a perfect example of how the DOJ and the FBI has become weaponized."[303]

When questioned by Democratic staff, however, O'Boyle admitted that he never worked on any matters related to school boards, that he did not work on any of the matters described in the letter by Republican staff, and that everything he knew about those matters was based on what Republican staff read to him.[304] He also confirmed that the FBI is obligated to investigate tips containing a threat of violence:

Q   In your role with the JTTF or otherwise with the FBI, did you ever have tips from the tip line referred to you?

A   I have.

Q   And was it your obligation to investigate those tips?

A   To some degree.

Q   If they contained a threat of violence, would you be obligated to investigate them?

A   To some degree, yes.[305]

With respect to Stephen Friend, as described above, during his interview, Friend detailed an instance in which he was asked to surveil an individual who was traveling to a school board meeting.[306] On cross-examination, Friend admitted that prior to being given this task, he was aware that the FBI had an open counterterrorism investigation into the individual in question related to their identification with the Three Percenters violent extremist group.[307] He also separately acknowledged that "there had to be a legitimate predication" for the open counterterrorism investigation on this individual.[308] Friend stated that he and his fellow agents never even entered the school board meeting.[309]

Committee Democrats thus conclude that the Republicans' investigation has failed to produce any evidence that either the FBI or the Justice Department have acted inappropriately in

---

2022), https://judiciary.house.gov/sites/evo-subsites/republicans-judiciary.house.gov/files/legacy_files/wp-content/uploads/2022/05/2022-05-11-JDJ-MJ-to-Garland-re-threat-tags_Redacted.pdf.

[300] Id.

[301] Id.

[302] Id.

[303] Garret O'Boyle Testimony at 84-85.

[304] Id. at 112-14.

[305] Id. at 114-15.

[306] Stephen Friend Testimony at 126-27.

[307] Id. at 139-40.

[308] Id. at 134.

[309] Id. at 127.

their work to protect school teachers, administrators, and other public officials from violence and threats of violence.

Committee Democrats are also deeply concerned about this talking point from Committee Republicans because it downplays the very real threats of violence which school employees face. In an American Psychological Association survey of nearly 15,000 school employees, "over 40% of school administrators reported verbal or threatening violence from parents" between March 2020 and June 2021.[310]

School administrators across the country have received increasing numbers of death threats since spring 2020. A school board member's child in Virginia received a letter that read, "It is too bad that your mama is an ugly communist whore. If she doesn't quit or resign before the end of the year, we will kill her, but first, we will kill you!"[311] Members of that same school board collectively received at least 22 death threats or messages which "said members should be or would be killed."[312] In Arizona, a principal received an email that threatened, "The next time it will be a barrel pointed at your Nazi face. Following the guidance you say? The Nazis were just following orders too. Guess we will have to see what side you choose. The Americans or the Nazis. Remember Tucson is a small community and you have a target on your back for enforcing unlawful orders."[313]

In some cases, threats have escalated to violence. The emailed threat to the Arizona principal came just after a parent and two others showed up at the elementary school with zip ties threatening to perform a "citizen's arrest" on the principal, who had asked a child to quarantine after a COVID-19 exposure.[314] A parent in California struck a teacher in the face when the teacher intervened in a confrontation between the parent and the school principal.[315] These are just a few examples of the threats being faced by teachers and school administrators. When Committee Republicans imply that threats of harm are not a serious issue, they excuse these attacks on educators and minimize a significant risk that school officials across the country are facing.

---

[310] Susan D. McMahon et al., *Violence Against Educators and School Personnel: Crisis During COVID*, AM. PSYCH. ASS'N (2022), https://www.apa.org/education-career/k12/violence-educators.pdf.

[311] Gabriella Borter, Joseph Ax & Joseph Tanfani, *School boards get death threats amid rage over race, gender, mask policies*, REUTERS (Feb. 15, 2022), https://www.reuters.com/investigates/special-report/usa-education-threats/.

[312] *Id.* These are just a few examples of threats that school boards have received across the country. Some threats are overtly antisemitic, such as a case in Pennsylvania, where school board members received an email which said, "This why hitler threw you c--ts in a gas chamber." *Id.*

[313] Mary Coleman, *Vail principal receiving death threats following viral incident with upset parent*, KOLD NEWS 13 (Sep. 4, 2021), https://www.kold.com/2021/09/04/vail-principal-receiving-death-threats-following-incident-with-upset-parent/.

[314] Andrea Salcedo, *A school ordered a student to quarantine. His dad and 2 men confronted the principal with zip ties, official says.*, WASH. POST (Sep. 3, 2021), https://www.washingtonpost.com/nation/2021/09/03/arizona-dad-confronts-principal-quarantine-zipties/.

[315] Lateshia Beachum and Andrea Salcedo, *Father injures teacher after arguing about masks, school says. Now he's banned from campus.*, WASH. POST (Aug. 13, 2021), https://www.washingtonpost.com/education/2021/08/13/california-mask-fight-school/.

Section II: Evidence Indicates That Extreme Far-Right Outside Activists – Not Committee Republicans – Are Driving the Republicans' Inquiry

I.   Evidence Suggests That Kash Patel Is Advancing the Committee's Work as Part of His Longtime Efforts to Protect President Trump

A.   Kash Patel Is a Longtime Trump Loyalist Who Has Described Himself as the "Lead Investigator for Russia Gate."

Kashyap P. Patel, known more commonly as Kash Patel, has been described as a "Trump loyalist"[316] who previously served as former House Intelligence Committee Chair Devin Nunes's "right-hand man ... trying to help the congressman undermine the Russia investigation."[317] Notably, he is reported to have written a "hopelessly misguided"[318] memo "widely dismissed as a biased argument of cherry-picked facts" which accused the FBI and Justice Department of abusing their powers[319]—substantially similar to the claims Committee Republicans are advancing in their current endeavor.

Former President Trump subsequently appointed Patel to the National Security Council (NSC) in 2019.[320] The NSC's Russia Director, Fiona Hill testified that Trump may have begun considering Patel to be his "Ukraine director" around the time of the events leading to Trump's first impeachment.[321] In addition, as journalist Tim Weiner noted in a recent *New York Times* opinion piece, Patel was "one of the Trump appointees who led the attempt to uncover the secrets of the 'deep state' that consumed the president during his last year in power."[322]

Following the 2020 election, Trump appointed Patel as chief of staff to Acting Secretary of Defense Christopher Miller at the Pentagon.[323] In this role, Patel reportedly "pursued the idea that Italian military satellites had been used to turn votes to Joe Biden in the presidential

[316] Courtney Kube & Carol E. Lee, *Trump loyalist Kash Patel blocking some Pentagon officials from helping Biden transition*, NBC NEWS (Dec. 5, 2020), https://www.nbcnews.com/politics/national-security/trump-loyalist-kash-patel-blocking-some-pentagon-officials-helping-biden-n1250053.

[317] Tim Weiner, *Trump just installed his own deep state at the Pentagon. What is it up to?*, WASH. POST (Nov. 13, 2020), https://www.washingtonpost.com/outlook/2020/11/13/deep-state-putsch-pentagon-trump/.

[318] Steve Benen, *Another member of Trump's inner circle reportedly takes the Fifth*, MSNBC (Oct. 26, 2022), https://www.msnbc.com/rachel-maddow-show/maddowblog/another-member-trumps-inner-circle-reportedly-takes-fifth-rcna54062.

[319] Julian E. Barnes, Adam Goldman & Nicholas Fandos *White House Aides Feared That Trump Had Another Ukraine Back Channel*, N.Y. TIMES (Oct. 13, 2019), https://www.nytimes.com/2019/10/23/us/politics/kash-patel-ukraine.html; Nicholas Fandos, Adam Goldman and Charlie Savage, *House Republicans Release Secret Memo Accusing Russia Investigators of Bias*, N.Y. TIMES (Feb. 2, 2018), https://www.nytimes.com/2018/02/02/us/politics/trump-fbi-memo.html.

[320] Julian E. Barnes, Adam Goldman & Nicholas Fandos *White House Aides Feared That Trump Had Another Ukraine Back Channel*, N.Y. TIMES (Oct. 13, 2019), https://www.nytimes.com/2019/10/23/us/politics/kash-patel-ukraine.html.

[321] *Id.*; Deposition of Fiona Hill, H. Permanent Select Comm. on Intel., H. Comm. on Oversight and Reform, H. Comm. on Foreign Affs. at 308-09 (Oct. 14, 2019).

[322] Tim Weiner, *The Mysteries of Mar-a-Lago*, N.Y. TIMES (Aug. 19, 2022), https://www.nytimes.com/2022/08/19/opinion/trump-mar-a-lago-records.html.

[323] Courtney Kube & Carol E. Lee, *Trump loyalist Kash Patel blocking some Pentagon officials from helping Biden transition*, NBC NEWS (Dec. 5, 2020), https://www.nbcnews.com/politics/national-security/trump-loyalist-kash-patel-blocking-some-pentagon-officials-helping-biden-n1250053.

election,"[324] blocked the Biden transition team's access to Defense Department officials, and "recast policy descriptions to include content that reflect[ed] favorably on Trump's policies before the information [was] shared with the Biden transition."[325]

After leaving government, Patel established the "Kash Patel Legal Offense Trust" using the WinRed Republican fundraising platform.[326] The fundraising pitch for Patel's Legal Offense Trust reads, in part:

> I know firsthand that the Fake News propaganda machine is working overtime to put American patriots on the defensive…
>
> I'm done playing defense. It's time to go on the offensive! That's why I'm fighting back.
>
> But to win, your support is critical to helping me reach my $250k goal to fund a top-notch legal defense team.[327]

Welcome to the Kash Patel Legal Offense Trust

My name is Kash Patel. As a former career national security official and senior Trump advisor, I know firsthand that the Fake News propaganda machine is working overtime to put American patriots on the defensive.

You see, among many others, *WaPo*, *CNN*, *Politico*, and the *NYT* falsely and viciously smeared me after I **discovered** and **exposed** their **Russian Collusion hoax**. Twitter has greenlit an account falsely impersonating me to, remain in operation.

I'm done playing defense. It's time to go on the offensive! That's why I'm fighting back.

But to win, your support is critical to helping me reach my $250k goal to fund a top-notch legal team.

So, make a gift now to help me strike a major blow to the far-Left media and Big Tech!

---

[324] Ryan Goodman, *Trump Associate's Stated Plan to Publicly Release "Declassified" Documents*, JUST SECURITY (Aug. 18, 2022), https://www.justsecurity.org/82723/trump-associates-stated-plan-to-publicly-release-declassified-documents/.

[325] Courtney Kube & Carol E. Lee, *Trump loyalist Kash Patel blocking some Pentagon officials from helping Biden transition*, NBC NEWS (Dec. 5, 2020), https://www.nbcnews.com/politics/national-security/trump-loyalist-kash-patel-blocking-some-pentagon-officials-helping-biden-n1250053.

[326] *Welcome to the Kash Patel Legal Offense Trust*, WINRED, https://secure.winred.com/donatetoday/kplot_don_bm_ams_lot-dt_na (last visited Mar. 1, 2023).

[327] *Id.*

In 2022, Patel expanded his operation to include Fight With Kash, whose website describes the organization as a nonprofit whose "charitable endeavors include: legal funds[,] education[, and] veteran and law enforcement financial support."[328] While the Fight With Kash "Donate" page states that the "FightWithKash Foundation is a 501(c)(3) nonprofit," no nonprofit organizations with that name can currently be found using the IRS's Tax Exempt Organization Search.[329] In July 2022, in a letter sent to an address which is in the same building as contact information found on the Fight With Kash website, the IRS granted 501(c)(3) tax-exempt status to the Kash Foundation Inc.[330] It is possible that Patel is confused by his own corporate structure; nevertheless, the Fight With Kash website continues to state that the organization is "Paid For By Kash Patel Legal Offense Trust."[331]

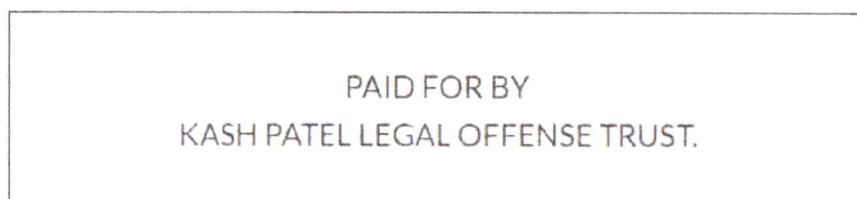

PAID FOR BY

KASH PATEL LEGAL OFFENSE TRUST.

PRIVACY POLICY

© 2023 FIGHT WITH KASH - ALL RIGHTS RESERVED.

In addition to running Fight With Kash and the Kash Patel Legal Offense Trust, Patel has focused on continuing to advance the false narrative of a "Deep State," including the FBI and the Justice Department, which is harming former President Trump and his allies. In April 2022, he reportedly spoke on a panel with former senior Trump administration lawyer Mark Paoletta in a conversation titled "Battling the Deep State" at a Trump-ally event near Mar-a-Lago.[332] Patel told the group of Trump donors and allies that the national security and intelligence community were "malevolently corrupt" and "had deliberately withheld important national security information from Trump."[333] Patel recounted how he had advised the former president "to fire senior officials in the Justice Department and he lamented the appointments of Deputy Attorney General Rod Rosenstein and FBI director Christopher Wray."[334] According to *Axios*, "Patel's message to the audience was that things would be different next time. A source in the room said

---

[328] FIGHT WITH KASH, https://www.fightwithkash.com/ (last visited Mar. 1, 2023).
[329] *Tax Exempt Organization Search*, IRS, https://apps.irs.gov/app/eos/ (search by organization name for "FightWithKash" or "Fight With Kash") (last visited Feb. 28, 2023).
[330] Letter from Stephen A. Martin, Director, Exempt Organizations, Rulings and Agreements, Internal Revenue Service to Kash Foundation Inc (Jul. 26, 2022); *Contact*, FIGHT WITH KASH, https://www.fightwithkash.com/contact (last visited Feb. 28, 2023).
[331] FIGHT WITH KASH, https://www.fightwithkash.com/ (last visited Mar. 1, 2023).
[332] Jonathan Swan, *A radical plan for Trump's second term*, AXIOS (Jul. 22, 2022), https://www.axios.com/2022/07/22/trump-2025-radical-plan-second-term.
[333] *Id*.
[334] *Id*.

later the takeaway from the session was that if Trump took office in 2025, he would target agencies that conservatives have not traditionally viewed as adversarial."[335]

In May 2022, Patel published a children's book entitled *The Plot Against the King*, which "perpetuates the false claim the Steele dossier sparked investigations into Russian collusion."[336] The story, written by Patel, follows "King Donald" and "Hillary Queenton" and provides "a revisionist account of the probe that dogged the first two years of the Trump presidency and eventually led to a special counsel investigation."[337]

Former President Trump named Patel as one of his representatives to the National Archives and Records Administration (NARA) in June 2022.[338] According to a statement by Trump spokesperson Liz Harrington, Patel's mission is "to make available to the American people previously declassified documents that reveal a clear conspiracy to unlawfully spy on candidate and then President Donald J. Trump — by the FBI, DOJ, and others — the largest state-sponsored criminality in American history."[339] This is an apparent reference to the "Spygate" conspiracy theory promulgated by Trump in an effort to discredit the Mueller investigation.[340] The Spygate conspiracy theory has itself been widely discredited, and Special Counsel John Durham, who has reportedly been investigating it, is now winding down his office without finding any evidence to support it.[341]

In August 2022, Patel identified himself on Truth Social as the "lead Investigator for Russia Gate."[342]

[335] *Id.*

[336] Hugo Lowell, *Former Trump official Kash Patel writes children's book repeating false claim over Steele dossier*, GUARDIAN (May 16, 2022), https://www.theguardian.com/us-news/2022/may/16/former-trump-official-kash-patel-writes-childrens-book-repeating-false-claim-over-steele-dossier.

[337] *Id.*

[338] Letter from Donald J. Trump, former President of the United States, to Debra Steidel Wall, Acting Archivist of the United States, U.S. National Archives and Records Administration (Jun. 19, 2022), https://www.archives.gov/files/trump-pra-representatives-designation-letter.06.19.2022.pdf.

[339] Betsy Woodruff Swan, *Trump greenlights Russia-related records access for conservative-favored journalist*, POLITICO (Jun. 24, 2022), https://www.politico.com/news/2022/06/24/trump-grants-records-access-to-conservative-favored-journalist-00042343.

[340] Kevin Roose, *How 'Spygate' Attacks Fizzled*, N.Y. TIMES (Oct. 20, 2020), https://www.nytimes.com/2020/10/20/technology/how-spygate-attacks-fizzled.html.

[341] *Id.*; Peter Stone, *How the Durham inquiry backfired to show weaponization of Trump DoJ*, GUARDIAN (Feb. 10, 2023), https://www.theguardian.com/us-news/2023/feb/10/donald-trump-fbi-durham-investigation.

[342] Kash Patel (@Kash), TRUTH SOCIAL (Aug. 12, 2022, 4:36 PM), https://truthsocial.com/@Kash/posts/108811817583790833.

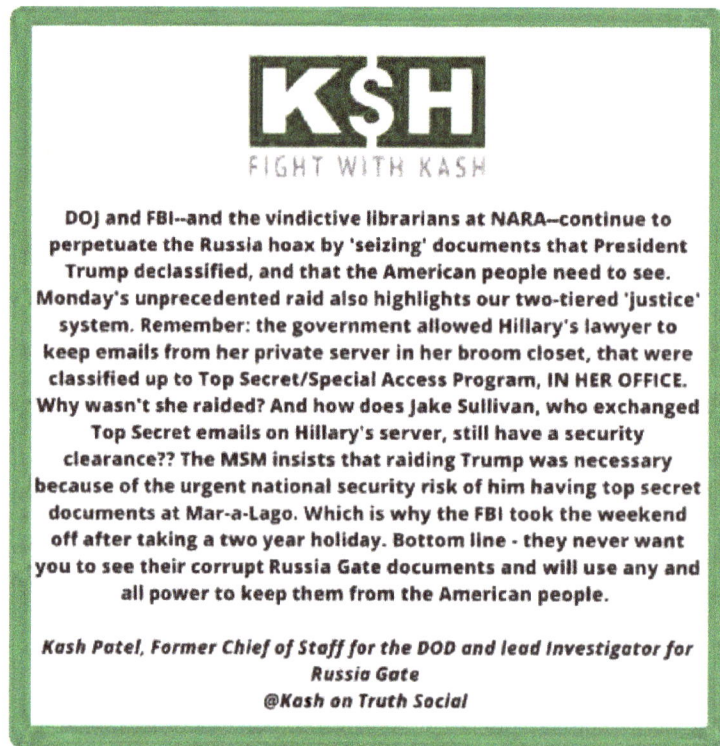

Committee Democrats have determined that Patel also has troubling sympathies for the QAnon conspiracy theory, which has been tied to multiple acts of violence, including a shooting at a pizza restaurant, an armed standoff with law enforcement, kidnapping, intentionally derailing a train, planning to attack politicians, and even murder.[343]

Patel has spoken favorably of QAnon and QAnon followers. During a media appearance in June 2022, he stated, "Whether it's the Qs of the world, who I agree with some of what he does and I disagree with some of what he does, if it allows people to gather and focus on the truth and the facts, I'm all for it."[344] In another interview, he said of QAnon, "There's a lot of good to a lot of it."[345] He also said of Q, the central figure of the QAnon conspiracy:

> He should get credit for all the things he has accomplished, because it's hard to establish a movement, let's call it that, because it's what it is. And he's put out so many names, you know, not just mine, but he's put out so many great American

---

[343] Jane Coaston, *QAnon, the scarily popular pro-Trump conspiracy theory, explained*, VOX (Aug. 21, 2020), https://www.vox.com/policy-and-politics/2018/8/1/17253444/qanon-trump-conspiracy-theory-4chan-explainer.
[344] Alex Kaplan, *How Devin Nunes and Kash Patel appealed to QAnon extremists to build Truth Social's user base*, MEDIA MATTERS (Aug. 1, 2022), https://www.mediamatters.org/truth-social/how-devin-nunes-and-kash-patel-appealed-qanon-extremists-build-truth-socials-user-base.
[345] *Id.*

figures who have been out there pounding – like the Johnny Ratcliffes of the world, the Whitakers, the Grenells, all these folks that were in the Trump administration that people barely knew about, they know because in large part because he was able to put out their work.[346]

On *GraceTimeTV* with Mary Grace, Patel said of QAnon supporters, "[W]e're just blown away at the amount of acumen some of these people have." He also said, "And if it's Q or whatever movement that's getting that information out, I am all for it, every day of the week."[347]

Patel, who sat on the board of Trump Media and Technology Group, the parent company of the social media platform Truth Social, from April 2022, until at least June 8, 2022,[348] has said that Truth Social has tried to incorporate QAnon into the company's "overall messaging scheme to capture audiences because whoever that person is has certainly captured a widespread breadth of the MAGA and the America First movement" and because "you can't ignore that group of people that has such a strong dominant following."[349] On Truth Social, Patel has regularly interacted with an account with the handle "@Q," which users believe may be linked to the QAnon central figure. This includes Patel posting that he was "having a beer with @Q," and the @Q account posting about hanging out with "@Kash."[350] The @Q account even posted a signed copy of Patel's children's book with the dedication "To Q."[351]

Similarly, the Truth Social account for the Patel's children's book has posted photographs of Patel signing copies of his book with "a special message in 10 books for some lucky patriots."[352] The accompanying photograph shows that Patel's "special message" read, "WWG1WGA!" underlined multiple times.[353] "WWG1WGA" is commonly used by those associated with the QAnon conspiracy theory to mean, "Where we go one, we go all."[354] In defending his use of the phrase, Patel said:

> And people keep asking me about all this Q stuff. I'm like, what does it matter? What I'm telling you is there is truth in a lot of things that many people say, and what I'm putting out there is the truth. And how about we have some fun along the

[346] *Id.*

[347] Media Matters Staff, *Trump official Kash Patel says he and Trump are "blown away" by the "acumen" of some QAnon supporters*, MEDIA MATTERS (Sep. 28, 2022), https://www.mediamatters.org/qanon-conspiracy-theory/trump-official-kash-patel-says-he-and-trump-are-blown-away-acumen-some.

[348] Matthew Goldstein, *Trump Media adds former Devin Nunes aides, Donald Jr. and 'Apprentice' contestant as officers*, N.Y. TIMES (Apr. 25, 2022), https://www.nytimes.com/2022/04/25/business/trump-media-truth-social.html; Chris Anderson, *Exclusive: Trump left Sarasota media company weeks before federal subpoenas were issued*, SARASOTA HERALD-TRIB. (Jul. 7, 2022), https://www.heraldtribune.com/story/news/2022/07/07/trump-leaves-boar, d-social-media-company-florida-federal-investigation/7828534001/.

[349] Alex Kaplan, *How Devin Nunes and Kash Patel appealed to QAnon extremists to build Truth Social's user base*, MEDIA MATTERS (Aug. 1, 2022), https://www.mediamatters.org/truth-social/how-devin-nunes-and-kash-patel-appealed-qanon-extremists-build-truth-socials-user-base.

[350] *Id.*

[351] @Q, TRUTH SOCIAL (Jun. 14, 2022, 12:23 PM), https://truthsocial.com/users/q/statuses/108476746478555731.

[352] Mary Papenfuss, *Trump Loyalist Kash Patel Touts QAnon Greeting In His 'King Donald' Children's Book*, HUFFPOST (Sep. 25, 2022), https://www.huffpost.com/entry/kash-patel-trump-qanon-kids-book-plot-against-king_n_632fc90ee4b0e2478903b814.

[353] *Id.*

[354] *Id.*

way? There's so many people who subscribe to the "where we go one, we go one all" mantra. And what's wrong with it?[355]

He continued, "But let's have fun with the truth."[356]

B. Patel Views the Weaponization Committee as a Tool to Destroy the "Deep State"

In recent months, Patel has suggested that the Weaponization Committee may be the means to destroy the "Deep State." On December 22, 2022, he posted, "LFG," an abbreviation for "Let's [expletive] Go," in response to a story about the Committee's anticipated investigations.[357]

Kash Patel ✓
@Kash · Dec 22, 2022

LFG #FWK

justthenews.com/accountability...

Incoming House Judiciary chairman vows to probe DOJ snooping on congressional investigators

Rep. Jim Jordan says the revelations by Just the News that DOJ subpoenaed phone and email records of House Intelligence investigators in 2017 make him wonder if DOJ is now clandestinely monitoring his...

🔗 justthenews.com

500 ReTruths **1.47k** Likes   Dec 22, 2022, 12:56 PM

On January 25, 2023, Patel wrote an opinion column in the *Daily Caller*.[358] The next day—just as the Committee's investigation was getting underway—he posted the article on Truth Social, commenting, "We can and will destroy the Deep State and

---

[355] Media Matters Staff, *Trump official Kash Patel defends signing book with QAnon slogan*, MEDIA MATTERS (Sep. 27, 2022), https://www.mediamatters.org/qanon-conspiracy-theory/trump-official-kash-patel-defends-signing-book-qanon-slogan.

[356] *Id.*

[357] Truth Social Post, @Kash, Dec. 22, 2022, 12:56 p.m. https://truthsocial.com/@Kash/posts/109558616190328922.

[358] Kash Patel, *Kash Patel: Hunter Biden's Access To Classified Docs Should Concern Everyone. Here's How We Get To The Bottom Of It*, DAILY CALLER (Jan. 25, 2023), https://dailycaller.com/2023/01/25/kash-patel-hunter-biden-joe-biden-classified-documents-robert-hur/.

#GovernmentGangsters."[359] In the article, he called for the "newly formed House Committee on the Weaponization of the Federal Government" to "subpoena critical documents from the FBI… so the world can see the actions of all the government gangsters involved in this cover-up."[360]

Kash Patel ✓
@Kash · Jan 26

We can and will destroy the Deep State and #GovernmentGangsters

dailycaller.com/2023/01/25/kas...

KASH PATEL: Hunter Biden's Access To Classified Docs Should Concern Everyone. Here's How We Get To The Bottom Of It

KASH PATEL: Hunter Biden's Access To Classified Docs Should Concern Everyone. Here's How We Get To The Bottom Of It

🔗 dailycaller.com

760 ReTruths **2.15k** Likes   Jan 26, 2023, 5:26 PM

On February 7, Patel reposted a Truth Social post from Donald Trump reading, "Republicans in Congress must investigate the abusive Weaponization of the FBI and Department of Injustice against the Democrats number one political opponent, ME (leading BIG in every Poll!), which has been going on for a long time, and is absolutely outrageous. Don't be afraid of the Marxists and Thugs. We must MAKE AMERICA GREAT AGAIN!!!"[361]

On February 10 – the day after the Select Subcommittee's first hearing – Patel posted, "Rockets fired by the Weaponization Committee… now make sure they hit the damn targets.

---

[359] Kash Patel (@Kash), TRUTH SOCIAL (Jan. 26, 2023, 5:26 PM), https://truthsocial.com/@Kash/posts/109757857821434055.

[360] Kash Patel, *Kash Patel: Hunter Biden's Access To Classified Docs Should Concern Everyone. Here's How We Get To The Bottom Of It*, DAILY CALLER (Jan. 25, 2023), https://dailycaller.com/2023/01/25/kash-patel-hunter-biden-joe-biden-classified-documents-robert-hur/.

[361] Donald J. Trump (@realDonaldTrump), TRUTH SOCIAL (Feb. 7, 2023, 6:47 PM), https://truthsocial.com/@realDonaldTrump/posts/109823292143955862.

Turn ON the subpoena machine NOW."[362] Five days after Patel's post, Judiciary Committee Republicans issued subpoenas to Apple, Amazon, Alphabet, Meta and Microsoft.[363]

Kash Patel ✓
@Kash · Feb 10

Rockets fired by Weaponization Committee... now make sure they hit the damn targets. Turn ON the subpoena machine NOW

663 ReTruths   **2.18k** Likes   Feb 10, 2023, 12:32 PM

On February 13 – two days before Friend testified before the Committee – Patel posted, "The FBI is not a joke, it's a political machine, an offshoot of the DNC.[364]

Kash Patel ✓
@Kash · Feb 13

The FBI is not a joke, its a political machine, an offshoot of the DNC

justthenews.com/accountability...

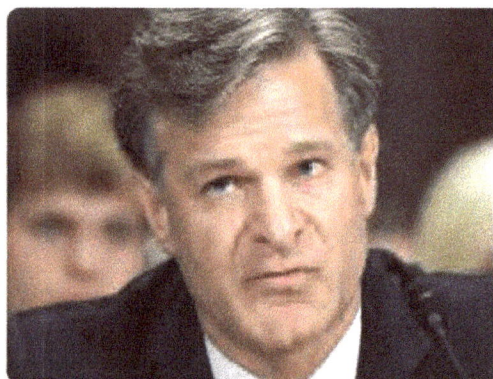

FBI keeps getting burned badly by reliance on liberal sources

Latest blunder involving Catholics has many questioning why the bureau keeps falling prey to political influence from the left.

🔗 justthenews.com

1.19k ReTruths   **2.66k** Likes   Feb 13, 2023, 9:00 AM

And on February 17, on his weekly EpochTV show, Patel described in extensive detail the steps that Committee Republicans should take to "set the trap" using subpoenas.[365] Patel said of this trap, "It's kind of what we [Republicans] did in Russiagate," to ensnare the FBI and

---

[362] Kash Patel (@Kash), TRUTH SOCIAL (Feb. 10, 2023, 12:32 PM), https://truthsocial.com/@Kash/posts/109841636912748890.

[363] Rachel Lerman, *As GOP plays up censorship allegations, House subpoenas Big Tech CEOs*, WASH. POST (Feb. 15, 2023), https://www.washingtonpost.com/technology/2023/02/15/house-republican-subpoena-big-tech/.

[364] Kash Patel (@Kash), TRUTH SOCIAL (Feb. 13, 2023, 9:00 AM), https://truthsocial.com/@Kash/posts/109857788097626810.

[365] Kash Patel and Jan Jekielek, *Kash Patel: Here's How Jim Jordan Can Set a Trap to Expose Collusion Between Big Tech and Intelligence Agencies*, EPOCHTV (Feb. 17, 2023), https://www.theepochtimes.com/kash-patel-heres-how-jim-jordan-can-set-trap-to-expose-collusion-between-big-tech-and-intelligence-agencies_5065846.html.

Department of Justice.[366] He urged the Committee to pursue both testimonial and documentary subpoenas, saying, "It's an extensive process, Jan. This is the first step. We'll see if this committee's willing to take the next two to three steps we have just outlined here."[367]

C.   Patel Has Provided Support and Publicity to Both Garret O'Boyle and Stephen Friend and Has Suggested That They Can Play a Key Role in Helping to Take Down the FBI

In a January 30 Truth Social Post, Patel detailed the spending of his Fight With Kash organization, which including providing financial support to "whistle blowers," "J6 families," "those maligned by fake news media," and others.[368]

Kash Patel ✓
@Kash · Jan 30

Fight With Kash 2022 roll up- what a year, we put the Mission first and gave away nearly $100K in financial assistance: everything from whistle blowers, active duty service members, J6 families, legal funds to bring defamation cases for those maligned by fake news mafia, and lots of holiday meals for families in need. Plus the monster free info vaults on website. Thank you @truthsocial and our entire #FWK warrior nation. We just warming up, lets go YUGE in 2023

fightwithkash.com

Welcome

...

⧉ www.fightwithkash.com

668 ReTruths   **2.27k** Likes   Jan 30, 2023, 2:00 PM

During their interviews, Garret O'Boyle and Stephen Friend both confirmed that they had received money from Patel.[369] Committee Democrats have determined that Patel's support for them extends beyond that to helping them secure legal counsel and promoting them and their causes.[370]

---

[366] *Id.*
[367] *Id.*
[368] Kash Patel (@Kash), Truth Social (Jan. 30, 2023, 2:00 PM), https://truthsocial.com/@Kash/posts/109779696419329570.
[369] Garret O'Boyle Testimony at 144-45; Stephen Friend Testimony at 77.
[370] Garret O'Boyle Testimony at 145; Stephen Friend Testimony at 78.

a) O'Boyle Initially Attempted to Conceal His Connection to Patel, Who Provided Him With Funding And Connected Him With Attorney Jesse Binnall

During his interview, O'Boyle repeatedly described the difficult financial situation he is in because of his suspension from the FBI.[371] Because of this, Democratic staff questioned how he was paying his attorney:

Q   How are you – are you paying your attorney?

A   I have a nonprofit that's paying for my legal fees.

Q   Okay. What nonprofit is that?

A   It's called Fight With Kash.

Q   Okay. How did you find out about them?

A   Another whistleblower.

Q   Okay. Who owns Fight for Kash, or who runs Fight for Kash, if you know?

A   I guess I don't know if it's ran by a board or an owner or –

Q   Do you know what other – what other type of claims, or what other type of – what other type of individuals they might be providing resources to?

A   I don't.[372]

Democratic Committee staff later clarified:

Q   You said it was Fight With Kash. Is that right?

A   Correct.

Q   How do you spell Kash?

A   K-a-s-h.

Q   And do you know who – who is Kash?

A   Kash Patel.

Q   Okay. Do you know Kash Patel?

A   I've spoken with him once or twice.

Q   And what has the content of your conversations with the Kash Patel been?

A   He asked me how he could help. So I told him a little bit of my situation. And he said that he thinks he could get the nonprofit to help.

---

[371] *See, e.g.*, Garret O'Boyle Testimony at 62.
[372] Garret O'Boyle Testimony at 125.

Q   When did you speak with Mr. Patel?

A   I think in November. Maybe December.

Q   Okay. How did you learn about Kash Patel? Or, I'm sorry, did you reach out to him, or did he reach out to you?

A   I don't recall. I think another whistleblower told me he was expecting my call or that – I don't recall exactly if I was given his number or if he was given mine.

Q   Okay. And you said you may have learned about him from another whistleblower?

A   Correct.

Q   Okay. And you told him – and so in November you spoke with him and you told him about your allegations?

A   Yeah. I'm not sure exactly when. Late November, sometime in December. Somewhere in there.

Q   And you said that he said he thought he could help.

A   Correct.

Q   What did you understand that to mean? …

A   …My understanding was that his nonprofit would try to help me.

Q   Help you in what way?

A   With legal counsel. And his nonprofit sent me and my family some money from the nonprofit. So in those ways.

Q   Did his nonprofit or did Kash Patel himself refer you to your legal counsel?

A   They did help with that, yeah.[373]

At the end of the interview, O'Boyle's attorney, Jesse Binnall, stated, "And, finally, although Mr. O'Boyle was not aware of this directly, his representation by counsel is actually not being paid by anybody because it's pro bono."[374]

Committee Democrats observe that O'Boyle's own testimony concerning his interactions with Kash Patel undercuts Binnall's apparent attempt to distance himself and his client from Patel. Committee Democrats note further that as recently as February 12—two days after

---

[373] *Id.* at 143-45.
[374] Garret O'Boyle Testimony at 157.

O'Boyle testified—Patel praised Binnall on Truth Social, calling him "Americas lawyer."[375] Binnall and Patel appear to operate out of the same Alexandria, VA, office building.[376]

Kash Patel ✓
@Kash · Feb 12

Thats why hes Americas lawyer 🇺🇸

Jesse Binnall ✓
@jbinnall · Feb 12

Don't forget, this is Arizona: they haven't counted the early touchdowns yet.

559 ReTruths **3.34k** Likes   Feb 12, 2023, 9:20 PM

b) Kash Patel Gave Stephen Friend Money, Promoted His Book, and Secured Employment for Him

In contrast to O'Boyle, Stephen Friend proudly admitted that Kash Patel gifted him $5,000 "immediately" after the two first connected.[377] But Patel did not just provide Friend with funding—he also connected him with the Center for Renewing America, the organization which now employs Friend:

Q   Have you received money from any other fundraising or other source not online?

A   Kash Patel's organization gifted me $5,000.

Q   Okay. Who is Kash Patel?

A   He is a former government representative and now runs an outside organization.

Q   …Have you spoken with Kash Patel?

A   Yes.

Q   How many times?

A   He called me originally and offered to gift me the money through his organization. And then he talked to me as a follow-up for trying to get me

---

[375] Kash Patel (@Kash), TRUTH SOCIAL (Feb. 12, 2023, 9:20 PM), https://truthsocial.com/@Kash/posts/109855035950406671.
[376] *See Jesse R. Binnall*, BINNALL LAW GROUP, https://www.binnall.com/our-team/jesse-r-binnall/ (last visited Feb. 28, 2023); *Contact*, FIGHT WITH KASH, https://www.fightwithkash.com/contact (last visited Feb. 28, 2023). The IRS determination letter to the Kash Foundation Inc is addressed to the office listed on Binnall's website.
[377] Stephen Friend Testimony at 78.

in touch with the Center for Renewing America. And then exchanged like text messages or something like that as an acquaintance.

Q   And you said he initially contacted you?

A   Yes.

Q   When was that?

A   That was, I believe, before -- somewhere around Thanksgiving. I know I was visiting family because I had to pull away from the dinner table to answer his call.

Q   Okay. And when did it come about that he gifted you $5,000?

A   He immediately did. So it was in the mail within a week, and I received it at the end – so in November, I believe, of 2022.

Q   And when he reached out to you in November, did he indicate how he had learned about you, how he got your information?

A   Well, he's, I know, in touch with Kyle, and Kyle told him about my situation. So that's who shared my contact information to Kash, was Kyle.[378]

Patel's financial support for Friend came roughly three weeks before Friend posted, "FBI is trying to 'fix the glitch' by stalling for time and hoping to bleed legitimate whistleblowers white until we just resign. They didn't plan on guys like @kyleseraphin and me having the financial IQ and means to last."[379] Committee Democrats understand this to mean that Friend is praising his own financial planning skills, which may have been supported by an alternate source of income that would allow him to continue pursuing baseless claims while suspended from the FBI.

Kash Patel ReTrutned

Steve Friend ✓
@Real_SteveFriend · Dec 16, 2022

Replying to @georgiapatriot45, @EmeraldRobinson, and 1 more

FBI is trying to "fix the glitch" by stalling for time and hoping to bleed legitimate whistleblowers white until we just resign. They didn't plan on guys like @kyleseraphin and me having the financial IQ and means to last. Sucks for them. We aren't going anywhere and people on the inside know it. We get more inside info pushed out to us every day. I like knowing Chris Wray knows our names.

○ 72   ⇄ 830   ♡ 2.38k   ↑   ···

---

[378] Id. at 77-78. "Kyle" refers to Kyle Seraphin, another suspended FBI agent.
[379] Steve Friend (@Real_SteveFriend), TRUTH SOCIAL (Dec. 16, 2022, 11:06 PM), https://truthsocial.com/@Real_SteveFriend/posts/109527040842556949.

Patel also helped to ensure that Friend was able to testify before the Committee. On January 24, Patel reposted a Truth Social post from Kyle Seraphin criticizing Committee Republicans for refusing to pay for a witness' transportation to Washington D.C. for his transcribed interview.[380]

Kash Patel ReTruthed

Kyle Seraphin ✓
@kyleseraphin · Jan 24

I need @JimJordan and the GOP House Judiciary committee to do better. They just asked my "indefinitely suspended" friend to "pay his own way to DC" for a transcribed deposition. Because "it isn't an open hearing." Are you guys fricken SERIOUS? Pay out of YOUR pockets. Un-Fricken-believable. You want people to believe you are serious, you better start acting serious. Cause that is beyond stupid and shameful behavior. Fix it.

💬 123   ⇄ 769   ♡ 2.05k   ⬆   ...

It appears that Patel's advocacy was effective: during Stephen Friend's interview, Committee Republicans acknowledged paying for Friend's transportation and lodging.[381]

Patel has also played an active role in helping to promote Friend's story. Notably, while Friend indicated that the two first connected in November 2022, Patel actually discussed Friend's allegations against the FBI in a livestream episode of his weekly show, *Kash's Corner*, on EpochTV, the *Epoch Times*'s video streaming platform, two months prior to that.[382]

Patel regularly reposts Friend's Truth Social posts, such as a January 9 one suggesting that "the FBI 7th Floor" – an apparent reference to the seventh floor of FBI headquarters, which contains FBI leadership offices – "is nervous @JimJordan, @repandybiggsaz, @ThomasMassie, @RepMattGaetz are about to expose some snakes in the grass…"[383] Patel reposted this, adding, "Couldn't agree more… maybe ill jump into the fight too."[384]

---

[380] Kyle Seraphin (@kyleseraphin), TRUTH SOCIAL (Jan. 24, 2023, 2:44 PM), https://truthsocial.com/@kyleseraphin/posts/109745897007691544.
[381] Stephen Friend Testimony at 73-74.
[382] Kash Patel and Jan Jekielek, *Kash's Corner: FBI Whistleblower Goes Public; Nord Stream Pipeline Explosions; 'CHS Corruption Cover Up Network'*, EPOCHTV (Sep. 30, 2022), https://www.theepochtimes.com/live-kashs-corner-fbi-whistleblower-goes-public-nord-stream-pipeline-explosions-chs-corruption-cover-up-network_4764029.html.
[383] Steve Friend (@Real_SteveFriend), TRUTH SOCIAL (Jan. 9, 2023, 2:20 PM), https://truthsocial.com/@Real_SteveFriend/posts/109660868019707923.
[384] Kash Patel (@Kash), TRUTH SOCIAL (Jan. 9, 2023, 2:25 PM), https://truthsocial.com/@Kash/posts/109660885067083134.

Kash Patel ✓
@Kash · Jan 9

Couldnt agree more... maybe ill jump into the fight too

Steve Friend ✓
@Real_SteveFriend · Jan 9

The fact that Chis Wray is going to @FoxNews is more telling than his 8th grade level English paper. I think the FBI 7th floor is nervous @JimJordan, @repandybiggsaz, @ThomasMassie, @RepMattGaetz are about to expose some snakes in the grass...
www-foxnews-com.cdn.ampproject...

America's crime problem is real. Tackling it requires respect for cops | Fox News

🔗 www-foxnews-com.cdn.ampproject.org

843 ReTruths 2.18k Likes   Jan 09, 2023, 2:25 PM

On January 31, 2023, Patel urged his Truth Social followers—more than 820,000 as of February 28, 2023—to order Friend's book: "A must buy, Steve unleashes the truth n exposes FBI corruption. Order now."[385]

Kash Patel ✓
@Kash · Jan 31

A must buy, Steve unleashes the truth n exposes FBI corruption. Order now

Steve Friend ✓
@Real_SteveFriend · Jan 31

I'm going on offense. Time to explain what's actually going on with the FBI and why I chose to expose the truth.
amazon.com/True-Blue-Journey-S...

342 ReTruths 979 Likes   Jan 31, 2023, 11:40 AM

[385] Kash Patel (@Kash). TRUTH SOCIAL (Jan. 31, 2023, 11:40 AM). https://truthsocial.com/@Kash/posts/109784808049917808.

On February 17, 2023, Patel posted a link to a Just the News interview in which Friend discussed his appearance before the Committee, stating, "Men like this is how we fix our FBI, thanks @Real_SteveFriend."[386]

And most recently, on February 26, 2023, Patel reposted a Truth Social post from Friend urging Fox News to ask FBI Director Christopher Wray certain questions which Friend and other suspended agents prepared, including questions concerning Ray Epps and pipe bomb-related January 6 conspiracy theories.[387]

Based on this evidence, Committed Democrats conclude that there is a strong likelihood that Kash Patel is encouraging the witnesses to continue pursuing their meritless claims, and in fact is using them to help propel his vendetta against the FBI, Justice Department, and Biden administration on behalf of himself and President Trump. He appears to see the potential for the Select Subcommittee to play a key role in this regard, and Committee Democrats have serious concerns about possible coordination between Patel and Committee Republicans.

II.   The Center for Renewing America, Which Pushed Republican Leadership to Establish the Weaponization Subcommittee, Appears to Exert Concerning Influence Over Committee Republicans

In addition to his other activities, Patel currently serves as a Senior Fellow for National Security and Intelligence at the Center for Renewing America (CRA), which also recently hired

---

[386] Kash Patel (@Kash), TRUTH SOCIAL (Feb. 17, 2023, 12:47 PM). https://truthsocial.com/@Kash/posts/109881332035008839.

[387] Steve Friend (@Real_SteveFriend), TRUTH SOCIAL (Feb. 26, 2023, 4:22 PM). https://truthsocial.com/@Real_SteveFriend/posts/109933135255526894.

Stephen Friend as a Fellow on Domestic Intelligence and Security Services, apparently on Patel's recommendation.[388]

The CRA appears to be funded in large part by the Conservative Partnership Institute (CPI).[389] Run by former Trump Chief of Staff Mark Meadows and former Sen. Jim DeMint, CPI has been described as a "who's-who of Trump's former administration and the 'America First' movement" who, among other things, "recruit, train and promote ideologically vetted staff for GOP offices on Capitol Hill and the next Republican administration."[390]

CPI launched CRA in 2021 to "bring cultural fights into the national spotlight, win the debate, and then use the resulting momentum to create policy change nationwide."[391] It has credited CRA for leading anti-FBI messaging and specifically for establishing the messaging around the words "woke" and "weaponized," as well as for being the first entity to call on Republican leadership to establish the Weaponization Subcommittee.[392] As CPI wrote in its 2022 annual report:

> When the FBI raided President Trump's home at Mar-a Lago, for example, CRA was already well into an effort to expose and take on the Deep State.
>
> Following the Mar-a-Lago raid, CRA was one of the first organizations to enter the national conversation and frame the event in terms of a secretive and powerful government that has been weaponized against American citizens. Two words—"woke and weaponized"—quickly became the standard for describing a federal government that up until now has just been "big" and "overreaching."
>
> Center for Renewing America was the first to publicly call on House Minority Leader Kevin McCarthy to set up a modern-day Church Committee to investigate systemic corruption at the FBI and ultimately break it up.[393]

In fact, ten days after the August 8, 2022, FBI search of Mar-a-Lago, CRA published an article entitled, "A Partisan, Weaponized FBI Must Be Broken Up."[394] In the article, CRA called for the creation of an investigatory committee and for Congress to "use its impeachment power

---

[388] *Our Staff*, CTR. FOR RENEWING AM. (2021), https://americarenewing.com/about/ (last visited Mar. 1, 2023); Stephen Friend Testimony at 78.

[389] In its 2021 IRS Form 990, CRA disclosed receiving $1,042,274 in contributions and grants. As a nonprofit, it is not required to disclose the sources of its funding. Jonathan Swan, A radical plan for Trump's second term, AXIOS (Jul. 22, 2022), https://www.axios.com/2022/07/22/trump-2025-radical-plan-second-term. However, the 2021 IRS Form 990 for the Conservative Partnership Institute indicates that CPI granted $583,701 to CRA, or a little more than half of CRA's total income.

[390] *CPI Staff*, CONSERVATIVE PARTNERSHIP INST., https://www.cpi.org/team/ (last visited Mar. 1, 2023); Jonathan Swan, *A radical plan for Trump's second term*, AXIOS (Jul. 22, 2022), https://www.axios.com/2022/07/22/trump-2025-radical-plan-second-term.

[391] 2021 Annual Report, *Where Conservatives Go to Win*, CONSERVATIVE PARTNERSHIP INST. at 38 (2022), https://whoscounting.us/wp-content/uploads/2022/03/CPIAnnualReport.pdf; 2022 Annual Report, *Building a Winning Conservative Culture*, CONSERVATIVE PARTNERSHIP INST. at 22 (2023), https://www.cpi.org/2022-annual-report/.

[392] 2022 Annual Report, *Building a Winning Conservative Culture*, CONSERVATIVE PARTNERSHIP INST. at 22 (2023), https://www.cpi.org/2022-annual-report/.

[393] *Id.*

[394] *A Partisan, Weaponized FBI Must Be Broken Up*, CTR. FOR RENEWING AM. (Aug. 18, 2022), https://americarenewing.com/a-partisan-weaponized-fbi-must-be-broken-up-2/.

to remove Attorney General Merrick Garland and FBI Director Christopher Wray."[395] CRA summarized:

> The FBI's unprecedented raid on a former president's residence is the most recent and stark example of the degree to which the federal law enforcement apparatus is being weaponized to protect the country's political left and to attack its political right. These actions reveal the need for serious action by Congress to protect the American people and restore self-government in this country.[396]

CRA's President, former Trump administration official Russ Vought, has embraced many of the themes laid out by the witnesses George Hill, Garret O'Boyle, and Stephen Friend, and Vought reportedly pushed Republican leadership to establish the Weaponization Subcommittee at the start of the 118th Congress.[397] In the forward to CRA's 2023 budget proposal for the federal government, entitled "A Commitment to End Woke and Weaponized Government," Vought wrote,

> On the heels of this wrenching national experience is the growing awareness that the national security apparatus itself is arrayed against that half of the country not willing to bend the knee to the people, institutions, and elite worldview that make up the current governing regime. Instead of fulfilling their intended purpose of keeping the American people safe, they are hard-wired now to keep the regime in power. And that includes the emergence of political prisoners, a weaponized, SWAT-swaggering FBI, the charges of "domestic terrorism" and "disinformation" in relation to adversaries' exercise of free speech, and the reality that the NSA is running a surveillance state behind the protective curtain of "national security." The immediate threat facing the nation is the fact that the people no longer govern the country; instead, the government itself is increasingly weaponized against the people it is meant to serve.[398]

Committee Democrats find the connections between Patel, CRA, and CPI deeply concerning. Evidence suggests that these entities were not just a driving force for creating the Weaponization Subcommittee, but are actively propelling its efforts to advance baseless, biased claims for political purposes. This evidence seriously discredits the work done by Committee Republicans and casts further doubt on the reliability of the witnesses they have put forth.

---

[395] *Id.*

[396] *Id.*

[397] Jeff Stein, Josh Dawsey & Isaac Arnsdorf, *The former Trump aide crafting the House GOP's debt ceiling playbook*, WASH. POST (Feb. 19, 2023), https://www.washingtonpost.com/us-policy/2023/02/19/russ-vought-republican-debt-ceiling-strategy/.

[398] 2023 Budget Proposal, *A Commitment to End Woke and Weaponized Government*, CTR. FOR RENEWING AM. at 3-4 (Dec. 7, 2022), https://americarenewing.com/wp-content/uploads/2021/04/Budget-Center-for-Renewing-America-FY23.pdf.

Footnote 42: According to the account header, Hill joined Twitter in August 2021, and as of March 1, 2023, he has tweeted or retweeted items 6,011 times.

Senior Chief
6,011 Tweets

Senior Chief
@SeniorChiefEXW

13 years active duty USMC. Another 13 years USNR post 9-11. ReTIRED FBI National Security Intelligence Supervisor and current Adjunct Professor.

⊙ Where you least expect.   ▦ Joined August 2021

681 Following   **1,541** Followers

Appendix A: Referenced Media

Footnote 45: Geroge Hill (@SeniorChiefEXW), Twitter (Jan. 6, 2023, 8:27 AM), https://twitter.com/SeniorChiefEXW/status/1611353706070409218.

Senior Chief
@SeniorChiefEXW

Happy Anniversary Ray Epps, from your friends in The Deep State. Job well done! #J6

HEY JAN. 6TH COMMISH. WHERE'S RAY EPPS?

WHY HAS HE NOT BEEN ARRESTED?

8:27 AM · Jan 6, 2023 · **134** Views

Appendix A: Referenced Media

Footnote 47: George Hill (@SeniorChiefEXW), Twitter (Jan. 8, 2023, 4:55 PM), https://twitter.com/SeniorChiefEXW/status/1612206373856493568.

Senior Chief
@SeniorChiefEXW

Someone knows the identity of #NWScaffoldCommander. Seek #Whistleblower protection and step-up. Be a #Patriot.

Glenn Beck @glennbeck · Jan 6

It's not just Ray Epps who the govt has ignored. @DarrenJBeattie tells me he "pulled out all the stops" to identify Jan 6 rioter "Scaffold Commander", but found NOTHING: "If his identity is actually uncovered, it's going to be one of the biggest scandals in the country."

2:51 136.7K views

4:55 PM · Jan 8, 2023 · **698** Views

Appendix A: Referenced Media

Footnote 48: George Hill (@SeniorChiefEXW), TWITTER (Jan. 19, 2023, 6:02 PM), https://twitter.com/SeniorChiefEXW/status/1616209590110019585.

Senior Chief
@SeniorChiefEXW

· · ·

#J6Entrapment

militarý.com
3 Active-Duty Marines Who Work in Intelligence Arrested for Alleged Particip...
Micah Coomer, Joshua Abate, and Dodge Dale Hellonen -- three men
identified by investigators as active-duty Marines -- were arrested on four ...

6:02 PM · Jan 19, 2023 · **87** Views

Appendix A: Referenced Media

Footnote 49: George Hill (@SeniorChiefEXW), TWITTER (Jan. 6, 2023, 5:44 PM),
https://twitter.com/SeniorChiefEXW/status/1611493962002432003.

Senior Chief
@SeniorChiefEXW

...

#Insurrection #RayEpps #Fedsurrection #j6

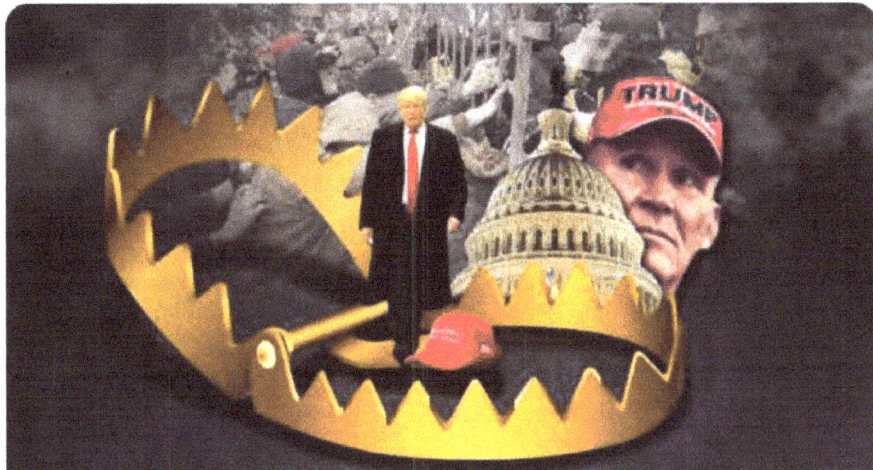

revolver.news
Meet Ray Epps, Part 2: Damning New Details Emerge Exposing Massive Web ...
Revolver blows open a network of still-unindicted operators who appear to
have been intimately involved in the initial Jan. 6 Capitol breach.

5:44 PM · Jan 6, 2023 · **82** Views

Appendix A: Referenced Media

Footnote 51: George Hill (@SeniorChiefEXW), TWITTER (Dec. 22, 2022, 6:16 PM), https://twitter.com/SeniorChiefEXW/status/1606066219987210242.

Senior Chief
@SeniorChiefEXW

justthenews.com/government/con...
@SpeakerPelosi and her staff have blood on their hands. #JS

justthenews.com
Pelosi's Jan. 6 story unravels as evidence mounts that Capitol breach was pre...
Contemporaneous emails and text messages show Pelosi staff involved in failed security planning ahead of Capitol riot.

6:16 PM · Dec 22, 2022 · **29** Views

Appendix A: Referenced Media

Footnote 8 and 53: George Hill (@SeniorChiefEXW), TWITTER (Dec. 28, 2022, 9:45 AM), https://twitter.com/SeniorChiefEXW/status/1608111891749937155.

Senior Chief
@SeniorChiefEXW

   ...

Insurrection my a$$. It was a set up and sadly, there's no shortage of idiots willing to take the bait.

Lynne 🦋 @LynneS700 · Dec 28, 2022
Patriots were the ONLY ones trying to STOP the Fake Insurrection violence being committed by implanted Antifa. (Pelosi's buddies)
twitter.com/GuntherEaglema...

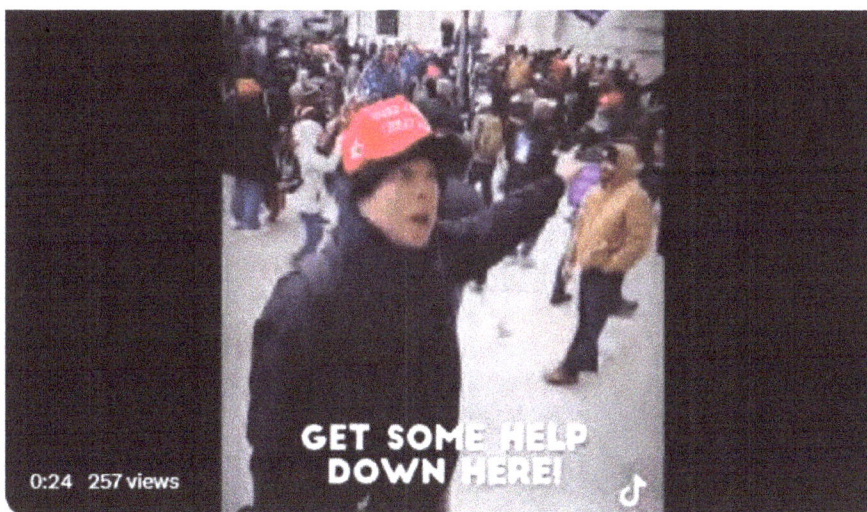

GET SOME HELP DOWN HERE!

0:24 257 views

9:45 AM · Dec 28, 2022 · **109** Views

Footnote 55: George Hill (@SeniorChiefEXW), TWITTER (Jun. 25, 2022, 10:44 PM), https://twitter.com/SeniorChiefEXW/status/1540888727152742400.

Senior Chief
@SeniorChiefEXW

···

The #FBI are the Brown Shirts of the #Democrat Party.
FBI Raids Home of Retired Texas Couple Who Attended Jan. 6 Capitol Rally theepochtimes.com/fbi-raids-home... via @epochtimes

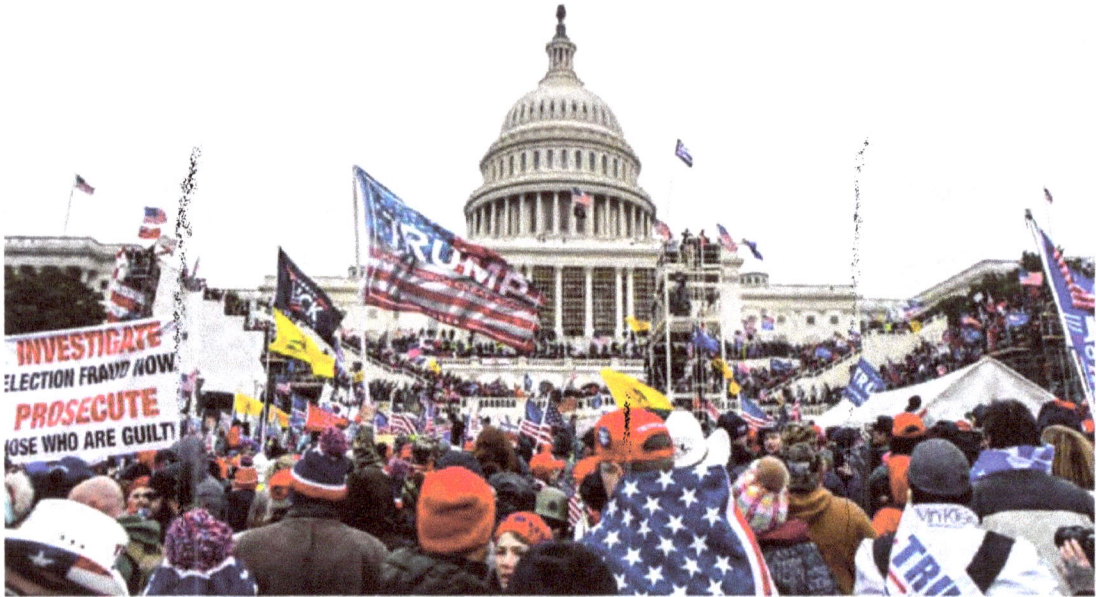

theepochtimes.com
FBI Raids Home of Retired Texas Couple Who Attended Jan. 6 Capitol Rally
A retired Texas couple says FBI agents on June 22 broke through the gate of their rural home, ...

10:44 PM · Jun 25, 2022

Appendix A: Referenced Media

Footnote 11, 57, and 58: George Hill (@SeniorChiefEXW), TWITTER (Nov. 30, 2022, 10:53 AM), https://twitter.com/SeniorChiefEXW/status/1597982151601160193.

Senior Chief
@SeniorChiefEXW

...

The #FBI are the Brown Shirt enforcers of the @DNC. By the Bureau's own policy, they are obligated to disrupt if innocent lives are at risk. But #Trump supporters aren't ever innocent - are they?

Rep. Marjorie Taylor Greene @RepMTG · Nov 30, 2022

If the FBI had so many informants inside a group, why don't they stop J6 from happening?

Ashley Babbit was killed on J6.

Roseann Boyland was beaten, trampled, and dragged down the hall away from life saving CPR being administered.

They would be alive if the FBI had stopped it. twitter.com/julie_kelly2/s...

10:53 AM · Nov 30, 2022

Appendix A: Referenced Media

Footnote 9, 59, and 60: George Hill (@SeniorChiefEXW), TWITTER (Nov. 26, 2022, 5:17 PM), https://twitter.com/SeniorChiefEXW/status/1596629184788721664.

Senior Chief @SeniorChiefEXW · Nov 26, 2022
The reason that bomber is not already in jail is because this is part of a larger #Democrat plan using their enforcement arm, the #FBI.

MR. JORDAN

theepochtimes.com
FBI Waited Over a Year to Fully Investigate Jan. 6 Pipe Bombs: House Judici...
As part of a gargantuan 1,050-page report detailing whistleblower findings from the FBI and Department of Justice (DOJ), ...

Senior Chief
@SeniorChiefEXW

The reason that bomber is not already in jail is because this is part of a larger #Democrat plan using their enforcement arm, the #FBI.

theepochtimes.com
FBI Waited Over a Year to Fully Investigate Jan. 6 Pipe Bom...
As part of a gargantuan 1,050-page report detailing whistleblower findings from the FBI and Department of ...

5:17 PM · Nov 26. 2022

Appendix A: Referenced Media

Footnote 64: George Hill (@SeniorChiefEXW), TWITTER (Jan. 19, 2023, 8:53 PM), https://twitter.com/SeniorChiefEXW/status/1616252459143282692.

Senior Chief
@SeniorChiefEXW
...

I'm disappointed @SpeakerMcCarthy ended the #J6 committee. There needs to be a real investigation. #RosanneBoyland
New Bodycam Footage Boosts Interest in Release of 14,000 Hours of Jan. 6 Video

theepochtimes.com
New Bodycam Footage Boosts Interest in Release of 14,000 Hours of Jan. 6 ...
Dramatic bodycam footage showing protesters doing CPR on the lifeless body of Jan. 6 protester Rosanne Boyland has ...

8:53 PM · Jan 19, 2023 · **306** Views

Footnote 10, 65, and 66: George Hill (@SeniorChiefEXW), TWITTER (Jan. 6, 2023, 8:29 AM), https://twitter.com/SeniorChiefEXW/status/1611354279851298816.

Senior Chief
@SeniorChiefEXW

\#J6

THIS NEEDS TO BE POSTED DAILY UNTIL THAT SOB IS ARRESTED & STANDS TRIAL

MICHAEL BYRD MURDERED ASHLI BABBITT JANUARY 6, 2021

8:29 AM · Jan 6, 2023 · **87** Views

Footnote 67: @GuntherEagleman, TWITTER (Jan. 2, 2023, 5:36 PM), https://twitter.com/SeniorChiefEXW/status/1610262756975935489.

↻ Senior Chief Retweeted

Gunther Eagleman™ ✓
@GuntherEagleman

FACT: Michael Byrd murdered Ashli Babbitt... The motherfucker should be in Prison.

5:36 PM · Jan 2, 2023 · **74.3K** Views

1,642 Retweets   **50** Quote Tweets   **7,793** Likes

Appendix A: Referenced Media

Footnote 74: George Hill (@SeniorChiefEXW), Twitter (Sep. 9, 2022, 11:38 AM),
https://twitter.com/SeniorChiefEXW/status/1568262516928815104.

Senior Chief
@SeniorChiefEXW   . . .

#Biden should be impeached but many #Republicans are still members
of the #UniParty or just gutless.
Most want Biden impeached, see GOP dropping ball

washingtonexaminer.com
Most want Biden impeached, see GOP dropping ball
A majority of voters, including a third of Democrats, support efforts to impeach
unpopular President Joe Biden, the latest president to face the nation's ...

11:38 AM · Sep 9, 2022

Appendix A: Referenced Media

Footnote 75: George Hill (@SeniorChiefEXW), TWITTER (Feb. 1, 2023, 7:09 AM),
https://twitter.com/SeniorChiefEXW/status/1620756320675667969.

7:09 AM · Feb 1, 2023 · **159** Views

Appendix A: Referenced Media

Footnote 76: George Hill (@SeniorChiefEXW), TWITTER (Nov. 27, 2022, 7:52 AM), https://twitter.com/SeniorChiefEXW/status/1596849524382711809.

Senior Chief
@SeniorChiefEXW

nypost.com/2022/11/26/bid...
#PedoJoe

nypost.com
'Creepy' Joe Biden roasted for strange selfies
"Here's Joey!"

7:52 AM · Nov 27, 2022

Appendix A: Referenced Media

Footnote 77: George Hill (@SeniorChiefEXW), TWITTER (Sep. 2, 2022, 10:23 PM), https://twitter.com/SeniorChiefEXW/status/1565525735086981123.

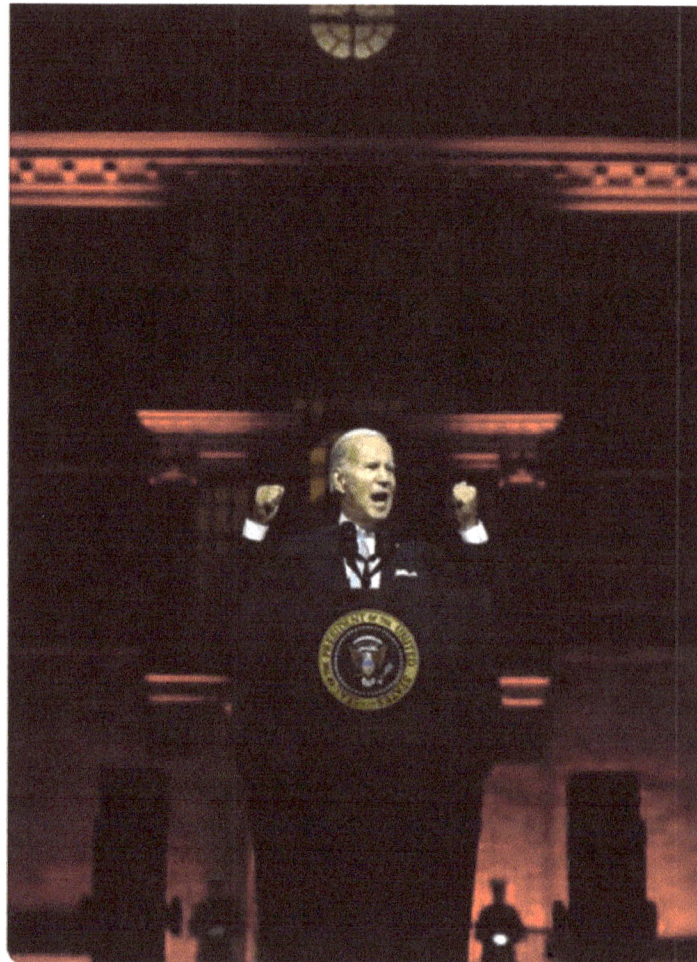

Senior Chief
@SeniorChiefEXW

Not a good look Joe Stalin, er, Joe Biden.
#bidenspeech

Mairead Elordi @JohnsonHildy · Sep 1, 2022
•• optics ••
Show this thread

10:23 PM · Sep 1, 2022

Footnote 78: George Hill (@SeniorChiefEXW), TWITTER (Jan. 27, 2023, 9:39 PM), https://twitter.com/SeniorChiefEXW/status/1619163281620619264.

Rep. Eric Swalwell ✓ @RepSwalwell · Jan 27   ···

This is what your inbox looks like when @SpeakerMcCarthy falsely smears you. We have told him his smears are inspiring death threats. Yet he continues. This is what he wants.

FW: Threatening Voicemail 1/27/2...

Congressman Eric Swalwell (CA-14)
174 Cannon HOB...

11:41 AM

FW: Threatening Voicemail 1/27/2...

11:41 AM

FW: Threatening Voicemail 1/27/2...

11:41 AM

FW: Threatening Voicemail 1/27/2...

💬 3,212　　🔁 4,024　　♡ 9,915　　📊 660.9K　　⬆

Senior Chief   ···
@SeniorChiefEXW

Replying to @RepSwalwell and @SpeakerMcCarthy

Don't be such a whiner. You slept with a PRCIS IO. You got off light (no pun intended).

9:39 PM · Jan 27, 2023 · 15 Views

Appendix A: Referenced Media

Footnote 79: George Hill (@SeniorChiefEXW), Twitter (Jan. 23, 2023, 5:53 AM), https://twitter.com/SeniorChiefEXW/status/1617475674922700802.

Senior Chief
@SeniorChiefEXW   ...

I've reached out to @RepKClark multiple times regarding her tacit support of #BLM, #Antifa and growing political violence. She has ignored every attempt for engagement. Now her child is facing serious charges. Reap what you sow.

5:53 AM · Jan 23, 2023 · **505** Views

Footnote 80: George Hill (@SeniorChiefEXW), Twitter (Jan. 31, 2023, 7:49 PM), https://twitter.com/SeniorChiefEXW/status/1620585152987467776.

Senior Chief
@SeniorChiefEXW   ...

@AOC

STOP KILLING GORILLAS
FOR GLUE AND TAPE!
made with mematic

7:49 PM · Jan 31, 2023 · **304** Views

Appendix A: Referenced Media

Footnote 80: George Hill (@SeniorChiefEXW), TWITTER (Jan. 31, 2023, 7:08 PM), https://twitter.com/SeniorChiefEXW/status/1620574897859694592.

Senior Chief
@SeniorChiefEXW

Calling political opponents #DomesticTerrorists gives license to Federal Law Enforcement to do whatever is necessary. @MaxineWaters

pjnewsletter.com
Maxine Waters Just Stepped Way Over the Line - She Slap...
How can she get away with this?

7:08 PM · Jan 31, 2023 · **108** Views

Footnote 80: George Hill (@SeniorChiefEXW), TWITTER (Jan. 26, 2023, 6:53 PM), https://twitter.com/SeniorChiefEXW/status/1618758963142729728.

Senior Chief
@SeniorChiefEXW

Poor Sparticus 😢 @CoryBooker

thepoliticalinsider.com
Cory Booker Mocked After Claiming More Americans Died from Gun Violence...
Senator Cory Booker was questioned by viewers after claiming to have witnessed more deaths from gun violence in his lifetime than "all of our wars ...

6:53 PM · Jan 26, 2023 · **91** Views

Footnote 80: George Hill (@SeniorChiefEXW), TWITTER (Jan. 31, 2023, 2:12 PM), https://twitter.com/SeniorChiefEXW/status/1620500316054503424.

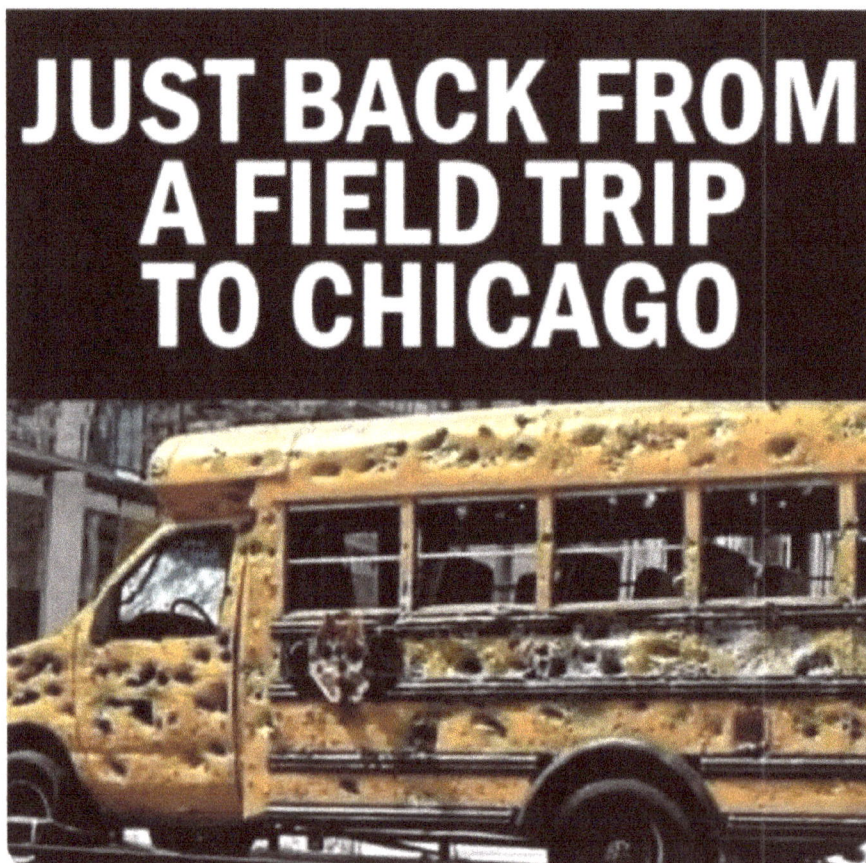

Appendix A: Referenced Media

Footnote 80: George Hill (@SeniorChiefEXW), Twitter (Sep. 9, 2022, 11:33 AM),
https://twitter.com/SeniorChiefEXW/status/1568261354989195270.

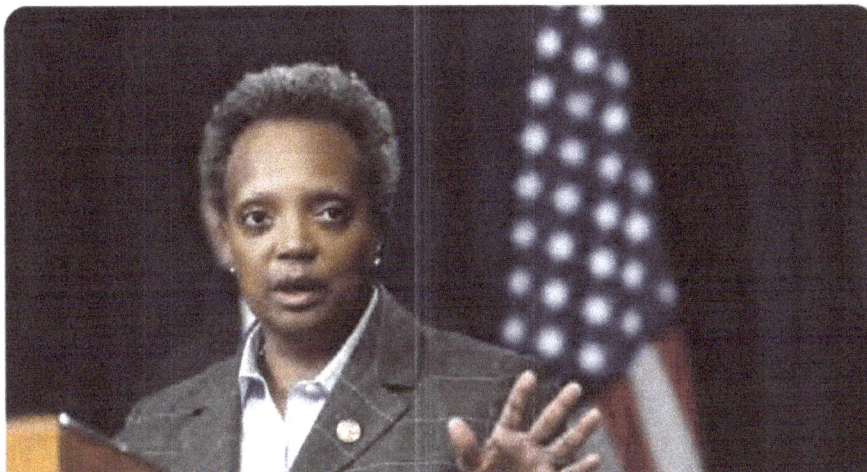

Senior Chief
@SeniorChiefEXW
...

@chicagosmayor is a real piece of work. She's a small angry person
throwing a snit.
Chicago's mayor Lightfoot is busing migrants to nearby Burr Ridge
without informing the mayor

hotair.com
Chicago's mayor Lightfoot is busing migrants to nearby Burr Ridge without
informing the mayor

11:33 AM · Sep 9, 2022

Appendix A: Referenced Media

Footnote 81: George Hill (@SeniorChiefEXW), TWITTER (Dec. 21, 2022, 9:38 AM),
https://twitter.com/SeniorChiefEXW/status/1605573408628129793.

Senior Chief
@SeniorChiefEXW

#DitchMitch This communist, along with his #CCP member wife, has to go!

Mollie ✔ @MZHemingway · Dec 21, 2022
So long as McConnell is top elected Republican, eagerly trashing voters,
vociferously advocating for Dem policy goals, pushing $1.7 trillion spending
packages, and weakly fighting for whatever he can be bothered to pursue,
Republicans have obvious problem.
thefederalist.com/2022/12/21/gop...

9:38 AM · Dec 21, 2022 · **62** Views

Footnote 82: George Hill (@SeniorChiefEXW), TWITTER (Jan. 28, 2023, 11:41 AM),
https://twitter.com/SeniorChiefEXW/status/1619375047445192706.

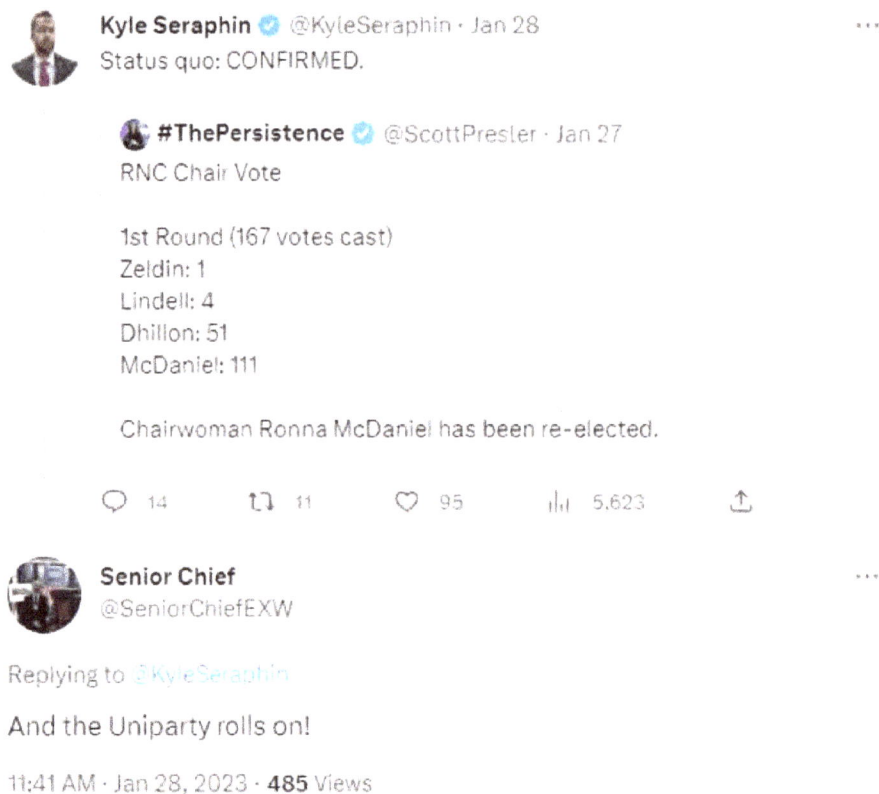

Kyle Seraphin ✔ @KyleSeraphin · Jan 28
Status quo: CONFIRMED.

#ThePersistence ✔ @ScottPresler · Jan 27
RNC Chair Vote

1st Round (167 votes cast)
Zeldin: 1
Lindell: 4
Dhillon: 51
McDaniel: 111

Chairwoman Ronna McDaniel has been re-elected.

○ 14   ⇄ 11   ♡ 95   ᴵᴵᵢ 5,623   ↑

Senior Chief
@SeniorChiefEXW

Replying to @KyleSeraphin

And the Uniparty rolls on!

11:41 AM · Jan 28, 2023 · **485** Views

Footnote 83: George Hill (@SeniorChiefEXW), TWITTER (Jan. 9, 2023, 5:19 PM), https://twitter.com/SeniorChiefEXW/status/1612574753881051174.

Senior Chief
@SeniorChiefEXW

Your feel good story of the Day. Sorry @DanCrenshawTX but when you carelessly throw around the #terrorist label, there are consequences. Mark Green beats Dan Crenshaw in race to chair Homeland Security Committee

washingtonexaminer.com
Mark Green beats Dan Crenshaw in race to chair Homeland Security Commit...
Rep. Mark Green (R-TN) won the coveted gavel for the House Committee on Homeland Security on Monday, beating Rep. Dan Crenshaw (R-TX) for the ...

5:19 PM · Jan 9, 2023 · **267** Views

Appendix A: Referenced Media

Footnote 83: George Hill (@SeniorChiefEXW), Twitter (Dec. 25, 2022, 10:44 AM), https://twitter.com/SeniorChiefEXW/status/1607039487179382785.

Senior Chief
@SeniorChiefEXW
...

I'm sure @RepDanCrenshaw is familiar with; did you sleep last night? Yes? Then you had time.
Crenshaw Blasts 'Lame Excuse' For Voting Against $1.7 Trillion Omnibus Package

townhall.com
Crenshaw Blasts 'Lame Excuse' For Voting Against $1.7 Trillion Omnibus Pack...

10:44 AM · Dec 25, 2022 · **33** Views

Footnote 87: George Hill (@SeniorChiefEXW), Twitter (Aug. 13, 2022, 10:13 AM), https://twitter.com/SeniorChiefEXW/status/1558456715556884480.

Senior Chief
@SeniorChiefEXW
...

Wray has never lost a minutes sleep over @ChuckGrassley @SenTedCruz or @Jim_Jordan - I'm sorry but it's true. No one in #DOJ or #FBI has ever paid a price for unlawful conduct and never will. Sad but true.
twitter.com/seannidav/statu...

This Tweet was deleted by the Tweet author. Learn more

10:13 AM · Aug 13, 2022

Appendix A: Referenced Media

Footnote 119: Garret O'Boyle (@GOBActual), TWITTER (Jan. 14, 2022, 12:15 AM).

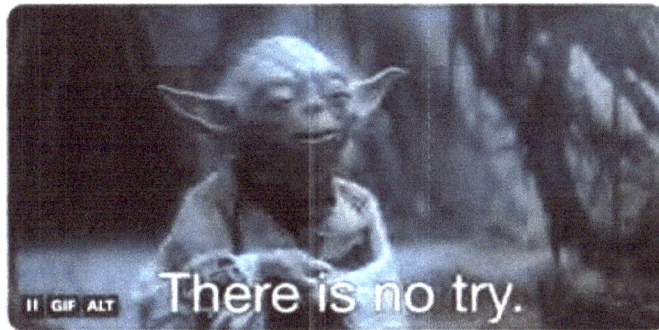

Alex Berenson ✓ @AlexBerenson Jan 14

I will try not to use the term pureblood anymore. It was necessary when unvaccinated people had to stand together against overwhelming pressure (I can't believe that actually happened, but it did). But no one is bragging about being jabbed anymore.

We won. Let's be graceful.

Garret O'Boyle
@GOBActual

Replying to @AlexBerenson

I'm still using it. It's true. We should never stop speaking the truth. There are still plenty bragging about being jabbed and still think we are killing people by not. Also this...

12:15 AM · Jan 15, 2023 · **9** Views

Appendix A: Referenced Media

Footnote 14 and 121: Garret O'Boyle (@GOBActual), TWITTER (Jan. 17, 2023, 10:10 AM).

Col. Rob Maness ret. 1776 🇺🇸 ✓ @RobManess · Jan 16
Would US military forces follow an order to attack American civilians?

Yes   48.3%

Hell no   51.7%

51,739 votes · Final results

Garret O'Boyle
@GOBactual

Replying to @RobManess

99% followed an order to harm themselves with mrna injections. It's a lot easier to follow orders to harm others. Reserve Police Battalion 101 comes to mind...

10:10 AM · Jan 17, 2023 · **30** Views

Footnote 149: Steve Friend (@RealStevefriend), TWITTER (Nov. 27, 2022, 9:05 AM), https://twitter.com/RealStevefriend/status/1596867895304519682.

Steve Friend
@RealStevefriend

Thank you @SharylAttkisson. I'm continuing to inform Americans about the FBI's improper activities regardless of OSC.

sharylattkisson.com
(READ) Office of Special Counsel dismisses FBI whistleblower complaint about the agency | Sharyl...

9:05 AM · Nov 27, 2022

Footnote 153: Steve Friend (@RealStevefriend), TWITTER (Dec. 20, 2022, 4:01 PM), https://twitter.com/RealStevefriend/status/1605307475497992193.

Steve Friend
@RealStevefriend

Worth a RT. @FBI Whistleblowers know where the bodies are buried @JudiciaryGOP. Prioritize protecting us in 2023 and more will come forward. Subpoenas and hearings aren't good enough. @KyleSeraphin @GOBactual @BreannaMorello @AbsoluteWithE

Kyle Seraphin ✓ @KyleSeraphin · Dec 2, 2022
🚨 Here we go folks. The Suspendables, FBI Agents who were suspended for upholding their oaths, have some questions for @FBI Dir Chris Wray. @dbongino @SebGorka @julie_kelly2 @mirandadevine @RichSementa @marklevinshow @DarrenJBeattie @TuckerCarlson @seanhannity @Jim_Jordan

Show this thread

4:01 PM · Dec 20, 2022 · **9,812** Views

Appendix A: Referenced Media

Footnote 154: Steve Friend (@RealStevefriend), TWITTER (Dec. 21, 2022, 9:37 PM), https://twitter.com/RealStevefriend/status/1605754480506519552.

Steve Friend
@RealStevefriend   ...

Yep. One of the disclosures I brought to Congress. Maybe @tedlieu missed it. Hoping @JudiciaryGOP will ask me about it in 2023

Breanna Morello ✓ @BreannaMorello · Dec 16, 2022

Hey @RealStevefriend, isn't this why you became a FBI whistleblower? twitter.com/mtaibbi/status...

9:37 PM · Dec 21, 2022 · **1,938** Views

Footnote 155: Steve Friend (@Real_SteveFriend), TRUTH SOCIAL (Dec. 24, 2022, 9:47 PM), https://truthsocial.com/@Real_SteveFriend/posts/109572026898527069.

Steve Friend ✓
@Real_SteveFriend · Dec 24, 2022

GOP House Judiciary Committee is tweeting out clips of @realDonaldTrump in Home Alone 2. President Trump is off Twitter guys. How about you DM some suspended FBI whistleblowers instead?

24 ReTruths **124** Likes   Dec 24, 2022, 9:47 PM

Appendix A: Referenced Media

Footnote 156: Steve Friend (@Real_SteveFriend), Truth Social (Dec. 25, 2022, 9:15 PM), https://truthsocial.com/@Real_SteveFriend/posts/109577563422431659.

Steve Friend ✔
@Real_SteveFriend · Dec 25, 2022

Trolling all day from the House GOP Judiciary Committee twitter account. Can they pretend to show an interest in protecting FBI whistleblowers like @kyleseraphin and me? Or does the committee exist solely for social media interns to "own the libs?"

Steve Friend ✔
@Real_SteveFriend · Dec 24, 2022

GOP House Judiciary Committee is tweeting out clips of @realDonaldTrump in Home Alone 2. President Trump is off Twitter guys. How about you DM some suspended FBI whistleblowers instead?

77 ReTruths   **296** Likes   Dec 25, 2022, 9:15 PM

Appendix A: Referenced Media

Footnote 157: Steve Friend (@Real_SteveFriend), TRUTH SOCIAL (Dec. 26, 2022, 8:47 PM),
https://truthsocial.com/@Real_SteveFriend/posts/109583116369352493.

Steve Friend ✓
@Real_SteveFriend · Dec 26, 2022

Spoiler: They took my whistleblower complaint. Used it for campaign rocket
fuel and 4 minute appearances on Fox News. Ignored me after I lost my
income. Focused on other dead end investigations that get no results but
deliver more tv appearances. I'm not alone either, @kyleseraphin

NTD Television ✓
@NTDTelevision · Dec 26, 2022

Republicans are vowing to investigate the cooperation between
#Twitter, the #FBI, and the federal government.

We look at what steps the GOP have taken thus far.
theepochtimes.com/ntd-evening-...

100 ReTruths   201 Likes   Dec 26, 2022, 8:47 PM

Appendix A: Referenced Media

Footnote 158: Steve Friend (@RealStevefriend), TWITTER (Dec. 26, 2022, 8:37 PM),
https://twitter.com/RealStevefriend/status/1607551304854904832.

Steve Friend
@RealStevefriend   . . .

We already know. Skip those headlines and focus on @FBI whistleblower
abuse

    ↑ **House Judiciary GOP** ✅ @JudiciaryGOP · Dec 26, 2022
    Fauci lied.

8:37 PM · Dec 26, 2022 · **2,652** Views

Footnote 165: Steve Friend (@RealStevefriend), TWITTER (Dec. 7, 2022, 12:35 PM),
https://twitter.com/RealStevefriend/status/1600544553878142986.

Steve Friend
@RealStevefriend   . . .

Looking forward to appearing on @NEWSMAX tonight with
@gregkellyusa at 9:30 ET.

12:35 PM · Dec 7, 2022

Footnote 165: Steve Friend (@RealSteveFriend), TWITTER (Dec. 7, 2022, 8:29 PM),
https://twitter.com/RealStevefriend/status/1600663729019842560.

Steve Friend
@RealStevefriend   . . .

Looking forward to appearing on American Sunrise tomorrow at 9:30ET
@RealAmVoice @edhenry @mrsflorida2016

8:29 PM · Dec 7, 2022

Footnote 168: @RealStevefriend, Twitter (Dec. 7, 2022),
https://web.archive.org/web/20221207205234/https://twitter.com/RealStevefriend.

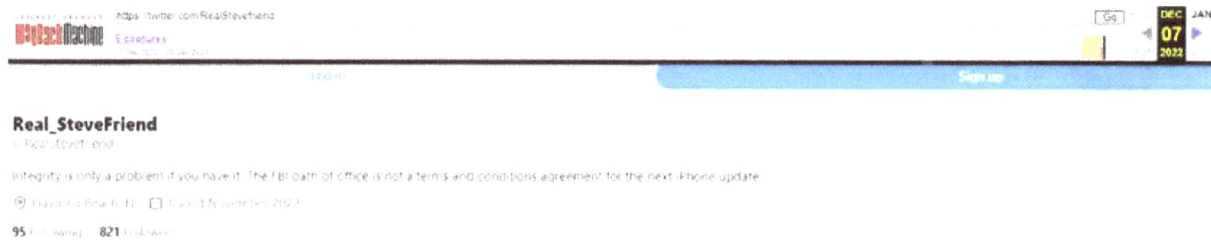

Footnote 168: @RealStevefriend, Twitter, https://twitter.com/RealStevefriend (last visited Mar. 1, 2023).

Appendix A: Referenced Media

Footnote 176: Russ Vought (@russvought), TWITTER (Jan. 27, 2023, 4:20 PM),
https://twitter.com/russvought/status/1619082843535323136.

Russ Vought ✓
@russvought

Excited to announce that FBI whistleblower Steve Friend is coming on board @amrenewctr to help uncover the full extent of the FBI's weaponization against the American people. @RealSteveFriend is going to play a huge role in maximizing the potential of the new Church committee!

4:20 PM · Jan 27, 2023 · **22K** Views

Footnote 220: Steve Friend (@Real_SteveFriend), TRUTH SOCIAL (Jan. 10, 2023, 9:09 AM), https://truthsocial.com/@Real_SteveFriend/posts/109665307137228963.

Steve Friend
@Real_SteveFriend · Jan 10

#OPRFiles Installment 39. I am on DAY 113 of suspension for improperly accessing the employee handbook... This FBI employee watched porn on the same computer system and got a letter of censure. Abolish the FBI @JimJordan @RepThomasMassie @HouseGOP

Misuse of Government Computer:
Employee used a Bureau computer to watch pornography while working the night shift. In mitigation, Employee has a positive performance history, maintains the support of the Division, and this appears to have been an isolated incident.

OFFENSE: Misuse of Government Computer, Offense Code 3.6

PENALTY: Letter of Censure

86 ReTruths 111 Likes   Jan 10, 2023, 9:09 AM

Appendix A: Referenced Media

Footnote 16 and 250: Steve Friend (@RealStevefriend), TWITTER (Feb. 21, 2023, 6:15 PM), https://twitter.com/RealStevefriend/status/1628171705586704387.

Steve Friend
@RealStevefriend   ...

Thanks @BrandonDrey for helping @KyleSeraphin and the Suspendables keep exposing the @FBI as a feckless, garbage institution. Waiting to hear any defense for massage recliners in a federal government workspace supposedly responsible for fighting major crime and terrorism.

Kyle Seraphin ✓ @KyleSeraphin · Feb 21 · ✏️
Honorary Suspendable @BrandonDrey for Daily Wire:

Former FBI Agents Slam Bureau For Wasting Tax Dollars On 'Wellness Room' For Employees
dailywire.com/news/former-fb...

6:15 PM · Feb 21, 2023 · **2,258** Views

Appendix A: Referenced Media

Footnote 18 and 251: Steve Friend (@RealStevefriend), TWITTER (Jan. 2, 2023, 10:10 AM), https://twitter.com/RealStevefriend/status/1609930175965270017.

Steve Friend
@RealStevefriend

...

#OPRFiles Installment 30. "Employee was involved in MULTIPLE domestic violence incidents." Defund the @FBI

Misuse of Position; Assault & Battery; Unprofessional Conduct; Failure to Report; Lack of Candor Under Oath: Employee was involved in multiple domestic violence incidents and failed to report his police contact. According to the Personnel Security Self-Reporting Requirements Policy, all FBI employees must report "[a]ny arrest, domestic violence incident report, driving while intoxicated/under the influence (DWI/DUI) offense, and/or other aggravated/unusual offense involving a law enforcement official." Employee located his wife at a hotel where she was staying with their children after she left him. Employee repeatedly attempted to gain access to her hotel room by telling hotel employees that he was in pursuit of a fugitive who was under FBI surveillance. When questioned by investigators during the OPR proceedings, Employee lacked candor when he claimed he only told hotel representatives that he needed to get into his wife's room to pick up clothes for their children.

OFFENSE: Lack of Candor - Under Oath, Offense Code 2.6 Misuse of Position, Offense Code 2.8 Assault/Battery, Offense Code 4.1 Failure to Report, Offense Code 5.8 Unprofessional Conduct - Off Duty, Offense Code 5.21

PENALTY: Dismissal

10:10 AM · Jan 2, 2023 · **13.5K** Views

Appendix A: Referenced Media

Footnote 19 and 252: Steve Friend (@RealStevefriend), TWITTER (Dec. 24, 2022, 9:04 PM), https://twitter.com/RealStevefriend/status/1606833333165596673.

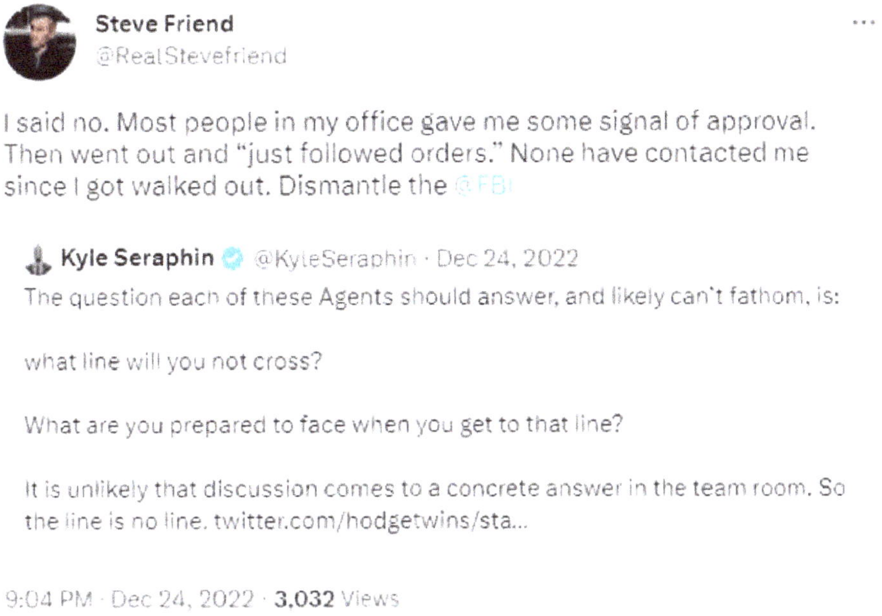

Steve Friend
@RealStevefriend
•••

I said no. Most people in my office gave me some signal of approval. Then went out and "just followed orders." None have contacted me since I got walked out. Dismantle the @FBI

Kyle Seraphin @KyleSeraphin · Dec 24, 2022
The question each of these Agents should answer, and likely can't fathom, is:

what line will you not cross?

What are you prepared to face when you get to that line?

It is unlikely that discussion comes to a concrete answer in the team room. So the line is no line. twitter.com/hodgetwins/sta...

9:04 PM · Dec 24, 2022 · **3,032** Views

Footnote 20 and 253: Steve Friend (@RealStevefriend), TWITTER (Dec. 16, 2022, 10:40 PM), https://twitter.com/RealStevefriend/status/1603958354694610944.

Steve Friend
@RealStevefriend
•••

Office of Special Counsel told me the @FBI has discretion to stray from its rules and procedures. It is too late for reform. The fix is in. Dissolve it all.

Richard Grenell @RichardGrenell · Dec 16, 2022
Agree. There must be a congressional investigation immediately. twitter.com/Stemic09/statu...

10:40 PM · Dec 16, 2022 **32K** Views

Appendix A: Referenced Media

Footnote 21 and 254: Steve Friend (@RealStevefriend), TWITTER (Dec. 26, 2022, 6:52 AM), https://twitter.com/RealStevefriend/status/1607343573615124482.

Steve Friend
@RealStevefriend

@FBI is beyond redemption. 4 consecutive scandalous Directors. Collusion with big tech. Entrapment. Persecution of political conservatives. Zero accountability and the unmitigated gall to call critics conspiracy theorists. Abort the @FBI

amgreatness.com
What Will the FBI Not Do? › American Greatness
The FBI on Wednesday finally broke its silence and responded to the revelations on Twitter of close ties between the bureau and the social media ...

6:52 AM · Dec 26, 2022 · **3,001** Views

Appendix A: Referenced Media

Footnote 22 and 255: Steve Friend (@RealStevefriend), TWITTER (Feb. 8, 2023, 7:26 PM), https://twitter.com/RealStevefriend/status/1623478351934418946.

Steve Friend
@RealStevefriend
...

The @FBI is targeting Catholics. And relying on left-wing news sources to substantiate their ridiculous, politicized "assessments." Abolish the FBI @KyleSeraphin @Tyler2ONeil @DailySignal

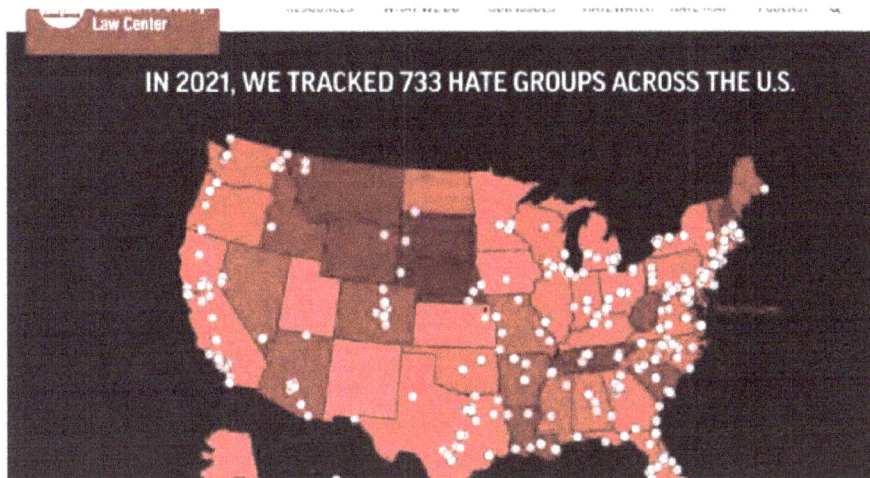

IN 2021, WE TRACKED 733 HATE GROUPS ACROSS THE U.S.

dailysignal.com
FBI Document Cites SPLC on 'Radical-Traditional Catholics'
FBI Richmond cited the Southern Poverty Law Center numerous times on what the SPLC calls "radical traditional Catholic hate groups."

7:26 PM · Feb 8, 2023 · **2,948** Views

Appendix A: Referenced Media

Footnote 23 and 256: Steve Friend (@RealStevefriend), TWITTER (Feb. 14, 2023, 7:42 PM), https://twitter.com/realstevefriend/status/1625656884626706433.

Steve Friend
@RealStevefriend

...

Propose an amendment to add @FBI

🌐 **Thomas Massie** ✓ @RepThomasMassie · Feb 14
I have introduced a bill to terminate the Department of Education.

There is no Constitutional authority for this federal bureaucracy to exist.

H.R.899 - To terminate the Department of Education.

118th Congress (2023-2024) | Get alerts

BILL	Hide Overview ✕
Sponsor:	Rep. Massie, Thomas [R-KY-4] (Introduced 02/09/2023)
Committees:	House - Education and the Workforce
Latest Action:	House - 02/09/2023 Referred to the House Committee on Education and the Workforce. (All Actions)
Tracker: ⓘ	Introduced / Passed House / Passed Senate / To President / Became Law

7:42 PM · Feb 14, 2023 · **3,071** Views

Footnote 258: Steve Friend (@Real_SteveFriend), TRUTH SOCIAL (Nov. 7, 2022, 7:47 PM), https://truthsocial.com/@Real_SteveFriend/posts/109305427771232937.

Steve Friend ✓
@Real_SteveFriend · Nov 7, 2022

The PC answer is that there are lots of good people doing good work. I'm done with it. The fact that 14k aren't standing next to @kyleseraphin and me means we need to Ctrl+Alt+Del the whole thing. Too many overpaid, underworked people resting on the laurels of those who came before and did real police work

Nin84
@Nin84 · Nov 7, 2022

Replying to @Real_SteveFriend

Hypothetically speaking, say two years ago or so a new agent from a conservative family & he or she is assigned to LA, I realized all are different, field office. How prevalent is the rot. Just curious on your thoughts.

29 ReTruths **107** Likes   Nov 07, 2022, 7:47 PM

Appendix A: Referenced Media

Footnote 260: Steve Friend, (@RealStevefriend), TWITTER (Dec. 25, 2022, 5:43 PM), https://twitter.com/RealStevefriend/status/1607145126505349120.

Steve Friend
@RealStevefriend
...

This must happen. No debate. Abort the @FBI

The Epoch Times ✓ @EpochTimes · Dec 25, 2022
"We've been looking at a Church-style committee to look at this," Rep. @Jim_Jordan said.

House Republicans are signaling a top-to-bottom invesigation of the #FBI in January.

"We need to hold people accountable," said Rep. @NancyMace. theepochtimes.com/gop-floats-chu...

5:43 PM · Dec 25, 2022 · **2,735** Views

Appendix A: Referenced Media

Footnote 261: Steve Friend (@Real_SteveFriend), TRUTH SOCIAL (Feb. 21, 2023, 8:15 AM), https://truthsocial.com/@Real_SteveFriend/posts/109902911518876069.

Steve Friend ✓
@Real_SteveFriend · 6d

Your tax dollars at work. Here is the announcement for a "wellness room" inside one of the FBI field offices. The room is a "quiet space" used to "decompress and take a break from the workday." Features massage recliners, lounge furniture, and a space for yoga!

BONUS! Here is a sign posted outside the FBI wellness room. This is not a serious law enforcement agency. At best the FBI is an insult to the taxpayer. At worst, an enemy.

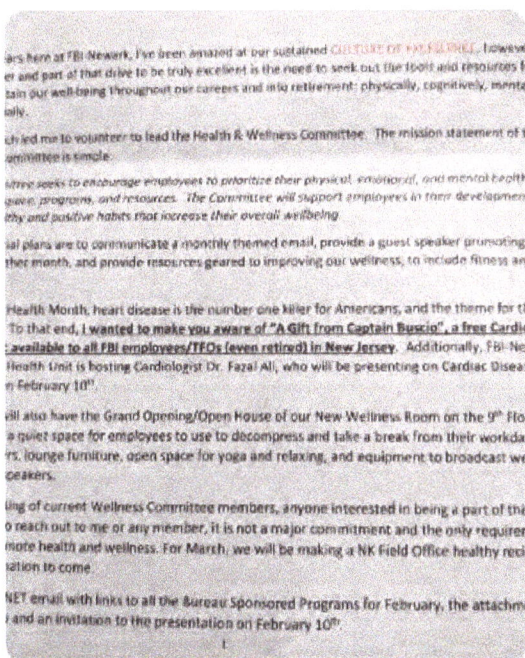

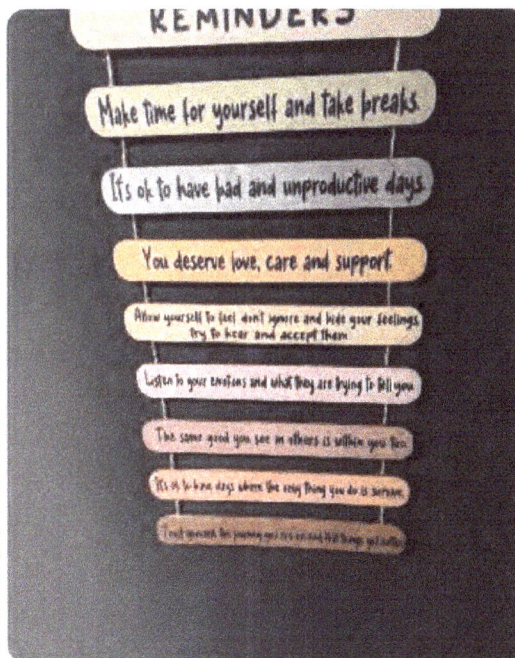

66 ReTruths   119 Likes   Feb 21, 2023, 8:15 AM

Footnote 262: Steve Friend (@RealStevefriend), TWITTER (Dec. 19, 2022, 6:48 PM), https://twitter.com/RealStevefriend/status/1604986983432048641.

Jesse Kelly ✔ @JesseKellyDC · Dec 19, 2022 · · ·
The FBI cannot continue to exist in any form. It will end this nation if it does.

Red states must immediately begin re-ordering themselves to stand between their citizens and the federal government. This is going to a dangerous place. And quickly.

Michael Shellenberger ✔ @ShellenbergerMD · Dec 19, 2022
1. TWITTER FILES: PART 7

The FBI & the Hunter Biden Laptop

How the FBI & intelligence community discredited factual information about Hunter Biden's foreign business dealings both after and *before* The New York Post revealed the contents of his laptop on October 14, 2020

Show this thread

○ 339   ⊔ 3,155   ♡ 9,524   �_ıl 454.9K   ↑

Steve Friend   · · ·
@RealStevefriend

Replying to @JesseKellyDC

Doctrine of Lesser Magistrates. @FBI has 14K agents. to police 400 million people. FBI requires manpower, intel, and casework from local law enforcement partners. Pressure your sheriffs to refuse to cooperate. Starve the FBI out. Turn your county into a FBI Sanctuary City.

6:48 PM · Dec 19, 2022 · **498** Views

Appendix A: Referenced Media

Footnote 263 and 265: Steve Friend (@RealStevefriend), TWITTER (Dec. 24, 2022, 11:56 PM), https://twitter.com/RealStevefriend/status/1606876566914580480.

Steve Friend
@RealStevefriend

$11.33 billion budget for next year. Don't talk to me about the "good men and women" of the @FBI. @KyleSeraphin is the ONLY other employee willing to speak out publicly? Defund the FBI. Breadlines for everyone. Including GOP senators voting to increase its budget

Hodgetwins @hodgetwins · Dec 24, 2022
The feds are still sending in armed combat ready SWAT teams to raid people who peacefully protested OUTSIDE the Capitol on Jan 6

Republican Senators voted to give them more money too

Show this thread

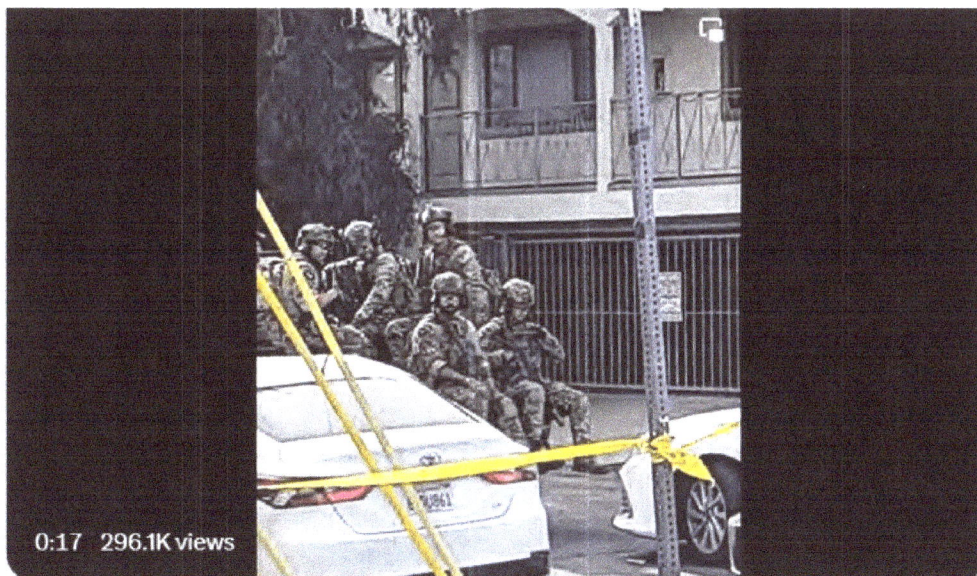

0:17   296.1K views

11:56 PM · Dec 24, 2022 · **12.4K** Views

Appendix A: Referenced Media

Footnote 264: Steve Friend (@RealStevefriend), TWITTER (Dec. 13, 2022, 12:55 PM), https://twitter.com/RealStevefriend/status/1602724023456120832.

Steve Friend
@RealStevefriend

· · ·

Can think of about 36k people at @FBI the @HouseGOP can lay off

Kyle Seraphin ✓ @KyleSeraphin · Dec 13, 2022
Weird flex. Who votes to fund the government? Oh... That's right. So get to work. This has been true my whole life and all of Jordan's political career. twitter.com/Jim_Jordan/sta...

12:55 PM · Dec 13, 2022

Footnote 326: *Welcome to the Kash Patel Legal Offense Trust*, WINRED, https://secure.winred.com/donatetoday/kplot_don_bm_ams_lot-dt_na (last visited Mar. 1, 2023).

Welcome to the Kash Patel Legal Offense Trust

My name is Kash Patel. As a former career national security official and senior Trump advisor, I know firsthand that the Fake News propaganda machine is working overtime to put American patriots on the defensive.

You see, among many others, *WaPo*, *CNN*, *Politico*, and the *NYT* falsely and viciously smeared me after I **discovered** and **exposed** their **Russian Collusion hoax**. Twitter has greenlit an account falsely impersonating me to remain in operation.

I'm done playing defense. It's time to go on the offensive! That's why I'm fighting back.

But to win, your support is critical to helping me reach my $250k goal to fund a top-notch legal team.

So, make a gift now to help me strike a major blow to the far-Left media and Big Tech!

Footnote 342: Kash Patel (@Kash), TRUTH SOCIAL (Aug. 12, 2022, 4:36 PM), https://truthsocial.com/@Kash/posts/108811817583790833.

Kash Patel ✓
@Kash · Aug 12, 2022

#FightWithKash Showing their hypocrisy

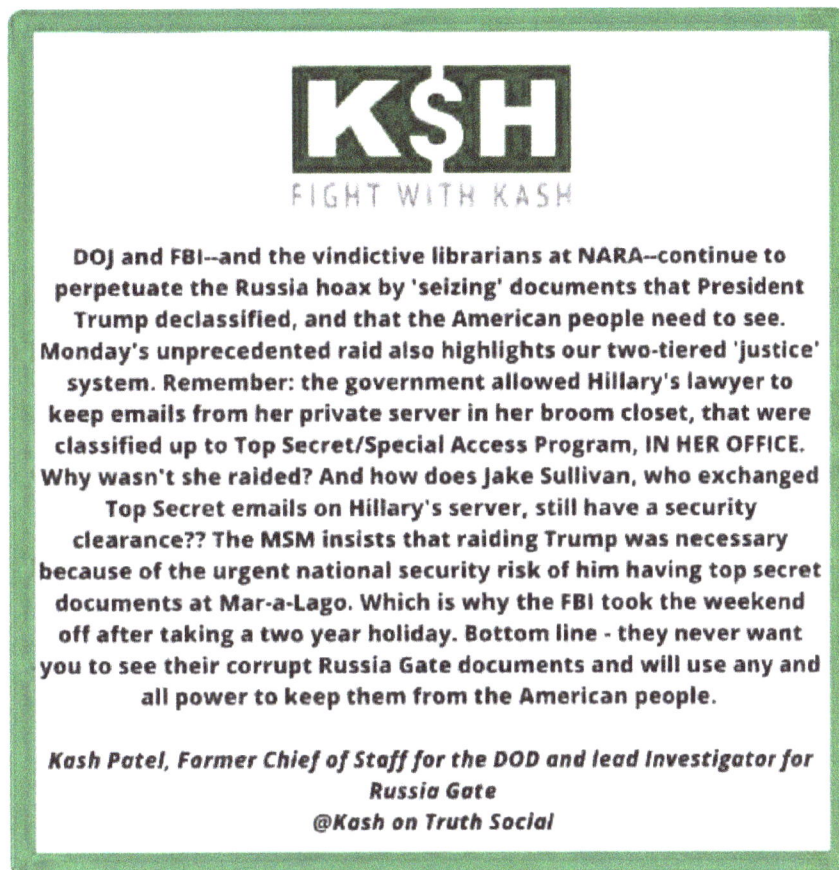

KSH
FIGHT WITH KASH

DOJ and FBI--and the vindictive librarians at NARA--continue to perpetuate the Russia hoax by 'seizing' documents that President Trump declassified, and that the American people need to see. Monday's unprecedented raid also highlights our two-tiered 'justice' system. Remember: the government allowed Hillary's lawyer to keep emails from her private server in her broom closet, that were classified up to Top Secret/Special Access Program, IN HER OFFICE. Why wasn't she raided? And how does Jake Sullivan, who exchanged Top Secret emails on Hillary's server, still have a security clearance?? The MSM insists that raiding Trump was necessary because of the urgent national security risk of him having top secret documents at Mar-a-Lago. Which is why the FBI took the weekend off after taking a two year holiday. Bottom line - they never want you to see their corrupt Russia Gate documents and will use any and all power to keep them from the American people.

Kash Patel, Former Chief of Staff for the DOD and lead Investigator for Russia Gate
@Kash on Truth Social

1.68k ReTruths 3.63k Likes   Aug 12, 2022, 4:36 PM

Footnote 351: @Q, Truth Social (Jun. 14, 2022, 12:23 PM), https://truthsocial.com/users/q/statuses/108476746478555731.

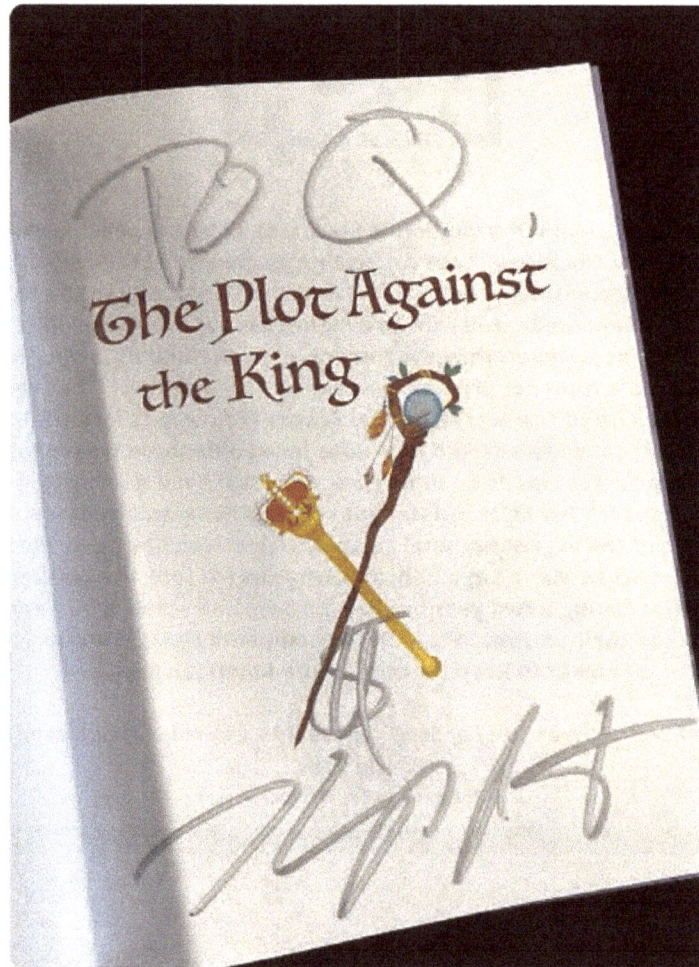

Q
@Q · Jun 14, 2022

Finally got my signed copy - thanks @Kash 🇺🇸 🙏

bravebooks.us/products/the-plo...

2.81k ReTruths   9.59k Likes   Jun 14, 2022, 12:23 PM

Appendix A: Referenced Media

Footnote 357: Truth Social Post, @Kash, Dec. 22, 2022, 12:56 p.m. https://truthsocial.com/@Kash/posts/109558616190328922.

Kash Patel ✓
@Kash · Dec 22, 2022

LFG #FWK

justthenews.com/accountability...

Incoming House Judiciary chairman vows to probe DOJ snooping on congressional investigators

Rep. Jim Jordan says the revelations by Just the News that DOJ subpoenaed phone and email records of House Intelligence investigators in 2017 make him wonder if DOJ is now clandestinely monitoring his...

⌀ justthenews.com

500 ReTruths **1.47k** Likes   Dec 22, 2022, 12:56 PM

Appendix A: Referenced Media

Footnote 359: Kash Patel (@Kash), Truth Social (Jan. 26, 2023, 5:26 PM),
https://truthsocial.com/@Kash/posts/109757857821434055.

Kash Patel ✓
@Kash · Jan 26

We can and will destroy the Deep State and #GovernmentGangsters

dailycaller.com/2023/01/25/kas...

KASH PATEL: Hunter Biden's Access To Classified Docs Should Concern Everyone. Here's How We Get To The Bottom Of It

KASH PATEL: Hunter Biden's Access To Classified Docs Should Concern Everyone. Here's How We Get To The Bottom Of It

🔗 dailycaller.com

760 ReTruths   **2.15k** Likes   Jan 26, 2023, 5:26 PM

Appendix A: Referenced Media

Footnote 361: Donald J. Trump (@realDonaldTrump), TRUTH SOCIAL (Feb. 7, 2023, 6:47 PM), https://truthsocial.com/@realDonaldTrump/posts/109823292143955862.

Kash Patel ReTruthed

Donald J. Trump ✓
@realDonaldTrump · Feb 7

Republicans in Congress must investigate the abusive Weaponization of the FBI and Department of Injustice against the Democrats number one political opponent, ME (leading BIG in every Poll!), which has been going on for a long time, and is absolutely outrageous. Don't be afraid of the Marxists and Thugs. We must MAKE AMERICA GREAT AGAIN!!!

Footnote 362: Kash Patel (@Kash), TRUTH SOCIAL (Feb. 10, 2023, 12:32 PM), https://truthsocial.com/@Kash/posts/109841636912748890.

Kash Patel ✓
@Kash · Feb 10

Rockets fired by Weaponization Committee... now make sure they hit the damn targets. Turn ON the subpoena machine NOW

663 ReTruths **2.18k** Likes   Feb 10, 2023, 12:32 PM

Appendix A: Referenced Media

Footnote 364: Kash Patel (@Kash), TRUTH SOCIAL (Feb. 13, 2023, 9:00 AM), https://truthsocial.com/@Kash/posts/109857788097626810.

Kash Patel ✓
@Kash · Feb 13

The FBI is not a joke, its a political machine, an offshoot of the DNC

justthenews.com/accountability...

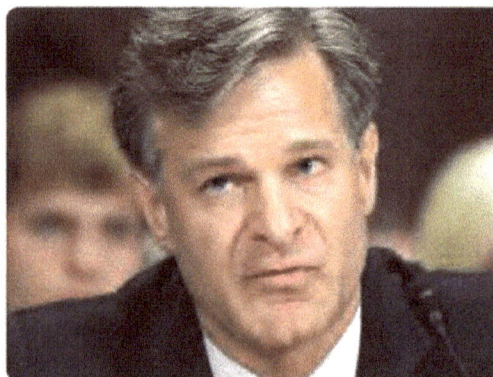

FBI keeps getting burned badly by reliance on liberal sources

Latest blunder involving Catholics has many questioning why the bureau keeps falling prey to political influence from the left.

🔗 justthenews.com

1.19k ReTruths   **2.66k** Likes   Feb 13, 2023, 9:00 AM

Appendix A: Referenced Media

Footnote 368: Kash Patel (@Kash), Truth Social (Jan. 30, 2023, 2:00 PM), https://truthsocial.com/@Kash/posts/109779696419329570.

Kash Patel ✓
@Kash · Jan 30

Fight With Kash 2022 roll up- what a year, we put the Mission first and gave away nearly $100K in financial assistance: everything from whistle blowers, active duty service members, J6 families, legal funds to bring defamation cases for those maligned by fake news mafia, and lots of holiday meals for families in need. Plus the monster free info vaults on website. Thank you @truthsocial and our entire #FWK warrior nation. We just warming up, lets go YUGE in 2023

fightwithkash.com

Welcome

...

⊘ www.fightwithkash.com

668 ReTruths   **2.27k** Likes   Jan 30, 2023, 2:00 PM

Footnote 375: Kash Patel (@Kash), Truth Social (Feb. 12, 2023, 9:20 PM), https://truthsocial.com/@Kash/posts/109855035950406671.

Kash Patel ✓
@Kash · Feb 12

Thats why hes Americas lawyer 🇺🇸

Jesse Binnall ✓
@jbinnall · Feb 12

Don't forget, this is Arizona: they haven't counted the early touchdowns yet.

559 ReTruths   **3.34k** Likes   Feb 12, 2023, 9:20 PM

Appendix A: Referenced Media

Footnote 379: Steve Friend (@Real_SteveFriend), TRUTH SOCIAL (Dec. 16, 2022, 11:06 PM), https://truthsocial.com/@Real_SteveFriend/posts/109527040842556949.

Appendix A: Referenced Media

Footnote 380: Kyle Seraphin (@kyleseraphin), TRUTH SOCIAL (Jan. 24, 2023, 2:44 PM), https://truthsocial.com/@kyleseraphin/posts/109745897007691544

Kyle Seraphin ✓
@kyleseraphin · Jan 24

I need @JimJordan and the GOP House Judiciary committee to do better. They just asked my "indefinitely suspended" friend to "pay his own way to DC" for a transcribed deposition. Because "it isn't an open hearing." Are you guys fricken SERIOUS? Pay out of YOUR pockets. Un-Fricken-believable. You want people to believe you are serious, you better start acting serious. Cause that is beyond stupid and shameful behavior. Fix it.

769 ReTruths **2.05k** Likes   Jan 24, 2023, 2:44 PM

Footnote 384 and 385: Kash Patel (@Kash), TRUTH SOCIAL (Jan. 9, 2023, 2:25 PM), https://truthsocial.com/@Kash/posts/109660885067083134.

Kash Patel ✓
@Kash · Jan 9

Couldnt agree more... maybe ill jump into the fight too

Steve Friend ✓
@Real_SteveFriend · Jan 9

The fact that Chis Wray is going to @FoxNews is more telling than his 8th grade level English paper. I think the FBI 7th floor is nervous @JimJordan, @repandybiggsaz, @ThomasMassie, @RepMattGaetz are about to expose some snakes in the grass...
www-foxnews-com.cdn.ampproject...

America's crime problem is real. Tackling it requires respect for cops | Fox News

🔗 www-foxnews-com.cdn.ampproject.org

843 ReTruths **2.18k** Likes   Jan 09, 2023, 2:25 PM

Appendix A: Referenced Media

Footnote 385: Kash Patel (@Kash), TRUTH SOCIAL (Jan. 31, 2023, 11:40 AM), https://truthsocial.com/@Kash/posts/109784808049917808.

Kash Patel ✔
@Kash · Jan 31

A must buy, Steve unleashes the truth n exposes FBI corruption. Order now

Steve Friend ✔
@Real_SteveFriend · Jan 31

I'm going on offense. Time to explain what's actually going on with the FBI and why I chose to expose the truth.
amazon.com/True-Blue-Journey-S...

342 ReTruths **979** Likes   Jan 31, 2023, 11:40 AM

Footnote 386: Kash Patel (@Kash), TRUTH SOCIAL (Feb. 17, 2023, 12:47 PM), https://truthsocial.com/@Kash/posts/109881332035008839.

Kash Patel ✔
@Kash · Feb 17

Men like this is how we fix our FBI, thanks @Real_SteveFriend

justthenews.com/accountability...

FBI whistleblower resigns from bureau, warns Congress about dangers of case 'quota system'

Bureau is "setting metrics for itself, setting a quota and pressuring its workforce to meet that quota," Agent Steve Friend told Just the News.

🔗 justthenews.com

783 ReTruths **1.76k** Likes   Feb 17, 2023, 12:47 PM

Appendix A: Referenced Media

Footnote 15 and 387: Steve Friend (@Real_SteveFriend), TRUTH SOCIAL (Feb. 26, 2023, 4:22 PM), https://truthsocial.com/@Real_SteveFriend/posts/109933135255526894.

Steve Friend
@Real_SteveFriend · 2d

Here are some suggested questions for @FoxNews to ask FBI Director Chris Wray during his interview on Tuesday. Tough but fair questions from The Suspendables

and sexual abuse to state authorities even if those authorities already have identical reports from local police was made required training on FBI Virtual Academy. Was this duplicative and wasteful mandate simply a "cover your ass" token reform as all FBI Agents are made aware they are "mandated reporters" of any allegations of child abuse?

35. Is Ray Epps a confidential human source? Has he ever been a CHS? Was he a CHS on January 6, 2021? If not for the FBI was he reporting to another agency that requested the FBI to leave him alone?

36. Did the FBI have CHS and/or undercover agents stationed inside the Capitol on January 6 before the protestors entered the building? Were they dressed as Trump voters? Was this a danger to them when Washington Field SWAT Agents entered the building to help establish order?

37. Why has the Washington Field Office SWAT team shot more of themselves in preventable weapons "accidents" than violent subjects? Should a team that has a history of negligent discharges to include wounding Agents on their own team be trusted with the types of "high risk warrants" they serve in the National Capitol Region?

38. Why didn't the FBI open a civil rights violation investigation concerning the killing of Ashley Babbitt?

39. How many agents were sent to investigate the garage door pull rope in Talladega? Was that a full investigation? Is it closed? What was the closing code?

40. Why didn't the FBI investigate and arrest individuals protesting in front of Supreme Court justices homes in an attempt to intimidate them and influence their decisions? Who made this decision?

695 ReTruths 1.68k Likes   Feb 26, 2023, 4:22 PM

THE SUSPENDABLES

December 2, 2022

The Honorable Christopher A. Wray
Director, Director's Office
935 Pennsylvania Avenue, NW
Washington, DC, 20535

Director Wray,

In light of "all hands" meeting scheduled for December 7, 2022, the Suspendables would respectfully request (but we obviously don't expect) answers to the following questions. Due to administrators acting on your authority, the FBI has failed to provide the protections guaranteed to FBI whistleblowers under 5 USC 2303. Despite statements to the contrary, the FBI has systematically engaged in targeted harassment and prohibited employment actions to include the suspension of our clearances as the Office of General Counsel continues to argue the FBI is immune from judicial review of these decisions under *Navy v Egan (1989)*. This should cause you great shame for representing false statements in front of the People's representatives AND the American people via statements made on your behalf. Please consider the following questions:

1. Will you promise to immediately resign if any of the whistleblower allegations outlined in the 11/4/2022 House Judiciary Committee letter are proven to be true?
2. Will you terminate the employment of SES employees who have leveraged adverse personnel actions as retaliation for disfavored political speech, vaccination status and/or whistleblowing to Congress?
3. Why are you leaking medical records of whistleblowers to the New York Times? Has there been an investigation to learn the identity of the leaker? What was the outcome? Have they been referred for prosecution?
4. Why are unvaccinated conservative/Christian men being targeted with sudden adverse personnel actions while "Kneel Team six" participants are being promoted?
5. Is their any truth to the belief that your Deputy Director, Paul Abbate, has engaged in sexual relationships with an employee who is being paid for a no-show position?
6. Since the Director's plane and detail members will wait for you indefinitely, why did you lie to Congress on August 4th that you "had a plane to catch" and doubling down on that lie on November 17th?
7. Will you cease the mandatory trip to the Holocaust Museum since, based on protected disclosures and whistleblower retaliation occurring as we speak, it is clear that the point of the trip has been lost?

8. Will you commit to educating executive management personnel that J6 protestors did not kill any police officers?
9. Where can one find the written documentation justifying your departure from DIOG rules regarding case indexing and management of J6?
10. Can you please rank the priority order: Oath of Office, loyalty to FBI, loyalty to political party in power?
11. Why did you make the unprecedented decision to name a successor to WFO ADIC D'Antuano (the executive who oversaw the J6 and Whitmer entrapment cases) prior to his 11/30/2022 retirement?
12. Why is EM sending emails about the importance of whistleblower training when the FBI clearly attacks and retaliates against whistleblowers?
13. Why is diversity and inclusion training being forced on employees when the FBI should clearly be talking about ethics and morality?
14. Why is the SAC in Jackson still employed when he has, on record, made racist statements about white people, including discussing his discriminatory hiring and promotion plans?
15. Is it accurate that the agent who originally interviewed Tony Bobulinski has risen to Unit Chief in less than two years? If so, why?
16. Why aren't we investigating everyone from Epstein's island?
17. What's the status update on the J6 DNC/RNC pipe bomb investigation? Why did the FBI release manipulated surveillance footage to the public? Will you release the full video so the public can view and assist in the investigation?
18. How many VCAC investigations have been closed or were declined to be further investigated as a result of resources being directed to Jan 6?
19. Provide specific details on how unvaccinated employees can confirm that coerced medical information (i.e. our mandated testing results) are being removed from the myMedLink system in compliance with the Privacy Act.
20. Please provide an exact figure or close estimation of the taxpayer funding costs associated with vetting, hiring and training those FBI employees that have been unjustly fired or put on administrative leave as a result of COVID vaccine mandates.
21. When exactly will the FBI be resuming processing of religious and medical exemptions to the COVID vaccine mandate currently "paused"?
22. Why have all-employee management surveys conducted annually (until the illegal COVID vaccine mandates began) been suspended?
23. How many administrative investigations have you opened in retaliation against FBI whistleblowers?
24. Did any FBI Agents overhear what was discussed between Bill Clinton and Loretta Lynch on the tarmac that day?
25. Why did Miami SAC George Piro retire only weeks before the FBI raid on Mar-A-Lago, and why was he demoted beforehand? Is there any truth to the rumor that he was the senior official caught by DOJ OIG outlined in Investigative Summary 22-107 in a Bucar accident with a subordinate who was performing a sexual act on him? ("The OIG investigation substantiated the allegation that the SAC engaged in sexual contact with a subordinate in an official government vehicle and had communications that were sexual in nature with that subordinate and two other subordinate staff members, in violation of FBI policy.")
26. Why was mandatory LGBTQ+ virtual training scrapped? As a show of transparency, will you make the slideshow available to Congress (which may not be necessary since we have)?
27. Is the FBI working with Facebook to spy on the private messages of FBI whistleblowers and their spouses?

28. Did the FBI pressure the employer of a whistleblower's spouse to fire said spouse?
29. Is Security Division planning or in the process of reviewing employees' FBI phone search history with the intention of pursuing Hatch Act violations if employees read news articles from certain sources during work hours?
30. When can we expect your written responses to Congressman Jordan and Senators Johnson and Grassley?
31. Will you commit to reinstating personnel who were suspended after making legally protected whistleblower disclosures as described in 5 USC 2303?
32. Have you offered mental health counseling to Jacksonville Special Agent in Charge Sherry Onks for the anxiety she reported feeling while working at the Hoover building on January 6, 2021?
33. Will you explain to the American public why FBI Washington Field Executive managers were "gleefully" telling each other that the events on January 6, 2021 were "our 9/11" and what they meant by that?
34. Following the failed Larry Nassar case, the decision to require Special Agents to report physical and sexual abuse to state authorities even if those authorities already have identical reports from local police was made required training on FBI Virtual Academy. Was this duplicative and wasteful mandate simply a "cover your ass" token reform as all FBI Agents are made aware they are "mandated reporters" of any allegations of child abuse?
35. Is Ray Epps a confidential human source? Has he ever been a CHS? Was he a CHS on January 6, 2021? If not for the FBI, was he reporting to another agency that requested the FBI to leave him alone?
36. Did the FBI have CHS and/or undercover agents stationed inside the Capitol on January 6 before the protestors entered the building? Were they dressed as Trump voters? Was this a danger to them when Washington Field SWAT Agents entered the building to help establish order?
37. Why has the Washington Field Office SWAT team shot more of themselves in preventable weapons "accidents" than violent subjects? Should a team that has a history of negligent discharges to include wounding Agents on their own team be trusted with the types of "high risk warrants" they serve in the National Capitol Region?
38. Why didn't the FBI open a civil rights violation investigation concerning the killing of Ashley Babbitt?
39. How many agents were sent to investigate the garage door pull rope in Talladega? Was that a full investigation? Is it closed? What was the closing code?
40. Why didn't the FBI investigate and arrest individuals protesting in front of Supreme Court justices homes in an attempt to intimidate them and influence their decisions? Who made the decision?
41. How many Indian Country CHS were tapped with requests for collection related to threats to the Dakota Access Pipeline? Were these CHS asked questions simply because they were Native Americans and regardless of the fact that they were living in different areas of the country and members of different tribes?
42. Why was a domestic terrorism agent the affiant on the arrest complaint for David DePape? Is that investigation a national security case?
43. Why did the FBI change fitness test requirements for new agents so individuals can begin training without having passed the fitness test? Who made that decision?
44. Why is the FBI only investigating FACE Act violations pertaining to abortion clinics? What about impediments to accessing houses of worship?
45. Why have so many whistleblowers spoken out in recent months? Is this an indication that the rank and file agents are unhappy with your leadership?

The Office of General Counsel has our attorneys' information should you chose to respond.

Footnote 23 and 256: From when he joined Twitter on November 16, 2022, through February 14, 2023, Friend posted over 20 times calling for the FBI to be defunded, dismantled, dissolved, aborted, abolished, or otherwise ended.

Steve Friend
@RealStevefriend

· · ·

Propose an amendment to add @FBI

Thomas Massie @RepThomasMassie · Feb 14
I have introduced a bill to terminate the Department of Education.

There is no Constitutional authority for this federal bureaucracy to exist.

H.R.899 - To terminate the Department of Education.

118th Congress (2023-2024) | Get alerts

BILL	Hide Overview ✖
Sponsor:	Rep. Massie, Thomas [R-KY-4] (Introduced 02/09/2023)
Committees:	House - Education and the Workforce
Latest Action:	House - 02/09/2023 Referred to the House Committee on Education and the Workforce. (All Actions)
Tracker: ❶	Introduced / Passed House / Passed Senate / To President / Became Law

7:42 PM · Feb 14, 2023 · **3,033** Views

Appendix A: Referenced Media

Steve Friend
@RealStevefriend

···

The @FBI is targeting Catholics. And relying on left-wing news sources to substantiate their ridiculous, politicized "assessments." Abolish the FBI @KyleSeraphin @Tyler2ONeil @DailySignal

Law Center

IN 2021, WE TRACKED 733 HATE GROUPS ACROSS THE U.S.

dailysignal.com
FBI Document Cites SPLC on 'Radical-Traditional Catholics'
FBI Richmond cited the Southern Poverty Law Center numerous times on what the SPLC calls "radical traditional Catholic hate groups."

7:26 PM · Feb 8, 2023 · **2,946** Views

Appendix A: Referenced Media

Steve Friend
@RealStevefriend

···

My buddy @KyleSeraphin likes to call the @FBI "law enforcement cosplay." He is correct. Whether it's this empty motto or the SELF DESCRIBED "premier law enforcement agency" moniker, the FBI's sloganeering can't hide its fecklessness and politicization. Abolish the FBI

FBI ✓ @FBI · Feb 5

F B I: These initials stand for the Federal Bureau of Investigation, but they also stand for "Fidelity - Bravery - Integrity," ideals the Bureau, its special agents, its professional staff, and its partners strive to represent every day. fbi.gov/history/seal-m...

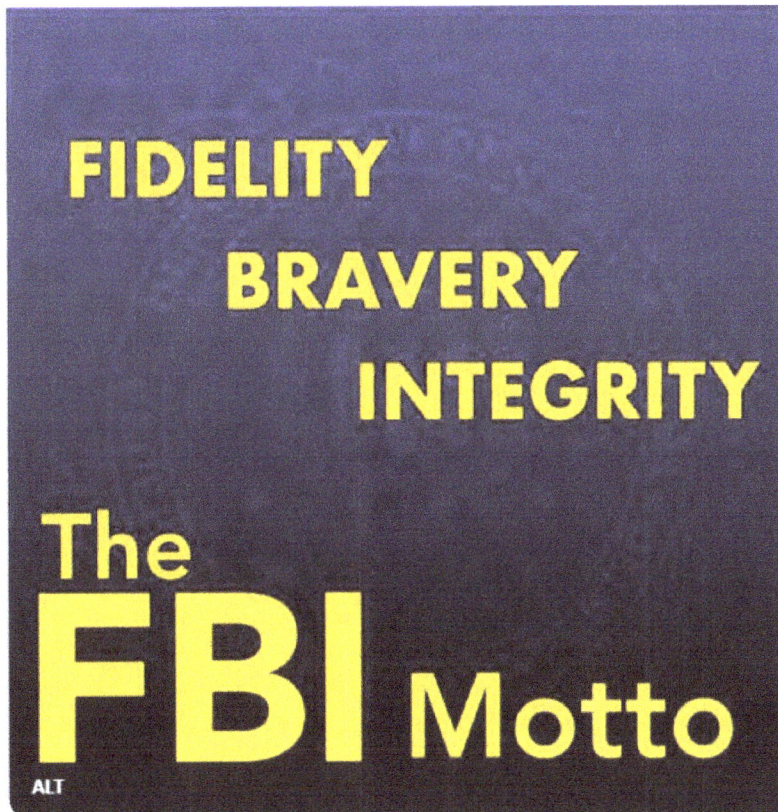

FIDELITY
BRAVERY
INTEGRITY
The FBI Motto
ALT

6:34 AM · Feb 6, 2023 · **6,602** Views

Steve Friend
@RealStevefriend

· · ·

Idea for you @SebGorka. Can we just abolish the @FBI and sell plain navy blue t-shirts instead?

Sebastian Gorka DrG ✔ @SebGorka · Feb 4
The new FBI twitter.com/SebGorka/statu...

6:02 PM · Feb 4, 2023 · **2,131** Views

Steve Friend
@RealStevefriend

· · ·

The @FBI quartered Twitter informants as proxy digital soldiers (3A) in your home to spy on free speech (1A) without a warrant (4A) in violation of due process (6A) in the hope of falsely imprisoning you (8A). Abolish the FBI

Tom Fitton ✔ @TomFitton · Feb 2
The FBI was reading your tweets...to get them censored by @Twitter

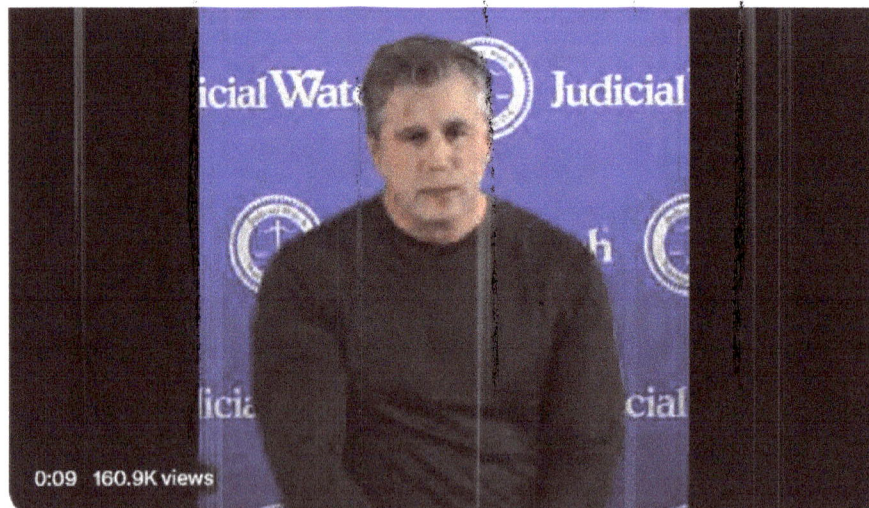

0:09 160.9K views

11:24 PM · Feb 2, 2023 · **2,937** Views

Appendix A: Referenced Media

Steve Friend
@RealStevefriend

...

#QHPFiles installment 39. I am on DAY 113 of suspension for improperly accessing the employee handbook... This FBI employee watched porn on the same computer system and got a letter of censure. Abolish the FBI.
@Jim_Jordan @RepThomasMassie @JudiciaryGOP

Misuse of Government Computer:
Employee used a Bureau computer to watch pornography while working the night shift. In mitigation, Employee has a positive performance history, maintains the support of the Division, and this appears to have been an isolated incident.

OFFENSE: Misuse of Government Computer, Offense Code 3.6

PENALTY: Letter of Censure

9:08 AM · Jan 10, 2023 · **3,448** Views

Appendix A: Referenced Media

Steve Friend
@RealStevefriend

@FBI underreported how frequently armed citizens stop active shooters. This agency is completely politicized and must be abolished.

firearmsnews.com
FBI Underreports Defensive Gun Use to Congress - Firear...
The Crime Prevention Research Center reveals the FBI has underreported how frequently armed citizens stop active ...

11:01 PM · Jan 8, 2023 · **125** Views

Steve Friend
@RealStevefriend

The process IS the punishment @julie_kelly2. Abolish the @FBI.

> **Julie Kelly** 🇺🇸 @julie_kelly2 · Jan 4
> FBI investigating couples who went into Capitol on Jan 6 and DOJ charging them with low level crimes to destroy their lives and family.
>
> This happened right before Christmas

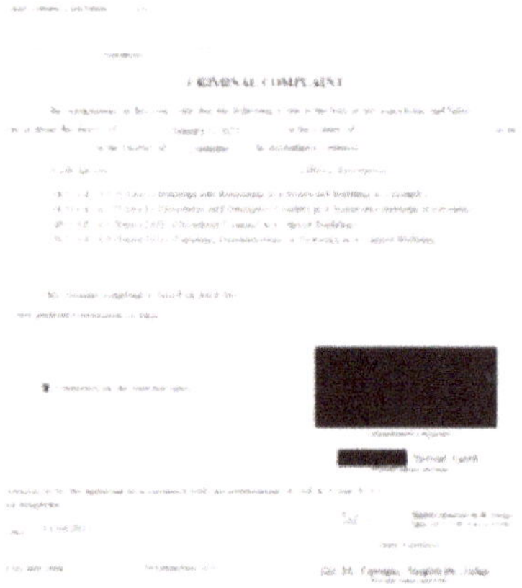

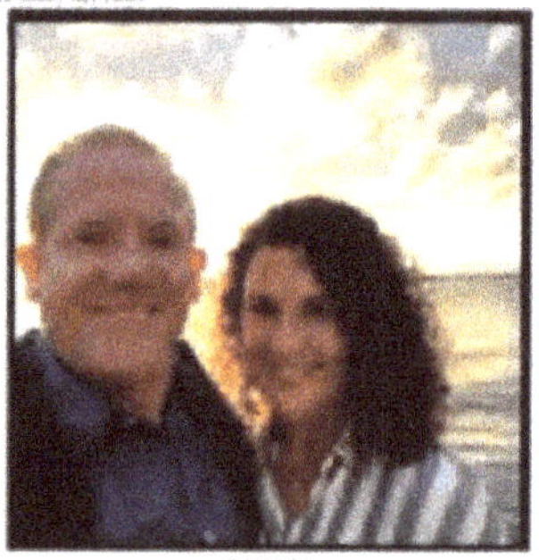

12:51 PM · Jan 4, 2023 · **18.5K** Views

Appendix A: Referenced Media

Steve Friend
@RealStevefriend

...

Flawed @FBI data undercounts anti-semitism. Same folks inflating domestic terrorism with January 6 cases. Abolish the FBI.

dailywire.com
Watchdog Calls For Congressional Investigation Into 'Useless' FBI Stats Showing Decline In Anti-S...

7:38 PM · Jan 3, 2023 · **15.6K** Views

Steve Friend
@RealStevefriend

...

#OPRFiles Installment 30. "Employee was involved in MULTIPLE domestic violence incidents." Defund the @FBI

Misuse of Position; Assault & Battery; Unprofessional Conduct; Failure to Report; Lack of Candor Under Oath: Employee was involved in multiple domestic violence incidents and failed to report his police contact. According to the Personnel Security Self-Reporting Requirements Policy, all FBI employees must report "[a]ny arrest, domestic violence incident report, driving while intoxicated/under the influence (DWI/DUI) offense, and/or other aggravated/unusual offense involving a law enforcement official." Employee located his wife at a hotel where she was staying with their children after she left him. Employee repeatedly attempted to gain access to her hotel room by telling hotel employees that he was in pursuit of a fugitive who was under FBI surveillance. When questioned by investigators during the OPR proceedings, Employee lacked candor when he claimed he only told hotel representatives that he needed to get into his wife's room to pick up clothes for their children.

OFFENSE: Lack of Candor - Under Oath, Offense Code 2.6 Misuse of Position, Offense Code 2.8 Assault/Battery, Offense Code 4.1 Failure to Report, Offense Code 5.8 Unprofessional Conduct - Off Duty, Offense Code 5.21

PENALTY: Dismissal

10:10 AM · Jan 2, 2023 · **13.5K** Views

Appendix A: Referenced Media

Steve Friend
@RealStevefriend

···

#OPRFiles Installment 25. Cyber threats, harassment, assaulting a servant of the court...25 days. I'm on day 100 for saying my duty to the Constitution outweighs loyalty to @FBI managers. This agency deserves nothing short of dissolution.

Unprofessional Conduct; Failure to Report:
Employee sent a threatening and vile email to his girlfriend's ex-husband. Following the threats, the ex-husband obtained a temporary protective order against Employee. A process server attempted to serve a subpoena on Employee. When the process server knocked on Employee's door, Employee threatened to shoot him. Employee failed to report to his supervisor or SecD that a temporary protective order had been issued against him and that he had an upcoming hearing.

OFFENSE: Failure to Report, Offense Code 5.8 Unprofessional Conduct - Off Duty, Offense Code 5.21

PENALTY: 25-day suspension

6:40 AM · Dec 28, 2022 · **2,362** Views

Appendix A: Referenced Media

Steve Friend
@RealStevefriend

@FBI is beyond redemption. 4 consecutive scandalous Directors. Collusion with big tech. Entrapment. Persecution of political conservatives. Zero accountability and the unmitigated gall to call critics conspiracy theorists. Abort the @FBI

amgreatness.com
What Will the FBI Not Do? › American Greatness
The FBI on Wednesday finally broke its silence and responded to the revelations on Twitter of close ties between the bureau and the social media ...

6:52 AM · Dec 26, 2022 · **2,999** Views

⮌ Steve Friend Retweeted

Mises Caucus
@LPMisesCaucus

Replying to @FBI

Merry Christmas! Your agency should be abolished

1:01 PM · Dec 25, 2022 · **10.7K** Views

Appendix A: Referenced Media

Steve Friend
@RealStevefriend

I said no. Most people in my office gave me some signal of approval. Then went out and "just followed orders." None have contacted me since I got walked out. Dismantle the @FBI

> **Kyle Seraphin** @KyleSeraphin · Dec 24, 2022
> The question each of these Agents should answer, and likely can't fathom, is:
>
> what line will you not cross?
>
> What are you prepared to face when you get to that line?
>
> It is unlikely that discussion comes to a concrete answer in the team room. So the line is no line. twitter.com/hodgetwins/sta...

9:04 PM · Dec 24, 2022 · **3,029** Views

House Judiciary GOP @JudiciaryGOP · Dec 25, 2022
Fa la la la la la la fang fang.

💬 519   🔁 213   ♡ 1,391   ⅲ 226.8K   ⬆

Steve Friend
@RealStevefriend

Replying to @JudiciaryGOP

Less trolling. More defunding the @FBI

6:40 PM · Dec 25, 2022 · **2,081** Views

Appendix A: Referenced Media

Steve Friend
@RealStevefriend

···

This must happen. No debate. Abort the @FBI

The Epoch Times ✅ @EpochTimes · Dec 25, 2022
"We've been looking at a Church-style committee to look at this," Rep. @Jim_Jordan said.

House Republicans are signaling a top-to-bottom invesigation of the #FBI in January.

"We need to hold people accountable," said Rep. @NancyMace.
theepochtimes.com/gop-floats-chu...

5:43 PM · Dec 25, 2022 · **2,740** Views

Steve Friend
@RealStevefriend

...

$11.33 billion budget for next year. Don't talk to me about the "good men and women" of the @FBI. @KyleSeraphin is the ONLY other employee willing to speak out publicly? Defund the FBI. Breadlines for everyone. Including GOP senators voting to increase its budget

> **Hodgetwins** ✓ @hodgetwins · Dec 24, 2022
> The feds are still sending in armed combat ready SWAT teams to raid people who peacefully protested OUTSIDE the Capitol on Jan 6
>
> Republican Senators voted to give them more money too
>
> Show this thread

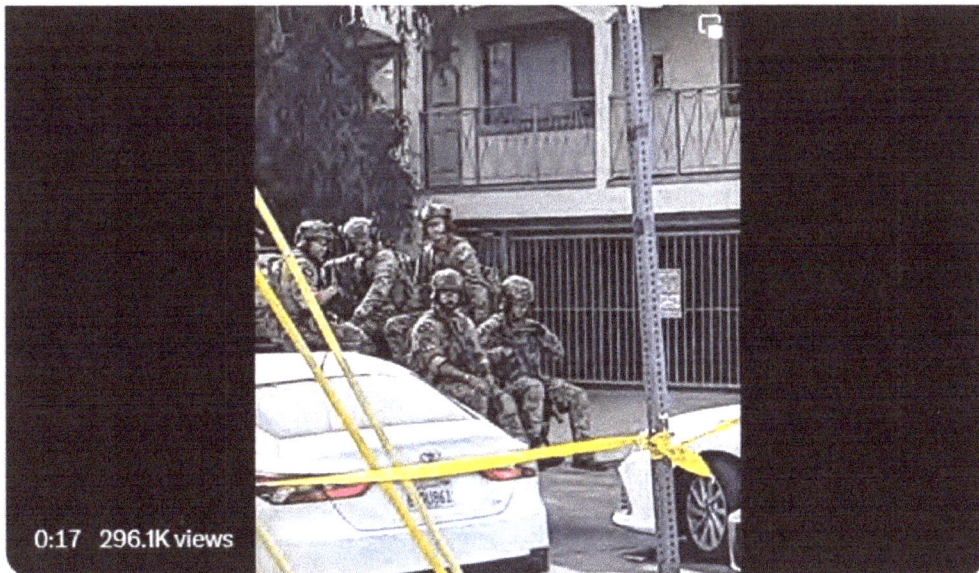

0:17 296.1K views

11:56 PM · Dec 24, 2022 · **12.4K** Views

Jesse Kelly ✔ @JesseKellyDC · Dec 19, 2022 ···

The FBI cannot continue to exist in any form. It will end this nation if it does.

Red states must immediately begin re-ordering themselves to stand between their citizens and the federal government. This is going to a dangerous place. And quickly.

> **Michael Shellenberger** ✔ @ShellenbergerMD · Dec 19, 2022
>
> 1. TWITTER FILES: PART 7
>
> The FBI & the Hunter Biden Laptop
>
> How the FBI & intelligence community discredited factual information about Hunter Biden's foreign business dealings both after and *before* The New York Post revealed the contents of his laptop on October 14, 2020
>
> Show this thread

💬 339   🔁 3,155   ♡ 9,524   � 454.9K   ⬆

Steve Friend   ···
@RealStevefriend

Replying to @JesseKellyDC

Doctrine of Lesser Magistrates. @FBI has 14K agents. to police 400 million people. FBI requires manpower, intel, and casework from local law enforcement partners. Pressure your sheriffs to refuse to cooperate. Starve the FBI out. Turn your county into a FBI Sanctuary City.

6:48 PM · Dec 19, 2022 · **498** Views

Appendix A: Referenced Media

Steve Friend @RealStevefriend · Dec 14, 2022

I told my supervisors my duty was to protect the Constitution. They responded that my duty was to the @FBI

> **Dinesh D'Souza** ✔ @DineshDSouza · Dec 14, 2022
>
> I'm not saying the ordinary FBI agent is corrupt. The agents are just "following orders" the way Germans did in the 1930s. This is how corruption and gangsterism trickles down through the agencies of the state. The bad people make the good people carry out their nefarious schemes

💬 58   🔁 281   ♡ 1,084   📊   ⬆️

Neolithe @denonklipsch · Dec 18, 2022

Replying to @RealStevefriend and @FBI

And that's when you say, "No, my duty is to my oath I swore.

💬 1   🔁   ♡ 2   📊 52   ⬆️

Steve Friend
@RealStevefriend

Replying to @denonklipsch and @FBI

I did. I've been indefinitely suspended for 90 days and counting. Dismantle the @FBI. The oath is nothing more than clicking "Agree" on the latest iOS terms of service.

sharylattkisson.com
'The Oath of Office is Not an iPhone User Agreement' by FBI Special Agent and Whistleblower Stephen...

1:47 PM · Dec 18, 2022 · **80** Views

Steve Friend
@RealStevefriend

#OPRFiles, Installment 13. I'm on day 89 of suspension. @KyleSeraphin is over 200. This guy is a supervisor who tunes up his child and gets a 40 day hiatus. I don't doubt he was promoted when the smoke cleared. DISMANTLE the @FBI

Assault and Battery: Supervisory Employee hit his minor child. The child's school noticed bruises and contacted Child Protective Services. In mitigation, Employee has 15 years of FBI service, no prior disciplinary matters, and has taken parenting classes. In aggravation, the victim was a minor and the child appeared to have been coached to minimize what happened.

OFFENSE: Assault/Battery, Offense Code 4.1

PENALTY: 40-day suspension

3:54 PM · Dec 17, 2022 · **72.3K** Views

Steve Friend
@RealStevefriend

Office of Special Counsel told me the @FBI has discretion to stray from its rules and procedures. It is too late for reform. The fix is in. Dissolve it all.

> **Richard Grenell** ✓ @RichardGrenell · Dec 16, 2022
> Agree. There must be a congressional investigation immediately.
> twitter.com/Stemic09/statu...

10:40 PM · Dec 16, 2022 · **32K** Views

Steve Friend
@RealStevefriend

Can think of about 36k people at @FBI the @HouseGOP can lay off

> **Kyle Seraphin** ✓ @KyleSeraphin · Dec 13, 2022
> Weird flex. Who votes to fund the government? Oh... That's right. So get to work. This has been true my whole life and all of Jordan's political career.
> twitter.com/Jim_Jordan/sta...

12:55 PM · Dec 13, 2022

Steve Friend
@RealStevefriend

...

I had glimpses into January 6 and the Wolverine Watchmen cases. This was true across the board. Defund and dismantle the @FBI

Kyle Seraphin @KyleSeraphin · Nov 27, 2022
Read it all. This is how FBI Domestic AND International Counterterrorism cases are done. Period.
Show this thread

line ideology and radical speech, but he was never in any place to be a terrorist." Childs wrote. "If I had not been encouraged to 'turn him in' or threatened to keep him on course, he would not be in prison now and no attack would have ever been perpetrated by him. He's in prison because I was too coward to tell and had become frustrated that they couldn't move the case forward. I was able to confirm independently that the FBI had even sent another informant to meet Abdul-Latif, but nothing came of the encounters. "They made a comment to me that they had been watching him for a while." Childs recalled. "and now

was coming forward now, as he embarked on a life sentence, because he no longer feared the FBI. "I have tried to relay this information before," Childs wrote in his letter, "but was always cut off and threatened with losing my freedom as well."

"I took that as an order to wipe my phone before it was collected," Childs said. "In order to protect everyone, I claimed that I had a bunch of porn on it that could have gotten me in trouble."

In court filings, the Justice Department acknowledged that DeJesus deleted his

6:18 PM · Nov 27, 2022

Steve Friend
@RealStevefriend

⋯

Defund the @FBI. I'll pay to fly Director Wray anywhere he want, one-way trip. You want to go halves @KyleSeraphin?

Josh Hawley ✓ @HawleyMO · Nov 18, 2022
Watch it here
Show this thread

2:37 PM · Nov 18, 2022

Steve Friend
@RealStevefriend

⋯

Defund the @FBI. Breadline for everyone in leadership

The Epoch Times ✓ @EpochTimes · Nov 17, 2022
"You left a statutorily required oversight hearing in order to go on a personal vacation?" @HawleyMO asked.

#FBI Director Chris Wray defended leaving a congressional hearing abruptly to go on vacation after telling a senator he was attending to business.
theepochtimes.com/fbi-director-w...

9:16 PM · Nov 17, 2022

Appendix A: Referenced Media

Steve Friend
@RealStevefriend

⋯

Defund the @FBI

11:00 AM · Nov 16, 2022

1. Letter from Jim Jordan, Ranking Member, H. Comm. on the Judiciary, to Christopher A. Wray, Director, Fed. Bureau of Investigation (Sep. 14, 2022).

2. Decl. of Stephen M. Friend (Sep. 21, 2022).

3. Letter from Jason Foster, Founder & President, Empower Oversight, to the Office of Inspector General, Dep't of Justice (Jan. 31, 2023).

4. *U.S. v. Cole et al.*, Case no. 1:22-mj-184-RMM, Doc. No. 5-1 (Statement of Facts) (Aug. 29, 2022).

5. *Prepublication Review Policy Guide*, FED. BUREAU OF INVESTIGATION § 3 (Jan. 8, 2020).

6. FARA Exhibit B Filing, Federal State Unitary Enterprise Rossiya Segodnya International Information Agency, Reg. No. 6869 (Aug. 2, 2022).

7. Catrina Doxsee, Seth G. Jones, Jared Thompson, Kateryna Halstead & Grace Hwang, *Pushed to Extremes: Domestic Terrorism amid Polarization and Protest*, CTR. FOR STRATEGIC & INT'L STUDIES (May 17, 2022).

8. Seth G. Jones, Catrina Doxsee, Grace Hwang & Jared Thompson, *The Military, Police, and the Rise of Terrorism in the United States*, CTR. FOR STRATEGIC & INT'L STUDIES (Apr. 12, 2021).

9. Merrick Garland, *Partnership Among Federal, State, Local, Tribal, and Territorial Law Enforcement to Address Threats Against School Administrators, Board Members, Teachers, and Staff*, OFF. OF THE ATT'Y GEN. (Oct. 4, 2021).

10. Letter from Jim Jordan, Ranking Member, H. Comm. on the Judiciary, and Mike Johnson, Ranking Member, Subcomm. on the Const., C.R. and C.L., et al to Attorney General Merrick B. Garland, Att'y Gen. (May 11, 2022).

11. Gabriella Borter, Joseph Ax & Joseph Tanfani, *School boards get death threats amid rage over race, gender, mask policies*, REUTERS (Feb. 15, 2022).

12. Letter from Jim Jordan, Ranking Member, H. Comm. on the Judiciary, and Mike Johnson, Ranking Member, Subcomm. on the Const., C.R. and C.L., (Aug. 10, 2022).

13. Letter from Stephen A. Martin, Director, Exempt Organizations, Rulings and Agreements, Internal Revenue Service to Kash Foundation Inc (Jul. 26, 2022).

14. Letter from Donald J. Trump, former President of the United States, to Debra Steidel Wall, Acting Archivist of the United States, U.S. National Archives and Records Administration (Jun. 19, 2022).

15. Center for Renewing America, Inc., *Return of Organization Exempt From Income Tax* [Form 990], INTERNAL REVENUE SERV. at 1 (2021).

16. Conservative Partnership Institute, *Return of Organization Exempt From Income Tax* [Form 990], INTERNAL REVENUE SERV. at 1, 30-32 (2021).

ONE HUNDRED SEVENTEENTH CONGRESS

Congress of the United States
House of Representatives

COMMITTEE ON THE JUDICIARY

2138 RAYBURN HOUSE OFFICE BUILDING

WASHINGTON, DC 20515-6216

(202) 225-3951
judiciary.house.gov

September 14, 2022

The Honorable Christopher A. Wray
Director
Federal Bureau of Investigation
935 Pennsylvania Avenue, N.W.
Washington, DC 20535

Dear Director Wray:

On July 27, 2022, we wrote to you about whistleblower disclosures that FBI officials were pressuring agents to reclassify cases as "domestic violent extremism" (DVEs) even if the cases do not meet the criteria for such a classification.[1] You have failed to acknowledge our letter or even begin to respond substantively. Since our letter, new publicly available information and additional protected whistleblower disclosures suggest the FBI's actions are far more pervasive than previously known.

On August 2, 2022, a media organization obtained a copy, which new whistleblower disclosures have authenticated, of the FBI's "Domestic Terrorism Symbols Guide" on "Militia Violent Extremists" (MVEs).[2] The FBI's document included symbols like "2A" and states that "MVEs justify their existence with the Second Amendment, due to the mention of a 'well regulated Militia,' as well as the right to bear arms."[3] The document also includes "commonly referenced historical imagery or quotes," like the "Betsy Ross Flag" and the "Gadsden Flag," as symbols of so-called terrorists.[4] Additionally, the FBI document includes a section labeled "symbols of militia networks some MVEs may self-identify with," and describes one group, called American Contingency, as "[m]ainstream media, nationwide, mostly online activity, low history of violence."[5] American Contingency is a company founded by former U.S. servicemember Mike Glover, who has publicly rejected the FBI's accusations that he is a

---

[1] Letter from Jim Jordan, Ranking Member, H. Comm. on the Judiciary, to Christopher A. Wray, Dir., Fed. Bureau of Investigation (July 27, 2022).

[2] Press Release, *FBI Whistleblower LEAKS Bureau's 'Domestic Terrorism Symbols Guide' on 'Militia Violent Extremists' Citing Ashli Babbitt as MVE Martyr*, PROJECT VERITAS (Aug. 2, 2022). The FBI document states "[t]he use or sharing of these symbols should not independently be considered evidence of MVE presence or affiliation or serve as an indicator of illegal activity, as many individuals use these symbols for their original, historic meaning, or other non-violent purposes." *Id.*

[3] *Id.*

[4] *Id.*

[5] *Id.*

terrorist and has described American Contingency's charitable work on behalf of communities devastated by natural disasters.[6]

The FBI's recent characterization of American Contingency as a DVE organization is striking in light of new whistleblower disclosures that show that the FBI had concluded as recently as 2020 that the group was not a threat. According to whistleblower information, in July 2020, an FBI employee in northern Virginia flagged American Contingency as a "domestic terrorist group" because Glover "appears to be rallying individuals to 'take action'" and "speaks about his distaste for how the government is handling the current situations in the US and encourages people to 'join' his cause." Notes made in the FBI's e-Guardian incident reporting system, reflected below, show how the FBI rifled through Glover's life—obtaining his military records, his veteran's disability rating, and even his monthly disability benefit—before concluding that American Contingency "desires to assist Americans in preparing themselves for catastrophic events and not to overthrow the United States Government. A background investigation and review of Glover's social media failed to support the allegation that Glover is a threat to the United States or its citizens."

Authorized Method:	Administrative note for informational purposes.
Description:	Glover is a decorated Veteran of the United States. His videos posted on Youtube.com and his military record attest to his patriotism for the United States. Glover desires to assist Americans in preparing themselves for catastrophic events and not to overthrow the United States Government. A background investigation and review of Glover's social media failed to support the allegation that Glover is a threat to the United States or its citizens. Therefore, it is requested captioned lead be closed for information only.
Status:	Completed
History:	08/26/2020 12:09:42 PM Created Note: Request lead be closed for information only

This whistleblower information suggests that the FBI opened an investigation into an American citizen—and deemed him a potential "threat"—simply because he exercised his First Amendment right to speak out in protest of the government. As the whistleblower commented:

> It doesn't take a First Amendment scholar to realize what is protected speech and what isn't . . . . It seems clear that this is an instance where an FBI employee reported something because it didn't align with their own woke ideology. . . . I think this is a primary example of how woke and corrupt the FBI has become.

Even after the FBI determined in 2020 that American Contingency was not a threat, the FBI still labeled the group as a violent extremist group in an official FBI alert. This disclosure comports with other whistleblowers who have described how the FBI is pressuring its employees to

---

[6] American Contingency, https://www.americancontingency.com/ (last accessed Aug. 18, 2022). The FieldCraft Survival Channel, I am NOT a terrorist, YouTube (Aug. 4, 2022), https://www.youtube.com/watch?v=p4JBDcN7YFo. *See also* American Contingency, How We Got Here, https://www.americancontingency.com/how-we-got-here/ (last visited Aug. 18, 2022).

recharacterize cases as DVE cases to artificially pad its data and advance a misleading political narrative.

This whistleblower information further reinforces our concerns—about which we have written to you several times—about the FBI's politicization. One whistleblower described the level of politicization within the FBI's leadership as "rotted at its core." As we have detailed, multiple whistleblowers have disclosed how the Biden FBI is conducting a "purge" of FBI employees holding conservative views. You have ignored these concerns and instead suggested the FBI is above any criticism or accountability.[7] The front-line men and women of the FBI—many of whom have come forward as whistleblowers—deserve our respect and gratitude. But the FBI leadership in Washington is in desperate need of accountability and reform.

To inform our ongoing oversight of the FBI, please provide the following documents and information:

1. All documents and communications referring or relating to the FBI's Domestic Terrorism Symbols Guide on Militia Violent Extremism, for the period of January 1, 2020, to the present; and

2. A full and complete explanation as to why the FBI's Domestic Terrorism Strategic Unit did not include symbols, images, phrases, events, and individuals about left-wing violent extremists' group in the FBI's Domestic Terrorism Symbols Guide.

Please provide this information as soon as possible, but no later than 5:00 p.m. on September 28, 2022. In addition, our earlier requests made in the July 27 letter remain outstanding, and we once more reiterate these requests. We remind you that whistleblower disclosures to Congress are protected by law and that we will not tolerate any effort to retaliate against whistleblowers for their disclosures.

Sincerely,

Jim Jordan
Ranking Member

cc: The Honorable Jerrold L. Nadler, Chairman

---

[7] Email from the Hon. Christopher A Wray, Dir., Fed. Bureau of Investigation (Aug. 11, 2022 2:26 PM). ("There has been a lot of commentary about the FBI this week questioning our work and motives. Much of it is from critics and pundits on the outside who don't know what we know and don't see what we see.").

Declaration of Stephen M. Friend

I, Stephen M. Friend, pursuant to 28 U.S.C. §1746, hereby declares as follows:

1. I am a person over eighteen (18) years of age and competent to testify. Upon my belief and information, I make this Declaration on personal knowledge and in support of my complaint of reprisal and disclosure to the Office of Special Counsel, and against the Federal Bureau of Investigation (hereinafter the "FBI").

2. I am an FBI Special Agent currently on suspension. I graduated from the University of Notre Dame in 2007 and was employed as an accountant in private practice between 2007 and 2008. In 2009 I was sworn in as a Peace Officer for the Savannah Chatham Metro Police Department in Savannah Chatham Georgia. I served as a Peace Officer for said Department until 2012 when I joined my father's accounting firm for one year. In 2013 I joined the Pooler Police Department in Pooler Georgia as a Peace Officer until 2014.

3. On June 14, 2014, I joined the FBI as a new agent trainee. Following my graduation from Quantico's New Agent Academy I was posted to the FBI's Omaha Division/Sioux City Resident Agency tasked with investigating violent crimes and major offenses occurring in Indian Country. I was also a member of the FBI's Omaha SWAT Team. While in that posting I also served as an acting Special Supervisory Special Agent.

4. In June of 2021 I was transferred to the FBI's Jacksonville Florida Field Office/Daytona Beach Residency Agency as a Special Agent tasked with investigating child exploitation and human trafficking. In October of 2021, an Assistant Special Agent in Charge (ASAC) informed my supervisor that I was reassigned as a member of the Joint Terrorism Task Force (hereinafter "JTTF") and directed to concentrate my time towards domestic terrorism investigations. The ASAC communicated that the reassignment was necessary due to the voluminous number of J6 investigations and rising threats of "domestic violent extremism."

5. I was also told that child sexual abuse material investigations were no longer an FBI priority and should be referred to local law enforcement agencies. Prior to the incidents described below I received exemplary performance

reviews and numerous awards throughout my eight-year FBI career. Most recently, in July of 2022 the FBI conferred me with an "On-The-Spot" financial award.

6. **My concerns are as follows**: Stephen M. Friend, made a disclosure, of which an acting responsible official had knowledge, after which I was subjected to an adverse action.

7. As background information, full investigation casefiles within the FBI are labeled in three sections. The first section denotes the nature of the criminal offense. The second section identifies the FBI Field Office with responsibility for investigating. The third section is a unique case number populated by the FBI's SENTINEL case management system and attributable to the investigation. Additionally, if the investigating Case Agent requires assistance from another field office (i.e., interviewing a subject or witness who resides out of the Case Agent's geographical area of responsibility), investigative policy guides the Case Agent to "cut a lead" to Special Agents in another Field Office requesting that they take certain investigative action to assist the Case Agent. The "lead" facilitates timely investigation without forcing the Case Agent to engage in costly and time-consuming travel to areas beyond his area of responsibility.

* Domestic Investigations and Operations Guide (DIOG) Appendix J: (U) Case File Management and Indexing

  * J.1.2 (U) Investigative Leads and Lead Office (LO)

    (U//FOUO) Leads are sent by EC, or a Lead Request document, to offices and assigned to individuals/organizations in order to aid investigations. When the OO sets a lead to another office, that office is considered a Lead Office (LO). (U//FOUO) There are only two types of investigative leads: "Action Required" and "Information Only."

  * J.1.2.1 (U) Action Required Lead

    (U//FOUO) An action required lead must be used if the sending office <u>requires</u> the receiving LO to take some type of investigative action.

    (U//FOUO) An action required lead may <u>only</u> be set out of an open investigative file, including an:

      A) (U) Assessment file;

B) (U) Predicated investigation file;

C) (U) Pending inactive investigation file; or

D) (U) Unaddressed work file...

8. Accordingly, investigations stemming from the January 6, 2021, Capitol Hill protest (hereinafter "J6") could be assigned, according to Domestic Investigations and Operations Guide (DIOG) Appendix J, to Special Agents working at the "Office of Origin (OO)." Per DIOG guidance, Washington D.C. Field Office (WFO) is a logical OO because WFO's area of responsibility includes Washington D.C. If deemed the appropriate OO, any investigations or assessments opened by WFO would be marked with the second section casefile label of "WF." Should investigative actions be necessary outside of Washington D.C., the WFO Case Agent should "cut a lead" to the appropriate FBI Field Office. In the event that an alternative FBI Field Office assumed the role as OO (i.e., because a subject resides in the OO's area of responsibility) any investigations or assessment opened would be marked with the second section casefile label attributable to that Field Office (i.e., "DL" for FBI Dallas). Should investigative actions be necessary outside of the OO's area of the responsibility, the Case Agent should "cut a lead" to the appropriate FBI Field Office. Regardless of the particular OO and according to DIOG Appendix J, the assigned Case Agent assumes management responsibilities for all aspects of the assessment or investigation.

* Domestic Investigations and Operations Guide (DIOG) Appendix J: (U) Case File Management and Indexing.

o J.1 (U) Investigative File Management

o J.1.1 (U) Office of Origin (OO)

o (U/FOUO) Generally the Office of Origin (OO) is determined by:

A) (U//FOUO) The residence, location or destination of the subject of the investigation;

B) (U//FOUO) The office in which the complaint is first received;

C) (U//FOUO) The office designated by FBIHQ as OO in any investigation.

* Domestic Investigations and Operations Guide (DIOG) Appendix J: (U) Case File Management and Indexing

o J.1 (U) Investigative File Management

o J.1.3 (U) Office of Origin's (OO) Supervision of Cases
(U//FOUO) The OO is responsible for proper supervision
of Assessments and investigations in its own territory
and being conducted in a LO. The FBI employee,
usually an FBI Special Agent, to whom an investigation
is assigned, is often referred to as the "Case Agent."
An FBI employee is personally responsible for ensuring
all logical investigation is initiated without undue
delay, whether the employee is assigned in the OO or
in a LO; this includes setting forth Action Required
or Information Only leads as appropriate for other
offices or other FBI employees in his/her own office.
The OO Case Agent has overall responsibility for
supervision of the investigation...

The FBI is following an atypical procedure. J6 task force
members in Washington D.C. identify potential subjects and
possible locations where these individuals reside. The task
force disseminates information packets to Field Offices around
the country. If an assessment or investigation is opened for a
J6 subject, the recipient Field Offices become the official OO.
However, while Special Agents and Task Force Officers in these
Field Offices are assigned the role of "Case Agent," the J6 task
force effectively manages the cases and performs the bulk of
investigative work. The Case Agents perform investigative
actions at the direction of the J6 task force. The J6 task
force has the preeminent role for presenting J6 cases to the
United States Attorney's Office for prosecution.

9. In October of 2021, I was assigned to J6 cases on
behalf of Special Agents working in Washington D.C. On these
occasions, the J6 Task Force members disseminated information to
my office with instructions to perform logical investigative
actions (such as surveillance or subject interviews). Members
of the Daytona Beach Resident Agency (DBRA) Joint Terrorism Task
Force (JTTF) completed and documented these tasks. Later, J6
Task Force members in Washington D.C. reviewed the work and
requested additional investigative actions be performed or
pressured members of my local JTTF to open full investigations.
The J6 Task Force members assured the JTTF that once the case
was opened, they would perform future investigative work and
paperwork for the casefile. In accordance supervisor roles and
responsibilities outlined in the DIOG, the J6 Task Force
supervisors approved this work before it was submitted to the
casefile. Resultantly, there are active criminal investigations

of J6 subjects in which I am listed as the "Case Agent," but have not done any investigative work. Additionally, my supervisor has not approved any paperwork within the file. J6 Task Force members are serving as Affiants on search and arrest warrant affidavits for subjects whom I have never investigated or even interviewed but am listed as a "Case Agent." The J6 Task Force tasked the DBRA JTTF with executing these warrants.

* Domestic Investigations and Operations Guide (DIOG) 3.5 (U) Supervisor Roles and Responsibilities

* 3.5.2.1 (U) Approval/Review of Investigative or Collection Activities

> (U//FOUO) Anyone in a supervisory role who approves/reviews investigative or collection activity must determine whether the standards for opening, approving, conducting, and closing an investigative activity, collection activity or investigative method, as provided in the DIOG, have been satisfied. (U//FOUO) Only FBI supervisory employees and representatives from other government agencies (OGA) assigned to the FBI under the Joint Duty Assignment Program or the Intergovernmental Personnel Act as supervisors (as defined in DIOG subsection 3.5.1) may approve the serialization of investigative records into Sentinel. Additionally, whenever an OGA supervisor (as described above) approves an investigative record, an FBI supervisor must also approve the record into Sentinel. An OGA supervisor may not approve investigative methods (i.e., DIOG Section 18 methods) or investigative activities (e.g., UDP and OIA).

* Domestic Investigations and Operations Guide (DIOG) Appendix J: (U) Case File Management and Indexing

o J.1 (U) Investigative File Management
J.1.3 (U) Office of Origin's (OO) Supervision of Cases
(U//FOUO) The OO is responsible for proper supervision of Assessments and investigations in its own territory and being conducted in a LO. The FBI employee, usually an FBI Special Agent, to whom an investigation is assigned, is often referred to as the "Case Agent." An FBI employee is personally responsible for ensuring

all logical investigation is initiated without undue delay, whether the employee is assigned in the OO or in a LO; this includes setting forth Action Required or Information Only leads as appropriate for other offices or other FBI employees in his/her own office. The OO Case Agent has overall responsibility for supervision of the investigation...

10.   During the week of August 15, 2022, I became aware of imminent arrests of J6 subjects and searches of their respective residences within the FBI's Jacksonville and Tampa Field Office areas of responsibility. Simultaneous takedowns were scheduled to occur on August 24, 2022. Due to perceived threats levels, an FBI SWAT team was enlisted to arrest one of the arrests. On Friday, August 19, 2022, I spoke with my front-line supervisor, SSRA Greg Federico, on two separate occasions to disclose my concerns about potential DIOG policy violations employed during the investigative processes. SSRA Federico listened to my concerns but emphasized that the warrants were lawful court orders. He said that these operations were one step in the process and that the subjects would be afforded all due process.

11.   I responded that it was inappropriate to use an FBI SWAT team to arrest a subject for misdemeanor offenses and opined that the subject would likely face extended detainment and biased jury pools in Washington D.C. I suggested alternatives such as the issuance of a court summons or utilizing surveillance groups to determine an optimal, safe time for a local sheriff deputy to contact the subjects and advise them about the existence of the arrest warrant. SSRA Federico told me that FBI executive management considered all potential alternatives and determined the SWAT takedown was the appropriate course of action. SSRA Federico noted that I appeared to be under stress and suggested speaking to the FBI's employee assistance program. SSRA Federico told me that he respected how I was standing on principle, but I was putting him in a difficult situation because Special Agents cannot refuse to participate in specific cases. He stated that he wished I just "called in sick" for this warrant but his hands were tied now that I told him that I was going to refuse to participate in any J6 cases. Per the Office of Personnel Management, "an employee is entitled to use sick leave for: personal medical needs, family care or bereavement, care of a family member with a serious health condition, and adoption-related purposes." SSRA Federico told me that the FBI plans to prosecute every subject

associated with J6 and he expected "another wave" of J6 subjects would be referred to the Daytona Beach Resident Agency for investigation and arrest. SSRA Federico asked how I thought the Special Agent in Charge (SAC) of FBI Jacksonville would react to my position. He told me that it sounded like my concerns were with FBI leadership and the overall nature of the J6 investigations. SSRA Federico threatened reprisal indirectly by asking how long I saw myself continuing to work for the FBI. He asked me to reconsider my position and told me that he would decide on his actions over the course of the weekend.

12. On August 22, 2022, I was contacted by Jacksonville's Assistant Special Agent in Charge (ASAC) Coult Markovsky, who requested that I attend a meeting at the FBI Jacksonville office the following afternoon. On August 23, 2022, I met with ASAC Markovksy and ASAC Sean Ryan. I again disclosed my concerns about potential DIOG policy violations employed during the J6 investigative processes. I told that the irregular case dissemination, labeling, and management processes could be considered exculpatory evidence the must be disclosed to defendants in accordance with the Brady rule. I expressed my concerns about violating citizens' Sixth Amendment rights due overzealous charging by the DOJ and biased jury pools in Washington D.C. I cautioned about the similarities between Ruby Ridge, the Governor Whitmer kidnapping case, and the J6 investigation. ASAC Markovsky said that I lacked perspective on the J6 prosecutions because I was not principally involved in the day-to-day investigations. He added that it is the FBI's job to gather facts, but we are not responsible for determining if an individual should be prosecuted. I countered that former FBI Director James Comey's actions indicated this was no longer an FBI practice when he stated that "no reasonable prosecutor" would bring charges against former Secretary of State Hillary Clinton.

13. The ASACs asked if I believed the J6 rioters committed a crime. I responded that some of the people who entered the Capitol committed crimes, but others were innocent. I elaborated that I believed some innocent individuals had been unjustly prosecuted, convicted, and sentenced. ASAC Markovsky unironically asked if I thought that the individuals who "killed police officers" should be prosecuted. I replied that there were no police officers killed on January 6, 2021. ASAC Markovsky told me that I was being a bad teammate to my colleagues. The ASACs threatened reprisal again by warning that my refusal could

amount to insubordination. References were made to my future career prospects with the FBI. ASAC Ryan suggested I might want to speak with the FBI's employee assistance program about my emotional concerns with J6 cases. The ASACs informed me that I could not refuse to participate if FBI leadership was comfortable that an operation is Constitutional, within FBI guidelines, and did not present an unnecessary risk to my safety.

14. I responded by again disclosing that the facts and concerns I presented demonstrated how the J6 investigations violate all three elements. I told them that I would not participate in any of these operations. At the conclusion of the meeting, the ASACs opined that they did not know how they would proceed with me from a disciplinary perspective. They emphasized that any punitive action would be a slow process. However, four hours later ASAC Markovsky emailed me the following act of reprisal: "After multiple conversations with SSRA Greg Federico and our continued conversations today with myself and ASAC Ryan, you continue to refuse to participate in an FBI mission to serve a lawful court order issued by a Federal Judge. You are not to report to the Daytona Beach RA tomorrow, August 24, 2022, and you will be placed on AWOL (Absent Without Leave) status. AWOL in itself is not disciplinary, but can lead to disciplinary charges, such as removal." ASAC Markovksy and ASAC Ryan stated that all the details of our meeting were Unclassified.

15. On September 1, 2022, I met with FBI Jacksonville Special Agent in Charge (SAC) Sherry Onks. SAC Onks told me that I had a reputation as a good Special Agent and expressed disappointment with my refusal to participate in the January 6th investigations. SAC Onks suggested that I do "some soul searching" and decide if I wanted to work for the FBI. SAC Onks said that it "sounded like I lost faith in the FBI and its leadership." SAC Onks stated that the J6 investigations were all legal, ethical, and in accordance with FBI procedure. She said that my refusal to participate in the cases meant that I did not trust my colleagues' work and indicated that I believed the Special Agents working on J6 were coopted into behaving unethically and immorally. I again disclosed by informing SAC Onks that I believed the investigations were inconsistent with FBI procedure and resulted in the violation of citizens' Sixth and Eighth Amendment rights. I added that many of my colleagues expressed similar concerns to me but had not vocalized their objections to FBI Executive Management. SAC Onks disagreed with

my premise and said that my views represented an extremely small minority of the FBI workforce. SAC Onks told me that she had never encountered my situation during her career. She recalled the fear she felt while sitting on the seventh floor of the J. Edgar Hoover Building on January 6, 2021 when protestors "seized the Capitol" and threatened the United States' democracy. SAC Onks reprised against me and admitted as much, when she informed me that she referred me to the FBI's Office of Professional Responsibility and Security Division. SAC Onks told me that the Security Division was assessing my security clearance.

16. In addition to the atypical Originating Office identification process for J6 cases, the process potentially violates Case Manager and Case File Management and Indexing policies listed in the FBI's Domestic Investigations and Operations Guide (DIOG). These potential violations include:

- Domestic Investigations and Operations Guide (DIOG) 3.3 (U) Special Agent/Task Force Officer (TFO)/Task Force Member (TFM)/Task Force Participant (TFP)/FBI Contractor/Others -- Roles and Responsibilities
  - 3.3.1.10 (U) Serve as Investigation ("Case") Manager: (U//FOUO) If assigned responsibility for an investigation, manage all aspects of that investigation, until it is assigned to another person. It is the case manager's responsibility to ensure compliance with all applicable laws, rules, regulations, and guidelines, both investigative and administrative, from the opening of the investigation through disposition of the evidence, until the investigation is assigned to another person...
- Domestic Investigations and Operations Guide (DIOG) Appendix J: (U) Case File Management and Indexing
  - J.1 (U) Investigative File Management
    J.1.3 (U) Office of Origin's (OO) Supervision of Cases (U//FOUO) The OO is responsible for proper supervision of Assessments and investigations in its own territory and being conducted in a LO. The FBI employee, usually an FBI Special Agent, to whom an investigation is assigned, is often referred to as the "Case Agent." An FBI employee is personally responsible for ensuring all logical investigation is initiated without undue delay, whether the employee is assigned in the OO or in a LO; this includes setting forth Action Required or

Information Only leads as appropriate for other offices or other FBI employees in his/her own office. The OO Case Agent has overall responsibility for supervision of the investigation...

The manipulative casefile practice creates false and misleading crime statistics, constituting false official federal statements 18 U.S.C. §1001. Instead of hundreds of investigations stemming from an isolated incident at the Capitol on January 6, 2021, FBI and DOJ officials point to significant increases in domestic violent extremism and terrorism around the United States. At no point was I advised or counseled on where to take my disclosure beyond the reprising officials above; the threatened reprisal constituted a *de facto* gag on my whistleblowing.

17. The acting officials who had knowledge of my disclosures as set forth above included SSRA Greg Federico, Jacksonville's Assistant Special Agent in Charge (ASAC) Coult Markovsky, ASAC Sean Ryan, and FBI Jacksonville Special Agent in Charge (SAC) Sherry Onks.

18. I was reprised against and instructed to not report to the Daytona Beach RA on August 24, 2022, and was placed on AWOL status. When I arrived at the FBI's Daytona Beach Field Office on the morning of September 19, 2022, I was brought into a meeting with my supervisor, ASAC, SAC, and security officer. I was told that my security clearance was suspended pending an investigation. My credentials, firearm, and badge were confiscated, and I was escorted from the building.

19. I also received the letter annexed hereto and made a part hereof dated September 16, 2022.

I do solemnly affirm under the penalties of perjury and upon personal knowledge that the contents of the above statement are true to the best of my knowledge.

Stephen M. Friend L.S.

Stephen M. Friend
September 21, 2022

EMPOWER OVERSIGHT
Whistleblowers & Research

EMPOWR.us

January 31, 2023

VIA ELECTRONIC TRANSMISSION: OIGFOIA@USDOJ.GOV

Office of Inspector General
U.S. Department of Justice
441 G Street, N.W.
6th Floor
Washington, DC 20530

RE: **Request for Records Relating to DOJ-OIG's Decision Not to Investigate a Whistleblower Allegations of Systemic Abuses by the FBI**

Dear FOIA Officer:

INTRODUCTION

Empower Oversight Whistleblowers & Research ("Empower Oversight") is a nonpartisan, nonprofit educational organization dedicated to enhancing independent oversight of government and corporate wrongdoing. We work to help insiders safely and legally report waste, fraud, abuse, corruption, and misconduct to the proper authorities, and seek to hold those authorities accountable to act on such reports by, among other means, publishing information concerning the same.

BACKGROUND

On August 19, 2022, Steve Friend, an eight-year veteran of the Federal Bureau of Investigation ("FBI") who was stationed in the Daytona Beach Resident Office, which reports to the Jacksonville Field Office, made protected disclosures (under 5 U.S.C. § 2303) to his supervisor concerning alleged violations of the Constitution, laws, and FBI policy in connection with the planned execution of arrest and search warrants the following week. [Declaration of Steve M. Friend ("Declaration") at ¶¶ 3, 4, and 10, attached.]

His supervisor claimed to Special Agent Friend that he appeared to be under stress and suggested that he pursue counseling; characterized his disclosures as a refusal to participate in a class of cases,[1] which he would have to report up the chain of command; asked Special Agent Friend how he reckoned the Special Agent in Charge ("SAC") of the field office would react to his disclosure; and inquired how he perceived his future working for the FBI. [Declaration at ¶¶ 10 and 11.]

---

[1] Special Agent Friend never refused to participate. Instead, he made a protected disclosure and asked to be assigned to alternative duties on the date of the execution of the arrest and search warrants. Ultimately, one day before the planned execution of the arrest and search warrants, he was directed by FBI management not to report to duty the following day.

On August 22, 2022, Special Agent Friend was instructed to report to the FBI's Jacksonville Field Office the following day. [Declaration at ¶¶ 12, 13, and 14.] As directed, on August 23, 2022, Special Agent Friend met with two Assistant Special Agents in Charge ("ASACs") in Jacksonville. He repeated and elaborated on the protected disclosure that he made the prior week to his supervisor. *Id.* The ASACs asked about his personal views on the class of cases in controversy; characterized him as a "bad teammate;" threatened to punish him if he refused to participate in the planned arrest and search warrants;[2] questioned his career prospects in the FBI; recommended counseling; and ruminated aloud that they did not know how the FBI would proceed against him, given that formal discipline is a slow process. *Id.* Approximately four hours after the meeting in Jacksonville, one of the two ASACs emailed Special Agent Friend, instructed him not to report for duty the next day, and notified him that the FBI was placing him on Absent Without Leave ("AWOL") status on August 24, 2022, the date of the planned execution of the arrest and search warrants. Additionally, the ASAC informed him that AWOL status could lead to disciplinary charges. *Id.* Special Agent Friend complied with the directive, did not report for duty pursuant to the instruction, and was recorded in the FBI personnel system as AWOL for that day as a result, despite having offered to perform other assigned duties.

On September 1, 2022, Special Agent Friend met with the SAC of the Jacksonville Field Office. [Declaration at ¶ 15.] She advised Special Agent Friend that, given his heretofore good reputation, she was disappointed with his refusal to participate in the arrest and search warrants on August 24th,[3] and suggested that he needed to do some "soul searching" regarding whether he wanted to work for the FBI; theorized that Special Agent Friend's concerns about the class of cases in controversy exposed a belief that his colleagues were coopted by leadership priorities, which caused them to cross ethical and moral boundaries; expressed her personal support for the class of cases; and informed Special Agent Friend that she had referred him to the FBI's Office of Professional Responsibility and its Security Division, the latter of which was assessing his security clearance. *Id.*

On the evening of September 14, 2022, an ASAC in the Jacksonville Field Office called him and directed him to report to the field office the next morning (September 15, 2022) to attend a Security Awareness Briefing ("SAB"). Because he had already successfully completed the FBI's annual SAB requirement, he asked why he was being directed to attend a duplicative one-on-one SAB lecture. The ASAC responded "because you have made different choices than other people." Special Agent Friend then asked whether he could bring a lawyer with him to the meeting. The ASAC said he did not think so, but would ask and get back to him. By the next morning the ASAC had not resolved the question about his attorney attending the SAB, and Special Agent Friend called in sick.

On September 16, 2022, the Executive Assistant Director of the FBI's Human Resources Branch informed Special Agent Friend that, as the FBI's Security Programs Manager, she had suspended his security clearance. The suspension of Special Agent Friend's security clearance precludes him from entering FBI space and, thus, suspends his "authority to fulfill the duties and responsibilities of" his position. As grounds for her suspension of his clearance, the Executive Assistant Director claimed:

> On 08/24/2022, you advised your supervisors of your objection to participating in the court authorized search and arrest of a criminal subject. During your communications, you espoused beliefs which demonstrate

---

[2] Again, Special Agent Friend did not refuse to participate. He made a protected disclosure and asked to be assigned to alternative duties on the date of the execution of the arrest and search warrants.

[3] *See,* footnotes 1 and 2.

questionable judgement.[4] On 09/03/2022, you entered FBI space and downloaded documents from FBI computer systems to an unauthorized flash drive and you subsequently failed to cooperate with a Security Awareness Briefing, demonstrating an unwillingness to comply with rules and regulations.

The Assistant Director of the FBI's Human Resources Branch's suspension of Special Agent Friend's security clearance halted his paycheck, achieving the exact same effect as a disciplinary adverse personnel action would have, but without any independent oversight or meaningful review.

I.   Special Agent Friend's Complaint

On September 21, 2022, Special Agent Friend submitted to the Department of Justice, Office of Inspector General ("DOJ-OIG"), a complaint that, in addition to detailing numerous acts of whistleblower retaliation against him, includes allegations of systemic abuses of the Constitution, laws, and policy by the FBI. Specifically, Special Agent Friend's complaint includes allegations of four systemic abuses by the FBI:

- Evasion of case management policies to drive a false narrative supporting an FBI priority;

- Defiance of the Department of Justice's ("DOJ") Use of Force policy and FBI policy to send a message to disfavored actors;

- Retaliation against whistleblowers; and

- Exploitation of security clearances to avoid due process procedures applicable to disciplinary proceedings.

Evasion of Case Management Policies to Drive a False Narrative in Support of an FBI Priority

On January 7, 2021, just hours after thousands of critics of the results of the 2020 presidential election descended on the Capitol building, FBI Director Christopher Wray stated:

> The violence and destruction of property at the U.S. Capitol building yesterday showed a blatant and appalling disregard for our institutions of government and the orderly administration of the democratic process. As we've said consistently, we do not tolerate violent agitators and extremists who use the guise of First Amendment-protected activity to incite violence and wreak havoc. Such behavior betrays the values of our democracy. Make no mistake: With our partners, we will hold accountable those who participated in yesterday's siege of the Capitol.

> Let me assure the American people the FBI has deployed our full investigative resources and is working closely with our federal, state, and local partners to aggressively pursue those involved in criminal activity during the events of January 6. Our agents and analysts have been hard at work through the night gathering evidence, sharing intelligence, and working with federal prosecutors to bring charges. Members of the public can help by providing tips, information,

---

[4] Special Agent Friend did not communicate with his managers on August 24, 2022. On that date, he complied with his ASAC's direction not to report for duty, and was placed on AWOL as a result of his compliance.

and videos of illegal activity at fbi.gov/USCapitol. We are determined to find those responsible and ensure justice is served.[5]

Two years later, Attorney General Merrick Garland characterized the FBI's investigation of the riot at the Capitol as "one of the largest, most complex, and most resource-intensive investigations in our history."[6] He also advised that the investigation has been and is being led by, the FBI's Washington, D.C. Field Office ("WFO"), *id.*, and had previously stated that prosecutors "will hold accountable anyone who is criminally responsible for attempting to interfere with the . . . lawful transfer of power from one administration to the next,"[7] which is inherently not confined to participation in riot at the Capitol.

Additionally, on June 15, 2021, Attorney General Garland announced the *National Strategy for Countering Domestic Terrorism*, a government-wide program designed to study, deter, disrupt, and prevent the full range of domestic terrorism threats.[8] Introducing the national strategy, he explained that during President Biden's first week in office, he directed the Administration to undertake an assessment of the domestic terrorism threat, and to use it to develop a strategy. *Id.* The assessment was completed in March of 2021, and concluded that domestic violent extremists "pose an elevated threat to the Homeland in 2021." *Id.* He added that his experience on the ground confirms the assessment, noting that the number of the FBI's open domestic terrorism investigations had increased significantly during the fledgling year. *Id.*

The FBI defines "domestic terrorism" as activities that involve danger to human life; violate Federal or state criminal laws; appear to be intended to intimidate or coerce a civilian population, influence government, or affect the government operations; and occur primarily within the United States' territory.[9] The FBI continually reviews and evaluates intelligence data to ensure that it identifies "Domestic Violent Extremist" operating with the United States' territory whose advocacy for particular ideological positions escalates to a threat of violence. *Id.* Currently, the government focuses on threats emanating from racial or ethnic, anti-government, environmental, and abortion-related biases. *Id.*[10]

According to case management and indexing procedures set forth at appendix J of the FBI's Domestic Investigations and Operations Guide ("DIOG"), the "Office of Origin" ("OO") of an investigative action is determined by, among various means, the residence of the subject of the investigation, the office that first received a complaint comprising the subject of the

---

[5] FBI, Director Wray's Statement on Violent Activity at the U.S. Capitol Building (January 7, 2021), available at https://www.fbi.gov/wanted/capitol-violence?utm_medium=email&utm_source=govdelivery#Director's-Statement.

[6] DOJ, Attorney General Merrick B. Garland Statement on the Second Anniversary of the January 6 Attack on the Capitol (January 4, 2023), available at https://www.justice.gov/opa/pr/attorney-general-merrick-b-garland-statement-second-anniversary-january-6-attack-capitol.

[7] Johnson, Kevin; Jansen, Bart, Garland Vows to Pursue Charges on 'Anyone' Criminally Responsible for Jan. 6 When Pressed on Trump (July 26, 2022), available at https://www.usatoday.com/story/news/politics/2022/07/26/merrick-garland-charges-jan-6/10151899002/.

[8] DOJ, Attorney General Merrick B. Garland Remarks: Domestic Terrorism Policy Address (June 15, 2021), available at https://www.justice.gov/opa/speech/attorney-general-merrick-b-garland-remarks-domestic-terrorism-policy-address.

[9] FBI, DHS, Domestic Terrorism: Definitions, Terminology, and Methodology (Updated), available at https://www.fbi.gov/file-repository/fbi-dhs-domestic-terrorism-definitions-terminology-methodology.pdf/view.

[10] During his June 15th speech, Attorney General Garland singled out racially-, ethnically-, and anti-government motivated extremists as posing the greatest threat to society. *See* DOJ, Attorney General Merrick B. Garland Remarks: Domestic Terrorism Policy Address (June 15, 2021), available at https://www.justice.gov/opa/speech/attorney-general-merrick-b-garland-remarks-domestic-terrorism-policy-address.

investigation, or a location designated by the FBI's headquarters. [Declaration at ¶ 8.][11] Typically, a special agent within the OO is assigned responsibility for the investigation, including ensuring that it is conducted without delay. *Id.* If the OO develops a lead (*e.g.*, the need to interview a subject or witness who resides beyond the boundaries of the OO's geographic area of jurisdiction), then it should "cut a lead" to another field office which is then called the Lead Office ("LO"), which will assign a special agent to execute the lead on behalf of the OO. [Declaration at ¶ 7.]

Additionally, according to the case management and indexing procedures of DIOG at appendix J, the OO—and the special agent it assigned—is responsible for the "proper supervision" of the investigation, whether such investigation is carried out within boundaries of the OO or at a geographically remote LO to which a lead has been sent. [Declaration at ¶ 8.] Similarly, a special agent's supervisor is responsible to ensure that "all investigative activity, collection activity, and use of investigative methods [by the agent] comply with the Constitution, Federal law," the DIOG, and other applicable legal and policy requirements; confirm that the agent creates and maintains reliable and trustworthy files; and to review the agent's investigative files every 90 days to verify efficiency and compliance with applicable law. DIOG, §§ 3.4.2.4, 3.4.2.9, and 3.4.4.1 – 3.4.4.3.

Special Agent Friend explained that, deviating from the FBI's Domestic Investigations and Operations Guide ("DIOG"), officials in the FBI's Washington, D.C. Field Office ("WFO") identified subjects to investigate in connection with the January 6, 2021, riot at the Capitol and/or interference with the transition of executive power, and sent information packets concerning such subjects to field offices nationwide with instructions to open investigations. [Declaration at ¶ 8.][12] As directed by the WFO, the recipient field offices opened investigations, designating themselves as the Offices of Origin ("OOs"), and assigned local special agents as the responsible case agents. *Id.* Thereafter, the WFO managed the cases and performed the bulk of the investigative work, including presenting cases to the offices of the United States Attorneys for prosecution. *Id.* For their part, the nominally responsible case agents assigned to the cases performed such functions as the WFO directed, *Id.*, and field office supervisors effectively had no role in monitoring compliance with the Constitution, laws, and the DIOG, [Declaration at ¶ 9]. WFO supervisors exercised *de facto* control of the cases despite documentation indicating that the OOs were other field offices. *Id.*

Not only is Special Agent Friend's disclosure fully consistent with Attorney General Garland's assertion that the WFO controls the FBI's investigation of the January 6th riot at the Capitol and interference with the transition of executive power,[13] it adds important context to the Attorney General's assertion concerning the sharp increase in domestic terrorism cases in 2021.[14]

---

[11] Unless it is an emergency and an official with approval authority is unavailable, approval for all deliberate deviations from the DIOG must be requested in writing addressed to an Assistant Director of the appropriate operational program and to the Office of Integrity and Compliance, with a notice to the General Counsel. DIOG, § 2.7.2. Of course, one may not deviate from the DIOG until after the requested approval is granted. *Id.*

[12] FBI employees are required to report in writing all instances of substantial non-compliance with the DIOG (*e.g.*, noncompliance that has the potential to adversely affect an individual's rights or liberties, or failure to obtain supervisory approval). DIOG, § 2.8.2. If the non-compliance occurs in a field office, the writing must be routed through the Division Compliance Officer to the SAC or Assistant Director In Charge. DIOG, § 2.8.3.

[13] *See* DOJ, Attorney General Merrick B. Garland Statement on the Second Anniversary of the January 6 Attack on the Capitol (January 4, 2023), available at https://www.justice.gov/opa/pr/attorney-general-merrick-b-garland-statement-second-anniversary-january-6-attack-capitol.

[14] *See* DOJ, Attorney General Merrick B. Garland Remarks: Domestic Terrorism Policy Address (June 15, 2021), available at https://www.justice.gov/opa/speech/attorney-general-merrick-b-garland-remarks-domestic-terrorism-policy-address.

601 KING STREET, SUITE 200 | ALEXANDRIA, VA 22314-3151   PAGE 5 OF 14

176 of 315

Special Agent Friend pointed out that by departing from the DOIG in this way, FBI headquarters and the WFO would create false and misleading crime statistics reports to Congress. [Declaration at ¶ 16]. Instead of hundreds of domestic terrorism cases isolated in the WFO, as a consequence of events occurring on a single day, and the FBI's extraordinary effort to investigate anyone remotely associated—even passively—with the riot at the Capitol on January 6ᵗʰ, the FBI has disbursed the cases throughout its field offices, *Id.*, causing a statistical surge nationwide.

Defiance of Use of Force Policy to Send a Message to Politically Disfavored Actors

The DIOG notes that FBI's law enforcement authorities are conditioned on "rigorous obedience to the Constitution," and accordingly the Attorney General established a set of basic principles "that serve as the foundation of all FBI mission-related activities."[15] These principles include protecting individual rights and using "the least intrusive means that do not otherwise compromise FBI operations."[16] For intelligence and evidence gathering (*e.g.*, the execution of a search warrant) considerations that must be balanced to ensure that the means used are the least intrusive means include the:

- Seriousness of the crime or national security threat;

- Strength and significance of the intelligence/information to be gained;

- Amount of information already known about the subject or group under investigation; and

- Requirements of operational security, including protection of sources and methods.[17]

Similarly, regarding the execution of an arrest warrant, the DIOG limits the use of physical force to the threshold "reasonable and necessary to take custody and overcome all resistance of the arrestee, and to ensure the safety of the arresting agents, the arrestee and others in the vicinity of the arrest."[18]

Effective July 19, 2022, Attorney General Garland updated the "Use-of-Force" policy applicable to DOJ and its sub-agencies (*e.g.*, the FBI).[19] According to the updated policy, FBI officials:

> may use only the force that is objectively reasonable to effectively gain control of an incident, while protecting [FBI officials] and others. . . . Officers may use force only when no reasonably effective, safe, and feasible alternative appears to exist and may use only the level of force that a reasonable officer on the scene would use under the same or similar circumstances.

---

[15] DIOG, § 4.1.1.

[16] DIOG, §§ 4.1.1, 18.2.

[17] DIOG, § 4.4.4.

[18] DIOG, § 19.5.2.

[19] Memorandum from Attorney General Garland, *Subject: Department's Updated Use-of-Force Policy* (May 20, 2022), available at https://www.justice.gov/ag/page/file/1507826/download#:~:text=Officers%20may%20use%20force%20only,the%20same%20or%20%20similar%20circumstances.

Id. As guidance for discerning the "reasonableness" of required force, the policy cites careful attention to the facts and circumstances of particular cases, the severity of the crime at issue, whether the subject poses an immediate threat to the safety of the arresting officer or others, and whether the subject resists or attempts to evade arrest. *Id.*

During the week of August 15, 2022, Special Agent Friend became the aware of the FBI's imminent execution of arrest and search warrants of numerous persons who resided in the geographic jurisdiction of the FBI's Jacksonville and Tampa field offices and were subjects of investigation for participating in the January 6th riot at the Capitol and/or interfering with the transition of executive power. [Declaration at ¶ 10]. The executions of the warrants were scheduled for August 24, 2022, and the plans of execution included the use of an FBI SWAT team for at least one of the arrests. *Id.*

On Friday, August 19, 2022, Special Agent Friend approached his supervisor in the Daytona Beach Resident Office, and advised him that he was concerned that the plans for the executions of the warrants applicable to subjects of investigations of the riot at the Capitol appeared to violate DOJ and FBI policies and by extension the Constitution. [Declaration at ¶¶ 10 and 11]. Specifically, he stated that the execution plans for the warrants threatened to compromise the subjects' due process rights (*i.e.*, overzealous charges, biased jury pools in the District of Columbia, and excessive pre-trial detention) and to violate the DOJ's Use of Force and the FBI's least intrusive methods policies. [Declaration at ¶ 11]. In the latter regard, he believed, based on his experience, that it would be inappropriate to use FBI SWAT teams to arrest a subject of a misdemeanor offense, *Id.*, someone who had previously cooperated with the investigation, or someone who could more safely be apprehended in another manner. Alternatively, he proposed that in lieu of using force to arrest subjects at their homes, the FBI or local law enforcement could issue court summons, as many of the subjects were represented by counsel and had cooperated with FBI interview requests; or the subjects could be arrested away from their homes as they traveled from points A to B. *Id.* His supervisor dismissed his concerns, by replying that the warrants were lawful court orders, [Declaration at ¶¶ 10], suggesting that his supervisor does not understand that DOJ/FBI policy and Constitutional standards apply to the application of court orders; and proceeded to retaliate against him, suggesting that he is unaware of statutory protections applicable to whistleblowers.

Subsequently, on August 23, 2022, and September 1, 2022, Special Agent Friend met with his ASACs and SAC in the Jacksonville Field Office, and repeated the concerns that he had discussed with his supervisor on August 19th. [Declaration at ¶¶ 12 – 15]. Like his supervisor before them, the ASACs and SAC dismissed his concerns and retaliated against him. *Id.*

Special Agent Friend's concerns about the FBI violating applicable Use of Force and least intrusive means policies when executing warrants are not limited to the particular operation imminent at the time he made his protected disclosures, or even to arrests and searches of Capitol rioters. Recently, the media has extensively covered the FBI's selective use of unnecessarily intrusive tactics such as its use of tactical teams and equipment to arrest non-violent subjects like Roger Stone and Mark Houck and its unprecedented search of Mar-A-Lago.[20] The selective use of such tactics to send a message of intimidation to politically disfavored subjects would be improper. Thus, Special Agent Friend had a reasonable basis to

---

[20] *See, e.g.,* Dwinell, Joe, *FBI's Roger Stone Raid Sends Chilling Message* ((January 26, 2019), available at https://www.bostonherald.com/2019/01/26/fbis-roger-stone-raid-sends-chilling-message/; Catholic News Agency, *FBI Raids Home of Pro-life Leader on Questionable Charges* (September 23, 2022), available at https://www.catholicnewsagency.com/news/252380/fbi-raids-home-of-pro-life-leader-on-questionable-charges; McGurn, William, *Justice for Mark Houck* (January 30, 2023), available at https://www.wsj.com/articles/justice-for-mark-houck-fbi-abortion-pro-life-planned-parenthood-face-act-not-guilty-crime-arrest-11675113079 (Mr. Houck is a pro-life advocate who had cooperated with the FBI's investigation and who had agreed to accept a summons and surrender himself, but whom the FBI arrested at his home "as though he were John Dillinger); Miller, Tucker, and Balsamo, *FBI's Search of Trump's Florida Estate: Why Now?* (August 9, 2022), available at https://apnews.com/article/donald-trump-mar-a-lago-fbi-search-99097089194e736315c366a0e8fbafee.

object and make protected disclosures about the resulting threats to public safety resulting from political motives apparently creeping into what should be strictly tactical law enforcement decisions on the merits.

Retaliation Against Whistleblowers

Section 2303 of Title 5 of the United State Code prohibits the FBI's management from taking an adverse personnel action (*e.g.*, demotion, removal, or suspension) against an employee, or failing to take a beneficial personnel action (*e.g.*, hiring or promotion) against an applicant for employment or an employee, "as a reprisal for a disclosure of information" to appropriate authorities, when the applicant or employee reasonably believes that the content of the information:

- Involves the violation of laws, rules, or regulations, or

- Evidences gross mismanagement, gross waste of funds, an abuse of authority, or a substantial and specific danger to public health or safety.[21]

At a minimum, Special Agent Friend's immediate supervisor, his ASACs, his SAC, and the Executive Assistant Director of the FBI's Human Resources Branch retaliated against him because he had the audacity to make protected disclosures about his concerns that the FBI's approach to the investigation (including the execution of search warrants) and arrest of alleged participants in the January 6th riot at the Capitol and/or persons who allegedly interfered with the transition of executive power. In response to his disclosures, his supervisor questioned his fitness for duty, suggested that he pursue counseling, asked how he reckoned the SAC would react to his disclosure, and implied that he had imperiled his career. [Declaration at ¶¶ 10 and 11.]

His ASACs characterized him as a "bad teammate," threatened to punish him if he refused to participate in planned execution of arrest and search warrants, questioned his future career prospects in the FBI, recommended counseling, and placed him on AWOL status on August 24th (after directing him not to report for duty on that date). [Declaration at ¶¶ 12, 13, and 14.]

His SAC expressed disappointment that he "refused" to participate in the arrest and search warrants on the date he was placed on AWOL, suggested that he reconsider his career in the FBI, questioned his belief system and his opinions of his colleagues, and referred him to the FBI's Office of Professional Responsibility and its Security Division. [Declaration at ¶ 15.]

The Executive Assistant Director of the FBI's Human Resources Branch suspended his security clearance. Among other reasons for her decision, she cited an erroneous August 24, 2022, conversation with his supervisors. In fact, he did not tell his supervisors on August 24th that he objected to participating in searches or arrests. He had been instructed not to report for duty, was placed on AWOL, and had no contact with his supervisors that day.

Further, Special Agent Friend may not be the only FBI employee who was retaliated against for questioning the FBI's approach to the investigation (including the execution of search warrants) and arrest of alleged participants in the January 6th riot at the Capitol and/or persons who allegedly interfered with the transition of executive power. During their meeting on September 1st, Special Agent Friend advised his SAC that many of his colleagues had expressed to him similar concerns about the FBI's approach. His SAC disputed his contention, claiming that Special Agent Friend's views represented an extremely small minority of the FBI's

---

[21] 5 U.S.C. § 2303(a).

workforce. Her rejoinder implies that management was aware—through receipt of other protected disclosures or by surveillance—that Special Agent Friend's concerns were shared by some "minority" of the FBI's staff. Moreover, her rebuttal signifies that she refused to acknowledge or failed to comprehend that there could be more special agents who shared his concerns but were too scared of retaliation to voice those concerns. Indeed, disclosing concerns about the FBI's violations of the Constitution, laws, and regulations is widely perceived to pose a serious risk to one's career and invites whistleblower retaliation by the FBI's management, for which there are woefully inadequate remedies.

Abuse of Security Clearance Inquiries to Avoid Due Process Procedures Applicable to Disciplinary Proceedings

Towards the conclusion of Special Agent Friend's meeting with the two ASACs on August 23rd, the ASACs ruminated aloud that they did not know how the FBI would proceed against him from a disciplinary perspective. [Declaration at ¶¶ 12, 13, and 14.] Specifically, the ASACs' groused that formal discipline is a slow process. *Id.*

From the perspective of an FBI manager who wants to be quickly and efficiently resolve personnel issues, the ASACs' critique of the FBI's procedures for "adverse actions" (*i.e.*, suspensions for more than 14 days, demotions, and removals) is on target. The process is slow and cedes the manager's decision-making. Indeed, DOJ-OIG reports that the FBI's goal—not actual experience—is "to complete the investigation and adjudication of misconduct cases in 180 days."[22] However, as DOJ-OIG notes, this period excludes appeals of adjudications; the FBI has an informal goal of resolving appeals of adjudications in an additional 120 days. Moreover, once a manager initiates a disciplinary process, he/she loses the ability to control of not only the timing of the final action, but also of the proposed action itself.

The FBI's disciplinary process consists of four phases:

- Reporting misconduct allegations,

- Investigating allegations,

- Adjudicating investigations, and

- Appealing adjudications.[23]

The FBI's Inspection Division ("ID") and Office of Professional Responsibility ("OPR")—offices with the FBI's headquarters—are responsible for the administration of the four phases. *Id.*

First, according to the FBI's Manual of Administrative Operations and Procedures ("MOAP"), all allegations of employee misconduct must be reported to OPR, which will "determine and advise who will conduct the investigation" of the alleged misconduct.[24] Typically, OPR will assign the investigation to the Assistant Director, SAC, or Legal Attache of the office of the subject of the investigation. *Id.*

---

[22] DOJ-OIG, *Report No. I-2009-002: Review of the Federal Bureau of Investigation's Disciplinary System*, pp. 3, 24, (May 2009), available at https://www.oversight.gov/sites/default/files/oig-reports/final_4.pdf.

[23] DOJ-OIG, *Report No. 21-127: Review of the Federal Bureau of Investigation's Adjudication Process for Misconduct Investigations*, p. 4., (September 2021), available at https://oig.justice.gov/sites/default/files/reports/21-127.pdf.

[24] MOAP, Part 1, § 13.2.

Second, the investigation must be initiated promptly, and generally "every logical lead which will establish the true facts should be completely run out."[25] The record of the investigation should include "the initial allegation; the investigative results; aggravating or mitigating circumstances; statement of specific charge(s) and the employee's answer(s) including defenses to the specific charge(s), if any." *Id.* The investigation shall not be "complete until the specific allegations that may justify disciplinary action are made known the employee who may be disciplined and the employee is afforded reasonable time to answer the specific allegations." *Id.*

During the pendency of the investigation, it is not a foregone conclusion that the subject of the investigation will be prevented from performing his/her duties. Rather, the Assistant Director, SAC, or Legal Attache assigned to conduct the investigation is authorized to temporarily assign the subject to other duties, "if the circumstances surrounding the allegation indicate that such action warranted."[26] However, all such reassignment decisions must be made on a case-by-case basis; they "should not be made automatically." *Id.*

Investigation findings are recorded in written reports that are filed in the subject's personnel file in the field office and at the FBI's headquarters.[27] The report format includes recommendations for what, if any, administrative action is appropriate.[28]

Third, disciplinary recommendations are guided by a MOAP schedule, but—except for certain minor offenses delegated to management in FBI's field offices—final determinations of the appropriate discipline to propose against an employee accused of misconduct is reserved to the FBI's headquarters,[29] specifically it is reserved to the OPR's Adjudication Units.[30] The Assistant Director of OPR reviews the determinations of the Adjudication Units and if he/she agrees that discipline is warranted, then "the action is taken and the employee notified."[31]

Fourth, if the Assistant Director of OPR agrees that discipline is warranted and takes an adverse action, then the employee may appeal the decision to the Assistant Director of ID.[32]

To circumvent these formal disciplinary procedures, the FBI can rapidly, and without meaningful, if any, due process, suspend special agents' security clearances and place them in a leave without pay status. On September 1st Special Agent Friend's SAC advised him that she had referred him to the FBI's Security Division for a review of his clearance. Fifteen days later—not the combined 300-day goal set forth in the FBI's discipline procedures (*i.e.*, 180 days for investigation and adjudication and 120 days for appeal of the adjudication), the Executive Assistant Director of the FBI's Human Resources Branch suspended his security clearance and

---

[25] MOAP, Part 1, § 13.3.

[26] MOAP, Part 1, § 13.1.

[27] MOAP, Part 1, §§ 13.7, 13.7.1, and 13.7.2.

[28] MOAP, Part 1, § 13.7.1.

[29] MOAP, Part 1, § 13.13.

[30] DOJ-OIG, *A Review of Allegations of a Double Standard of Discipline at the FBI* (November 21, 2022), available at https://oig.justice.gov/sites/default/files/archive/special/0211/chapter2.htm.

[31] MOAP, Part 1, § 14-4.2; *see also*, DOJ-OIG, *A Review of Allegations of a Double Standard of Discipline at the FBI* (November 21, 2022), available at https://oig.justice.gov/sites/default/files/archive/special/0211/chapter2.htm.

[32] DOJ-OIG, *A Review of Allegations of a Double Standard of Discipline at the FBI* (November 21, 2022), available at https://oig.justice.gov/sites/default/files/archive/special/0211/chapter2.htm.

halted his paycheck. It has the exact same effect as a disciplinary adverse personnel action would have, but without any independent oversight or meaningful review.

It often seems like the Nation's two principal political parties cannot agree on anything. At least one exception, however, is a shared belief that the Executive branch of government has grown less inhibited about improperly revoking security clearances to silence its detractors. For example, Senator Warner accused former President Trump of "abusing" the security clearance process "to punish his political opponents," in particular John Brennan.[33] On the other side of the aisle, former Representative Hunter complained about the Army's retaliation against retired Lt. Colonel Jason Amerine, including the suspension of his security clearance at the FBI's urging, for revealing to Congress bureaucratic infighting that impaired the Nation's efforts to recover hostages.[34] And, indeed, in connection with Special Agent Friend's circumstances, Senators Grassley and Johnson admonished Attorney General Garland and FBI Director Wray that "The FBI should never suspend security clearances as a form of punishment or to retaliate against patriotic whistleblowers for stepping forward to report potential wrongdoing."[35]

Further, following the revocation of Mr. Brennan's security clearance, the Project on Government Oversight ("POGO") reported:

> The revocation of Mr. Brennan's individual clearance, though conspicuous and newsworthy, isn't immediately detrimental to Mr. Brennan or to the public. In fact, it isn't even clear if the former director has actually lost it yet. Rather, what's more concerning is what the loss represents: the escalating weaponization of security clearances as a form of reprisal.

> Whistleblowers have felt this weaponization for years—many have lost clearances because of retaliatory investigations initiated under false pretenses by their supervisors after speaking out against waste, fraud, or abuse. To make matters worse, others who would have come forward with additional life-saving disclosures remain silent observers of abuse for fear of losing their livelihoods.[36]

In other words, what the FBI has done to Special Agent Friend does not appear to be an isolated event. It very well may be an example of a widespread FBI practice—one that the Office of Inspector General should be reviewing for systemic abuses.

II.   DOJ-OIG's Response to Special Agent Friend's September 21st Complaint

On December 2, 2022, DOJ-OIG advised Daniel Meyer, Special Agent Friend's legal counsel, that "[a]fter careful consideration and in view of the limited resources of the OIG, we

---

[33] Sen. Mark Warner, *On Senate Floor, Warner Warns Trump: Stop Abusing Security Clearance Process to Punish Critics* (August 21, 2018), available at https://www.warner.senate.gov/public/index.cfm/2018/8/on-senate-floor-warner-warns-trump-stop-abusing-security-clearance-process-to-punish-critics.

[34] Rep. Duncan Hunter, *Make No Mistake: The FBI and Army Retaliated Against a Hero* (December 17, 2015), available at https://warontherocks.com/2015/12/make-no-mistake-the-fbi-and-army-retaliated-against-a-hero/; *see also*, Brian, Danielle, and Smithberger, Mandy, *How the System Went After a War Hero: Jason Amerine Goes to Washington* (December 10, 2015), available at https://warontherocks.com/2015/12/how-the-system-went-after-a-war-hero-jason-amerine-goes-to-washington/.

[35] September 26, 2022, letter to Attorney General Garland and FBI Director Wray from Senators Charles E. Grassley and Ron Johnson, p. 3, available at https://www.grassley.senate.gov/imo/media/doc/grassley_johnson_to_doj_fbi_stephen_friend.pdf.

[36] Jones, Rebecca, *Revoking Clearances on a Whim Hurts Whistleblowers—and the Rest of Us* (September 14, 2018), available at https://www.pogo.org/analysis/2018/09/revoking-clearances-on-a-whim-hurts-whistleblowers-and-the-rest-of-us.

have decided not to open an investigation of the allegations that you raise." Nonetheless, in its letter, DOJ-OIG went on:

- Effectively to affirm the importance of Special Agent Friend's allegations of the FBI's systemic abuses;

- Expressed its desire to refer his allegations to the FBI's "Inspection Division[37] for further action;" and

- Threatened to "<u>close the matter and take no further action</u>" (emphasis original), if Special Agent Friend refused to consent to the DOJ-OIG's referring his allegations of the FBI's systemic abuses back to the FBI.

In addition to threatening to close Special Agent Friend's complaint unless he consents to the referral of his complaint of systematic abuses back to the alleged abuser, DOJ-OIG's refusal to investigate his allegations—which it agrees are important—on the basis of resource grounds is bafflingly unpersuasive. Inquiries at the heart of great national political controversies like this are the subjects most in need of the sort of independent, nonpartisan, factually grounded, objective review that inspectors general were created to provide.

Could the DOJ-OIG, with its hundreds of agents, attorney, and multiple field offices around the country really be so overextended that it has no capacity to investigate whether:

(1) the FBI's investigative statistics are being skewed to support a false narrative of a nationwide surge in domestic terrorism;

(2) the FBI is selectively using unreasonable force and/or intrusive measures against politically disfavored subjects;

(3) the FBI is retaliating against whistleblowers who disclose and object to 1 and 2; or

(4) the FBI is abusing security clearance processes to avoid following the FBI's standard disciplinary processes?

RECORDS REQUEST

To shed light on the rationale for the DOJ-OIG's refusal to investigate Special Agent Friend's allegations of the FBI's systemic abuses of the Constitution, laws, and policy, pursuant to the Freedom of Information Act ("FOIA"),[38] Empower Oversight requests:

1. All communications between and among DOJ-OIG personnel relative to the information Special Agent Friend submitted on or about September 21, 2022.

2. Any investigative activities undertaken DOJ-OIG to follow-up on or confirm/refute information that Special Agent Friend submitted on or about September 21, 2022.

---

[37] The FBI's Inspection Division "conducts internal investigations, reviews operation performance and use-of-enforcement authorities in all investigative programs, and conducts special inquiries." FBI, *Suzanne Turner Named Assistant Director of the Inspection Division* (February 16, 2022), available at https://www.fbi.gov/news/press-releases/suzanne-turner-named-assistant-director-of-the-inspection-division. The division is currently headed by an assistant director with substantial prior immersion in the FBI's counterterrorism, intelligence, and national security programs. *Id.*

[38] 5 U.S.C. § 552.

3. All information supporting DOJ-OIG's rationale for concluding that the information Special Agent Friend submitted on or about September 21, 2022, did not warrant investigation by DOJ-OIG.

DEFINITIONS

"COMMUNICATION(S)" means every manner or method of disclosure, exchange of information, statement, or discussion between or among two or more persons, including but not limited to, face-to-face and telephone conversations, correspondence, memoranda, telegrams, telexes, email messages, voice-mail messages, text messages, Slack messages, meeting minutes, discussions, releases, statements, reports, publications, and any recordings or reproductions thereof.

"DOCUMENT(S)" or "RECORD(S)" mean any kind of written, graphic, or recorded matter, however produced or reproduced, of any kind or description, whether sent, received, or neither, including drafts, originals, non-identical copies, and information stored magnetically, electronically, photographically or otherwise. As used herein, the terms "DOCUMENT(S)" or "RECORD(S)" include, but are not limited to, studies, papers, books, accounts, letters, diagrams, pictures, drawings, photographs, correspondence, telegrams, cables, text messages, emails, memoranda, notes, notations, work papers, intra-office and inter-office communications, communications to, between and among employees, contracts, financial agreements, grants, proposals, transcripts, minutes, orders, reports, recordings, or other documentation of telephone or other conversations, interviews, affidavits, slides, statement summaries, opinions, indices, analyses, publications, questionnaires, answers to questionnaires, statistical records, ledgers, journals, lists, logs, tabulations, charts, graphs, maps, surveys, sound recordings, data sheets, computer printouts, tapes, discs, microfilm, and all other records kept, regardless of the title, author, or origin.

"PERSON" means individuals, entities, firms, organizations, groups, committees, regulatory agencies, governmental entities, business entities, corporations, partnerships, trusts, and estates.

"REFERS," "REFERRING TO," "REGARDS," REGARDING," "RELATES," "RELATING TO," "CONCERNS," "BEARS UPON," or "PERTAINS TO" mean containing, alluding to, responding to, commenting upon, discussing, showing, disclosing, explaining, mentioning, analyzing, constituting, comprising, evidencing, setting forth, summarizing, or characterizing, either directly or indirectly, in whole or in part.

"INCLUDING" means comprising part of, but not being limited to, the whole.

INSTRUCTIONS

The time period of the requested records is January 6, 2021, through the present.

The words "and" and "or" shall be construed in the conjunctive or disjunctive, whichever is most inclusive.

The singular form shall include the plural form and vice versa.

The present tense shall include the past tense and vice versa.

In producing the records described above, you shall segregate them by reference to each of the numbered items of this FOIA request.

If you have any questions about this request, please contact Bryan Saddler by e-mail at bsaddler@empowr.us.

FEE WAIVER REQUEST

Empower Oversight agrees to pay up to $25.00 in applicable fees, but notes that it qualifies as a "representative of the news media"[39] and requests a waiver of any fees that may be associated with processing this request, in keeping with 5 U.S.C. § 552 (a)(4)(A)(iii).

Empower Oversight is a non-profit educational organization as defined under Section 501(c)(3) of the Internal Revenue Code, which helps insiders safely and legally report waste, fraud, abuse, corruption, and misconduct to the proper authorities, and seeks to hold those authorities accountable to act on such reports by, among other means, publishing information concerning the same. Empower Oversight has no commercial interest in making this request.

Further, the information that Empower Oversight seeks is in the public interest because it is likely to contribute significantly to the public's understanding of the rationale for the DOJ-OIG's refusal to investigate Special Agent Friend's allegations of the FBI's systemic abuses of the Constitution, laws, and policy.

Empower Oversight is committed to government accountability, public integrity, and transparency. In the latter regard, the information that that Empower Oversight receives that tends to explain the subject matter of this FOIA request will be disclosed publicly via its website, and copies will be shared with other news media for public dissemination.

For ease of administration and to conserve resources, we ask that documents be produced in a readily accessible electronic format. Thank you for your time and consideration. Please don't hesitate to contact me with any questions.

Cordially,

/Jason Foster/

Jason Foster
Founder & President

---

[39] On September 23, 2021, in connection with a FOIA appeal arising from Empower Oversight's August 12, 2022, FOIA request, the Securities Exchange Commission conceded that Empower Oversight qualifies as a news media requester for purposes of fees assessed pursuant to the FOIA. *See*, "Empower Oversight Wins Appeal of Erroneous SEC Fee Decision: Must be treated as a "media requestor" in seeking ethics records of senior officials," Empower Oversight Press Release (Sep 24, 2021), https://empowr.us/empower-oversight-wins-appeal-of-erroneous-sec-fee-decision-must-be-treated-as-a-media-requestor-in-seeking-ethics-records-of-senior-officials/. Thereafter, numerous other agencies recognized Empower Oversight as a media requester.

Declaration of Stephen M. Friend

I, Stephen M. Friend, pursuant to 28 U.S.C. §1746, hereby declares as follows:

1. I am a person over eighteen (18) years of age and competent to testify. Upon my belief and information, I make this Declaration on personal knowledge and in support of my complaint of reprisal and disclosure to the Office of Special Counsel, and against the Federal Bureau of Investigation (hereinafter the "FBI").

2. I am an FBI Special Agent currently on suspension. I graduated from the University of Notre Dame in 2007 and was employed as an accountant in private practice between 2007 and 2008. In 2009 I was sworn in as a Peace Officer for the Savannah Chatham Metro Police Department in Savannah Chatham Georgia. I served as a Peace Officer for said Department until 2012 when I joined my father's accounting firm for one year. In 2013 I joined the Pooler Police Department in Pooler Georgia as a Peace Officer until 2014.

3. On June 14, 2014, I joined the FBI as a new agent trainee. Following my graduation from Quantico's New Agent Academy I was posted to the FBI's Omaha Division/Sioux City Resident Agency tasked with investigating violent crimes and major offenses occurring in Indian Country. I was also a member of the FBI's Omaha SWAT Team. While in that posting I also served as an acting Special Supervisory Special Agent.

4. In June of 2021 I was transferred to the FBI's Jacksonville Florida Field Office/Daytona Beach Residency Agency as a Special Agent tasked with investigating child exploitation and human trafficking. In October of 2021, an Assistant Special Agent in Charge (ASAC) informed my supervisor that I was reassigned as a member of the Joint Terrorism Task Force (hereinafter "JTTF") and directed to concentrate my time towards domestic terrorism investigations. The ASAC communicated that the reassignment was necessary due to the voluminous number of J6 investigations and rising threats of "domestic violent extremism."

5. I was also told that child sexual abuse material investigations were no longer an FBI priority and should be referred to local law enforcement agencies. Prior to the incidents described below I received exemplary performance

reviews and numerous awards throughout my eight-year FBI career. Most recently, in July of 2022 the FBI conferred me with an "On-The-Spot" financial award.

6. **My concerns are as follows**: Stephen M. Friend, made a disclosure, of which an acting responsible official had knowledge, after which I was subjected to an adverse action.

7. As background information, full investigation casefiles within the FBI are labeled in three sections. The first section denotes the nature of the criminal offense. The second section identifies the FBI Field Office with responsibility for investigating. The third section is a unique case number populated by the FBI's SENTINEL case management system and attributable to the investigation. Additionally, if the investigating Case Agent requires assistance from another field office (i.e., interviewing a subject or witness who resides out of the Case Agent's geographical area of responsibility), investigative policy guides the Case Agent to "cut a lead" to Special Agents in another Field Office requesting that they take certain investigative action to assist the Case Agent. The "lead" facilitates timely investigation without forcing the Case Agent to engage in costly and time-consuming travel to areas beyond his area of responsibility.

* Domestic Investigations and Operations Guide (DIOG) Appendix J: (U) Case File Management and Indexing

* J.1.2 (U) Investigative Leads and Lead Office (LO)

> (U//FOUO) Leads are sent by EC, or a Lead Request document, to offices and assigned to individuals/organizations in order to aid investigations. When the OO sets a lead to another office, that office is considered a Lead Office (LO). (U//FOUO) There are only two types of investigative leads: "Action Required" and "Information Only."

* J.1.2.1 (U) Action Required Lead

> (U//FOUO) An action required lead must be used if the sending office requires the receiving LO to take some type of investigative action.

> (U//FOUO) An action required lead may only be set out of an open investigative file, including an:

> A) (U) Assessment file;

B) (U) Predicated investigation file;

C) (U) Pending inactive investigation file; or

D) (U) Unaddressed work file...

8. Accordingly, investigations stemming from the January 6, 2021, Capitol Hill protest (hereinafter "J6") could be assigned, according to Domestic Investigations and Operations Guide (DIOG) Appendix J, to Special Agents working at the "Office of Origin (OO)." Per DIOG guidance, Washington D.C. Field Office (WFO) is a logical OO because WFO's area of responsibility includes Washington D.C. If deemed the appropriate OO, any investigations or assessments opened by WFO would be marked with the second section casefile label of "WF." Should investigative actions be necessary outside of Washington D.C., the WFO Case Agent should "cut a lead" to the appropriate FBI Field Office. In the event that an alternative FBI Field Office assumed the role as OO (i.e., because a subject resides in the OO's area of responsibility) any investigations or assessment opened would be marked with the second section casefile label attributable to that Field Office (i.e., "DL" for FBI Dallas). Should investigative actions be necessary outside of the OO's area of the responsibility, the Case Agent should "cut a lead" to the appropriate FBI Field Office. Regardless of the particular OO and according to DIOG Appendix J, the assigned Case Agent assumes management responsibilities for all aspects of the assessment or investigation.

* Domestic Investigations and Operations Guide (DIOG) Appendix J: (U) Case File Management and Indexing.

- o J.1 (U) Investigative File Management
- o J.1.1 (U) Office of Origin (OO)
- o (U/FOUO) Generally the Office of Origin (OO) is determined by:
  - A) (U//FOUO) The residence, location or destination of the subject of the investigation;
  - B) (U//FOUO) The office in which the complaint is first received;
  - C) (U//FOUO) The office designated by FBIHQ as OO in any investigation.

* Domestic Investigations and Operations Guide (DIOG) Appendix J: (U) Case File Management and Indexing

- o J.1 (U) Investigative File Management

o J.1.3 (U) Office of Origin's (OO) Supervision of Cases
   (U//FOUO) The OO is responsible for proper supervision
   of Assessments and investigations in its own territory
   and being conducted in a LO. The FBI employee,
   usually an FBI Special Agent, to whom an investigation
   is assigned, is often referred to as the "Case Agent."
   An FBI employee is personally responsible for ensuring
   all logical investigation is initiated without undue
   delay, whether the employee is assigned in the OO or
   in a LO; this includes setting forth Action Required
   or Information Only leads as appropriate for other
   offices or other FBI employees in his/her own office.
   The OO Case Agent has overall responsibility for
   supervision of the investigation...

The FBI is following an atypical procedure. J6 task force
members in Washington D.C. identify potential subjects and
possible locations where these individuals reside. The task
force disseminates information packets to Field Offices around
the country. If an assessment or investigation is opened for a
J6 subject, the recipient Field Offices become the official OO.
However, while Special Agents and Task Force Officers in these
Field Offices are assigned the role of "Case Agent," the J6 task
force effectively manages the cases and performs the bulk of
investigative work. The Case Agents perform investigative
actions at the direction of the J6 task force. The J6 task
force has the preeminent role for presenting J6 cases to the
United States Attorney's Office for prosecution.

        9.   In October of 2021, I was assigned to J6 cases on
behalf of Special Agents working in Washington D.C. On these
occasions, the J6 Task Force members disseminated information to
my office with instructions to perform logical investigative
actions (such as surveillance or subject interviews). Members
of the Daytona Beach Resident Agency (DBRA) Joint Terrorism Task
Force (JTTF) completed and documented these tasks. Later, J6
Task Force members in Washington D.C. reviewed the work and
requested additional investigative actions be performed or
pressured members of my local JTTF to open full investigations.
The J6 Task Force members assured the JTTF that once the case
was opened, they would perform future investigative work and
paperwork for the casefile. In accordance supervisor roles and
responsibilities outlined in the DIOG, the J6 Task Force
supervisors approved this work before it was submitted to the
casefile. Resultantly, there are active criminal investigations

of J6 subjects in which I am listed as the "Case Agent," but have not done any investigative work. Additionally, my supervisor has not approved any paperwork within the file. J6 Task Force members are serving as Affiants on search and arrest warrant affidavits for subjects whom I have never investigated or even interviewed but am listed as a "Case Agent." The J6 Task Force tasked the DBRA JTTF with executing these warrants.

* Domestic Investigations and Operations Guide (DIOG) 3.5 (U) Supervisor Roles and Responsibilities

* 3.5.2.1 (U) Approval/Review of Investigative or Collection Activities

> (U//FOUO) Anyone in a supervisory role who approves/reviews investigative or collection activity must determine whether the standards for opening, approving, conducting, and closing an investigative activity, collection activity or investigative method, as provided in the DIOG, have been satisfied. (U//FOUO) Only FBI supervisory employees and representatives from other government agencies (OGA) assigned to the FBI under the Joint Duty Assignment Program or the Intergovernmental Personnel Act as supervisors (as defined in DIOG subsection 3.5.1) may approve the serialization of investigative records into Sentinel. Additionally, whenever an OGA supervisor (as described above) approves an investigative record, an FBI supervisor must also approve the record into Sentinel. An OGA supervisor may not approve investigative methods (i.e., DIOG Section 18 methods) or investigative activities (e.g., UDP and OIA).

* Domestic Investigations and Operations Guide (DIOG) Appendix J: (U) Case File Management and Indexing

> o J.1 (U) Investigative File Management
> J.1.3 (U) Office of Origin's (OO) Supervision of Cases
> (U//FOUO) The OO is responsible for proper supervision of Assessments and investigations in its own territory and being conducted in a LO. The FBI employee, usually an FBI Special Agent, to whom an investigation is assigned, is often referred to as the "Case Agent." An FBI employee is personally responsible for ensuring

all logical investigation is initiated without undue delay, whether the employee is assigned in the OO or in a LO; this includes setting forth Action Required or Information Only leads as appropriate for other offices or other FBI employees in his/her own office. The OO Case Agent has overall responsibility for supervision of the investigation…

10.   During the week of August 15, 2022, I became aware of imminent arrests of J6 subjects and searches of their respective residences within the FBI's Jacksonville and Tampa Field Office areas of responsibility. Simultaneous takedowns were scheduled to occur on August 24, 2022. Due to perceived threats levels, an FBI SWAT team was enlisted to arrest one of the arrests. On Friday, August 19, 2022, I spoke with my front-line supervisor, SSRA Greg Federico, on two separate occasions to disclose my concerns about potential DIOG policy violations employed during the investigative processes. SSRA Federico listened to my concerns but emphasized that the warrants were lawful court orders. He said that these operations were one step in the process and that the subjects would be afforded all due process.

11.   I responded that it was inappropriate to use an FBI SWAT team to arrest a subject for misdemeanor offenses and opined that the subject would likely face extended detainment and biased jury pools in Washington D.C. I suggested alternatives such as the issuance of a court summons or utilizing surveillance groups to determine an optimal, safe time for a local sheriff deputy to contact the subjects and advise them about the existence of the arrest warrant. SSRA Federico told me that FBI executive management considered all potential alternatives and determined the SWAT takedown was the appropriate course of action. SSRA Federico noted that I appeared to be under stress and suggested speaking to the FBI's employee assistance program. SSRA Federico told me that he respected how I was standing on principle, but I was putting him in a difficult situation because Special Agents cannot refuse to participate in specific cases. He stated that he wished I just "called in sick" for this warrant but his hands were tied now that I told him that I was going to refuse to participate in any J6 cases. Per the Office of Personnel Management, "an employee is entitled to use sick leave for: personal medical needs, family care or bereavement, care of a family member with a serious health condition, and adoption-related purposes." SSRA Federico told me that the FBI plans to prosecute every subject

associated with J6 and he expected "another wave" of J6 subjects would be referred to the Daytona Beach Resident Agency for investigation and arrest. SSRA Federico asked how I thought the Special Agent in Charge (SAC) of FBI Jacksonville would react to my position. He told me that it sounded like my concerns were with FBI leadership and the overall nature of the J6 investigations. SSRA Federico threatened reprisal indirectly by asking how long I saw myself continuing to work for the FBI. He asked me to reconsider my position and told me that he would decide on his actions over the course of the weekend.

12.   On August 22, 2022, I was contacted by Jacksonville's Assistant Special Agent in Charge (ASAC) Coult Markovsky, who requested that I attend a meeting at the FBI Jacksonville office the following afternoon. On August 23, 2022, I met with ASAC Markovksy and ASAC Sean Ryan. I again disclosed my concerns about potential DIOG policy violations employed during the J6 investigative processes. I told that the irregular case dissemination, labeling, and management processes could be considered exculpatory evidence the must be disclosed to defendants in accordance with the Brady rule. I expressed my concerns about violating citizens' Sixth Amendment rights due overzealous charging by the DOJ and biased jury pools in Washington D.C. I cautioned about the similarities between Ruby Ridge, the Governor Whitmer kidnapping case, and the J6 investigation. ASAC Markovsky said that I lacked perspective on the J6 prosecutions because I was not principally involved in the day-to-day investigations. He added that it is the FBI's job to gather facts, but we are not responsible for determining if an individual should be prosecuted. I countered that former FBI Director James Comey's actions indicated this was no longer an FBI practice when he stated that "no reasonable prosecutor" would bring charges against former Secretary of State Hillary Clinton.

13.   The ASACs asked if I believed the J6 rioters committed a crime. I responded that some of the people who entered the Capitol committed crimes, but others were innocent. I elaborated that I believed some innocent individuals had been unjustly prosecuted, convicted, and sentenced. ASAC Markovsky unironically asked if I thought that the individuals who "killed police officers" should be prosecuted. I replied that there were no police officers killed on January 6, 2021. ASAC Markovsky told me that I was being a bad teammate to my colleagues. The ASACs threatened reprisal again by warning that my refusal could

amount to insubordination. References were made to my future career prospects with the FBI. ASAC Ryan suggested I might want to speak with the FBI's employee assistance program about my emotional concerns with J6 cases. The ASACs informed me that I could not refuse to participate if FBI leadership was comfortable that an operation is Constitutional, within FBI guidelines, and did not present an unnecessary risk to my safety.

14. I responded by again disclosing that the facts and concerns I presented demonstrated how the J6 investigations violate all three elements. I told them that I would not participate in any of these operations. At the conclusion of the meeting, the ASACs opined that they did not know how they would proceed with me from a disciplinary perspective. They emphasized that any punitive action would be a slow process. However, four hours later ASAC Markovsky emailed me the following act of reprisal: "After multiple conversations with SSRA Greg Federico and our continued conversations today with myself and ASAC Ryan, you continue to refuse to participate in an FBI mission to serve a lawful court order issued by a Federal Judge. You are not to report to the Daytona Beach RA tomorrow, August 24, 2022, and you will be placed on AWOL (Absent Without Leave) status. AWOL in itself is not disciplinary, but can lead to disciplinary charges, such as removal." ASAC Markovksy and ASAC Ryan stated that all the details of our meeting were Unclassified.

15. On September 1, 2022, I met with FBI Jacksonville Special Agent in Charge (SAC) Sherry Onks. SAC Onks told me that I had a reputation as a good Special Agent and expressed disappointment with my refusal to participate in the January 6th investigations. SAC Onks suggested that I do "some soul searching" and decide if I wanted to work for the FBI. SAC Onks said that it "sounded like I lost faith in the FBI and its leadership." SAC Onks stated that the J6 investigations were all legal, ethical, and in accordance with FBI procedure. She said that my refusal to participate in the cases meant that I did not trust my colleagues' work and indicated that I believed the Special Agents working on J6 were coopted into behaving unethically and immorally. I again disclosed by informing SAC Onks that I believed the investigations were inconsistent with FBI procedure and resulted in the violation of citizens' Sixth and Eighth Amendment rights. I added that many of my colleagues expressed similar concerns to me but had not vocalized their objections to FBI Executive Management. SAC Onks disagreed with

my premise and said that my views represented an extremely small minority of the FBI workforce. SAC Onks told me that she had never encountered my situation during her career. She recalled the fear she felt while sitting on the seventh floor of the J. Edgar Hoover Building on January 6, 2021 when protestors "seized the Capitol" and threatened the United States' democracy. SAC Onks reprised against me and admitted as much, when she informed me that she referred me to the FBI's Office of Professional Responsibility and Security Division. SAC Onks told me that the Security Division was assessing my security clearance.

16.   In addition to the atypical Originating Office identification process for J6 cases, the process potentially violates Case Manager and Case File Management and Indexing policies listed in the FBI's Domestic Investigations and Operations Guide (DIOG). These potential violations include:

- Domestic Investigations and Operations Guide (DIOG) 3.3 (U) Special Agent/Task Force Officer (TFO)/Task Force Member (TFM)/Task Force Participant (TFP)/FBI Contractor/Others – Roles and Responsibilities
    - 3.3.1.10 (U) Serve as Investigation ("Case") Manager: (U//FOUO) If assigned responsibility for an investigation, manage all aspects of that investigation, until it is assigned to another person. It is the case manager's responsibility to ensure compliance with all applicable laws, rules, regulations, and guidelines, both investigative and administrative, from the opening of the investigation through disposition of the evidence, until the investigation is assigned to another person…
- Domestic Investigations and Operations Guide (DIOG) Appendix J: (U) Case File Management and Indexing
    - J.1 (U) Investigative File Management
      J.1.3 (U) Office of Origin's (OO) Supervision of Cases (U//FOUO) The OO is responsible for proper supervision of Assessments and investigations in its own territory and being conducted in a LO. The FBI employee, usually an FBI Special Agent, to whom an investigation is assigned, is often referred to as the "Case Agent." An FBI employee is personally responsible for ensuring all logical investigation is initiated without undue delay, whether the employee is assigned in the OO or in a LO; this includes setting forth Action Required or

Information Only leads as appropriate for other offices or other FBI employees in his/her own office. The OO Case Agent has overall responsibility for supervision of the investigation...

The manipulative casefile practice creates false and misleading crime statistics, constituting false official federal statements 18 U.S.C. §1001. Instead of hundreds of investigations stemming from an isolated incident at the Capitol on January 6, 2021, FBI and DOJ officials point to significant increases in domestic violent extremism and terrorism around the United States. At no point was I advised or counseled on where to take my disclosure beyond the reprising officials above; the threatened reprisal constituted a *de facto* gag on my whistleblowing.

17. The acting officials who had knowledge of my disclosures as set forth above included SSRA Greg Federico, Jacksonville's Assistant Special Agent in Charge (ASAC) Coult Markovsky, ASAC Sean Ryan, and FBI Jacksonville Special Agent in Charge (SAC) Sherry Onks.

18. I was reprised against and instructed to not report to the Daytona Beach RA on August 24, 2022, and was placed on AWOL status. When I arrived at the FBI's Daytona Beach Field Office on the morning of September 19, 2022, I was brought into a meeting with my supervisor, ASAC, SAC, and security officer. I was told that my security clearance was suspended pending an investigation. My credentials, firearm, and badge were confiscated, and I was escorted from the building.

19. I also received the letter annexed hereto and made a part hereof dated September 16, 2022.

I do solemnly affirm under the penalties of perjury and upon personal knowledge that the contents of the above statement are true to the best of my knowledge.

Stephen M. Friend L.S.

Stephen M. Friend
September 21, 2022

STATEMENT OF FACTS

Your affiant, ███████████ is a Special Agent assigned to the Federal Bureau of Investigation Washington Field Office Joint Terrorism Task Force. In my duties as a Special Agent, I investigate criminal activity pertaining to international and domestic terrorism. Currently, I am tasked with investigating criminal activity in and around the United States Capitol and its grounds on January 6, 2021. As a Special Agent, I am authorized by law or by a government agency to engage in or supervise the prevention, detection, investigation, or prosecution of a violation of Federal criminal laws.

The Capitol is secured twenty-four hours a day by United States Capitol Police. Restrictions around the Capitol include permanent and temporary security barriers and posts manned by USCP. Only authorized people with appropriate identification were allowed access inside the Capitol. On January 6, 2021, the exterior plaza of the Capitol was closed to members of the public.

On January 6, 2021, a joint session of the United States Congress convened at the Capitol, located at First Street, SE, in Washington, D.C. During the joint session, elected members of the United States House of Representatives and the United States Senate were meeting in separate chambers of the Capitol to certify the vote count of the Electoral College of the 2020 Presidential Election, which had taken place on Tuesday, November 3, 2020. The joint session began at approximately 1:00 p.m. Shortly thereafter, by approximately 1:30 p.m., the House and Senate adjourned to separate chambers to resolve a particular objection. Vice President Mike Pence was present and presiding, first in the joint session, and then in the Senate chamber.

As the proceedings continued in both the House and the Senate, and with Vice President Michael R. Pence present and presiding over the Senate, a large crowd gathered outside the Capitol. As noted above, temporary barricades and permanent barricades were in place around the exterior of the Capitol. USCP officers were present and attempting to keep the crowd away from the Capitol and the certification proceedings underway inside.

While the certification proceedings were underway, the exterior doors and windows of the Capitol were locked or otherwise secured. USCP officers attempted to maintain order and keep the crowd from entering the Capitol. Around 2:00 p.m., however, individuals in the crowd forced entry into the Capitol, including by breaking windows and by assaulting USCP officers. Others in the crowd encouraged and assisted those acts.

Shortly thereafter, at approximately 2:20 p.m., members of the House of Representatives and Senate, including the President of the Senate, Vice President Pence, were instructed to—and did—evacuate the chambers. Accordingly, the joint session of Congress was effectively suspended until shortly after 8:00 p.m. Vice President Pence remained in the Capitol from the time he was evacuated from the Senate Chamber to the time the session resumed.

During national news coverage of the aforementioned events, video footage which appeared to be captured on mobile devices of persons present on the scene depicted evidence of violations of local and federal law, including scores of individuals inside the Capitol without authority to be there.

B SQUAD

Organization

The FBI is investigating a group of individuals that self-identify as B SQUAD, referred to collectively herein as B SQUAD. The following interchange occurred on social media on December 2, 2020, between an individual whose identity is known to the FBI and another individual who acts as one of the leaders of B SQUAD—subsequently referred to herein as B Leader.

Individual 1:   Now, I think it would be hysterical if you got morale patches that said "plan B" or "B squad" because I think it's one of the top 3 funniest things I've personally ever heard from politicians as they try to dance around the M word lmao

Obviously

B Leader: Hahahahaha

I am going to name DC operation plan B[1]

The individuals of B Squad that are being charged via Criminal Complaint to include this affidavit are the following—[1] BENJAMIN COLE, [2] BRIAN PRELLER, [3] JOHN EDWARD CROWLEY, [4] JONATHAN ROCKHOLT, and [5] TYLER QUINTIN BENSCH. The facts included below are intended to show that on January 6, 2021, these five individuals engaged in criminal behavior in connection with the riot at the U.S. Capitol on January 6, 2021. Specifically, the first four named individuals (Cole, Preller, Crowley, Rockholt) are each alleged to have knowingly committed an act or attempted to commit an act with the intended purpose of obstructing, impeding, or interfering with one or more law enforcement officers while the law enforcement officers were engaged in the lawful performance of their official duties incident to and during a civil disorder, and that this civil disorder in any way or degree obstructed, delayed, or adversely affected either commerce or the movement of any article or commodity in commerce.

The five individuals, including Bensch, are also alleged to have knowingly entered or remained in a restricted building or on restricted grounds without lawful authority to do so. The five individuals are further alleged to have engaged in disorderly or disruptive conduct in, or within such proximity to, any restricted building or grounds at a time that such conduct, in fact, impeded or disrupted the orderly conduct of Government business or official functions; and did so

---

[1] Based on information gained through the course of this investigation, I believe that when Individual 1 referred to the "M word," they are referring to militias. I further believe that when they discuss a plan B/B Squad, they are referring to an alternate plan to be in place if they do not get the desired electoral outcome (i.e., the former president remaining in power).

knowingly, and with intent to impede or disrupt the orderly conduct of Government business or official functions.

The individuals named herein self-identify as "three percenters" (AKA "3%ers", "III%ers", or "Threepers") based on their adherence to the sub-ideology or common belief known as Three Percenterism. Many of the individual militia-style organizations have local chapters and names, such as the Georgia Security Force, the Michigan United Patriots Three Percent, the California Patriots—DC Brigade, and—in this case—the Guardians of Freedom. As explained below, Cole, Preller, Crowley, Rockholt, and Bensch are also self-identified members of a Guardians of Freedom subgroup called B SQUAD. [2] Below is how the Guardians of Freedom logo appeared on and prior to January 6 (*left*) and how it appears now.

---

[2] Three Percenters Militia violent extremists sometimes self-identify as three percenters ("III%ers" or "threepers") based on the myth that only three percent of American colonists took up arms against the British during the American Revolution. Some III%ers regard the present-day U.S. Government as analogous to British authorities during the Revolution in terms of infringements on civil liberties. While many independent or multi-state militia groups incorporate III% in their unit names, the term is less indicative of membership in a single overarching group than it is representative of a common belief in the notion that a small force (three percent of the population) that is armed and prepared, and with a just cause, can overthrow a perceived tyrannical government.

See also https://www.splcenter.org/fighting-hate/extremist-files/group/three-percenters, https://www.adl.org/resources/backgrounders/three-percenters.

Pursuant to a search warrant that was executed on the account of a known B SQUAD member, the following image or flyer was sent to a B SQUAD distribution list on or about December 24, 2020.

CALLING ALL PATRIOTS!!

On Jan 6th, 2021, the March for Trump Bus tour, powered by Women for America First, is rolling into Washington D.C. to demand transparency and election integrity.

The Guardians of Freedom III% are responding to the call from President Donald J. Trump to assist in the security, protection, and support of the people as we all protest the fraudulent election and re-establish liberty for our nation. JOIN US & Thousands of other Patriots!

We are ALL in this fight because we have seen imminent destruction of the United States of America. We will not let the infrastructure of our nation fall by the left as they control the people by muzzling them with masks, instilling fear, and forced into lockdown. This is about control. You are witnessing the destruction of our Constitutional Republic our forefathers fought and died for 244 years ago.

Remember this, it comes straight from our Declaration of Independence, that whenever any form of government becomes destructive, it is the right & duty of the people to alter or to abolish it. That is why YOU are here. For massive change to occur, massive action must be taken. Patriots, we are the lifeblood of this great nation & its time we prove that.

For the Guardians of Freedom members to deploy, help secure & defend the people at the January 6th event, it will take tremendous support from all of you to assist with the sharing and contributing to our events, missions, and fundraisers.

Please consider donating to assist with our next critical mission on January 6th, 2021

Thank you & God Bless America.

Donation Link: https://cash.app/$PatriotGOF#

www.threepercent-gof.com

An individual whose identity is known to the FBI and who is referenced to as "B Leader" for purposes of this affidavit, coordinated the group's travel from Florida to Washington, D.C., and their lodging in Washington, D.C. B Leader reserved a block of rooms at a hotel that is near to the U.S. Capitol, and he, the five individuals named in this Statement of Facts, and approximately forty other members of B SQUAD stayed on the same floor of that hotel on January 5, 2021.

The government sought and obtained a search warrant for B Leader's Facebook account. On or about December 30, 2021, B Leader posted the following graphic on his Facebook account.

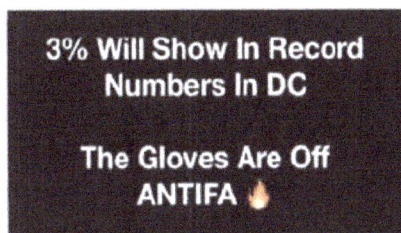

> 3% Will Show In Record Numbers In DC
>
> The Gloves Are Off ANTIFA 🔥

In Facebook communications on or about January 3 and 4, 2021, B Leader discussed meeting with one or more other individuals at an event in Freedom Plaza in Washington, D.C., on January 5, 2021. B Leader spoke at a rally in Freedom Plaza on January 5, 2021.

On January 3, 2021, B Leader published a video on his Facebook account intended for those traveling to Washington, D.C. The video was accompanied by the following written comment: "Quick safety video for your trip to DC! […] See you all January 6th #patriotsriseup."

In the January 3 video, B Leader wore a black tactical vest displaying the words "B SQUAD" and a patch associated with the "Three Percenters" movement (i.e., "III") on the front. During the video, B Leader:

1. Advised that the video was for "all of you Patriots out there that are going to Washington, D.C., [. . .] to support Trump, to have your voices heard" and that "we are going to have four more years of Trump, we all know that";

2. Warned that "we all know in D.C., once the sun goes down, things get a little bit violent and the reason why things get a little bit violent is because you have socialist, leftist, Marxist, communist agitators like Black Lives Matter and Antifa […]";

3. Described so-called "defensive tools" to take to Washington, D.C., including "the strongest pepper spray commercially available to use," an ASP baton (i.e., an expandable metal baton), knives with blades that were 3 inches or less, a walking cane, and a taser, all items that B Leader incorrectly claimed were legal in Washington, D.C.; and

4. Said that he was "super excited about DC on the 6th of January," and he advised "patriots [to] keep up the fight."

Throughout the video, B Leader stands in front of a group of individuals wearing military-style gear and face coverings, many of whom appeared to possess assault rifles.

Below are images of B Leader in the January 3 video displaying some of the "defensive tools" he suggested others bring to Washington, D.C., including an expandable metal baton, a walking cane, and a folding knife.

On January 6, 2021, on the restricted grounds of the U.S. Capitol, a group of B SQUAD members, including [1] BENJAMIN COLE, [2] BRIAN PRELLER, [3] JOHN EDWARD CROWLEY, [4] JONATHAN ROCKHOLT, and [5] TYLER QUINTIN BENSCH:

1. displayed various indicia of membership in the III%-ers, Guardians of Freedom, or B SQUAD on their clothing while committing criminal acts; and

2. wore riot gear—including tactical vests and helmets—and possessed expandable metal batons, chemical irritants, knives, and walking sticks. Those with walking sticks appeared to intend to use them as impact weapons, as opposed to being mere walking aids. None of the individuals who carried the long wooden poles are known to have a condition that requires the use of a walking stick.

The Inaugural Stage

During each presidential inauguration, the Architect of the Capitol (AOC) coordinates with the Joint Congressional Committee on Inaugural Ceremonies, Secret Service, the military, Department of Homeland Security, Presidential Inaugural Committee, District Government, and all of the AOC's Congressional partners to prepare the Capitol for the Inauguration. One such task is the creation from scratch of the 10,000 square foot Inaugural platform. One part of that process includes turning a west entrance to the Capitol, into a smaller, tighter, tunnel-like area that has commonly been referred to as "The Tunnel" in investigations and prosecutions surrounding January 6, 2021. The two photos below show the West Side of the Capitol as set up for Inauguration Day (*top*) and a closer view of The Tunnel (*bottom*).

At 12:53 p.m., rioters breached their first barricade at the Peace Circle onto Pennsylvania Walkway. Just under two hours later, at approximately 2:41 p.m., the rioters made their way past several additional lines of police officers and barricades to The Tunnel, which provides direct access into the Capitol. The siege on The Tunnel lasted for over two hours, until approximately 5:00 p.m.

Rioters attempted on multiple occasions to forcibly enter the Capitol through the line of USCP and Metropolitan Police Department (MPD) officers who gathered in The Tunnel and successfully repelled the attack. During the two plus hours, rioters assaulted the officers with blunt objects, including poles and crutches, and they used chemical irritants against the officers. Rioters also attempted to use their numbers and collective mass in a heave-ho effort to push the officers back. At times, the rioters forcibly pressed the officers' bodies against each other and against the doorway, crushing them. Subgroup B members [1] Benjamin James Cole, [2] John Edward Crowley, [3] Brian Michael Preller, and [4] Jonathan Alan Rockholt participated in at least one attempt by rioters to force their way through into the Capitol through the line of police officers. [5] Tyler Quintin Bensch moved with the other four B SQUAD members and was present when one of the heave-ho pushes against the officers occurred.

[1] Benjamin James Cole

On January 6, 2021, a 38-year-old white male named Benjamin James Cole had a full beard and a mustache. Cole was wearing the following items:

1. a red flannel-type shirt and tan/brownish pants;
2. sunglasses and a green knit hat under a green baseball cap bearing a patch with the words "pedophile hunter" and a rifle graphic in orange;
3. tactical vest and a drab colored scarf with a distinct pattern; and
4. a backpack with the word "THREE PERCENTER."

Cole also possessed, what appears to be, a black expandable metal baton in his back pocket.

The following are images of Cole obtained from open-source videos or images taken from within the restricted Capitol Grounds on January 6, 2021:

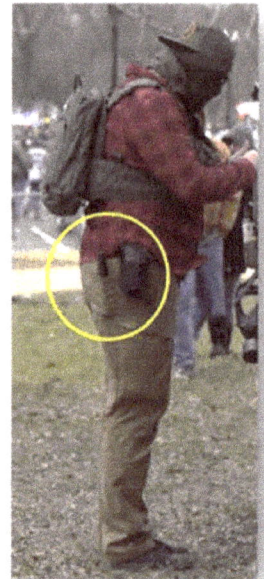

[2] John Edward Crowley

On January 6, 2021, a 50-year-old white male named John Edward Crowley was pictured wearing the following items while on restricted Capitol grounds:

1. a black and gray jacket;
2. a grayish and white baseball cap with the letters "USA" in red on the front;
3. a black scarf or neck gaiter; and
4. a large drab scarf with a distinct design.

The following are images of Crowley obtained from U.S. Capitol surveillance and open-source videos or images taken from within the restricted Capitol Grounds:

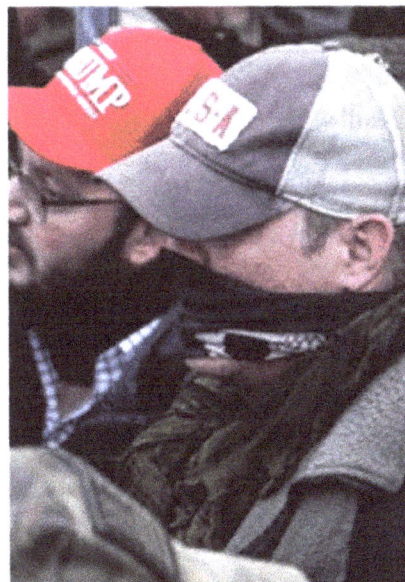

[3] Brian Michael Preller

On January 6, 2021, a 32-year-old white male named Brian Michael Preller was pictured wearing the following items while on restricted Capitol grounds:

1. a blue shirt with the words "WATERBOARDING INSTRUCTOR," blue jeans, black gloves, a black belt, and a black neck gaiter or turtleneck shirt (under his blue shirt);
2. large goggles and a green helmet with the word "monster" on the back in white; and
3. green tactical vest with a chemical irritant spray attached to the front.

Preller also possessed a long black walking stick. Preller had the phrase "B SQUAD" on the back of his tactical vest armor. The following are images of Preller obtained from open-source videos and/or images taken from within the restricted Capitol Grounds:

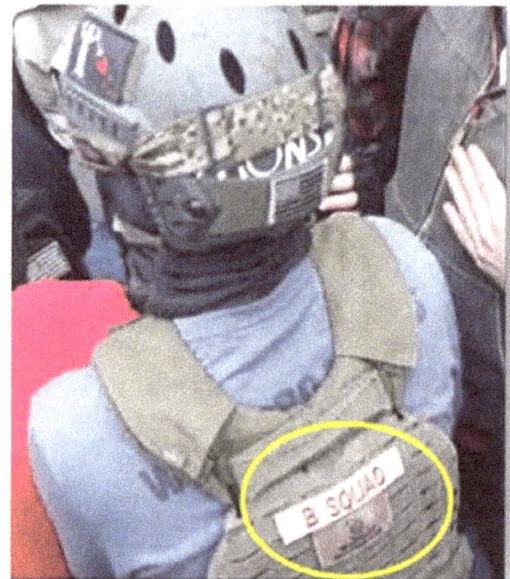

[4] Jonathan Alan Rockholt

On January 6, 2021, a 37-year-old white male named Johnathan Alan Rockholt was pictured wearing the following items while on restricted Capitol grounds:

1. an olive-green quilted jacket, blue jeans, and black gloves;
2. a tactical vest with a patch associated with the "Three Percenters" movement (i.e., "III");
3. a drab neck gaiter and sunglasses;
4. a grayish baseball helmet with a red, white, and blue skull on the back, yellow Gadsden flag[3] symbols on the sides, what appears to be, the logo for "GoF" (described below) and a U.S. flag on the front; and
5. what appears to be a knife in his front right pocket.

The following are images of Rockholt obtained from open-source videos and/or images taken from within the restricted Capitol Grounds:

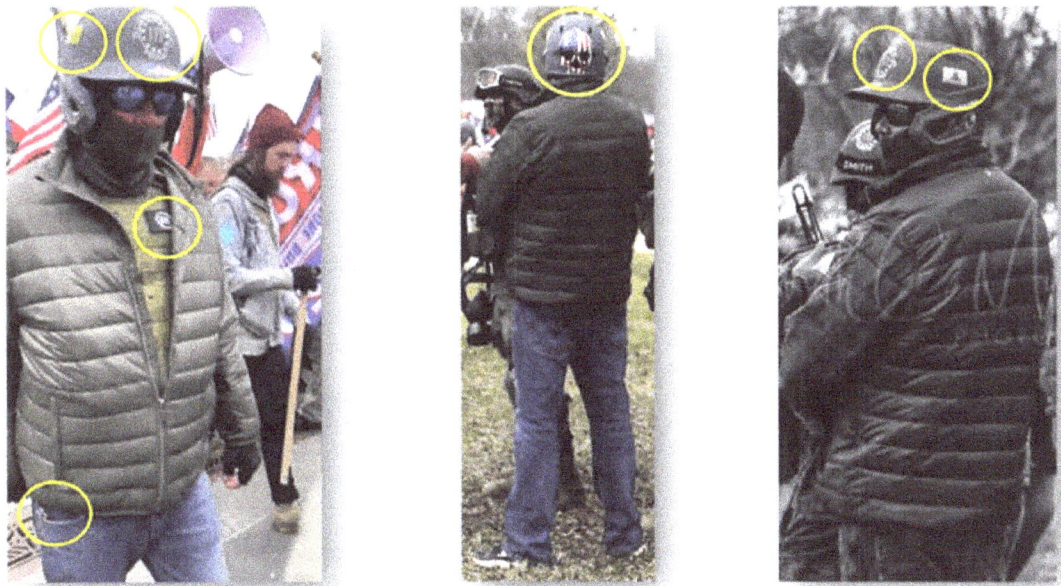

---

[3] The Gadsden flag is a historical American flag with a yellow background. Depicted on the flag is a coiled rattlesnake and the words "Dont [or, Don't] Tread on Me."

[5] Tyler Quintin Bensch

On January 6, 2021, a 20-year-old white male named Tyler Quintin Bensch was pictured wearing the following items while on restricted Capitol grounds:

1. green military fatigues and tan gloves;
2. a military-type helmet and goggles with the brand name "SMITH" in white on a black strap;
3. a tactical vest with a patch associated with the "Three Percenters" movement (i.e., "III");
4. a black gas mask with a green filter; and
5. a drab colored scarf with a distinct pattern.

Bensch also possessed:

1. one or more chemical irritant canisters on the front of his tactical vest;
2. a black radio and antennae on his left side; and
3. a GoPro style camera mounted on his right shoulder.

The following are images of Bensch obtained from open-source videos or images taken within the restricted Capitol Grounds:

Actions of Subgroup B at The Tunnel

Cole, Preller, Crowley, Rockholt, and Bensch were present on the Lower West Terrace and in The Tunnel on January 6, 2021. Each of the individuals joined the group of rioters who were attempting to force their way past the officers responsible for securing The Tunnel, an entry to the Capitol that provides immediate and unobstructed access to sensitive areas and offices used by Members of Congress. The following images depict B SQUAD members Cole, Preller, Crowley, and Rockholt preparing to enter and then entering The Tunnel. In the top left image below, Bensch is using a digital device in a manner consistent with taking pictures or recording video of the area, of the crowd, and of The Tunnel.

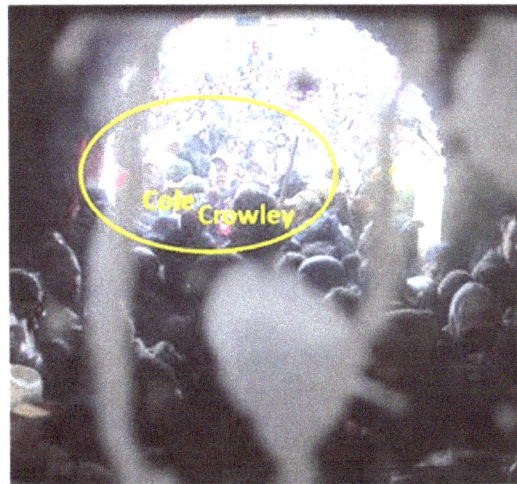

During the siege of The Tunnel that stretched from 2:41 p.m. for more than two hours, rioters pushed into The Tunnel and were repelled in a constant back-and-forth of heave-ho efforts by the rioters and resistance by the officers. Some members of Congress were sheltering in place near that entrance. The effort ultimately failed.

A full review of the applicable surveillance footage, including video of such individuals approaching the entrance to the tunnel, shows that Cole, Preller, Crowley, and Rockholt went into The Tunnel while Bensch remained only just outside. While inside The Tunnel, Cole, Preller, Crowley, and Rockholt confronted and assisted the crowd in confronting the police officers that were preventing The Tunnel and the Capitol from being breached. Specifically, while inside The Tunnel, Cole, Preller, Crowley, and Rockholt added their force, momentum, bodies, and efforts to the other rioters in a "heave-ho" effort. This put intense aggregate pressure on the police line in front of the rioters.

On the south side of The Tunnel, Preller was the closest in proximity to police, pushing his way forward to a point where Preller was essentially the person behind the person who was directly against police officers. Also, on the south side of The Tunnel, Crowley and Cole were in what is roughly equivalent to the third and fourth rows of rioters behind the police line. On the north side of The Tunnel, Rockholt was similarly in the third or fourth row, joining the rioters in pushing against the police line. Due to the tightly packed nature of the rioters in The Tunnel, Cole, Preller, Crowley, and Rockholt were all within a matter of feet of the police line when they lent their bodies to the rioters' collective "heave-ho" efforts to breach the line of police officers and force their way into the Capitol.

As a direct result of the combined actions of Cole, Preller, Crowley, Rockholt, and the other rioters in The Tunnel at that time, the rioters penetrated deeper into The Tunnel, the police line in was pushed farther back, and the rioters came closer to breaching that entry into the Capitol than at any other point on January 6, 2021.

After the officers succeeded in repelling Cole, Preller, Crowley, Rockholt, and other rioters out of The Tunnel, Rockholt picked up a clear riot shield with a USCP seal that appears to have been taken from officers by other rioters. The five made their way from The Tunnel to the west side of the Lower West Terrace where Bensch rinsed out Rockholt's eyes.

The following images show Cole, Preller, Crowley, Rockholt, and Bensch leaving The Tunnel, Rockholt picking up the USCP riot shield, and Bensch member rinsing out Rockholt's eyes following deployment of chemical irritants in the area.

While on the Lower West Terrace, Bensch used one of his chemical irritants to spray the face of an individual who an unknown member of the crowd claimed was "Antifa." Based on a review of a video of this incident, it does not appear that the individual who was sprayed by Bensch posed any type of threat to Bensch or others. The following images show Bensch spraying the other individual, the victim appearing to be in pain after being sprayed, and Bensch looking in the direction of the victim.

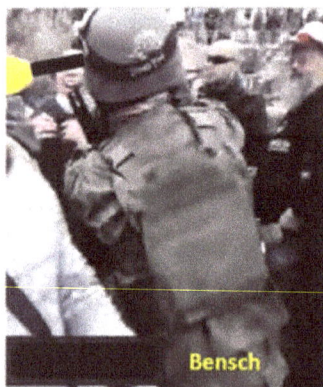

Video from various sources shows Crowley and Rockholt heading west, towards First Street, NW. In the surveillance video, it appears that Bensch carried the riot shield Rockholt took from the Lower West Terrace.

The Identification of Certain B Squad Members

According to records and information obtained from Hilton Corporation employees, including those employed at the Hampton Inn Washington-Downtown-Convention Center located in Washington, D.C.:

1. Between on or about December 23 to 25, 2021, a client called the "Black Group" reserved fifteen hotel rooms for January 5 to 7, 2021, at the Hampton Inn Washington-Downtown Convention Center. The "Client Representative" for the group was B Leader (whose identity is known to the FBI). A credit card in B Leader's name was used to reserve the rooms.

2. Between on or about January 4 and 5, 2021, approximately forty individuals associated with the group's reservation checked into the hotel and were given approximately twenty rooms on the hotel's third floor, including B Leader, Cole, Crowley, Rockholt, and Bensch. The group checked out on January 7, 2021.

3. According to Witness 1, a hotel employee, the group used white and gray Chrysler minivans, and, on January 6, 2021, group members were wearing tactical gear such as military style vests, zip ties, pepper spray, and clip-on knives, and had police-type batons, helmets, and masks.[4]

Benjamin Cole

Cole has been identified as engaging in the conduct attributed to him above based on, among other things, the following:

1. In or around March and May 2021, Cole was interviewed by the FBI regarding the events of January 6. During the initial interview (in-person), Cole admitted being in Washington, D.C., on January 6, 2021. Cole denied that he or anyone that he was with was close to the Capitol. Cole believed that the closest he got was a road in front of the Capitol. During a second interview, Cole admitted that he was within a "courtyard area" and saw ten to twelve riot shields on the ground. Cole denied picking up or taking any of the riot shields. Based on the context of Cole's statement, as well as open source and other video of police riot shields within the restricted Capitol Grounds, it appears Cole's admission to being within a "courtyard area" and seeing riot shields on the ground was a reference to being within the restricted Capitol Grounds.

---

[4] Another hotel employee, who said he/she had a medical condition that caused memory problems, advised agents that a couple members of the group were wearing clothing that resembled armor, but the group did not have weapons. This employee also believed that the group was driving a white SUV displaying a window decal of former President Trump.

2. Based on a comparison of Cole's Florida driver's license image and the video and images of Cole's exposed face with sunglasses, it appears that Cole is the person identified as Cole above.

3. Hotels records reflect Cole as one of the guests associated with the Black Group reservation. Cole was in the same room as Crowley.

4. An FBI agent interviewed Cole in person on March 18, 2021, and May 11, 2021. That same agent viewed photographs of Cole on January 6,2021, showing Cole leaving The Tunnel and at other times on that same date. The agent identifies that Cole, the person he interviewed, is the same individual in the photos from January 6, 2021.

5. On January 15, 2022, Your Affiant interviewed a tipster. This tipster had interacted with Cole in a friendly, social setting (a bar) numerous times. When I showed the tipster photos of Cole on January 6, 2021, the tipster responded, "Yes, that looks like him."

6. According to Verizon records, telephone number (352) 360-XXXX was subscribed to Benjamin Cole ("Cole Phone") between approximately August 2017 and April 2021. The address listed for Cole in the Verizon records is the same as Cole's address according to Florida driver's license records. According to information obtained pursuant to a search warrant, Cole Phone was identified as having utilized a cell site consistent with providing service to a geographic area that included the interior of the United States Capitol building on January 6, 2021.

7. Based on a review of public images on Cole Instagram, there is an image of Cole in which a tattoo of small yellow rectangles is visible on Cole's right wrist. A similar tattoo is visible on the right wrist of the individual identified above as Cole on January 6. The image on the left below is from Cole Instagram. The image on the right is an image from a video of Cole at the entrance of the tunnel on the Capitol's west side.

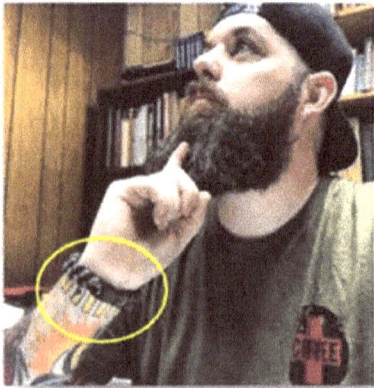

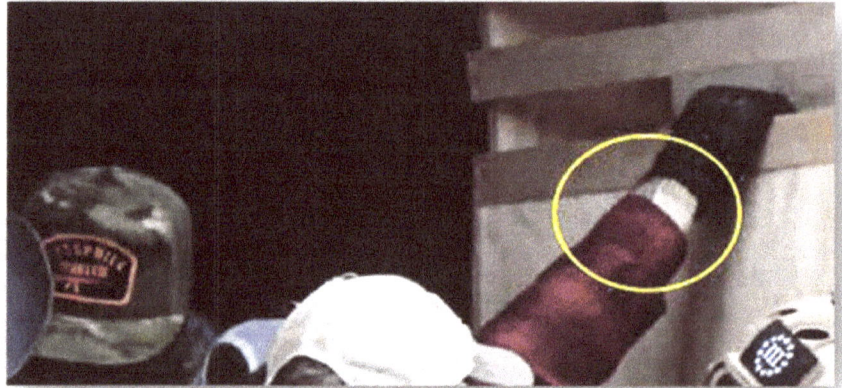

8. Another image from Cole Instagram appears to depict Cole wearing body armor with a unique patch on the upper right portion of Cole's chest (left image below). Cole wore similar body armor with what appears to be the same unique patch on the upper right portion of his chest at the Capitol on January 6 (right image below).

9. According to Facebook records, Cole Instagram is registered to an individual with the first name of "Ben" (i.e., Cole's first name) and no last name was provided. The account's vanity name and account identifier is "i_am_zombenji" and Cole Phone is listed as the accounts verified phone number. In addition, as referenced above, public postings on the account appear to contain images of Cole.

10. On or about January 2022, the following message was posted on Cole's Facebook account apparently regarding his conduct on January 6 and the instant investigation. The message states:

> This isn't really a post I want to make, but I will make it because it's funny to me . . . .
>
> I just want the FBI agent that's still investing [sic] me know . . . . . most anyone you call knows absolutely nothing about what I did in January of 2021. I also did nothing wrong while I was where I was. I would further like to add that you are wasting tax payer dollars by continuing to investigate something that will lead you to absolutely nothing.
>
> My closing arguments are will forever include that, you are a joke and you're [sic] bureau is a joke. Why don't you do something productive with your time and investigate the members of Congress for insider trading? Because I really want to know how someone who's [sic] salary is $174,000 a year, was able to increase their net worth into the millions in less than a decade.
>
> Thank you for your time. I'm glad it was wasted on me 😋

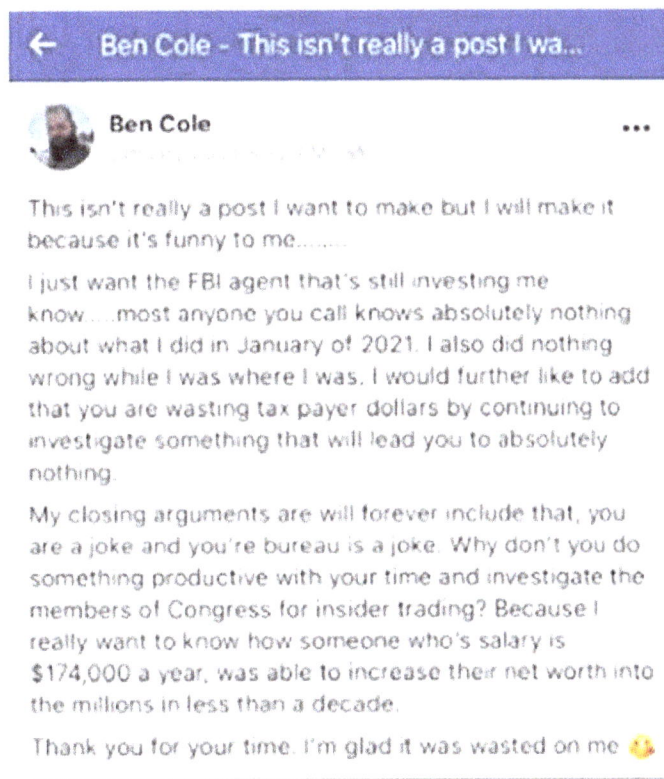

← Ben Cole - This isn't really a post I wa...

Ben Cole ...

This isn't really a post I want to make but I will make it because it's funny to me........

I just want the FBI agent that's still investing me know....most anyone you call knows absolutely nothing about what I did in January of 2021. I also did nothing wrong while I was where I was. I would further like to add that you are wasting tax payer dollars by continuing to investigate something that will lead you to absolutely nothing.

My closing arguments are will forever include that, you are a joke and you're bureau is a joke. Why don't you do something productive with your time and investigate the members of Congress for insider trading? Because I really want to know how someone who's salary is $174,000 a year, was able to increase their net worth into the millions in less than a decade.

Thank you for your time. I'm glad it was wasted on me 😋

Brian Preller

Preller has been identified as engaging in the conduct attributed to him above based on, among other things, the following:

1. As part of this investigation, Witness 3, an individual whose identity is known to the FBI, who has known Preller for more than a decade, and who is familiar with Preller's appearance, was shown one or more images of the individual identified above as Preller at the Capitol on January 6. Witness 3 identified the individual in the photos as Preller.

2. According to records obtained from Enterprise Rent-a-Car, Preller rented a gray 2020 Chrysler Pacifica in Leesburg, Florida, from January 5-8, 2021. The vehicle's mileage when returned was approximately 1,728 more than when it was provided to Preller. Of note, the distance between Leesburg, Florida, and Washington, D.C., is approximately 845 miles. Preller's phone number associated with the reservation was (352) 551-XXXX ("Preller Phone 1").

3. According to Witness 3, Preller Phone 1 was a phone number previously used by Preller in early 2021. According to T-Mobile records, Preller Phone 1 was subscribed to Corporate Resources Investments from approximately May 2018 until September 2021. As described above, according to Florida Department of State, Division of Corporations' online records, Corporate Resources Investments, Inc., is an inactive Florida corporation who registered agent and only officer/director is the individual named herein as B Leader.

4. According to cell site location information, Preller Phone 1 was in the vicinity of the U.S. Capitol during the afternoon on January 6.

5. According to Facebook records, an account with the vanity name and account identifier of "brian.preller.37" is registered to "Brian Preller" ("Preller Facebook"), and associated with a telephone number that was at that time subscribed to Preller's ex-wife, according to T-Mobile records ("Preller Phone 2"). Public postings on this account appear to reflect Preller's connection to events at the Capitol on January 6, 2021, including:

    a. A picture from April 9, 2021, showing Preller on a bed, underneath an American flag, and holding an object that appears to be the same type of walking stick Preller carried at the Capitol on January 6th. The image on the left below is from Preller Facebook. The image on the right below is from open-source video of Preller at the Capitol on January 6. During an interview of Witness 3, Witness 3 identified both individuals pictured as Preller.

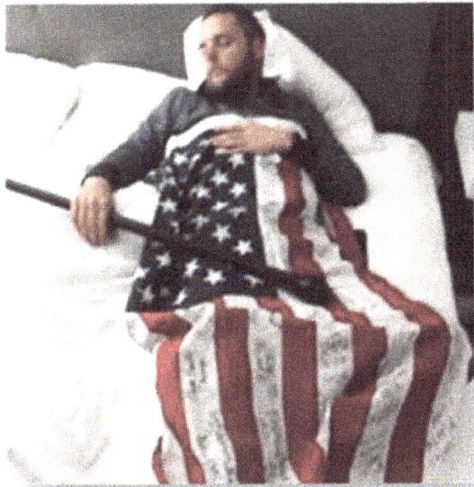

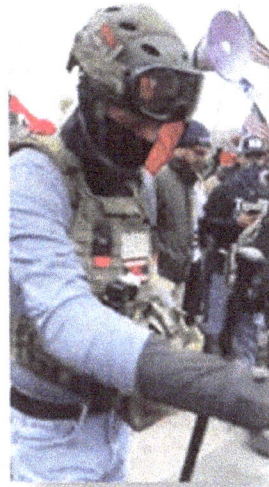

b. In December 2021, Preller sent the image above of him laying underneath a U.S. flag to a female acquaintance. In the related messages, Preller wrote, "Washington DC January 6th […] I was one of the ones in the capital."

c. A posting from June 7, 2021, shows an image of Preller with what appears to be a black flag on a black flagpole. The black flag appears to be the same as the one B Leader and other members of B SQUAD carried on January 6. During an interview of Witness 3, Witness 3 identified Preller as the individual in this image.

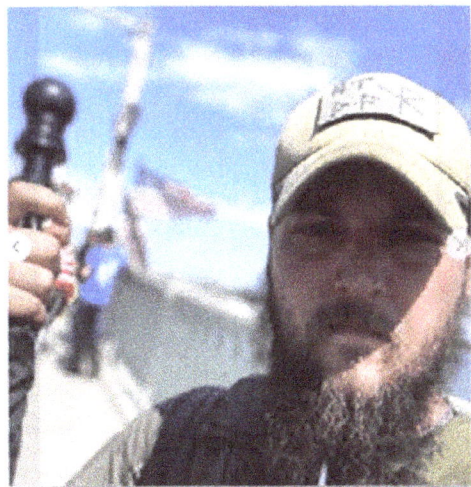

d. Accompanying the image of Preller with the black flag and flagpole was the following comment from Preller, which appears to contain a reference to Preller, the flag, and others being at the Capitol in coded language: "Still got the flag my dude. The one that we carried together, at that one place when we followed our oaths."

e.   In November 2021, Preller messaged another female acquaintance that his divorce was being finalized and "Yeah that tends to happen when the FBI shows up at your door." When the female asked, "What dumb shit did you do now," Preller responded, "January 6 2021 […] Yeah…lol fun ride […] Still got the shield." [This is likely a reference to the riot shield Rockholt picked up on the Lower West Terrace.]

f.   In June 2021, Preller messaged with a male acquaintance that he was "building an army of 3% patriots that I'm commanding officer for also connect to the CIA DHS and Q anon." When the other individual asked what the army did, Preller responded, "'community outreach' […] Invade the capital building […] You know Stuff."

g.   In July 2021, when a male acquaintance asked what Preller was "doing these days anyway," Preller responded that he was working at a "Gunshop" and "[c]ontinuing to build my 3% army so I can overthrow the federal government."

h.   In September 2021, Preller wrote to another individual, "I had the room flooded with 3% Patriots right before I made that little statement. . . . Lvl 4s deep concealment trained by yours truly under very specific orders that no one, no one goes to jail at all cost." The individual responded, "Fuck that man let em arrest you for doin nothing wrong. Lawsuit + makes them look bad." Preller wrote back, "Flagler county sherrifs is on our side 80/20. But I'm not ever seeing the inside of a cell brother. Ever."

i.   According to records obtained from the social media company TikTok, the account assigned username "odinsmonster" is subscribed to Preller Phone 2 ("Preller TikTok"). A review of publicly available portions of the Preller TikTok appears to contain multiple videos and images of Preller, including a video July 25, 2021 that appears to depict Preller inside of the Preller Vehicle. The video appears to have been created or edited using a mirror effect (i.e., the images in the video are reversed). Visible in the video is a patch attached to the interior headliner of the vehicle that appears very similar to the "B SQUAD" patch Preller wore on his back on January 6, 2021, at the Capitol. Below for comparison are a cropped image of the patch from the vehicle (which is reversed due to the mirror effect) and an image of the patch on Preller's back on January 6.

John Edward Crowley

Crowley has been identified as engaging in the conduct attributed to him above based on, among other things, the following:

1. Hotel records reflect that Crowley was one of the guests associated with the Black Group reservation and was in the same room as Cole.

2. According to AT&T records, telephone number (352) 494-XXXX ("Crowley Phone") was subscribed to "Edward Crowley" from at least July 2011 to April 2022. The address associated with Crowley Phone is the same address associated with Crowley's Florida driver's license.

3. According to information obtained pursuant to a search warrant, Crowley Phone was identified as having utilized a cell site consistent with providing service to a geographic area that included the interior of the United States Capitol building on January 6, 2021.

4. The image of Crowley associated with his Florida driver's license is consistent with the partially obstructed facial images of the individual identified above as Crowley above from January 6, 2021.

5. Witness 4, an individual whose identity is known to the FBI and a former member of the Guardians of Freedom, is listed in the hotel records as having been part of the Black Group reservation. Witness 4 is also familiar with members of Subgroup B. During an interview with Witness 4, they identified a Florida driver's license image of Crowley as an individual they know. When shown an image of Crowley on January 6, Witness 4 identified the pictured individual known to them as "Ed" or Eddie or the nickname "Palm Fronds." Witness 4 identified Ed Palm Fronds as one of the members of Guardians of Freedom.

6. In February 2022, an FBI Task Force Officer surveilled and interacted with Crowley. When I showed the TFO photographs of Crowley from January 6, 2021, the TFO stated that the individual in the pictures is the same as the individual that he surveilled and with whom he interacted.

7. Agents have identified an Instagram account with the display name of "eddiepalmfronds." The @eddiepalmfronds account was used pre-January 6, 2021, to post information regarding the belief that the results of the 2020 presidential election were fraudulent and that action needed to be taken. Specifically, in or around December 24, 2020, @eddiepalmfronds posted the following comment in relation to an advertisement for a Guardians of Freedom fundraiser purportedly intended to "assist with our next critical mission on January 6th, 2021":

> All, Please consider donating for a great cause. Patriots will go to DC Jan. 6th to show their patriotism and support during the time Congress will count Electoral College votes as this was of course a fraudulent election. We want to protect the people and Trump supporters as we stand up for our liberty and our Constitution. We are in need of you all to help us fundraise for this event. We are also in need of tremendous support from all of you for our members to deploy, help secure and

defend the people. Please consider donating as we are in need of financial support. Donations will be going towards hotel stays, vehicle rentals, transportation gas fees, food, tactical gear, etc. Link in bio.

Thanks, Good Bless

Edward

> **eddiepalmfronds** All. Please consider donating for a great cause. Patriots will go to DC Jan. 6th to show their patriotism and support during the time Congress will count Electoral College votes as this was of course a fraudulent election. We want to protect the people and Trump supporters as we stand up for our liberty and our Constitution. We are in need of you all to help us fundraise for this event. We also are in need of tremendous support from all of you for our members to deploy, help secure and defend the people. Please consider donating as we are in need of financial support. Donations will be going towards hotel stays, vehicle rentals, transportation gas fees, food, tactical gear, etc.
> Link in bio.
> Thanks, Good Bless
> Edward

8. @eddiepalmfronds posted comments reflecting the accountholder's belief that the results of the 2020 presidential election were fraudulent. For example, approximately 3 weeks after the posting above, when another poster commented that President Biden was "elected democratically," @eddiepalmfronds responded, "elected hahaha, fraud." In another posting, the account referred to President Biden as "pedophile China Joe, fraud election."

9. According to Facebook records, the "eddiepalmfronds" Instagram account is registered to "Eddie Palm Fronds" and the account's vanity name and account identifier is "eddiepalmfronds" ("Crowley Instagram"). As noted above, Crowley's middle name is Edward and Witness 4 identified Crowley's Guardians of Freedom nickname as "Palm Fronds."[5] In addition, according to Facebook records, the registered email address for the account is edward@edwardcrowley.com and the verified phone number is Crowley Phone.

---

[5] In the affidavits in support of the search warrants referenced in paragraph 56 above, Crowley's first name was erroneously identified as "Edward," which is Crowley's middle name.

Jonathan Rockholt

Rockholt has been identified as engaging in the conduct attributed to him above based on, among other things, the following:

1. Hotel records reflect that Rockholt was one of the guests associated with the Black Group reservation.

2. Investigators have reviewed images of Rockholt from his Florida driver's license, booking photos from a 2016 arrest in Flagler County, Florida, and images that appear to be of Rockholt from the publicly available portions of the Rockholt Facebook account. Investigators have also compared open-source images and videos of the individual believed to be Rockholt on January 6 (as described above) and images and video that appear to be Rockholt at other events. While no individual image or video was dispositive as to Rockholt's identity as the member of Subgroup B attributed to him above, the cumulative result of such comparisons and the information described below indicates that there is at least probable cause to believe that Rockholt is such person.

3. For example, investigators reviewed an image from a Facebook website of a group of individuals at an unidentified event. On the right side of the group is an individual who appears to be Rockholt based on a comparison of the known/suspected images of Rockholt. In the picture, Rockholt and the others appear to be standing in front of a III% related flag and Rockholt appears to be wearing a shirt with a skull like the skull logo associated with the Marvel character the Punisher. In addition, Rockholt is standing in front of a Gadsden flag based on another image from the Facebook website that shows the flag unobstructed. As described above, the tactical vest believed to be worn by Rockholt on January 6 contained a III% logo on the front, and his helmet had a Gadsden flag on the side and a skull like the skull logo associated with the Punisher on the back. Cropped portions of the referenced Facebook images are below.

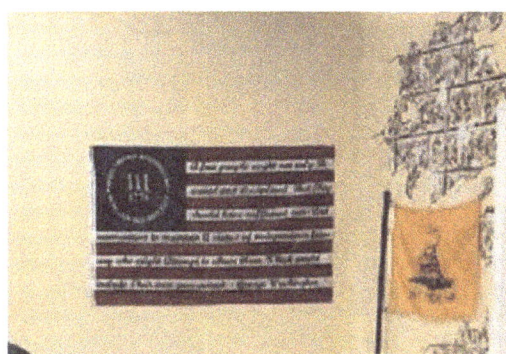

4. An open-source video posted on August 2, 2021, which appears to be of an anti-vaccine protest in Orlando, Florida, appears to depict Rockholt wearing shoes like the ones worn by the individual believed to be Rockholt at the Capitol on January 6. Specifically, in the video, Rockholt appears to be wearing black gym shoes with a white sole, black bottom, and a logo consistent with an "S." On the left below is an image of Rockholt at the Orlando protest. The images to the right depict Rockholt's shoes on January 6 at the Capitol.

5. Investigators reviewed an image from a Facebook page that appears to depict a group of individuals, including Rockholt, exhibiting support for former President Trump on a bridge, on or before July 22, 2020. In such image, Rockholt appears to be wearing the same or similar sunglasses to those he wore at the Capitol on January 6. On the left below is an image of Rockholt on the bridge. The image on the right depicts Rockholt's sunglasses on January 6 at the Capitol. The nose and the profile of Rockholt as seen in the Facebook page are also the same as the nose and profile of the individual seen at the Capitol on January 6, 2021.

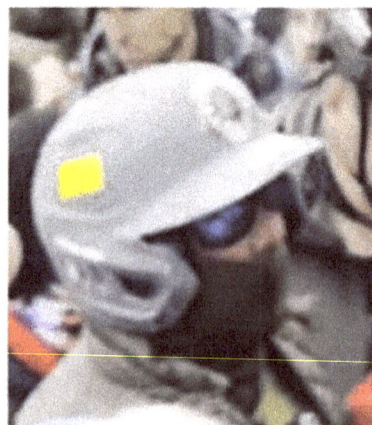

6. Investigators reviewed open-source video that appears to depict Rockholt walking in Washington, D.C., on January 6, 2021, prior to the attack on the Capitol. In such video, Rockholt appears to be wearing sunglasses like those referenced in the subparagraph above and a thick red wristwatch. Images depicting Rockholt at the Capitol on January 6 appear to show him wearing the same or a similar red wristwatch. On the left below is an image that appears to be Rockholt walking in Washington, D.C., on January 6. The image on the right depicts Rockholt's wristwatch on January 6 at the Capitol. The image below is taken from Rockholt Facebook.

7. Investigators compared open-source video and images that appear to depict Rockholt at the Capitol riot to images obtained from the search warrant executed upon the Rockholt Facebook. In the former, the individual believed to be Rockholt wears a green gaiter with a vertical seam on the front:

8. Investigators compared this image with one taken from the Rockholt Facebook, which is an apparent selfie. The image below was sent by Rockholt to an associate on January 5, 2021, accompanying a statement indicating he was enroute to Washington D.C.

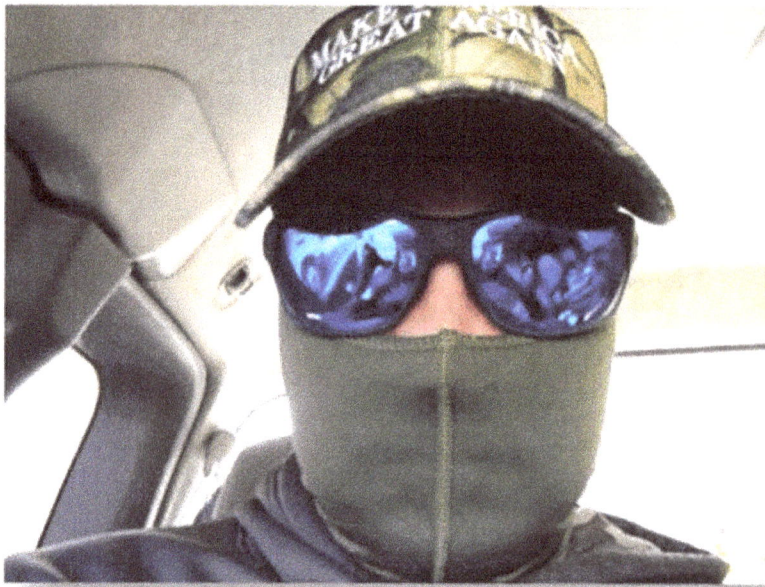

9. A video recovered from the Rockholt Instagram account[6] appeared to show Rockholt wearing a green puffy jacket identifiable with that from January 6 shown in paragraph (7) above. Rockholt sent this video on or about February 1, 2021. A screenshot from this video is below:

10. According to Verizon records, Rockholt Phone is currently subscribed to an individual who shares Rockholt's last name and appears to be a relative of Rockholt. The billing address for the account is the same as the address listed for Rockholt in connection with his Florida driver's license. The records also indicate that "Johnathan Rockholt" and two others with the Rockholt last name are authorized users and/or account managers with "FULL ACCESS" on the Rockholt Phone account. As described below, Rockholt Phone had contact with other members of B SQUAD in December 2020 and January 2021.

   a. According to Verizon records, Network Element records for Rockholt Phone show:

   b. The Network Elements associated with 3G wireless calls between November 1, 2020, and January 4, 2021, consistently appear to have been in Florida (e.g., "Orlando 2" and "Jacksonville2").

   c. The Network Elements associated with 3G wireless calls between January 5, 2021, and January 7, 2021, appear to be consistent with the phone traveling from Florida to Washington, D.C., and back to Florida, namely: (1) the use of Network Elements on January 5, 2021, that appear to be located in Florida ("Orlando2"), Georgia ("Macon_MTX01"), South Carolina ("Charleston_MTX4"), North Carolina ("Raleigh") and ("Raleigh_MTX08"), Virginia ("Richmond"), and Washington, D.C. ("Washington"); (2) the use of Network Elements on January 6, 2021, that appear to be located in Washington, D.C. ("Washington"); and (3) the use of

---

[6] On or about July 6, 2022, Magistrate Judge Harvey of the District of Columbia signed a search warrant numbered 22sc1789 for an Instagram account used by Jonathan Rockholt (*Rockholt Instagram*).

Network Elements on January 7, 2021, that appear to be located in Washington, D.C. ("Washington"), North Carolina ("Raleigh_MTX08") and ("Raleigh"), South Carolina ("Charleston_MTX4"), and Florida ("Jacksonville2").

d. According to Facebook records, Rockholt Facebook (i.e., "jonny.rockholt") is subscribed to an individual using the name "Jonny Rocky," whose registered email addresses are "jonnyrockholt@[…].com" and "jonny.rockholt@facebook.com." A review of public portions of Rockholt Facebook identified, among other things: (1) a November 3, 2020 posting (i.e., on the day of the 2020 presidential election) of an image of a Gadsden flag flying at, what appears to be the residence associated with Rockholt's address, based on open source images of the residence (see below); (2) an April 6, 2021 posting relating to and critical of the investigation and prosecution of those involved in the attack on the Capitol (see below); and (3) images of Rockholt's unconcealed face.

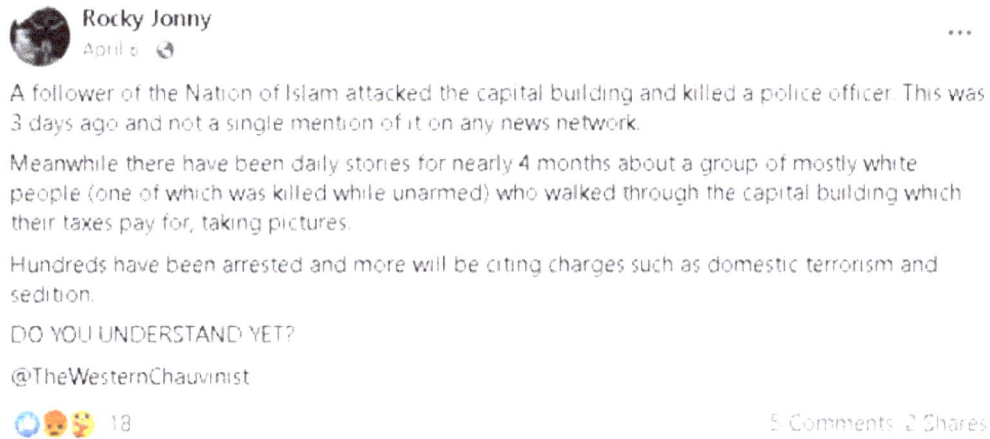

Rocky Jonny
April 8

A follower of the Nation of Islam attacked the capital building and killed a police officer. This was 3 days ago and not a single mention of it on any news network.

Meanwhile there have been daily stories for nearly 4 months about a group of mostly white people (one of which was killed while unarmed) who walked through the capital building which their taxes pay for, taking pictures.

Hundreds have been arrested and more will be citing charges such as domestic terrorism and sedition.

DO YOU UNDERSTAND YET?

@TheWesternChauvinist

18   5 Comments 2 Shares

11. A search of the Rockholt Facebook account identified, among other things, items relating to the Guardians of Freedom, an image with the text "Hampton Inn Washington Convention Center in Downtown DC – Hilton," and image that appears to be Rockholt in front of the Washington Monument, which appears to be from a Trump rally in Washington, D.C., and a Florida security officer license bearing Rockholt's name and date of birth.

Tyler Bensch

Bensch has been identified as engaging in the conduct attributed to him above based on, among other things, the following:

1. Hotel records reflect that Bensch was one of the guests associated with the Black Group reservation.

2. As part of this investigation, Witness 2—an individual whose identity is known to the FBI and who previously had an online relationship with Bensch—informed agents that they previously communicated with Bensch via different social media. According to Witness 2, on January 6, 2021, Bensch posted videos on his Snapchat account – "yoitztylerr"[7] – which appeared to show Bensch, with his face concealed, at the Capitol with a gas mask, body armor vest, all black or camouflage attire, and an AR-style rifle.[8] On January 6, 2021, Bensch also posted to Snapchat that his location was in Washington, D.C.

3. Witness 2 informed agents that Bensch used a photo of himself posing in front of the Capitol building with what appeared to be an AR-style rifle as his Facebook profile photo. Witness 2 also provided agents with a copy of the following image which was posted on Bensch's Facebook account on or about December 15, 2020. The image depicts two individuals pointing at the camera in the middle of a street with the Capitol in the background. The individual on the right is wearing or possessing the same or a very similar helmet, goggles, body armor, military fatigues, and gas mask as Bensch was did the images from January 6.[9]

---

[7] Witness 2 initially identified Bensch's Snapchat account as "yoitztylerr" (with two 'r's) but through legal process, I confirmed that Bensch's actual Snapchat account is "yoitztylerrr" (with three 'r's).

[8] Your affiant notes there has been no other information obtained in this investigation which indicates Bensch was armed while at the Capitol. However, in the January 3rd Video, an individual believed to be Bensch appears to be holding an assault rifle.

[9] Near the conclusion of the interview, Witness 2 asked whether they could receive a $1,000 reward for providing this information. The witness was advised that no reward would be provided.

4. On or about December 12, 2020, three days before the image above was posted to Bensch's Facebook account, a pro-Trump rally was held in Washington, D.C., which resulted in violent clashes between Trump supporters and counter protestors. Open-source videos associated with the event contain images of Bensch—based on that individuals' helmet, goggles, body armor, military fatigues, drab scarf, and right shoulder camera as the individual identified as Bensch in the images above. The two bottom photos are Bench on January 6, 2021.

5. In addition, at least one video from December 12, 2020, appears to depict this individual wearing a ring on his right forefinger. The ring matches the ring Bensch is wearing in images from Bensch Facebook. The image on the left below is from one such video. The two images on the right were taken from public postings on Bensch Facebook. Although the video is from December 12, 2020, the helmet, goggles, and scarf match the items that Bensch wore at the Capitol on January 6, 2021.

6. According to a search of the website www.backstage.com, which is used to, among other things, find professional acting roles, Bensch has a public profile on which it appears that he has posted images of himself wearing, what appear to be the same or very similar military fatigues and drab scarf as those he wore on January 6, 2021.

7. Using legal process, I have identified a Snapchat account that is owned and operated by Bensch. Bensch's Snapchat account contains videos and images Bensch in the gear he wore at the Capitol on January 6, as well as video and images of Bensch in such gear.

8. The following flyer was posted around Washington, D.C. The flyer includes a screen capture from B Leader's January 3rd Video. In the one of Bensch's Snapchat videos, a voice believed to Bensch is heard saying, "Hey, that looks familiar!" The video then zooms in on an individual believed to be Bensch in the January 3rd Video. From left to right, the photos below show the flyer of which Bensch recorded a video, a cropped closeup from the flyer, a screenshot from the video that B Leader recorded and posted to the internet on January 3, 2021, and a photo of Bensch on restricted Capitol grounds on January 6, 2021.

9. Bensch's Snapchat account also has an image of a patch that appears to be sewn to the type of camouflage worn by Bensch. The patch displays a III% logo, the year "1776", and the phrase "When Tyranny Becomes Law Rebellion Becomes Duty." The account also contains an audio file in which Bensch's voice says, in sum and substance, that he joined a militia instead of the Marines because he wanted to be in the infantry and would have been assigned to be a mailman in the Marines.

Probable Cause for Criminal Offenses

18 U.S.C. § 231

Based on the foregoing, your affiant submits there is probable cause to believe that **[1] Benjamin Cole, [2] Brian Preller, [3] John Edward Crowley,** and **[4] Jonathan Rockholt** violated 18 U.S.C. § 231(a)(3), which makes it unlawful to commit or attempt to commit any act to obstruct, impede, or interfere with any fireman or law enforcement officer lawfully engaged in the lawful performance of his official duties incident to and during the commission of a civil disorder which in any way or degree obstructs, delays, or adversely affects commerce or the movement of any article or commodity in commerce or the conduct or performance of any federally protected function.

For purposes of 18 U.S.C. § 231, a federally protected function means any function, operation, or action carried out, under the laws of the United States, by any department, agency, or instrumentality of the United States or by an officer or employee thereof. This includes the Joint Session of Congress where the Senate and House count Electoral College votes.

18 U.S.C. § 1752

Based on the foregoing, your affiant submits that there is probable cause to believe that **[1] Benjamin Cole, [2] Brian Preller, [3] John Edward Crowley, [4] Jonathan Rockholt,** and **[5] Tyler Bensch** violated 18 U.S.C. § 1752(a)(1) and (2), which make it a crime to (1) knowingly enter or remain in any restricted building or grounds without lawful authority to do; and (2) knowingly, and with intent to impede or disrupt the orderly conduct of Government business or official functions, engage in disorderly or disruptive conduct in, or within such proximity to, any restricted building or grounds when, or so that, such conduct, in fact, impedes or disrupts the orderly conduct of Government business or official functions, or attempt or conspire to do so.

For purposes of 18 U.S.C. § 1752, a "restricted building" includes a posted, cordoned off, or otherwise restricted area of a building or grounds where the President or other person protected by the Secret Service, including the Vice President, is or will be temporarily visiting; or any building or grounds so restricted in conjunction with an event designated as a special event of national significance.

FEDERAL BUREAU OF INVESTIGATION

Attested to by the applicant in accordance with the requirements of Fed. R. Crim. P. 4.1 by telephone, this 16th day of August 2022.

ROBIN MERIWEATHER
U.S. MAGISTRATE JUDGE

Prepublication Review Policy Guide

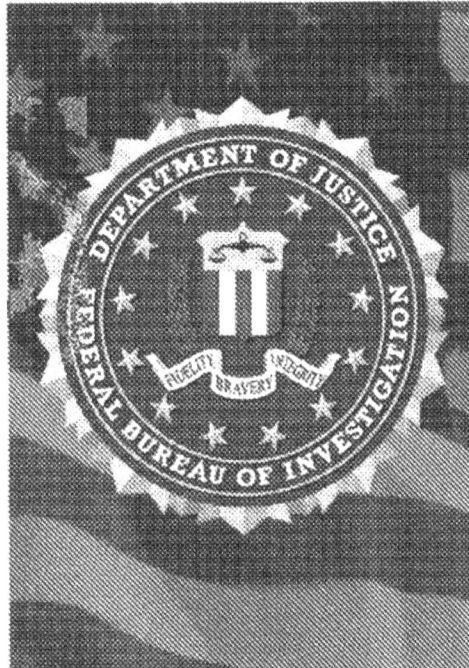

Federal Bureau of Investigation

Information Management Division

1065PG

January 8, 2020

Approvals

Policy Information	
Last Updated	N/A
Effective Date	2020-01-08
Review Date	2023-01-08

Approval Information	
Sponsoring Executive Approval	**Marlin L. Ritzman** Assistant Director Information Management Division
Final Approval	**Paul M. Abbate** Associate Deputy Director

General Information

Questions or comments pertaining to this policy guide (PG) can be directed to:

Federal Bureau of Investigation Headquarters (FBIHQ),
Information Management Division (IMD)

Prepublication Review Office, [ ] or FBIPREPUB@fbi.gov

b7E

Supersession Information

This document supersedes the *Prepublication Review Policy Guide* (0792PG).

Revision Log

The revision log documents substantive changes made to the previous version of this policy, the *Prepublication Review Policy Guide*, 0792PG, published on June 4, 2015.

The numbers and titles in the "Revised" column refer to the subsections as they currently appear in this updated policy. "Deleted" subsection numbers refer to those in the previous published version of the policy.

Revised Section Number and Title	Deleted Section Number and Title
1.1 "Background" is now in Section 3	
4.1.2. Extemporaneous Oral Disclosures	
4.1.4. Prohibited Disclosures	
4.2.1. Submission of Prepublication Review Requests	
4.2.4. Submissions Involving Human-Based Research	
4.3.1. IMD Response Time	
6. Recordkeeping Requirements	

Table of Contents

List of Appendices

1. Introduction

1.1. Purpose

This policy guide (PG) outlines specific policies and procedures regarding prepublication review and establishes requirements regulating individual conduct.

Under the First Amendment to the United States Constitution, Americans enjoy the right to free speech, which includes a right to publish. However, with regard to public employees, specifically, Federal Bureau of Investigation (FBI) personnel, this right must comport with the FBI's significant law enforcement and national security responsibilities and the FBI's interest in maintaining effective and efficient operations. Accordingly, in matters concerning the use of FBI information, it is necessary for the FBI to protect its information from disclosures that could endanger substantial government interests. This policy sets forth program guidance relating to disclosure of FBI information outside of official use and ensures adequate protections for FBI personnel's constitutionally protected rights as citizens.

1.2. Scope

This PG applies to all FBI personnel.

1.3. Exemptions

There are no exemptions to this PG.

2. Roles and Responsibilities

2.1. Information Management Division (IMD)

IMD is responsible for providing guidance on all prepublication review issues, including those not explicitly covered in this PG.

2.2. IMD Assistant Director (AD)

The IMD AD must:

- Oversee a comprehensive, FBI-wide prepublication review program.

- Serve as the final decision maker on adverse decision appeals, subject to the exceptions in subsection 4.3.2. below.

2.3. Prepublication Review Office, Record/Information Dissemination Section (RIDS), IMD

The Prepublication Review Office must:

- Establish and disseminate policies, procedures, and training relating to the development, coordination, and overall management of the prepublication review program.

- Review and adjudicate prepublication submissions.

2.4. Federal Bureau of Investigation Headquarters (FBIHQ) Division, Field Offices (FO), and Legal Attachés (Legat) Heads

FBIHQ division, FO, and Legat heads, or their designees, must designate subject matter experts (SME) to review prepublication submissions upon request from IMD.

2.5. FBI Personnel

FBI personnel must:

- Comply with prepublication review requirements and with the following agreements:

  o FD 291, "FBI Employment Agreement," signed by all FBI personnel as a condition of employment

  o Analogous forms, such as the FD-868, "Nondisclosure Agreement for Joint Task Force Members, Contractors, Detailees, Assignees, and Interns," signed by task force members, contractors, and the like

  o FD-857, "Sensitive Information Nondisclosure Agreement"

  o Standard Form (SF)-312, "Classified Information Nondisclosure Agreement," signed by all FBI personnel as a condition of being granted access to classified information

  o Form 4414, "Sensitive Compartmented Information Nondisclosure Agreement," signed by all FBI personnel with access to Sensitive Compartmented Information (SCI) information as a condition of this access

- Contact their respective chief division counsel (CDC) or the Office of the General Counsel (OGC), and comply with the *Self-Reporting Requirements Policy Guide (1037PG)*, before making any court appearances or responses to subpoenas in a personal capacity that could require them to divulge FBI information set forth in Title 28 Code of Federal Regulations (CFR) Part 16, Subpart B.

3. Policy Statement

All information created and acquired by current and former FBI personnel in connection with official FBI duties, as well as all official material to which FBI personnel have access, is the property of the United States. FBI personnel must surrender all materials in their possession that contain FBI information upon FBI demand or upon separation from the FBI. Unauthorized disclosure, misuse, or negligent handling of FBI information could adversely affect national security, place human life in jeopardy, result in the denial of due process, obstruct justice, prevent the FBI from effectively discharging its responsibilities, or violate federal law.

Before disclosing FBI information outside of their official duty requirements, FBI personnel must submit the proposed disclosures to the Prepublication Review Office, RIDS, IMD for review. This prepublication review affords the FBI the opportunity to (1) assess whether the proposed disclosure includes prohibited information, (2) advise submitting FBI personnel of any such concerns, and (3) work with the submitter to resolve such concerns.

The legality or propriety of a proposed disclosure will be reviewed during the prepublication review. The FBI prepublication review process does not encompass factual accuracy or grammar checks of the proposed disclosure. Completion of the prepublication review process does not constitute an FBI endorsement of the author or the material disclosed. FBI personnel who fail to comply with the prepublication review process or who make prohibited disclosures are subject to administrative actions, clearance revocations, disciplinary actions, civil suits, and/or criminal sanctions, as appropriate.

Compliance with this PG does not relieve FBI personnel from the obligation to comply with FBI outside employment rules or 5 CFR Part 2635 (Standards of Ethical Conduct for Employees of the Executive Branch), including any applicable limitations on compensation. It is FBI personnel's obligation to seek guidance from IMD and the Office of Integrity and Compliance (OIC) on all prepublication review issues not explicitly covered in this section.

All provisions of this PG are severable. If a court should determine that any provision is unenforceable, that provision would be void, but the remainder would continue in full force.

4. Processes and Procedures

4.1. Scope of Prepublication

4.1.1. Oral, Written, or Electronic Disclosures

This policy applies to any public disclosure by FBI personnel, including oral, written, or electronic, of any information identified in subsection 4.1.4. of this PG. Methods of disclosure include, but are not limited to, résumés, blogs, Web sites, articles, and books. This PG also applies to disclosures of drafts, initial manuscripts, and similar preliminary works to anyone, including non-FBI attorneys, ghost writers, co-authors, and publishers. The only exception to this rule is for disclosures by FBI personnel who are testifying as defendants in criminal cases in the United States. In that limited situation, this policy does not cover disclosures made during testimony or during privileged conversations between FBI personnel and their attorneys.

FBI personnel who wish to make court appearances or respond to subpoenas in their personal capacities, which could require them to divulge FBI information, should contact their CDCs or the OGC for additional guidance. Disclosure of Department of Justice (DOJ)/FBI information in federal or state proceedings is subject to the provisions of 28 CFR Part 16, Subpart B.

4.1.2. Extemporaneous Oral Disclosures

Advance review of contemporaneous oral disclosures in general cannot be done; however, this does not mean that FBI personnel may disregard the requirements of review when making planned oral disclosures. At a minimum, FBI personnel must provide outlines of their presentations. Except in those rare instances in which deferring comment would not be practicable due to unusually compelling circumstances beyond an individual's control, FBI personnel must defer comment until they can comply with this policy by providing an outline prior to public disclosure. If an individual makes a disclosure without the appropriate review, he or she may be subject to post-disclosure administrative action, clearance revocation, disciplinary action, civil suits, and/or criminal sanctions, if warranted by the content of the disclosure.

4.1.3. Disclosures Not Subject to Prepublication Policy

Official speeches, writings, presentations, and publications made in the performance of official duties are outside the scope of this PG. Personnel should consult the *Public Affairs Policy Guide: Media Relations, External Communications, and Personal Use of Social Media (1002PG)* for guidance.

Disclosures that clearly have nothing to do with the FBI or its activities, investigations, missions, or operations and are not otherwise related to any FBI information are not subject to this PG.

Disclosures protected by law include disclosures to Congress (including by members of the military) regarding illegality, waste, fraud, abuse, mismanagement, public health or safety threats that could expose confidential government agents or compromise national security (see Section 5).

4.1.4. Prohibited Disclosures

FBI personnel who fail to comply with the prepublication review process or who make prohibited disclosures are subject to administrative actions, clearance revocations, disciplinary actions, civil suits, and/or criminal sanctions, as appropriate. FBI personnel must not disclose to unauthorized recipients.

- Information protected from disclosure by the Privacy Act of 1974, as amended.

- Classified information, the disclosure of which could harm national security. To the extent that proposed disclosures involve classified information, prepublication review processing will be conducted in conformance with 28 CFR § 17.18, in addition to 28 CFR Part 16.

- Information that reveals sensitive law enforcement, intelligence, counterintelligence, or counterterrorism techniques, sources, or methods of the FBI or any other governmental entity.

- Information that would reveal grand jury material protected from disclosure by Rule 6(e) of the Federal Rules of Criminal Procedure (FRCP).

- Information that would tend to reveal the identity of a confidential human source (CHS) or the identity of a private institution or a government agency or authority when the information was furnished on a confidential basis.

- Information that relates to any sensitive operational details or the substantive merits of any ongoing or open investigation or case.

- Proprietary information and trade secrets.

- Information pertaining to wiretaps or intercepts, electronic communications (including storage mechanisms), or foreign intelligence protected or regulated by Title III (Title 18 United States Code [U.S.C.] §§ 2510-2520) or the Foreign Intelligence Surveillance Act (FISA) (50 U.S.C. §§ 1801-1862).

- Information pertaining to currency transaction reports regulated or protected by 31 U.S.C. §§ 5313-5319.

- Tax return information regulated or protected by 26 U.S.C. § 6103.

- Information pertaining to contractor bids or proposals or source-selection information before the award of the procurement contract to which the information relates.

- Any other information that is prohibited by executive order (EO), law, statute, or regulation.

- Any other information that the FBI would have discretion to withhold from disclosure pursuant to civil discovery obligations, court orders, the Freedom of Information Act (FOIA), or any other statute, law, or regulation

4.1.5. Accountability for Permitted Disclosures

Disclosures will not be prohibited, pursuant to this PG, solely because they are critical or disparaging of the FBI, the government, or any individual. Any disclosures by current FBI personnel, however, that adversely affect the ability to effectively and efficiently fulfill their official responsibilities or that interfere with FBI operations may subject the individuals to administrative or disciplinary actions for the consequences of the disclosures. Examples of disclosures that are not prohibited under this PG, but still may subject FBI personnel to disciplinary actions, are the disclosures of private grievances and disclosures that significantly impair discipline or harmony among coworkers. These types of disclosures could have detrimental effects on close working relationships where personal loyalty or confidence is necessary, impede the performance of the duties of FBI personnel, or interfere with regular FBI operations. In such cases, FBI personnel will not be prohibited from making such disclosures, but they may be held accountable for the consequences of the disclosures. This subsection does not apply to disclosures not subject to the prepublication review policy (see subsection 4.1.3.).

FBI personnel may ordinarily speak or write about matters unrelated to their employment if they are expressing their personal views. However, when expressing such views to an audience that is aware of an individual's FBI employment, FBI personnel must make clear that they are stating their personal opinions, not the opinions of the FBI, and not their official opinions as FBI employees, contractors, or other members of FBI personnel.

Certain matters of significant public concern are so closely related to the responsibilities and missions of the FBI that there is a significant likelihood that any comments on such matters by FBI personnel will be perceived as reflecting an individual's official view in his or her official capacity with the FBI. Therefore, when communicating on matters closely related to the responsibilities, missions, or operations of the FBI, FBI personnel must make absolutely clear that they are expressing their personal opinions. Further, certain personnel may be precluded from publicly communicating their personal opinions on particular matters. For example, it may be inappropriate for a senior FBI official to publicly express his or her personal view regarding matters within the jurisdiction of the FBI. This is because others are likely to perceive the personal views of a senior management employee possessing substantial policy-making authority as indistinguishable from his or her official position as a senior FBI manager.

4.2. Administration and Management of Prepublication

4.2.1. Submission of Prepublication Review Requests

In general, FBI personnel must submit to IMD the full text of all proposed disclosures containing FBI information at least 30 working days in advance of the proposed disclosure. Prepublication review submissions must be made in writing, even if oral disclosure is contemplated. FBI personnel must first submit prepublication requests to their supervisors or the relevant SMEs prior to submitting them to IMD. Approval from the individual's supervisor or SME must be submitted to IMD with the prepublication request. FBI personnel should consult the Prepublication Review Office BUNET page for additional guidance. Material should be submitted either by unclassified e-mail at FBIPREPUB@fbi.gov or by mail addressed to the Prepublication Review Office, Information Management Division, 170 Marcel Drive, Winchester, VA 22602-4842

b7E

4.2.2. Submissions That Contain Operational or Intelligence Matters

Submissions that contain operational or intelligence matters by nature require review outside the prepublication review office. Accordingly, submitters should not expect proposed disclosures of such material to be reviewed within 30 working days. Although IMD will endeavor to review materials in a timely manner, the prepublication review requirement will not be satisfied until reviews are complete and FBI personnel have been notified.

4.2.3. Submissions Developed in Pursuit of Academic Degrees

During their FBI employment, FBI personnel occasionally elect to pursue academic degrees that require them to conduct research-based studies, write thesis papers, or create other projects as part of their educational pursuits. To the extent that information contained in an education-related product is the type of FBI information prohibited from disclosure under subsection 4.1.4, that document constitutes an oral, written, or electronic disclosure within the scope of this PG and must be submitted for prepublication review. Because of the nature of academic studies and the deadlines often associated with completing academic work, FBI personnel are highly advised to submit, in accordance with subsection 4.2.1, any abstracts that describe, in sufficient detail, the scope of work to be completed in order to secure preliminary approval of the desired submission's subject, as well as information reasonably foreseen to be contained in any resulting publication. Upon the FBI personnel member's finalization of the submission, he or she must submit the document for final review and approval via the prepublication review process.

4.2.4. Submissions Involving Human-Based Research

FBI personnel seeking publication based on research conducted on human subjects are required to receive approval by the FBI Institutional Review Board [for Human Subject Research] (IRB) prior to conducting the research or submitting any publications for review to IMD. The IRB is responsible for the prior review of all research projects that are conducted or supported by the FBI and that involve human subjects and are not otherwise exempt. Research involves human subjects under FBI regulations even if it only includes the use of nonpublic information about living human beings. For an overview of the IRB, see the "Overview of the Institutional Review Board."

The IRB may approve the project, reject the project, or require modifications in order for the project to be approved. Approved projects involving human-based research are subject to continuing review by the IRB at least once per year. If the IRB determines that an approved project has failed to meet the yearly continued review requirement in a timely manner, has not been conducted in accordance with its requirements, or has resulted in unexpected, serious harm to the subjects, the project may be suspended. IMD will not review any publication that has failed to receive initial IRB approval or any subsequent requisite IRB approvals.

4.3. Information Management Division Prepublication Review

IMD must conduct the prepublication review, answer questions from FBI personnel about the prepublication review process, and review and process all requests as follows:

- IMD may consult or coordinate with FBI personnel who can assist in determining how to proceed with the prepublication review process. This may include seeking assistance to assess the content or potential impact of the proposed disclosure or to initiate appropriate responses to the proposed disclosure. In such instances, the proposed disclosure will be forwarded to the FBIHQ division(s) that has subject matter expertise concerning the proposed disclosure. FBIHQ division heads must designate points of contact (POC) for prepublication review coordination.

- IMD may consult with other government agencies (OGA) as needed.

- IMD should inform the Office of Congressional Affairs (OCA) and the Office of Public Affairs (OPA) of the likely publication so that OCA and OPA may be prepared for subsequent congressional or press inquiries.

- If the proposed disclosure includes material that IMD finds cannot be disclosed, IMD must notify the submitter and propose modifications that would make the material acceptable. IMD must work with the individual and attempt to resolve all concerns.

4.3.1. Information Management Division Response Time

IMD will respond substantively to prepublication review requests within 30 working days from receipt of the written requests, per 28 CFR § 17.18. Additional time may be necessary for outside consultations with specific FBI sections and OGAs, as well as for sensitive, large, or technical submissions. If the review requires additional time, IMD will provide periodic progress reports.

4.3.2. Appealing an Adverse Decision

FBI personnel who receive adverse decisions may appeal those decisions to IMD's AD, who will act pursuant to a delegation of authority from the Director and process the appeals within 15 working days of receipt. The decision of IMD's AD is final, with the exception of decisions relating to the deletion of classified information, which may be appealed to the deputy Attorney General (DAG) pursuant to 28 CFR § 17.18(j)(3).

4.3.3. Post-Disclosure Reviews

Actual disclosures are subject to post-disclosure reviews. As set forth in subsection 4.1.5, an individual may be subject to a post-disclosure administrative or disciplinary action if the disclosure adversely affects the ability of other FBI personnel to effectively and efficiently fulfill their official responsibilities (including disclosures of private grievances or information that impairs discipline or harmony among coworkers) and thus has a detrimental effect on the work environment, impedes the performance of FBI personnel's duties, or interferes with the regular operations of the FBI.

5. Authorities

The following legal summaries pertain to the authorities cited in this PG and provide additional information for understanding the policies and procedures set forth in this PG.

- 28 CFR § 17.18 (Prepublication Review) (Includes provisions governing appeals of prepublication decisions. See subsection 4.3.2.)

- 5 CFR Parts 2635 (Standards of Ethical Conduct for Employees of the Executive Branch)

- 5 CFR Part 3801 (Supplemental Standards of Ethical Conduct for Employees of the Department of Justice)

The following legal authorities provide guidance with respect to certain prohibited disclosures (see subsection 4.1.4.):

- 5 U.S.C. § 552a (Privacy Act of 1974)

- Federal Rules of Criminal Procedure Rule 6(e)

- 18 U.S.C. §§ 2510-2520 (Wire and electronic communications interception and interception of oral communications) and 50 U.S.C. §§ 1801-1862 (FISA)

- 31 U.S.C. §§ 5313-5319 (Reports on domestic coins and currency transactions)

- 26 U.S.C. § 6103 (Confidentiality and disclosure of returns and return information)

- Any other information that the FBI would have discretion to withhold from disclosure pursuant to civil discovery obligations, the Freedom of Information Act (5 U.S.C. § 552), EO 13526 (Classification of National Security Information), or any other statute, law, or regulation.

Disclosures protected by law (see subsection 4.1.3.) include the following:

- 5 U.S.C. § 7211 (governing disclosures to Congress)

- 10 U.S.C. § 1034, as amended by the Military Whistleblower Protection Act (governing disclosure to Congress by members of the military)

- 5 U.S.C. § 2302(b)(8), as amended by the Whistleblower Protection Act (governing disclosures of illegality, waste, fraud, abuse, or public health or safety threats)

- 5 U.S.C. § 2303 and 28 CFR Part 27, the FBI Whistleblower Protection Act (governing disclosures of illegality, mismanagement, waste, fraud, abuse, or public health or safety threats)

- 50 U.S.C. § 421, et seq., the Intelligence Identities Protection Act of 1982 (governing disclosures that could expose confidential government agents)

- 18 U.S.C. §§ 641, 793, 794, 798, and 952 and Section 4(b) of the Subversive Activities Act of 1950 (50 U.S.C. § 783(b)) (statutes that protect against disclosure that may compromise national security)

6. Recordkeeping Requirements

The prepublication review files contain a copy of the proposed publication (e.g., manuscript, article, or pamphlet); correspondence between the prepublication review staff and SMEs; notes; and correspondence with the author, including objections to the release of certain information and/or requests to modify portions of the publication.

The prepublication review files are uploaded in Sentinel into a designated case file. A new case file is opened each year.

Appendix A: References

Applicable Policies and Other Guidance:

- *FBI Seal Name Initials and Special Agent Gold Badge Policy Directive (0625D)*

- *Work Schedule Directive and Policy Guide (0576DPG)*

- *FBI Ethics and Integrity Program Policy Directive and Policy Guide (0754DPG)*

- *Safeguarding Classified National Security Information Directive and Policy Guide (0632DPG)*

Applicable Forms:

- FD-291, "FBI Employment Agreement"

- FD-868, "Nondisclosure Agreement for Joint Task Force Members, Contractors, Detailees, Assignees, and Interns"

- FD-857, "Sensitive Information Nondisclosure Agreement"

- SF-312, "Classified Information Nondisclosure Agreement"

- Form 4414, "Sensitive Compartmented Information Nondisclosure Agreement"

Appendix B: Definitions and Acronyms

Definitions

Assignee: any person assigned a task with FBI-related material.

FBI employee: for the purposes of this policy, a full-time equivalent employee of the FBI who is authorized to represent the Bureau in matters involving official government business.

FBI information: any knowledge gained through FBI employment or assignments related to the FBI

FBI personnel: individuals employed by, detailed, or assigned to the FBI, including task force officers, members, and participants; members of the armed forces; experts and consultants to the FBI, industrial and commercial contractors, licensees, certificate holders, or grantees of the FBI, including all subcontractors; personal service contractors of the FBI; and any other category or person who acts for or on behalf of the FBI, as determined by the FBI Director.

Government contractor employee: an employee of a contractor organization conducting business with the FBI, the DOJ, or an OGA

Intern: a person working for the FBI under special appointment

Prepublication review: the process whereby FBI-related information is reviewed for potential approval for distribution to external sources.

Prohibited disclosure: specific information that is not releasable to external sources.

Proposed disclosure: FBI-related information for possible release to external sources.

Task force officer: see the *Domestic Investigations and Operations Guide* (DIOG), subsection 3.3.2.1.

Task force member: see DIOG subsection 3.3.2.2.

Task force participant: see DIOG subsection 3.3.2.3.

Unauthorized recipient: any person without appropriate clearance to review FBI-related information.

(U) Acronyms

AD	assistant director
CDC	chief division counsel
CFR	Code of Federal Regulations
CHS	confidential human source
DAG	deputy Attorney General
DIOG	*Domestic Investigations and Operations Guide*

DOJ	Department of Justice
EO	executive order
FBI	Federal Bureau of Investigation
FBIHQ	Federal Bureau of Investigation Headquarters
FISA	Foreign Intelligence Surveillance Act
FO	field office
FOIA	Freedom of Information Act
FRCP	Federal Rules of Criminal Procedure
IMD	Information Management Division
IRB	Institutional Review Board
Legat	legal attaché
OCA	Office of Congressional Affairs
OGA	other government agency
OGC	Office of the General Counsel
OIC	Office of Integrity and Compliance
OPA	Office of Public Affairs
PG	policy guide
POC	point of contact
RIDS	Record/Information Dissemination Section
SCI	Sensitive Compartmented Information
SF	standard form
SME	subject matter expert
U.S.C.	United States Code

OMB No. 1124-0004; Expires July 31, 2023

U.S. Department of Justice

Washington, DC 20530

Exhibit B to Registration Statement
Pursuant to the Foreign Agents Registration Act of 1938, as amended

INSTRUCTIONS. A registrant must furnish as an Exhibit B copies of each written agreement and the terms and conditions of each oral agreement with his foreign principal, including all modifications of such agreements, or, where no contract exists, a full statement of all the circumstances by reason of which the registrant is acting as an agent of a foreign principal. Compliance is accomplished by filing an electronic Exhibit B form at https://www.fara.gov.

Privacy Act Statement. The filing of this document is required for the Foreign Agents Registration Act of 1938, as amended, 22 U.S.C. § 611 *et seq.*, for the purposes of registration under the Act and public disclosure. Provision of the information requested is mandatory, and failure to provide the information is subject to the penalty and enforcement provisions established in Section 8 of the Act. Every registration statement, short form registration statement, supplemental statement, exhibit, amendment, copy of informational materials or other document or information filed with the Attorney General under this Act is a public record open to public examination, inspection and copying during the posted business hours of the FARA Unit in Washington, DC. Statements are also available online at the FARA Unit's webpage: https://www.fara.gov. One copy of every such document, other than informational materials, is automatically provided to the Secretary of State pursuant to Section 6(b) of the Act, and copies of any and all documents are routinely made available to other agencies, departments and Congress pursuant to Section 6(c) of the Act. The Attorney General also transmits a semi-annual report to Congress on the administration of the Act which lists the names of all agents registered under the Act and the foreign principals they represent. This report is available to the public in print and online at: https://www.fara.gov

Public Reporting Burden. Public reporting burden for this collection of information is estimated to average .32 hours per response, including the time for reviewing instructions, searching existing data sources, gathering and maintaining the data needed, and completing and reviewing the collection of information. Send comments regarding this burden estimate or any other aspect of this collection of information, including suggestions for reducing this burden to Chief, FARA Unit, Counterintelligence and Export Control Section, National Security Division, U.S. Department of Justice, Washington, DC 20530; and to the Office of Information and Regulatory Affairs, Office of Management and Budget, Washington, DC 20503.

1. Name of Registrant	2. Registration Number
Ghebi LLC	6869

3. Name of Foreign Principal

    Federal State Unitary Enterprise Rossiya Segodnya International Information Agency

Check Appropriate Box:

4. ☒ The agreement between the registrant and the above-named foreign principal is a formal written contract. If this box is checked, attach a copy of the contract to this exhibit.

5. ☐ There is no formal written contract between the registrant and the foreign principal. The agreement with the above-named foreign principal has resulted from an exchange of correspondence. If this box is checked, attach a copy of all pertinent correspondence, including a copy of any initial proposal which has been adopted by reference in such correspondence.

6. ☐ The agreement or understanding between the registrant and the foreign principal is the result of neither a formal written contract nor an exchange of correspondence between the parties. If this box is checked, give a complete description below of the terms and conditions of the oral agreement or understanding, its duration, the fees and expenses, if any, to be received.

7. What is the date of the contract or agreement with the foreign principal?   08/01/2022

8. Describe fully the nature and method of performance of the above indicated agreement or understanding.

    The nature and performance of the contract are set forth in the attached contract. Registrant produces radio shows, newswires and web articles which are predominantly distributed by other entities. Registrant has editorial control over these programs, newswires and web articles and journalists are given reasonable creative discretion.

FORM NSD-4
Revised 05/20

9. Describe fully the activities the registrant engages in or proposes to engage in on behalf of the above foreign principal.

Registrant produces radio shows, newswires and web articles which are predominantly distributed by other entities. Registrant has editorial control over these programs, newswires and web articles and journalists are given reasonable creative discretion.

10. Will the activities on behalf of the above foreign principal include political activities as defined in Section 1(o) of the Act[1].

Yes ☒   No ☐

If yes, describe all such political activities indicating, among other things, the relations, interests or policies to be influenced together with the means to be employed to achieve this purpose. The response must include, but not be limited to, activities involving lobbying, promotion, perception management, public relations, economic development, and preparation and dissemination of informational materials.

Registrant produces radio shows, newswires and web articles which are predominantly distributed by other entities. Registrant has editorial control over these programs, newswires and web articles and journalists are given reasonable creative discretion.

11. Prior to the date of registration[2] for this foreign principal has the registrant engaged in any registrable activities, such as political activities, for this foreign principal?

Yes ☐   No ☐   N/A - This statement is filed to update the registrant's agreement/contract with the foreign principal.

If yes, describe in full detail all such activities. The response should include, among other things, the relations, interests, and policies sought to be influenced and the means employed to achieve this purpose. If the registrant arranged, sponsored, or delivered speeches, lectures, social media, internet postings, or media broadcasts, give details as to dates, places of delivery, names of speakers, and subject matter. The response must also include, but not be limited to, activities involving lobbying, promotion, perception management, public relations, economic development, and preparation and dissemination of informational materials.

Set forth below a general description of the registrant's activities, including political activities.

Set forth below in the required detail the registrant's political activities.

Date	Contact	Method	Purpose

12. During the period beginning 60 days prior to the obligation to register[3] for this foreign principal, has the registrant received from the foreign principal, or from any other source, for or in the interests of the foreign principal, any contributions, income, money, or thing of value either as compensation, or for disbursement, or otherwise?

Yes ☐   No ☐   N/A - This statement is filed to update the registrant's agreement/contract with the foreign principal.

If yes, set forth below in the required detail an account of such monies or things of value.

Date Received	From Whom	Purpose	Amount/Thing of Value

13. During the period beginning 60 days prior to the obligation to register[4] for this foreign principal, has the registrant disbursed or expended monies in connection with activity on behalf of the foreign principal or transmitted monies to the foreign principal?

Yes ☐   No ☐   N/A - This statement is filed to update the registrant's agreement/contract with the foreign principal.

If yes, set forth below in the required detail and separately an account of such monies, including monies transmitted, if any.

Date	Recipient	Purpose	Amount

---

1 "Political activity," as defined in Section 1(o) of the Act, means any activity which the person engaging in believes will, or that the person intends to, in any way influence any agency or official of the Government of the United States or any section of the public within the United States with reference to formulating, adopting, or changing the domestic or foreign policies of the United States or with reference to the political or public interests, policies, or relations of a government of a foreign country or a foreign political party.

2,3,4 Pursuant to Section 2(a) of the Act, an agent must register within ten days of becoming an agent, and before acting as such.

EXECUTION

In accordance with 28 U.S.C. § 1746, and subject to the penalties of 18 U.S.C. § 1001 and 22 U.S.C. § 618, the undersigned swears or affirms under penalty of perjury that he/she has read the information set forth in this statement filed pursuant to the Foreign Agents Registration Act of 1938, as amended, 22 U.S.C. § 611 *et seq.*, that he/she is familiar with the contents thereof, and that such contents are in their entirety true and accurate to the best of his/her knowledge and belief.

Date	Printed Name	Signature
08/02/2022	Mindia Gavasheli	/s/Mindia Gavasheli

EXECUTION

In accordance with 28 U.S.C. § 1746, and subject to the penalties of 18 U.S.C. § 1001 and 22 U.S.C. § 618, the undersigned swears or affirms under penalty of perjury that he/she has read the information set forth in this statement filed pursuant to the Foreign Agents Registration Act of 1938, as amended, 22 U.S.C. § 611 *et seq.*, that he/she is familiar with the contents thereof, and that such contents are in their entirety true and accurate to the best of his/her knowledge and belief.

Date	Printed Name	Signature
08/02/2022	Mindia Gavasheli	

Pushed to Extremes

Domestic Terrorism amid Polarization and Protest

By Catrina Doxsee, Seth G. Jones, Jared Thompson, Grace Hwang, and Kateryna Halstead   MAY 2022

THE ISSUE

There has been a significant rise in the number of domestic terrorist attacks and plots at demonstrations in the United States, according to new CSIS data. The result is escalating violence in U.S. cities between extremists from opposing sides, a major break from historical trends. In 2021, over half of all domestic terrorist incidents occurred in the context of metropolitan demonstrations. In addition, the most frequent targets of attacks were government, military, and law enforcement agencies, who are increasingly at the center of domestic terrorism by extremists of all ideologies.

INTRODUCTION

On the evening of February 19, 2022, Benjamin Smith—who had become enraged at the Black Lives Matter movement, Covid-19 restrictions, and the local homeless population—opened fire on protesters that were demonstrating against police violence near Normandale Park in Portland, Oregon. One woman was killed, and four people were hospitalized with gunshot wounds.[1] In August 2020, only four miles away from Normandale Park, Michael Reinoehl, an anti-fascist, shot and killed Aaron "Jay" Danielson, a member of the far-right group Patriot Prayer.[2] These attacks unfolded against a backdrop of nearly two years of heightened protest activity in urban areas of the United States.[3] Although most demonstrations have been peaceful, some have devolved into violence.

Other acts of terrorism have occurred amid growing political polarization and the mainstreaming of extremist beliefs. Most recently, on May 14, 2022, Peyton Gendron, motivated by the far-right "Great Replacement" conspiracy theory, opened fire in a grocery store in Buffalo, New York, killing 10 people

and injuring 3.[4] This conspiracy theory—which alleges that immigration is being weaponized to diminish the influence and existence of the white population—has been shared on mainstream platforms with increasing frequency.[5] The Department of Justice (DOJ) is investigating the attack "as a hate crime and an act of racially-motivated violent extremism."[6]

To better understand the trends in U.S. domestic terrorism, CSIS compiled a data set of 1,040 terrorist attacks and plots in the United States between January 1, 1994, and December 31, 2021. The 2021 data are new, and they yield several main findings.

First, there was a significant increase in the number and percentage of domestic terrorist incidents at demonstrations in cities in 2020 and 2021. In 2019, only 2 percent of all U.S. terrorist attacks and plots occurred at demonstrations, but this portion rose to 47 percent in 2020 and 53 percent in 2021. The result is that some metropolitan areas of the United States—such as Portland, Seattle, New York, Los Angeles, and Washington, D.C.—are becoming focal points of domestic terrorism, where extremists from opposing sides square off against each other and against law enforcement agencies. This development has created a "security dilemma" in metropolitan areas, where attempts by one side to improve its own security threatens the security of others, leading to further escalation.

Second, U.S. law enforcement agencies have increasingly become a target of domestic terrorists from all sides of the political spectrum. The government, military, and especially law enforcement were the primary targets of domestic terrorist attacks and plots in 2021, composing 43 percent of all attacks. They were most likely to be targeted regardless of perpetrator ideology: they were selected in 48 percent of violent far-left events, 37 percent of violent far-right events, and all Salafi-jihadist events in 2021. This development indicates that U.S. security agencies—particularly law enforcement—are increasingly at risk from domestic terrorism.

Third, there was an increase in the percentage of attacks and plots by anarchists, anti-fascists, and other likeminded extremists in 2021. While white supremacists, anti-government militias, and likeminded extremists conducted the most attacks and plots in 2021 (49 percent), the percentage of attacks and plots by anarchists, anti-fascists, and likeminded extremists grew from 23 percent in 2020 to 40 percent in 2021. This rise has occurred alongside an increase in violence at demonstrations. However, although there was a historically high level of both far-right and far-left terrorist attacks in 2021, violent far-right incidents were significantly more likely to be lethal, both in terms of weapon choice and number of resulting fatalities.

The remainder of this brief is divided into four sections. The first provides an overview of terrorism and outlines the data set used in this analysis. The second examines trends in terrorist events in the United States that are related to public demonstrations. The third describes additional findings from the data set. The final section provides brief policy implications.

TERRORISM

This analysis focuses on terrorism, which is defined as the deliberate use—or threat—of violence by non-state actors in order to achieve political goals and create a broad psychological impact.[7] For inclusion in the data set, events had to meet all parts of this definition. This definition is consistent with the official U.S. government definition of domestic terrorism under 18 U.S. Code § 2331 as "acts dangerous to human life" that occur primarily within U.S.

territory and are intended "(i) to intimidate or coerce a civilian population; (ii) to influence the policy of a government by intimidation or coercion; or (iii) to affect the conduct of a government by mass destruction, assassination, or kidnapping."[8]

The brief does not analyze the broad topic of hate speech or hate crimes, though hate speech and hate crimes are clearly concerning. There is some overlap between hate crimes and terrorism since some hate crimes include the use or threat of violence. However, some hate incidents, such as graffiti, do not involve the use or threat of violence.[9] The brief also does not include other forms of civil disturbance or criminal activity outside of the definition of terrorism, such as looting or trespassing. Some of these disturbances do not involve violence, and many individuals that participate in these activities lack political goals or an intention to cause broad psychological impact. However, the data set does include terrorist attacks committed by demonstrators, attacks targeting demonstrators, and attacks intentionally timed to occur alongside demonstrations, often to obscure the identity or the intent of the perpetrators.

This brief discusses four categories of terrorist ideologies: violent far-right, violent far-left, religious, and ethnonationalist. Events for which a political motive was identified that did not fit into one of these categories were classified as "other." When discussing perpetrator ideologies, it is important to note that extremist ideologies do not correspond to mainstream political parties in the United States. *Violent far-right* terrorists are generally motivated by ideas of racial or ethnic supremacy; opposition to government authority, including perceived overreach related to issues such as Covid-19 policies; misogyny, including incels ("involuntary celibates"); hatred based on sexuality or gender identity; belief in the QAnon conspiracy theory; or opposition to certain policies, such as abortion.[10] *Violent far-left* terrorists are motivated by an opposition to capitalism, imperialism, or colonialism; Black nationalism; support for environmental causes or animal rights; pro-communist or pro-socialist beliefs; or support for decentralized political and social systems, such as anarchism.[11] *Religious* terrorists are motivated by a faith-based belief system, such as Christianity, Hinduism, Islam, Judaism, or other faiths. All attacks recorded in the CSIS data set that were coded as religious were inspired by a Salafi-jihadist ideology, so the terms are used interchangeably in this analysis. *Ethnonationalist* terrorists are motivated by ethnic or nationalist goals, including self-determination.

Finally, data suggest that violence is most often planned

and perpetrated by a single individual or small network rather than centralized, hierarchical terrorist groups. These individuals are frequently inspired by broader ideological movements or networks, and they often become radicalized and access resources through online platforms. Many networks are inspired by the concept of "leaderless resistance," which rejects large, structured organizations in favor of decentralized networks or individual activity.[12]

Using these definitions, CSIS compiled and analyzed a data set of 1,040 terrorist attacks and plots in the United States between January 1, 1994, and December 31, 2021.[13] The data set includes information such as the incident date, location, perpetrator ideology, target, weapons used, fatalities, relation to public demonstrations, and perpetrators' current or former affiliation with the military or law enforcement.[14] A full methodology and codebook for the data set is linked at the end of this brief.

THE SECURITY DILEMMA: DOMESTIC TERRORISM AND PUBLIC DEMONSTRATIONS

Over the past two years, there has been a rise in the percentage of domestic terrorism attacks and plots at demonstrations. This phenomenon is linked to the proliferation of demonstrations and counter-demonstrations in some urban areas of the United States caused by political polarization, Covid-19 mandates, racial injustice, elections, and other factors. As ideologically opposed individuals and groups organize against each another in urban areas of the United States, there has been a spiraling of radicalization, extreme rhetoric, and violence—a phenomenon often referred to as reciprocal radicalization.[15] As this situation increasingly provokes violent action, it can also be understood as a "security dilemma," in which one side's efforts to increase its own security, typically with firearms, melee weapons, or incendiaries, decreases the security of others.[16]

At the core of the dilemma is a situation of escalating violence in some metropolitan areas of the United States that pits such groups and loose networks as anti-fascists and anarchists against white supremacists, anti-government militias, and a host of others, such as the Three Percenters, Proud Boys, Patriot Prayer, and Oath Keepers. A condition of instability and spiraling violence makes security the first concern for groups and networks. When individuals seek to protect themselves by acquiring weapons, others react by acquiring arms of their own. As tensions rise, it becomes difficult to know the intentions

of others. The security dilemma has occurred overseas in situations of emerging anarchy, such as the collapse of a state.[17] Notably, this trend has emerged amid extremist rhetoric that increasingly portrays political conflict in the United States in martial or revolutionary terms—whether as a call to action to prevent violence by opponents or, as in accelerationist ideologies, in an attempt to hasten the violent collapse of the state.[18]

This phenomenon has triggered a spike in politically motivated violence in the United States. For instance, militia members have gathered with firearms and other weapons at protests over the past two years to "protect" local businesses from looters.[19] Meanwhile, anti-fascists have organized "direct action" campaigns to prevent far-right networks from demonstrating and, when that is impossible, to impose consequences, often through violence. On its website, Rose City Antifa—an anti-fascist coalition based in Portland, Oregon—explains that it does not rely on law enforcement to counter "fascist activity" because "[t]he state upholds white supremacy at every level of government and the police frequently work with far-right aggressors to brutalize people opposing state oppression and violence. We cannot count on state actors to push forward the cause of justice, equity, and community safety. It's up to us to keep us safe."[20] Although some of these mobilizations have included members of formal groups, most have involved loose ideological networks of individuals who have organized online.

Within this analysis, "demonstrations" may include protests, sit-ins, marches, and other public gatherings intended to advance a social or political cause. To be clear, the vast majority of demonstrations have been peaceful. As Bruce Hoffman and Jacob Ware argue with data from the Armed Conflict Location & Event Data Project (ACLED), "of the more than 10,600 demonstrations and protests held throughout the United States between May and August 2020, more than 10,000—nearly 93 percent—were peaceful, with demonstrators not engaging in violence."[21] Peaceful demonstrations and protests are important to exercise First Amendment rights. Nevertheless, the data show that in a politically charged climate—especially in metropolitan areas—some demonstrations are incubators of domestic terrorism. This is particularly concerning in light of recent studies indicating that a historically high percentage of Americans believe that violence against the government or against individuals with opposing views can be justified.[22]

The rest of this section analyzes the connection between

Figure 1: Percentage of U.S. Terrorist Attacks and Plots Related to Demonstrations, 1994–2021

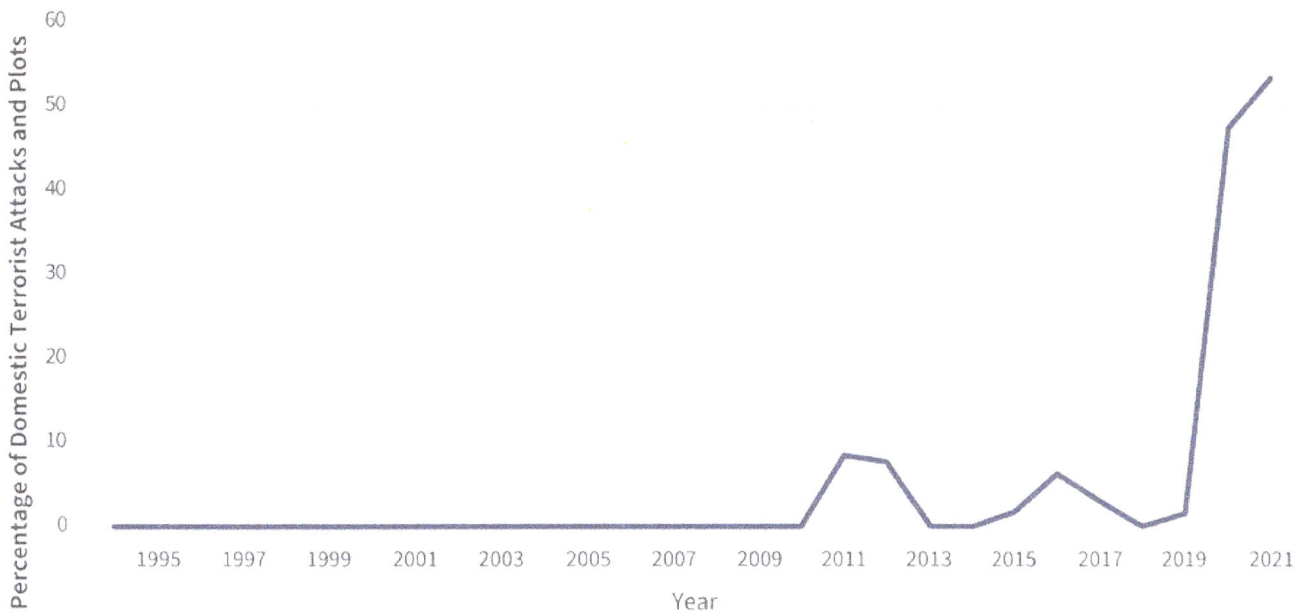

Source: Data compiled by CSIS Transnational Threats Project

domestic terrorist activity and demonstrations in the United States in three parts. First, it assesses the portion of terrorist attacks and plots related to demonstrations since 1994. Second, it evaluates the most common targets of attacks related to demonstrations in recent years, including whether attacks were more likely to be committed by demonstrators or to target them. Finally, it assesses the ideological motivation of individuals who have committed or planned domestic terrorist attacks in connection with demonstrations in 2020 and 2021.

PERCENTAGE OF TERRORIST ACTIVITY RELATED TO DEMONSTRATIONS

The United States began to see a rise in domestic terrorist activity linked to public demonstrations in 2020. By 2021, more than half of all domestic terrorist incidents occurred during public demonstrations. To better understand this changing context for domestic terrorism, this section examines trends in the subset of domestic terrorist attacks and plots that were related to demonstrations.

As shown in Figure 1, the data set recorded no terrorist incidents in the United States during demonstrations between 1994 and 2010.[23] Some domestic terrorism incidents occurred at demonstrations between 2011 to 2012 and 2015 to 2017, but the percentage of all terrorist attacks and plots at demonstrations did not exceed 8 percent in either period. For example, in October 2011, an individual threw a homemade chemical bomb into an Occupy Maine encampment in Portland, Maine.[24] In

July 2016, Micah Xavier Johnson opened fire at a peaceful march in Dallas, Texas, killing five police officers and wounding nine other officers and two civilians.[25] But the overall numbers were low.

There was a substantial increase in terrorist attacks and plots at demonstrations in 2020, with the percentage of all domestic terrorist activity jumping from 2 percent (1 of 65 incidents) in 2019 to 47 percent (52 of 110 incidents) in 2020. Although fewer attacks occurred in 2021 than in 2020, the percentage of all U.S. terrorist attacks and plots related to demonstrations continued to grow. In 2021, 53 percent of all domestic terrorist activity (41 of 77 incidents) occurred at demonstrations. For example, on August 22, 2021, anti-government and anti-vaccination extremists gathered in Portland, Oregon, for an event titled "Summer of Love: United We Stand Divided We Fall," which was intended to show opposition to Covid-19 vaccinations and demand the release of individuals arrested during the January 6 attack at the U.S. Capitol. During this event, Dennis G. Anderson reportedly showed lynching videos to counterprotesters, made racist remarks and threats with a knife, and then began shooting at counterprotesters.[26]

DEMONSTRATORS AS TARGETS AND PERPETRATORS

To better understand how terrorist attacks unfolded in the context of public demonstrations, CSIS analyzed data on the targets of attacks in 2020 and 2021 that occurred at demonstrations. Demonstrators were the targets of 41

Figure 2: Targets of U.S. Terrorist Attacks and Plots Related to Demonstrations, 2020–2021

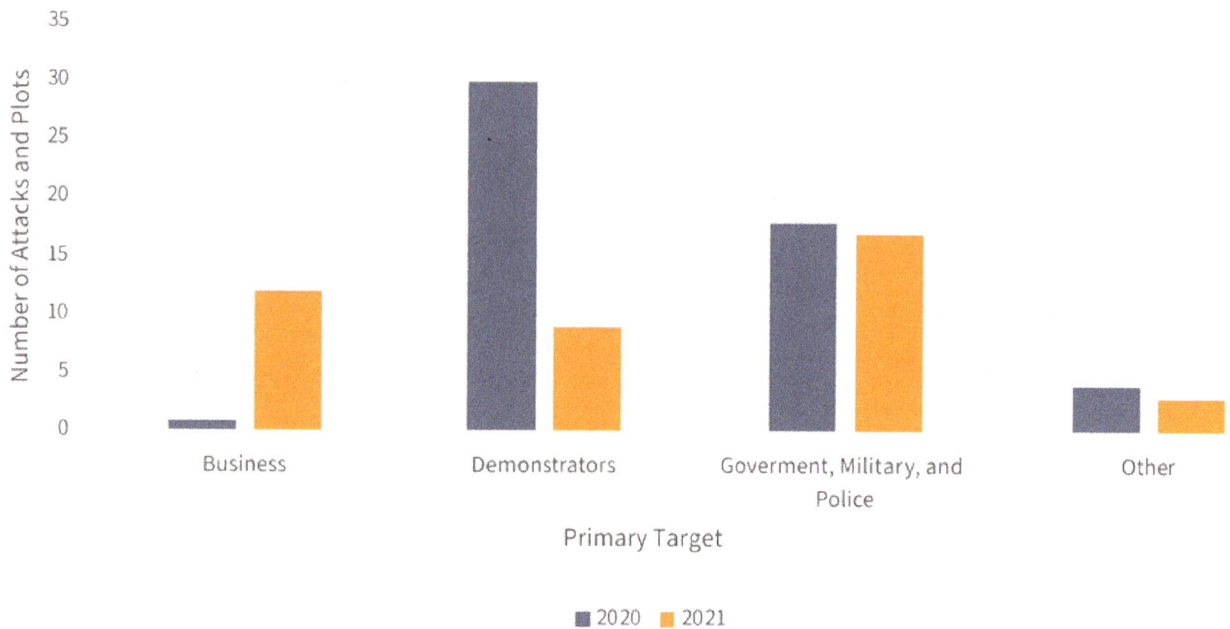

Source: Data compiled by CSIS Transnational Threats Project.

percent of all terrorist attacks and plots related to public demonstrations, making them the most common target of such incidents in 2020 and 2021. For example, in October 2021, William Aslaksen argued with members of a crowd protesting against the federal Covid-19 vaccination mandate in Palmdale, California, then intentionally drove his Jeep Wrangler into the crowd, injuring one woman.[27] Demonstrators were not targeted equally across the two years, however. In these types of attacks, demonstrators were the target in 30 cases in 2020 and 9 in 2021.

Government, military, and police locations and personnel were the second-most common target of terrorist incidents related to demonstrations from 2020 to 2021, composing 37 percent of all such incidents during the two-year period. They were the most common target in 2021. The most prominent instance was the violent storming of the U.S. Capitol on January 6, 2021, by individuals attempting to stop the certification of the 2020 presidential election results.[28] Between 2020 and 2021, businesses were targeted in 14 percent of terrorist events related to demonstrations, and the remaining 7 percent were directed against other targets, including journalists, private individuals, religious institutions, and infrastructure.

IDEOLOGIES BEHIND DEMONSTRATION-LINKED TERRORIST ATTACKS

In 2020, most attacks related to demonstrations (58 percent) were conducted by violent far-right

perpetrators, including white supremacists, militia members, and other anti-government extremists. Many of these attacks were related to the 2020 presidential election or opposition to racial justice protests and Covid-19 restrictions. In 2021, however, 73 percent of attacks related to demonstrations were orchestrated by violent far-left individuals, including anarchists, anti-fascist extremists, and violent environmentalists. These incidents were largely related to opposition to far-right ideologies and opposition to law enforcement, including perceptions that law enforcement was sympathetic to the far-right or operated with corruption or bias. While this ideological opposition has long existed, the sharp increase in violent far-left activity related to demonstrations likely is linked to the historically high level of far-right violence in 2020, which coincided with extensive media coverage of police violence against Black individuals and heightened tensions surrounding the Covid-19 pandemic and 2020 presidential election. As Rose City Antifa and other far-left groups have articulated, in the face of perceived state inaction or complicity, far-left extremists may see themselves as the only ones able to act.[29]

OTHER DATA FINDINGS

CSIS data also highlighted trends in the number and type of U.S. terrorist attacks and plots. This section analyzes the data in three parts: incidents and fatalities, perpetrator ideology, and types of weapons and targets.

Figure 3: U.S. Terrorist Attacks and Plots and Fatalities, 1994–2021

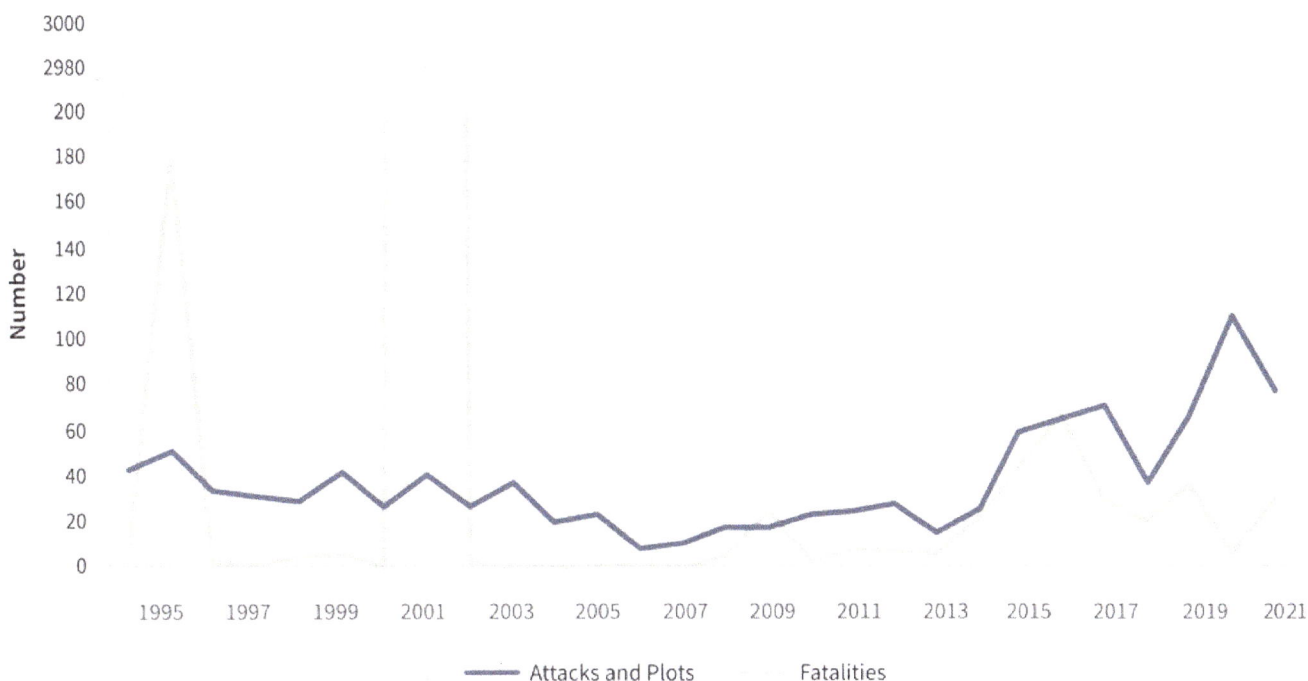

INCIDENTS AND FATALITIES

The total number of domestic terrorist attacks and plots decreased from its height in 2020, though 2021 still had the second-highest number of attacks and plots in the past three decades. In 2021, there were 77 terrorist attacks and plots in the United States, a decrease of 30 percent from the prior year.

However, the number of fatalities increased from 5 in 2020 to 30 in 2021, as shown in Figure 3. This level was roughly comparable to 2019, when there were 35 fatalities from terrorism in the United States. The recent increase in domestic terrorist activity began around 2014. From 2014 to 2021, there have been an average of 31 fatalities per year, indicating that the 30 deaths in 2021 were typical of this period. This is substantially more than the period from 1994 to 2013, when there were only three years in which more than eight individuals were killed in terrorist attacks in the United States: 1995, 2001, and 2009. These were primarily due to the Oklahoma City bombing, the 9/11 attacks, and the Fort Hood shooting, respectively.

The return to a higher level of fatalities in 2021 may indicate that the lower number of deaths in 2020 was an anomaly. For instance, this number may have been the result of the Covid-19 pandemic and related lockdown policies, which disrupted routines and reduced mass gatherings. Or it could

have been caused by perpetrators' prioritization of less lethal tactics, such as melee weapons and incendiary devices.

Terrorist attacks and plots in 2021 spanned 18 states and Washington, D.C., as shown in Figure 4. While many of these events took place in large metropolitan areas, these cities were dispersed across the continental United States. The highest concentration of incidents occurred in and around Portland, Oregon, where CSIS tracked 18 terrorist attacks and plots in 2021. The next highest number of terrorist incidents occurred in New York City, where there were 7 attacks and plots in 2021.

PERPETRATOR IDEOLOGY

Violent far-right attacks and plots remained the most frequent type of domestic terrorism in 2021, but violent far-left perpetrators committed a growing percentage of attacks. As shown in Figure 5, of the 77 terrorist events in 2021, 38 events (49 percent) were perpetrated by those on the violent far-right, 31 events (40 percent) by the violent far-left, 3 events (4 percent) by Salafi-jihadists, 2 events (3 percent) by ethnonationalists, and 3 events (4 percent) by those with other motives.

Most violent far-right perpetrators were motivated by white supremacist or anti-government sentiments, and they committed most of the fatal attacks in 2021. Of the 30 fatalities in 2021, 28 resulted from far-right terrorist attacks. White supremacists killed 13 people, a violent misogynist killed 8, anti-government extremists killed 4, and an anti-vaccination perpetrator killed 3. On June 26 in Winthrop, Massachusetts, for example, Nathan Allen shot and killed two Black individuals after crashing a stolen box truck. Allen had frequently read extremist material and had written journals filled with white nationalist beliefs, including calls for white people—who he believed to be "apex predators"—to kill Black people.[30]

Most violent far-left perpetrators were motivated by anarchism, anti-fascism, or anti-police stances. Although these actors committed a historically high number of terrorist attacks and plots in 2021, only one resulted in a fatality. On June 24 in Daytona Beach, Florida, Othal Wallace shot and killed local police officer Jason Raynor.

Figure 4: Location of U.S. Terrorist Attacks and Plots, 2021

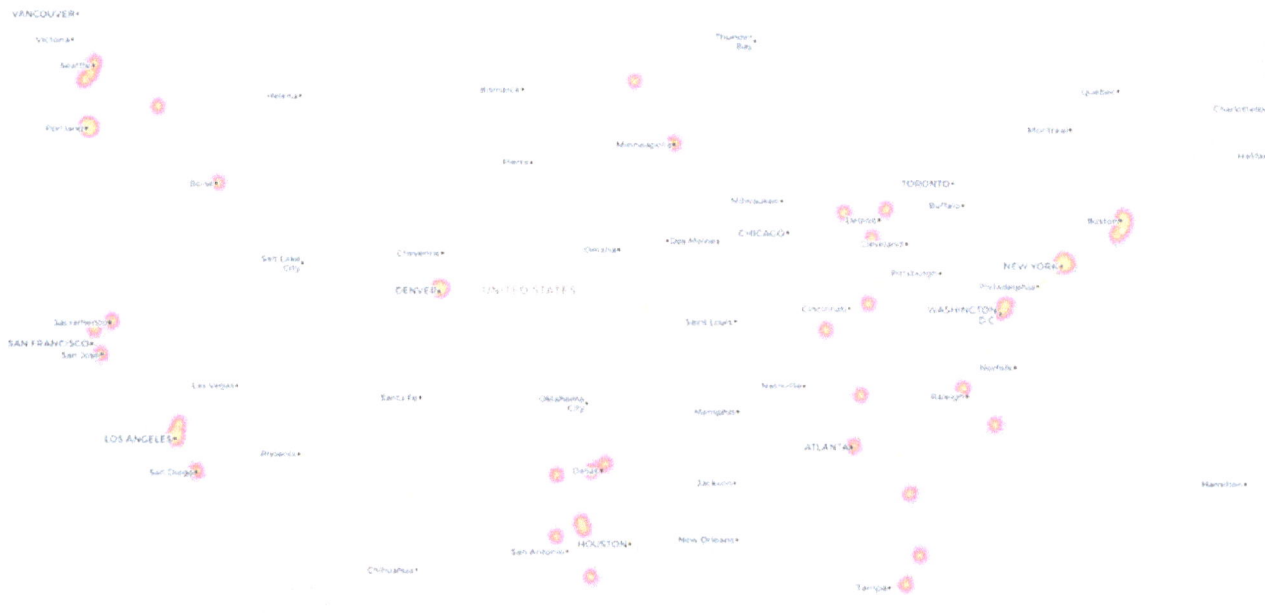

Source: Data compiled by the CSIS Transnational Threats Project.
Note: No attacks occurred in Hawaii, Alaska, or Puerto Rico in 2021.

Figure 5: U.S. Terrorist Attacks and Plots by Perpetrator Orientation, 1994–2021

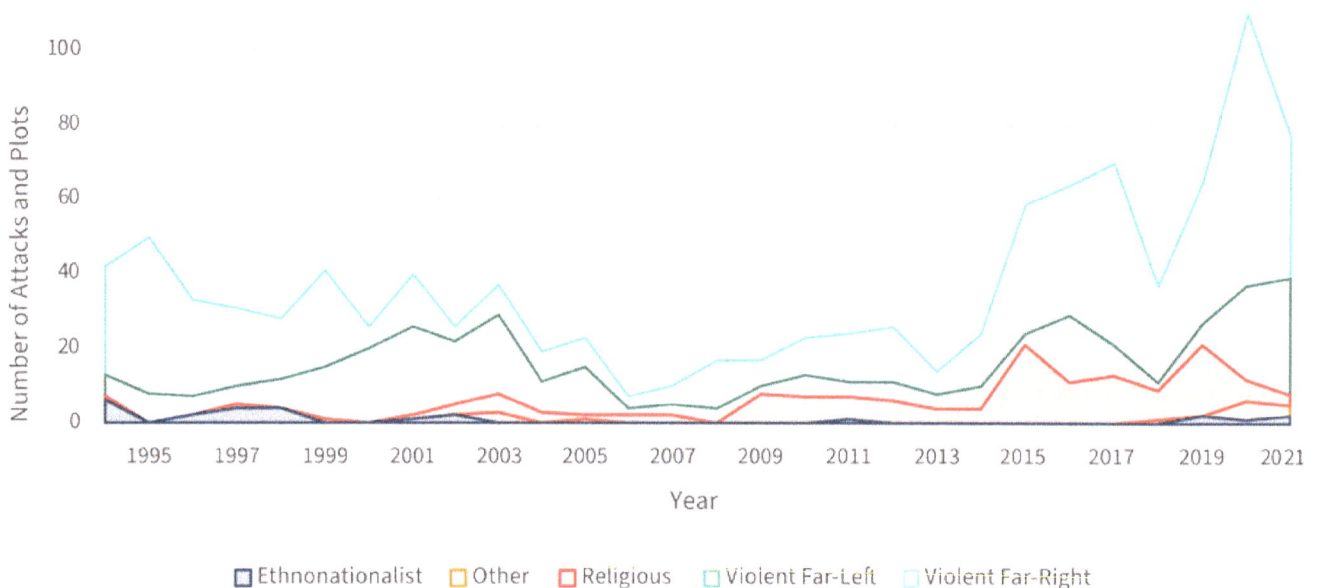

Source: Data compiled by the CSIS Transnational Threats Project.

Wallace had links to several Black nationalist paramilitary groups, including the Not F*****g Around Coalition and Black Nation, the latter of which he founded in early 2021.[31]

The three religious terrorist events in 2021, all of which were committed by individuals inspired by Salafi-jihadist beliefs, made up a relatively low percentage of all domestic terrorist activity. Two of these incidents were disrupted plots, but the third was an attack resulting in one fatality. On August 29, Imran Ali Rasheed shot and killed a Lyft driver in Garland, Texas, then opened fire inside a police office in Plano, Texas. The Federal Bureau of Investigation (FBI) revealed that Rasheed left a note indicating that he may have been inspired by a foreign terrorist organization and had previously been investigated for terrorist connections.[32]

WEAPONS AND TARGETS

In 2021, violent far-right attackers primarily used highly lethal weapons, such as firearms, while far-left attackers mainly used melee weapons, such as knives or bludgeoning weapons, which are less lethal. Regardless of perpetrator ideology, most terrorist fatalities in 2021 were from firearms: 9 of the 11 fatal attacks were committed with firearms, accounting for 26 of the 30 deaths.[33]

Of the 38 far-right terrorist attacks and plots in 2021, 16 used firearms, 9 involved explosives and incendiaries, 4 were melee attacks, and 2 were vehicular attacks. On March 16, for example, Robert Aaron Long conducted a shooting spree at three spas in the Atlanta metropolitan area, killing eight individuals and injuring one. Long viewed the women working at these spas as a "temptation" and aimed to help other men suffering from "sex addiction" by killing them.[34]

Of the 31 far-left terrorist attacks and plots in 2021, 19 were melee attacks, 3 primarily used explosives or incendiaries, 2 used firearms, and 1 was a vehicular attack. The large number of melee attacks was a diversion from the violent far-left's traditional reliance on explosives and incendiaries.[35] Most of these melee attacks involved deliberate property damage, and some attacks also included incendiaries as a secondary weapon. On October 12, after a memorial gathering for a local anarchist activist in Portland, Oregon, a group of approximately 100 individuals smashed windows, destroyed property, and set fires at banks, retail stores, and government buildings, causing over $500,000 in damage.[36] This attack was later shared on anarchist news websites.

Figure 6: Primary Weapon Used in U.S. Violent Far-Right and Violent Far-Left Terrorist Attacks and Plots, 2021

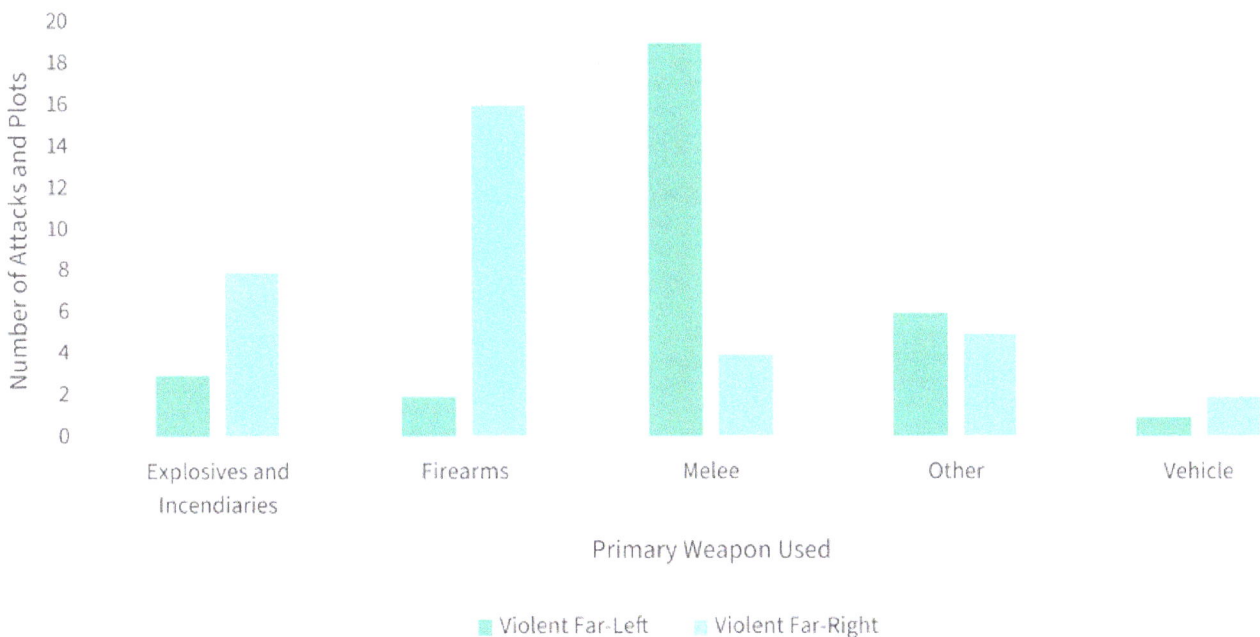

Government, military, and police locations and personnel were the most frequent targets of domestic terrorist attacks in 2021 regardless of perpetrator orientation. As seen in Figure 7, of the total 77 terrorist attacks and plots in 2021, 29 were directed against government, military, and police targets. These perpetrators identified with a range of ideologies and movements, including the QAnon conspiracy, the sovereign citizen movement, militia groups, anarchism, anti-fascism, environmentalism, and other anti-government and anti-authority philosophies. The next most common target for violent far-left perpetrators was businesses, while the next most common target for violent far-right individuals was private individuals, frequently targeted based on identity categories such as race, ethnicity, religion, or gender.

The reliance by violent far-right perpetrators on weapons such as guns, explosives, and incendiaries is consistent with their larger share of fatal attacks in 2021. These attacks often targeted people directly, particularly government personnel and private individuals. Meanwhile, violent far-left perpetrators primarily used melee weapons and incendiaries to cause property damage, particularly against government and police buildings and businesses. These data indicate that while both violent far-right and violent far-left actors

committed a historically large number of terrorist attacks in 2021, violent far-right actors were more likely to pursue their motives with lethal intent.

POLICY IMPLICATIONS

With domestic terrorism occurring at a high rate across the country, including in the context of public demonstrations, policymakers need access to comprehensive, objective data to better understand the threat, better assess what factors are causing an increase (or decrease) in the threat levels, and craft recommendations. Political polarization in the United States has grown in recent years, including among the general public, members of Congress, and within political parties.[37] Despite this political polarization, however, policymakers—including from the legislative branch—need to pursue bipartisan efforts to reject all forms of terrorism. By definition, terrorism involves the use or threat of violence and is illegal. Freedom of speech is protected by the First Amendment of the U.S. Constitution, but violence is not. In fact, violence and the threat of violence can undermine the ability and willingness of individuals to express their ideas in accordance with their First Amendment rights. As Portland commissioner Jo Ann Hardesty concluded in a statement after the February 2022 shooting, "We know this [violence

Figure 7: Targets of U.S. Violent Far-Right and Violent Far-Left Terrorist Attacks and Plots, 2021

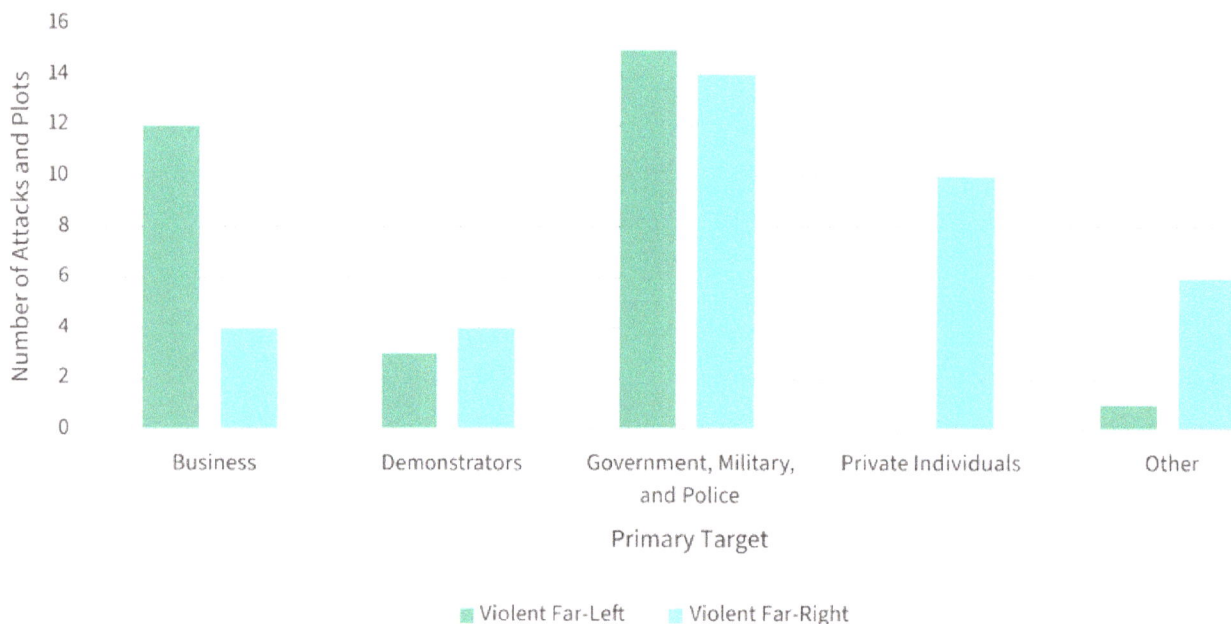

Source: Data compiled by the CSIS Transnational Threats Project.

against demonstrators] has a chilling effect on civic engagement."[38] Studies on public willingness to participate in demonstrations and voice political opinions have reached the same conclusion.[39]

The rest of this section outlines several recommendations for policymakers and law enforcement, with the goal of bridging ideological divides, gaining public trust, and establishing more effective counterterrorism policies.

First, the U.S. government should publicly release comprehensive data on terrorist attacks and plots, the characteristics of perpetrators, and other factors such as tactics and targets. Data analysis could offer an objective mechanism for apportioning counterterrorism resources and efforts relative to actual threats. The FBI (and more broadly the DOJ) or Department of Homeland Security (DHS) should issue annual or biannual reports to the House and Senate Judiciary, Homeland Security, and Intelligence Committees that assess the domestic terrorism threat; analyze domestic terrorism incidents that occurred in the previous six months or one year; and provide transparency through a public quantitative analysis of domestic terrorism-related assessments, investigations, incidents, arrests, indictments, prosecutions, convictions, and weapons recoveries.

It is concerning that the U.S. government does not publicly release comprehensive data on domestic terrorist attacks and plots. Without reliable data, it is virtually impossible to adopt effective counterterrorism policies. Instead, it has historically taken high-profile attacks, such as the 1995 Oklahoma City bombing or the 2021 attack on the U.S. Capitol, to trigger federal review and policy change. In the wake of the Capitol attack, several federal agencies are conducting internal reviews and policy updates. Now is an ideal time to bridge these activities by establishing a coordinated approach to data collection and management across relevant federal and state government bodies—such as the recommendations for data standardization across systems compiled by the U.S. Department of Defense (DOD) Countering Extremist Activity Working Group. Secretary Austin created the group in April 2021 to implement a set of counterextremism policy changes in the DOD and to develop recommendations for longer-term counterextremism efforts.[40]

Second, state, local, and tribal law enforcement agencies need additional help, including resources, to identify and respond to domestic terrorism "left of boom" (before an attack occurs). The DHS, DOJ, and FBI should continue to review their respective counterterrorism training and resource programs that are provided to federal, state, local, and tribal law enforcement agencies and ensure that such programs include sufficient training and resources in understanding, detecting, deterring, and investigating acts of domestic terrorism. Congress should also consider encouraging the DHS to increase funds for the Nonprofit Security Grant Program, which provides funding for nonprofit organizations, including houses of worship, to improve and upgrade their security.

Third, the U.S. government, its partners overseas, and the private sector need to continue to aggressively target individuals and groups that espouse violence on digital platforms. This is a war of ideas on virtual battlefields as much as on the streets of U.S. cities and towns. Virtually all domestic extremists use the internet and social media platforms to issue propaganda, coordinate training, raise funds, recruit members, and communicate with others. Policymakers should continue to demand that these digital platforms take down content that supports domestic terrorism and violates their terms of service.

Fourth, state and city officials should consider legislation banning or restricting the presence of firearms and other weapons at public demonstrations, which could ameliorate the security dilemma emerging in some U.S. cities. As CSIS analysis shows, firearms are used in most fatal domestic terrorist attacks, and a growing portion of terrorist attacks and plots are occurring at demonstrations. Furthermore, a recent study found that armed demonstrations are six times more likely to become violent or destructive than unarmed demonstrations.[41] Although the First and Second Amendments preserve the right to free speech—including symbolic speech—and to bear arms, respectively, judicial precedent suggests that armed protest may not fall under the umbrella of symbolic speech, and therefore may be restricted in the interest of public safety.[42]

In addition, a recent study found that the presence of firearms at demonstrations significantly reduces the likelihood of individuals attending the event and voicing their opinions due to a perceived threat from individuals with opposing views.[43] The study also found that the perception of danger from armed protests and the subsequent chilling effect were significant regardless of the ideology of respondents. This implies that legislation more closely governing the presence of weapons at demonstrations could be supported by policymakers from across the political spectrum if there is assurance and evidence that it will be enforced evenly, regardless of demonstrators' beliefs or motives.

Despite the worrying data trends, there is cause for hope.

Over the past year, a growing number of federal efforts to counter domestic extremism have prioritized better understanding the scope and nature of domestic extremism and developing long-term strategies to respond to and prevent terrorist activity. This indicates a willingness to take a methodical, research-driven approach to domestic counterterrorism efforts. With significant agreement that terrorism is illegal and a threat to the United States, policymakers must now find ways to collaborate to establish longer-term systemic responses that prioritize transparency to protect the security of all Americans. ■

Catrina Doxsee is an associate director and associate fellow with the Transnational Threats Project at the Center for Strategic and International Studies (CSIS) in Washington, D.C. *Seth G. Jones* is senior vice president and director of the International Security Program at CSIS and author most recently of Three Dangerous Men: Russia, China, Iran, and the Rise of Irregular Warfare *(W.W. Norton, 2021). Jared Thompson* is a research associate with the Transnational Threats Project at CSIS. *Grace Hwang* is a program coordinator and research assistant with the Burke Chair in Strategy and Transnational Threats Project at CSIS. *Kateryna Halstead* is a research assistant with the Transnational Threats Project at CSIS.

*The authors give special thanks to **Colin Clarke** for his review of the document—including the data set—and his helpful critique. They also thank CSIS colleagues **Michelle Macander, Brian McSorley,** and **Devi Nair** for their insightful comments. Finally, thanks to **Leena Marte** and **William Taylor** for their graphic design and to **Jeeah Lee, Katherine Stark,** and **Rayna Salam** for their publication support.*

For an overview of the methodology used in compiling the data set, please see **here.**

This brief is made possible by general support to CSIS. No direct sponsorship contributed to this brief.

ENDNOTES

1   Portland Police Bureau, "UPDATE #4: Normandale Park Murder Suspect Booked Into Jail," press release, March 23, 2022, https://www.portlandoregon.gov/police/news/read.cfm?id=402187; Bryan Pietsch, "Man Charged with Murder in Portland, Ore., Shooting at Protest Against Police Violence," *Washington Post*, February 23, 2022, https://www.washingtonpost.com/nation/2022/02/23/portland-oregon-shooting-benjamin-smith/; and Maxine Bernstein and Shane Dixon Kavanaugh, "Portland Man Under Suspicion in Mass Shooting Fixated on City's Protests, Homeless Problem, Neighbors and Family Say," *The Oregonian*, February 25, 2022, https://www.oregonlive.com/crime/2022/02/portland-man-under-suspicion-in-mass-shooting-fixated-on-citys-protests-homeless-problem-neighbors-and-family-say.html.

2   Lewis Kamb and Hal Bernton, "Portland Shooting Suspect Followed Right-wing Activists After Spotting Them Downtown, Unsealed Arrest Warrant Says," *Seattle Times*, September 5, 2020, https://www.seattletimes.com/seattle-news/portland-shooting-suspect-followed-right-wing-activists-after-spotting-them-downtown-unsealed-arrest-warrant-says/; Neil MacFarquhar, Mike Baker, and Adam Goldman, "In His Last Hours, Portland Murder Suspect Said He Feared Arrest," *New York Times*, September 4, 2020, https://www.nytimes.com/2020/09/04/us/portland-shooting-michael-reinoehl.html; and Destiny Johnson and Cassidy Quinn, "Unsealed Documents Shed Light on Moments Before Fatal Downtown Portland Shooting," KGW8, September 4, 2020, https://www.kgw.com/article/news/local/multnomah-county-district-attorney-provides-new-information-inhomicide-case/283-629b983a-620a-469e-bc03-4b365a99a547; and "Court Docs Reveal What Led Up to Deadly Mass Shooting at Portland, Oregon Protest," KATU, February 22, 2022, https://katu.com/news/local/court-docs-reveal-what-led-up-to-deadly-mass-shooting-at-portland-protest.

3   For comprehensive data on protest activity in the United States since May 2020, see "U.S. Crisis Monitor," Armed Conflict Location & Event Data Project (ACLED), https://acleddata.com/special-projects/us-crisis-monitor/.

4   Isaac Stanley-Becker and Drew Harwell, "Buffalo Suspect Allegedly Inspired by Racist Theory Fueling Global Carnage," *Washington Post*, May 15, 2022, https://www.washingtonpost.com/nation/2022/05/15/buffalo-shooter-great-replacement-extremism/.

5   Colin P. Clarke, "Op-Ed: The Buffalo Gunman Emerged from a Far-Right Ecosystem that's Gone Mainstream," *Los Angeles Times*, May 15, 2022, https://www.latimes.com/opinion/story/2022-05-15/buffalo-shooting-gunman-white-supremacist-great-replacement.

6   U.S. Department of Justice, "Justice Department Statement on the Mass Shooting in Buffalo, NY," Office of Public Affairs, Press Release, May 14, 2022, https://www.justice.gov/opa/pr/justice-department-statement-mass-shooting-buffalo-ny.

7   On definitions of terrorism, see, for example, Bruce Hoffman, *Inside Terrorism*, 2nd ed. (New York, NY: Columbia University Press, 2006), 1–41, https://www.rand.org/pubs/commercial_books/CB386.html; and Global Terrorism Database, *Codebook: Inclusion Criteria and Variables* (College Park, MD: University of Maryland, October 2019), https://www.start.umd.edu/gtd/downloads/Codebook.pdf.

8   18 U.S. Code § 2331.

9   On similarities and differences between terrorism and hate crimes, see Tore Bjørgo and Jacob Aasland Ravndal, *Extreme-Right Violence and Terrorism: Concepts, Patterns, and Responses* (The Hague, Belgium: International Centre for Counter-Terrorism, September 2019), https://icct.nl/publication/extreme-right-violence-and-terrorism-concepts-patterns-and-responses/; Daniel Koehler, *Violence and Terrorism from the Far-Right: Policy Options to Counter an Elusive Threat* (The Hague, Belgium: International Centre for Counter-Terrorism, February 2019), 9, https://icct.nl/wp-content/uploads/2019/02/Koehler-Violence-and-Terrorism-from-the-Far-Right-February-2019.pdf; James B. Jacobs and Kimberly Potter, *Hate Crimes: Criminal Law and Identity Politics* (New York, NY: Oxford University Press, 1998); Kathleen Deloughery, Ryan King, and Victor Asal, "Close Cousins or Distant Relatives? The Relationship Between Terrorism and Hate Crime," *Crime & Delinquency* 58, no. 5 (October 2012): 663–88, doi:10.1177/0011128712452956; Randy Blazak, "Isn't Every Crime a Hate Crime? The Case for Hate Crime Laws," *Sociology Compass* 5, no. 4 (April 2011): 244–55, https://www.researchgate.net/publication/260416492_Isn't_Every_Crime_a_Hate_Crime_The_Case_for_Hate_Crime_Laws; and Donald P. Green, Laurence H. McFalls, and Jennifer K. Smith, "Hate Crime: An Emergent Research Agenda," *Annual Review of Sociology* 27 (August 2001): 479–504, doi:10.1146/annurev.soc.27.1.479.

10 Far-right terrorists are often described as believing that social and racial inequality is inevitable, desirable, and natural. They also possess views that include anti-egalitarianism, nativism, and authoritarianism. See Jacob Aasland Ravndal et al., *RTV Trend Report 2019: Right Wing Terrorism and Violence in Western Europe, 1990-2018* (Oslo, Norway: Center for Research on Extremism, 2019), 3, https://www.sv.uio.no/c-rex/english/groups/rtv-dataset/trend-report-2019.pdf. Also see Jacob Aasland Ravndal and Tore Bjørgo, "Investigating Terrorism from the Extreme Right: A Review of Past and Present Research," *Perspectives on Terrorism* 12, no. 6 (December 2018): 5–22, https://www.universiteitleiden.nl/binaries/content/assets/customsites/perspectives-on-terrorism/2018/issue-6/a1-ravndal-and-bjorgo.pdf; Ehud Sprinzak, "Right-Wing Terrorism in a Comparative Perspective: the Case of Split Delegitimization," *Terrorism and Political Violence* 7, no. 1 (1995): 17–43, doi:10.1080/09546559508427284; and Cas Mudde, "Right-Wing Extremism Analyzed: A Comparative Analysis of the Ideologies of Three Alleged Right-Wing Extremist Parties (NPD, NDP, CP'86)," *European Journal of Political Research* 27, no. 2 (1995): 203–24, doi:10.1111/j.1475-6765.1995.tb00636.x.

11 Much of the literature on terrorism has classified Black nationalist groups as far left. Many adherents of Black nationalism have opposed colonialism and imperialism, supported Marxist-Leninist views, advocated anarchism, and cooperated with other far-left individuals and groups. See, for example, William Rosenau, "'Our Backs Are Against the Wall': The Black Liberation Army and Domestic Terrorism in 1970s America," *Studies in Conflict and Terrorism* 36, no. 2 (2013): 176–92, doi:10.1080/1057610X.2013.747074; Dana M. Williams, "Black Panther Radical Factionalization and the Development of Black Anarchism," *Journal of Black Studies* 46, no. 7 (2015): 678–703, doi:10.1177/0021934715593053; and Steven Windisch, Gina Scott Ligon, and Pete Simi, "Organizational [Dis]trust: Comparing Disengagement Among Former Left-Wing and Right-Wing Violent Extremists," *Studies in Conflict and Terrorism* 42, no. 6 (2019): 559–80, doi:10.1080/1057610X.2017.1404000.

12 See, for example, Louis Beam, "Leaderless Resistance," *The Seditionist* 12 (February 1992): 5.

13 Of the 1,040 terrorist events between January 1, 1994, and December 31, 2021, 831 were terrorist attacks and 209 were disrupted plots. Of the 77 terrorist events in 2021, 64 were terrorist attacks and 13 were disrupted plots.

14 A full methodology with codebook is linked at the end of the brief. CSIS drew events from the following databases and other sources: ACLED (2020–2021); the Anti-Defamation League's (ADL) Hate, Extremism, Anti-Semitism, and Terrorism (H.E.A.T.) Map (2002–2021); Janes Terrorism and Insurgency Events (2009–2021); START GTD (1994–2017); and press releases and reports from the Federal Bureau of Investigation and Department of Justice. TNT cross-referenced events against criminal complaints and affidavits, when possible, as well as local and national news sources such as the *New York Times*, *Washington Post*, and *Los Angeles Times*. For some of the external databases referenced, see Clionadh Raleigh, Andrew Linke, Håvard Hegre, and Joakim Karlsen, "Introducing ACLED-Armed Conflict Location and Event Data," *Journal of Peace Research* 47, no. 5 (2010): 651–60, doi:10.1177/0022343310378914; "ADL H.E.A.T. Map," ADL, Center on Extremism, https://www.adl.org/education-and-resources/resource-knowledge-base/adl-heat-map; and "Janes Terrorism and Insurgency Events," Janes, https://www.janes.com/military-threat-intelligence/terrorism-and-insurgency.

15 See, for example, Kim Knott, Ben Lee, and Simon Copeland, Briefings: Reciprocal Radicalisation (Lancaster, UK: Centre for Research and Evidence on Security Threats (CREST), September 2018), https://crestresearch.ac.uk/resources/reciprocal-radicalisation/; Jacob Davey and Mario Peuker, "How the Left and the Right Radicalize Each Other," Fair Observer, February 4, 2021, https://www.fairobserver.com/region/asia_pacific/jacob-davey-mario-peucker-far-left-far-right-reciprocal-radicalization-australia-news-14251/; and Roger Eatwell, "Community Cohesion and Cumulative Extremism Contemporary Britain," Political Quarterly 77, no. 2 (2006): 206–16, **doi:10.1111/j.1467-923X.2006.00763.x.**

16 The security dilemma has been most significantly developed in the international relations literature. See, for example, John Herz, "Idealist Internationalism and the Security Dilemma," *World Politics* 2, no. 2 (January 1950): 157–80, doi:10.2307/2009187; Robert Jervis, "Cooperation Under the Security Dilemma," *World Politics* 30, no. 2 (January 1978): 167–214, doi:10.2307/2009958; Charles L. Glaser, "Realists as Optimists: Cooperation as Self-Help," International Security 19, no. 3 (Winter 1994/95): 50–90, doi:10.2307/2539079; and Charles L. Glaser, "The Security Dilemma Revisited," World Politics 50, no. 1 (October 1997): 171–201, https://www.jstor.org/stable/25054031.

17 See, for example, Barry Posen, "The Security Dilemma and Ethnic Conflict," *Survival* 35, no. 1 (Spring 1993), 27–47, doi:10.1080/00396339308442672.

18 Daveed Gartenstein-Ross, Samuel Hodgson, and Colin Clarke, "The Growing Threat Posed by Accelerationism and Accelerationist Groups Worldwide," Foreign Policy Research Institute, April 2020, https://www.fpri.org/article/2020/04/the-growing-threat-posed-by-accelerationism-and-accelerationist-groups-worldwide/; Brian Hughes and Cynthia Miller-Idriss, "Uniting for Total Collapse: The January 6 Boost to Accelerationism," Combating Terrorism Center at West Point, *CTC Sentinel* 14, no. 4 (April/May 2021), https://ctc.westpoint.edu/uniting-for-total-collapse-the-january-6-boost-to-accelerationism/; and Luke Mogelson, "In the Streets with Antifa," *New Yorker*, October 25, 2020, https://www.newyorker.com/magazine/2020/11/02/trump-antifa-movement-portland.

19 See, for example, Isaac Stanley-Becker, "As Protests Spread to Small-Town America, Militia Groups Respond With Armed Intimidation and Online Threats," *Washington Post*, June 18, 2020, https://www.washingtonpost.com/national/as-protests-spread-to-small-town-america-militia-groups-respond-with-online-threats-and-armed-intimidation/2020/06/18/75c4655e-b0a1-11ea-8f56-63f38c990077_story.html.

20 "About: Frequently Asked Questions," Rose City Antifa, accessed February 7, 2022.

21 Bruce Hoffman and Jacob Ware, "Terrorism and Counterterrorism Challenges of the Biden Administration," Combating Terrorism Center at West Point, *CTC Sentinel* 14, no. 1 (January 2021): 6, https://ctc.westpoint.edu/wp-content/uploads/2021/01/CTC-SENTINEL-012021.pdf; and "US Crisis Monitor Releases Full Data For Summer 2020," ACLED, August 31, 2020, https://acleddata.com/2020/08/31/us-crisis-monitor-releases-full-data-for-summer-2020/.

22 Meryl Kornfield and Mariana Alfaro, "1 in 3 Americans Say Violence Against Government Can Be Justified, Citing Fears of Political Schism, Pandemic," *Washington Post*, January 1, 2022, https://www.washingtonpost.com/politics/2022/01/01/1-3-americans-say-violence-against-government-can-be-justified-citing-fears-political-schism-pandemic/; and Matthew S. Schwartz, "1 in 4 Americans Say Violence Against the Government is Sometimes OK," NPR, January 31, 2022, https://www.npr.org/2022/01/31/1076873172/one-in-four-americans-say-violence-against-the-government-is-sometimes-okay.

23 Although the absence of terrorist incidents in the United States during demonstrations between 1994 and 2010 may be due in part to methodological limitations in tracking events in the earliest period that the data set covers, any incidents overlooked were likely not part of a significant trend.

24 David Hench, "Chemical Bomb Tossed into Occupy Maine Encampment," *Portland Press Herald*, October 23, 2011, https://www.pressherald.com/2011/10/23/chemical-bomb-tossed-into-occupy-maine-encampment/; and "Chemical Bomb Thrown at Occupy Maine Camp," CBS, October 24, 2011, https://www.cbsnews.com/news/chemical-bomb-thrown-at-occupy-maine-camp/.

25 Manny Fernandez, Richard Pérez-Peña and Jonah Engel Bromwich, "Five Dallas Officers Were Killed as Payback, Police Chief Says," *New York Times*, July 8, 2016, https://www.nytimes.com/2016/07/09/us/dallas-police-shooting.html; and Merrit Kennedy and Tanya Ballard Brown, "What We Know About The Dallas Suspected Gunman," NPR, July 8, 2016, https://www.npr.org/sections/thetwo-way/2016/07/08/485239295/what-we-know-about-the-dallas-suspected-gunman.

26 Zane Sparling, "Police Arrest Gresham Man for Firing Gun Near Protesters," The Outlook, August 23, 2021, https://pamplinmedia.com/go/42-news/519509-415043-police-arrest-gresham-man-for-firing-gun-near-protesters; Ryan Haas and Jonathan Levinson, "Gunfire Erupts After Proud Boys and Anti-fascists Openly Brawl in Portland Without Police Intervention," Oregon Public Broadcasting (OPB), August 23, 2021, https://www.opb.org/article/2021/08/22/far-right-activists-counterprotesters-gather-in-portland/; and Suzette Smith and Justin Yau, "Downtown Shootout Follows Sunday's Dueling Demonstrations," *Willamette Week*, August 22, 2021, https://www.wweek.com/news/2021/08/22/downtown-shootout-follows-sundays-dueling-demonstrations/.

27 "Woman Struck by SUV at Palmdale Protest Against Federal Vaccine Mandate," *Antelope Valley* Times. October 25, 2021, https://theavtimes.com/2021/10/25/woman-struck-by-suv-at-palmdale-

protest-against-federal-vaccine-mandate/; and "Driver Hits Crowd at Vaccine Mandate Rally in Palmdale, Injures Woman," NBC Los Angeles, October 23, 2021, https://www.nbclosangeles.com/news/local/driver-hits-crowd-at-vaccine-mandate-rally-in-palmdale-injures-woman/2729737/.

28 "Capitol Riot Investigations," *New York Times*, accessed February 3, 2022, https://www.nytimes.com/spotlight/us-capitol-riots-investigations; and "Capitol Hill Siege," George Washington University Program on Extremism, accessed February 7, 2022, https://extremism.gwu.edu/Capitol-Hill-Cases.

29 "About: Frequently Asked Questions," Rose City Antifa.

30 Renee Algarin, "Nathan Allen In His Own Words," Suffolk County District Attorney, press release, July 7, 2021, https://www.suffolkdistrictattorney.com/press-releases/items/nathan-allen-diaries; Brian Vitagliano, Evan Simko-Bednarski, and Artemis Moshtaghian, "'Hate Fueled by White Supremacy' Behind Killing of Two Black People in Massachusetts, Authorities Say," CNN, July 8, 2021, https://www.cnn.com/2021/07/08/us/winthrop-massachusetts-shooting-white-supremacy/index.html; and Erin Tiernan, "Man Who 'Executed' Black Winthrop Residents Acted Alone, Authorities Say," *Boston Herald*, July 1, 2021, https://www.bostonherald.com/2021/06/28/man-who-executed-black-winthrop-residents-acted-alone-authorities-say/.

31 Spencer S. Hathaway, "State Attorney's Office to Seek the Death Penalty in Murder of Officer Raynor," Office of the State Attorney, Seventh Judicial Circuit of Florida, press release and charging document, August 18, 2021, https://www.documentcloud.org/documents/21045324-initial-othal-wallace-charging-documents-subsequent-press-release; Chris Joyner, "Man Arrested in Cop Shooting Had History With Extremism," *Atlanta Journal-Constitution*, June 30, 2021, https://www.ajc.com/news/man-arrested-in-cop-shooting-had-history-with-extremism/PNTI75NTPZAOXAKYBGI3ESMV3Y/; and Adrienne Cutway, "Body Camera Video Shows Officer Being Shot in Daytona Beach," WKMG News 6, July 2, 2021, https://www.clickorlando.com/news/local/2021/06/24/body-camera-video-shows-officer-being-shot-in-daytona-beach/.

32 Note that this investigation is ongoing, and the exact motive and content of the note is not publicly available. CSIS has classified this attack as an act of terrorism based on information released by authorities, including the FBI. See, for example, FBI Dallas (@FBIDallas), "#FBIDallas SAC DeSarno joined @GarlandPD & @PlanoPoliceDept at a press conference today regarding the murder investigation of a Lyft driver in Garland and subsequent shooting at the Plano Police department," Twitter post, August 30, 2021, 5:33 p.m., https://twitter.com/FBIDallas/status/1432456403420127233; Tom Steele, Francesca D'Annunzio, Maggie Prosser and Nataly Keomoungkhoun, "Man Who killed Lyft Driver, Opened Fire at Plano Police Station May Have Been Inspired by Terrorists," *Dallas Morning News*, August 30, 2021, https://www.dallasnews.com/news/crime/2021/08/30/authorities-identify-lyft-driver-killed-in-garland-before-gunman-shot-at-plano-police-headquarters/; "Man Who Killed Lyft Driver 'May Have Been Inspired By Foreign Terrorist Organization', Dallas FBI Says," CBS DFW, August 30, 2021, https://dfw.cbslocal.com/2021/08/30/dallas-fbi-man-shot-killed-garland-lyft-driver-inspired-foreign-terrorist-organization/; and "FBI: Texas Shooter Possibly Inspired by Foreign Terrorists," Associated Press, August 30, 2021, https://apnews.com/article/texas-744a0ad58ee3beb0b6fc8124fec4e1e2.

33 The finding that most fatal domestic terrorist attacks involve firearms—regardless of perpetrator ideology—is consistent with

past CSIS research. See, for example, Seth G. Jones, Catrina Doxsee, and Nicholas Harrington, "The Tactics and Targets of Domestic Terrorists," CSIS, *CSIS Briefs*, July 30, 2020, https://www.csis.org/analysis/tactics-and-targets-domestic-terrorists.

34 Kate Brumback, "Atlanta Spa-Shooting Suspect Pleads Not Guilty in 4 Killings," Associated Press, September 28, 2021, https://apnews.com/article/atlanta-spa-shootings-robert-aaron-long-a87456e5f25f34f0acc85c41f73ffbc6; "8 Dead in Atlanta Spa Shootings, With Fears of Anti-Asian Bias," *New York Times*, March 26, 2021, https://www.nytimes.com/live/2021/03/17/us/shooting-atlanta-acworth#the-suspect-in-the-spa-attacks-has-been-charged-with-eight-counts-of-murder; Alexis Stevens, "Cherokee DA Defends Plea Deal, Decision Not to Pursue Hate Crime," *Atlanta Journal-Constitution*, July 27, 2021, https://www.ajc.com/news/cherokee-da-defends-plea-deal-says-long-targeted-multiple-ethnicities-genders/WXOAD4JXHNGO3ML3WACU3NBV3E/; and Jina Moore, "How the Atlanta Shooting Shows the Dangers of American Evangelicalism's Trademark 'Purity Culture,'" Business Insider, March 20, 2021, https://www.businessinsider.com/the-atlanta-shooting-and-the-dangers-of-evangelical-purity-culture-2021-3.

35 Jones, Doxsee, and Harrington, "The Tactics and Targets of Domestic Terrorists."

36 David Mann, "Police: Crowd Causes $500K in Damage to Downtown Portland During Memorial for Activist Killed in 2019," KGW8, October 13, 2021, https://www.kgw.com/article/news/local/portland-memorial-vandalism/283-e5171a7b-be9a-49b5-902a-34da286bb966; and "Protesters Commemorating Activist's Death Damage Downtown Portland Windows, Leave Graffiti," *The Oregonian*, October 13, 2021, https://www.oregonlive.com/news/2021/10/protesters-commemorating-activists-death-damage-downtown-portland-windows-leave-graffiti.html.

37 See, for example, Michael Dimock and John Gramlich, "How America Changed During Donald Trump's Presidency," Pew Research Center, January 29, 2021, https://www.pewresearch.org/2021/01/29/how-america-changed-during-donald-trumps-presidency/; Drew DeSilver, "The Polarization In Today's Congress Has Roots That Go Back Decades," Pew Research Center, March 10, 2022, https://www.pewresearch.org/fact-tank/2022/03/10/the-polarization-in-todays-congress-has-roots-that-go-back-decades/; and "Beyond Red vs. Blue: The Political Typology," Pew Research Center, November 9, 2021, https://www.pewresearch.org/politics/2021/11/09/beyond-red-vs-blue-the-political-typology-2/.

38 "Court Docs Reveal What Led Up to Deadly Mass Shooting at Portland, Oregon Protest," KATU, February 22, 2022, https://katu.com/news/local/court-docs-reveal-what-led-up-to-deadly-mass-shooting-at-portland-protest.

39 See, for example, Diana Palmer, "Fired Up Or Shut Down: The Chilling Effect Of Open Carry On First Amendment Expression At Public Protests" (PhD diss., Northeastern University, 2021), https://repository.library.northeastern.edu/files/neu:bz611n382/fulltext.pdf.

40 For the full findings and recommendations of the Countering Extremist Activity Working Group, see *Report on Countering Extremist Activity Within the Department of Defense* (Washington, DC: Department of Defense, 2021), https://media.defense.gov/2021/Dec/20/2002912573/-1/-1/0/REPORT-ON-COUNTERING-EXTREMIST-ACTIVITY-WITHIN-THE-DEPARTMENT-OF-DEFENSE.PDF.

41 Roudabeh Kishi, Aaron Wolfson, Sam Jones, and Justin Wagner, "Armed Assembly: Guns, Demonstrations, and Political Violence in America," ACLED and Everytown for Gun Safety Support Fund,

August 23, 2021, https://acleddata.com/2021/08/23/armed-assembly-guns-demonstrations-and-political-violence-in-america/.

42 See, for example, Katlyn E. DeBoer, "Clash of the First and Second Amendments: Proposed Regulation of Armed Protests," *Hastings Constitutional Law Quarterly* 45, no. 2 (Winter 2018): 333–71, https://repository.uchastings.edu/hastings_constitutional_law_quaterly/vol45/iss2/5; and Palmer, "Fired Up Or Shut Down."

43 Palmer, "Fired Up Or Shut Down."

The Military, Police, and the Rise of Terrorism in the United States

By Seth G. Jones, Catrina Doxsee, Grace Hwang, and Jared Thompson
APRIL 2021

THE ISSUE

U.S. active-duty military personnel and reservists have participated in a growing number of domestic terrorist plots and attacks, according to new data from CSIS. The percentage of all domestic terrorist incidents linked to active-duty and reserve personnel rose in 2020 to 6.4 percent, up from 1.5 percent in 2019 and none in 2018. Similarly, a growing number of current and former law enforcement officers have been involved in domestic terrorism in recent years. But domestic terrorism is a double-edged sword. In 2020, extremists from all sides of the ideological spectrum increasingly targeted the military, law enforcement, and other government actors—putting U.S. security agencies in the crosshairs of domestic terrorists.

INTRODUCTION

There is growing concern about the extent to which U.S. military and law enforcement personnel have perpetrated—and been victims of—domestic terrorism.[1] In March 2021, the U.S. Department of Defense (DoD) sent a report to the House and Senate Armed Services Committees which concluded: "DoD is facing a threat from domestic extremists (DE), particularly those who espouse white supremacy or white nationalist ideologies." It continued that some domestic extremist networks "(a) actively attempt to recruit military personnel into their group or cause, (b) encourage their members to join the military, or (c) join, themselves, for the purpose of acquiring combat and tactical experience."[2] In 2020, the FBI alerted the DoD that it had opened 143 criminal investigations involving current or former service members—of which nearly half (68) were related to domestic extremism. Most investigations apparently involved veterans, some of whom had unfavorable discharge records.[3] The January 6, 2021, events at the U.S. Capitol raised additional concerns, since one reservist, one National Guard member, and at least 31 veterans were charged with conspiracy or other crimes.[4]

In addition, at least four police officers and three former officers faced federal charges for their involvement in storming the Capitol.[5]

In response to these developments, Secretary of Defense Lloyd Austin III pledged to intensify the DoD's effort to combat extremism in the military, remarking, "It concerns me to think that anyone wearing the uniform of a soldier, or a sailor, an airman, Marine, or Guardian or Coast Guardsman would espouse these [extremist] sorts of beliefs, let alone act on them. But they do. Some of them still do."[6] Secretary Austin also signed a memo directing commanding officers and supervisors to conduct a one-day "stand-down" to discuss extremism in the ranks with their personnel.[7] In addition, the DoD launched an investigation in January 2021 to determine the extent to which the department and military have implemented policies and procedures that prohibit advocacy and participation related to white supremacist, extremist, and criminal gang activity by active-duty personnel.[8]

Numerous police agencies also conducted investigations into extremism within their departments. As Mayor

CSIS | CENTER FOR STRATEGIC & INTERNATIONAL STUDIES

Bill de Blasio of New York City remarked, "Anyone who expresses racist views shouldn't be a police officer, anyone who expresses white supremacist views shouldn't be a police officer, anyone who encourages violence against our democratic institutions shouldn't be a police officer."[9]

While these steps are an important start, there has been little publicly available data about military or law enforcement involvement in domestic terrorism—as well as attacks against troops and police. In addition, some research is plagued by selection bias because it focuses on a single incident, such as the January 6 event at the U.S. Capitol.[10] Without more systematic data, it is hard to gauge the severity of the problem and to make useful recommendations. To help fill the gap, this analysis utilizes CSIS's data set of domestic terrorist plots and attacks since January 1, 1994, which was updated through the end of January 2021.

The data indicate that U.S. military personnel have been involved in a growing number of domestic terrorist plots and attacks. The percentage of attacks and plots committed by active-duty and reserve personnel rose in 2020 to 6.4 percent of all attacks and plots (7 of 110 total), up from 1.5 percent in 2019 (1 of 65 total) and none in 2018. Active-duty personnel perpetrated 4.5 percent of the attacks in 2020 (five incidents), and reservists conducted 1.8 percent (two incidents). While these individuals represent a tiny percentage of all current active-duty and reserve personnel, the increased number of incidents is still concerning.[11] The data also indicate a rise in law enforcement involvement in attacks. The growth is notable since individuals with a military or law enforcement background have skills that extremists want—such as proficiency in firing weapons, building explosive devices, conducting surveillance and reconnaissance, training personnel, practicing operational security, and performing other types of activities. The data should serve as a cautionary tale. While the numbers are relatively low, they are growing—and the military and law enforcement agencies need to take preventive action now.

There are several other notable findings from the data set. First, domestic extremists increasingly targeted the military, police, and other government agencies—putting security agencies in the crosshairs of domestic extremists. In 2020, government, military, and especially police personnel and facilities were the target of 38 percent of attacks, the most of any category. Second, there was a rise in the number of terrorist plots and attacks in 2020, despite a relatively low number of fatalities. This trend indicates that terrorism is a growing problem in the

United States; there were more terrorist plots and attacks in 2020 than in *any year* since the CSIS data set started in 1994. Third, the motivations for terrorism have shifted dramatically over the past two decades, from religious extremists inspired by al-Qaeda and the Islamic State after September 11, 2001, to white supremacists, anarchists, and others today. White supremacists, extremist militia supporters, and other like-minded individuals were involved in two-thirds of the attacks and plots in 2020. Anarchists, anti-fascists, and other like-minded individuals perpetrated roughly 23 percent of the plots and attacks in 2020, a notable increase from recent years. And Salafi-jihadists were involved in a mere 5 percent—their lowest share of incidents since 2008.

The rest of this brief is divided into four sections. The first provides an overview of terrorism and outlines the data set. The second section assesses the main findings on military personnel and law enforcement, both as perpetrators and targets. The third outlines other findings from the CSIS data set. The fourth section offers brief implications.

Domestic extremists increasingly targeted the military, police, and other government agencies— putting security agencies in the crosshairs of domestic extremists.

TERRORISM

This brief focuses on terrorism, which involves the deliberate use—or threat—of violence by non-state actors in order to achieve political goals and create a broad psychological impact.[12] Violence and the threat of violence are important components of terrorism. As Professor Bruce Hoffman of Georgetown University argues, terrorism is "the deliberate creation and exploitation of fear through violence or the threat of violence in the pursuit of political change."[13] U.S. Code, which is the official compilation of general and permanent laws of the United States, defines domestic terrorism under 18 U.S. Code § 2331 as "violent acts or acts dangerous to human life" that occur primarily within U.S. territory. It organizes terrorism acts into three components: the act is intended to "intimidate or coerce a civilian population," it aims to "influence the policy of a government by intimidation or coercion," and it involves "mass destruction, assassination, or kidnapping."[14]

In focusing on terrorism, this brief does not cover the broader categories of hate speech or hate crimes. There is some overlap between terrorism and hate crimes, since some hate crimes include the use or threat of violence.[15] But hate crimes can also include non-violent incidents, such as graffiti and verbal abuse. Hate crimes and hate speech are obviously concerning and a threat to society, but this analysis concentrates only on terrorism and the use—or threat—of violence to achieve political objectives. In addition, this analysis does not focus on protests, riots, looting, and broader civil disturbances—unless they meet the definition of terrorism. While these incidents are important to analyze, most are not terrorism. Some are not violent, while others lack a political motivation or the intention to create a broad psychological impact.[16]

Finally, while there is often a desire among government officials and academics to focus on terrorist *groups* and *organizations*, the terrorism landscape in the United States remains highly decentralized. Many are inspired by the concept of "leaderless resistance," which rejects a centralized, hierarchical organization in favor of decentralized networks or individual activity.[17] The decentralized nature of terrorism is particularly noteworthy regarding the use of violence, which CSIS data suggest is often planned and orchestrated by a single individual or small network.[18]

Based on this definition, the data set includes 980 cases of terrorist plots and attacks in the United States between January 1, 1994, and January 31, 2021. The data set includes such categories as the incident date, perpetrator, location, motivation, number of individuals wounded or killed, target, weapons used, and perpetrators' current or former affiliations with law enforcement and the military. The data set—including the codebook, definitions, and limitations—is explained in more detail in a methodology supplement linked at the end of this analysis.

MILITARY AND LAW ENFORCEMENT: PERPETRATORS AND TARGETS

This section begins with a historical overview of military and law enforcement personnel involved in terrorism. It then examines more recent data about military and law enforcement personnel as both perpetrators and targets of terrorism. To be clear, this analysis does not focus on the broader question of extremism in the military, including its pervasiveness and causes. Nor does it offer a systematic analysis of why these numbers have increased, though it does offer some hypotheses. While these are important issues, the data set focuses on terrorist incidents.

In addition, there are important distinctions between the types of military personnel. While active-duty members serve full time in the military, reservists serve only part time and cannot be charged under the Uniform Code of Military Justice (UCMJ) when they are off duty. The military has less authority to respond to veterans who become involved in extremist behavior, but if their conduct violates the UCMJ, the military may be able to respond with retroactive demotions and reduced pensions.[19]

Historical Trends: A small number of military and law enforcement personnel have been involved in domestic extremism over the years. In her study of the white power movement, for example, Professor Kathleen Belew of the University of Chicago argues that the Vietnam War and other political, economic, and social factors led to a consolidation and expansion of white power activists, who attempted to recruit active-duty soldiers, reservists, and veterans involved in the Vietnam War.[20] In 1970 alone, the U.S. Marine Corps recorded over 1,000 incidents of racial violence at installations in the United States and Vietnam, including violent altercations between black and white Marines at Camp Lejeune, North Carolina.[21] While most of these were not acts of terrorism, they still contributed to an enabling environment for extremist acts.

In addition, several influential extremists in the 1970s, 1980s, and 1990s served in the U.S. military or law enforcement agencies. One of the most prominent white supremacist figures was Louis Beam, who enlisted in the Army when he was 19 years old and fought in the Vietnam War.[22] In his speeches and writings—including his influential *Essays of a Klansman*—Beam argued that activists needed to continue waging the war on U.S. territory using guerrilla warfare.[23] Beam was not alone. Randy Duey, a member of the white supremacist group The Order, was an Air Force veteran and instructor at the survival school at Fairchild Air Force Base in Spokane, Washington.[24] Randy Weaver—a Christian Identity adherent who held white supremacist and anti-government views, and who was involved in the 1992 Ruby Ridge standoff near Naples, Idaho—was a former U.S. Army engineer.[25] Timothy McVeigh, who carried out the 1995 Oklahoma City bombing that killed 168 people and injured more than 680 others, enlisted in the U.S. Army in 1988 and fought in Iraq during Operation Desert Storm. There were also other veterans involved in extremism, such as William Potter Gale, Richard Butler, Bo Gritz, Frazier Glenn Miller, and Eric Rudolph.[26]

In addition, some former law enforcement officers were involved in domestic terrorism, including those that were members or sympathizers of the Ku Klux Klan.[27] Among the most prominent was Gerald "Jack" McLamb, a retired Phoenix police officer who urged resistance to those who supported a one-world government and wrote a 75-page manifesto titled, *Operation Vampire Killer 2000: American Police Action Plan for Stopping World Government Rule*.[28] White supremacist groups also attempted to infiltrate and recruit from law enforcement agencies, according to FBI assessments.[29]

Among the most prominent white power books during this period was *The Turner Diaries*, a dystopian novel that drew heavily on the concept of military and law enforcement personnel as white power soldiers. Written by William Pierce and published under the pseudonym Andrew Macdonald, *The Turner Diaries* depicts a violent revolution in the United States which leads to the overthrow of the federal government, a nuclear war, and a race war that results in the extermination of non-whites. In a reference to the U.S. military's experience fighting communist governments and insurgent groups across the globe, the protagonist, Earl Turner, notes, "We have had the example of decades of guerrilla warfare in Africa, Asia, and Latin American to instruct us."[30] William Pierce and his National Alliance, a white supremacist and neo-Nazi political organization, attempted to recruit military and law enforcement personnel.[31]

According to FBI data, 37 percent of lone offender terrorists in the United States between 1972 and 2015 served in the military.[32] But in the decade after September 11,

2001, there were few attacks by active-duty, reservist, or law enforcement personnel, though extremist groups attempted to infiltrate the military and law enforcement.[33] In June 2006, for example, Shayne Allyn Ziska, a state correctional officer in California, was sentenced to 17.5 years in prison for aiding a white supremacist prison gang called the Nazi Low Riders.[34] But the trends began to change over the past several years.

Military: As Figure 1 shows, there was an increase in the percentage of domestic terrorist plots and attacks perpetrated by active-duty and reserve personnel in recent years.[35] In 2020, 6.4 percent of all domestic terrorist attacks and plots (7 of 110 total) were committed by one or more active-duty or reserve members—an increase from 1.5 percent in 2019 (1 of 65 total) and none in 2018. While the attacks in 2021 account for only one month, the numbers in January 2021 showed another increase: 17.6 percent of domestic terrorism plots and attacks (3 of 17 total) were committed by active-duty or reserve personnel.

On January 19, 2021, for example, the FBI and U.S. Army Counterintelligence Coordinating Authority arrested a U.S. Army soldier, Cole James Bridges, at Fort Stewart after he conspired to blow up the 9/11 Memorial in New York and attempted to provide support to the Islamic State.[36] On May 30, 2020, authorities in Las Vegas, Nevada, arrested Andrew Lynam, an Army reservist, alongside Navy veteran Stephen T. Parshall and Air Force veteran

Figure 1: Percentage of U.S. Terrorist Attacks and Plots Perpetrated by Active-Duty or Reserve Service Members, 2015–2020

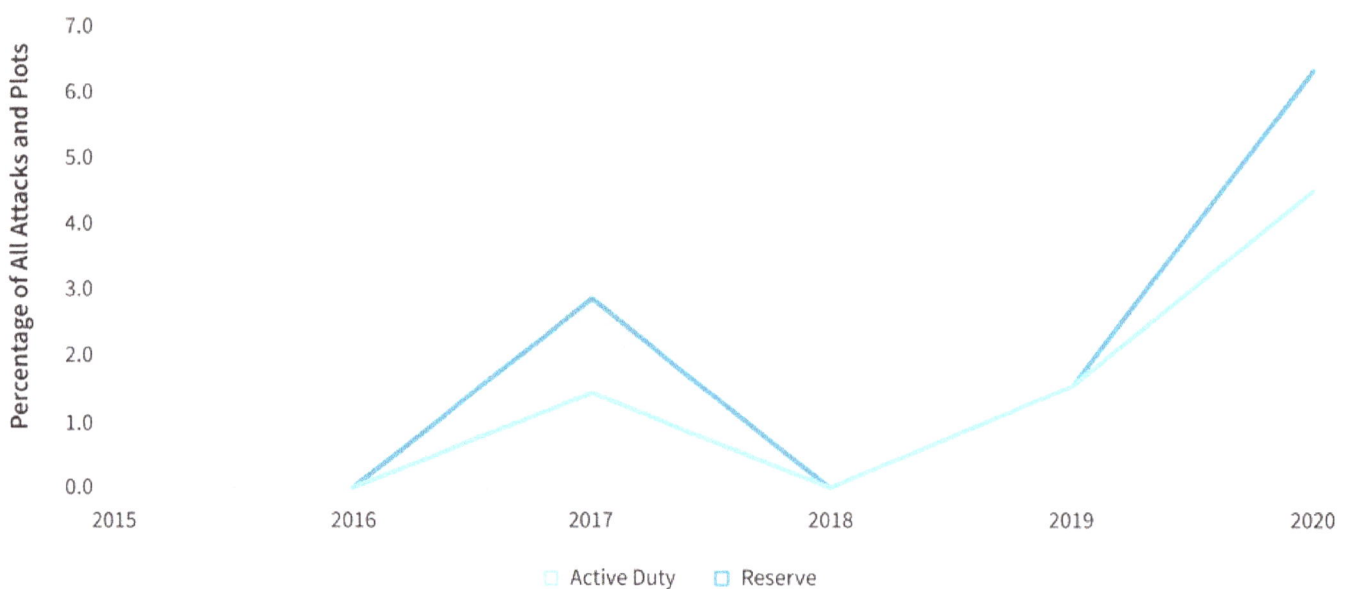

Source: Data compiled by CSIS Transnational Threats Project.

William L. Loomis—all self-identified Boogaloo Bois—for conspiring to firebomb a U.S. Forest Service building and a power substation to sow chaos during the protests held in response to the murder of George Floyd.[37] On June 10, 2020, the FBI arrested Army Private Ethan Melzer, who sent sensitive U.S. military information to the Order of the Nine Angles (O9A), an occult-based neo-Nazi and white supremacist group, in an attempt to facilitate a mass-casualty attack on Melzer's Army unit.[38] On May 29, 2020, Air Force Staff Sergeant Steven Carrillo, a supporter of the Boogaloo Bois who wanted to ignite a civil war, shot and killed Pat Underwood, a protective security officer, and wounded his partner in Oakland, California. Carrillo also killed a Santa Cruz County sheriff's deputy in Ben Lomond, California, with an assault rifle on June 6, 2020.[39]

In addition, the January 6, 2021, attack at the U.S. Capitol included veterans, reservists, a member of the National Guard, members of several militias and extremist organizations (such as the Sons of Liberty New Jersey, Groyper Army, Oath Keepers, Proud Boys, Boogaloo Bois, and Three Percenters), supporters of the extremist conspiracy QAnon, and other groups and networks. No participants have been identified as active-duty military personnel. On January 13, the FBI arrested Jacob Fracker, a U.S. Army National Guardsman, for his involvement in the Capitol attack.[40] As Fracker explained in an Instagram post, "Sorry I hate freedom? Sorry I fought for it and lost friends for it? . . . I can protest for what I believe in and still support your protest for what you believe in. Just saying . . . after all, I fought for your right to do it."[41]

Veterans have also been involved in domestic terrorist attacks and plots.[42] In October 2020, for example, the FBI arrested Adam Fox, Barry Croft, and several other accomplices in a plot to kidnap and potentially execute Michigan Governor Gretchen Whitmer. Members of this network, which had ties to militias in Michigan and other states, referred to Governor Whitmer as a "tyrant" and claimed that she had "uncontrolled power right now."[43] Paul Edward Bellar, a U.S. Army veteran who had been honorably discharged roughly a year before his arrest, trained the group on the use of firearms, medical care, and other tactical skills.[44] Veterans consistently committed more attacks and plots than active-duty and reserve troops—including 10 percent of all domestic terrorist attacks and plots since 2015, according to CSIS data.

Domestic extremist groups and networks have also attempted to recruit veterans, active-duty personnel, and reservists. To be clear, this analysis is not suggesting that individuals serving in the military or who are veterans are more inclined to embrace extremism than the general population or are attracted to extremist ideologies. Nevertheless, violent far-right and far-left networks have solicited military personnel because of their skill sets. According to one estimate, veterans and active-duty members of the military currently make up roughly 25 percent of active militia members.[45] Such organizations as the Proud Boys, Oath Keepers, and Three Percenters include active-duty personnel, reservists, veterans, and law enforcement personnel.[46] The Boogaloo Bois, anti-fascists, and extremists with other motivations have also included active-duty personnel, reservists, and veterans.

Law Enforcement: CSIS data identified six incidents since 1994 in which current or former law enforcement personnel committed domestic terrorist plots and attacks—though *all six cases* occurred since 2017. As with active-duty and reserve military personnel, this is an increase, despite representing a small fraction of all law enforcement professionals in the United States. Between October 2020 and January 2021, three domestic terrorist attacks or plots involved current law enforcement officers. For example, Joseph Wayne Fischer, an off-duty patrolman from Pennsylvania, participated in the January 6, 2021, Capitol attack and was reportedly in the front wave of rioters pushing back police officers. Fischer was charged with multiple criminal offenses, including obstruction of law enforcement and violent entry.[47] At least four current police officers and three former officers were allegedly involved in the January 6 incident at the Capitol.[48]

Former law enforcement officers were involved in two incidents in 2017 and one in 2020. On October 19, 2020, former Houston police captain Mark Anthony Aguirre ran a repairman off the road, pinned him to the ground, and threatened him at gunpoint, claiming that the man was transporting 750,000 false ballots as part of an election fraud scheme—a conspiracy theory pushed by the group Liberty Center for God and Country.[49]

Terrorist Targeting of Military and Law Enforcement: CSIS data also show that the U.S. government, military, and law enforcement were increasingly targeted by domestic terrorists. As shown in Figure 2, government, military, and police personnel and facilities were the targets of 34 of 89 attacks in 2020 from perpetrators of varying ideologies, making them the most frequent targets.[50] Of these 34 attacks, 19 targeted the government, 15 targeted law enforcement, and 1 targeted the military.[51] The attacks were led by perpetrators of various ideologies, including violent far-right,

Figure 2: Targets of U.S. Terrorist Attacks by Perpetrator Orientation, 2020

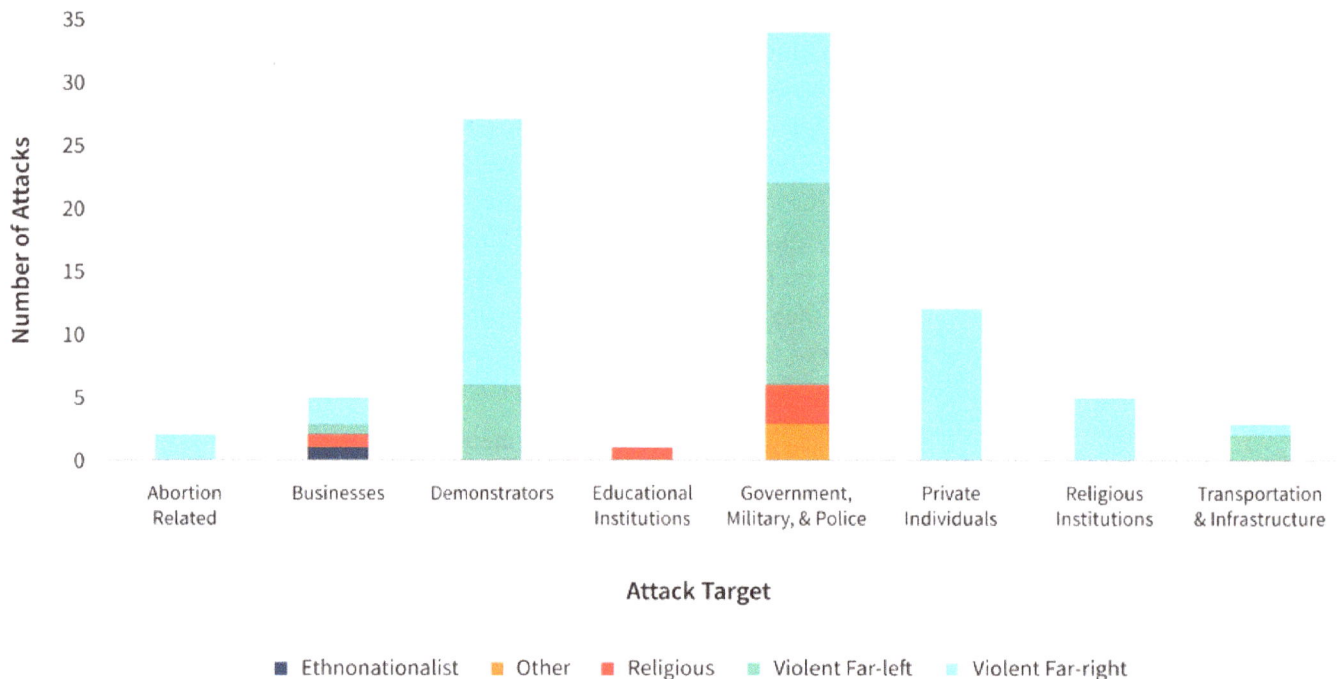

violent far-left, religious, and the Boogaloo Bois—who were responsible for all attacks coded as "other" in the 2020 data.

In addition, the percentage of domestic terrorist attacks against government, military, and police agencies *increased* over the past five years. In 2020, 38 percent of all domestic terrorist attacks targeted these institutions. This was the second-highest percentage since at least 1994—exceeded only in 2013, when attacks against government, military, and police targets comprised 46 percent of all attacks. The frequency of attacks against military and—in particular—law enforcement targets may be due, in part, to a growing belief by extremists that security agencies are the most visible arm of an illegitimate and oppressive government.

For some anti-fascists, the police are quintessential symbols of a repressive state—including against minority populations.[52] "As for the police . . . the historical record shows that along with the military they have also been among the most eager for a 'return to order,'" wrote Mark Bray in *Antifa: The Anti-fascist Handbook*.[53] This explains why some anti-fascists and anarchists conducted attacks against police stations and police vehicles during the protests in the summer of 2020. As highlighted by the events on

January 6, 2021, however, some on the violent far-right also consider law enforcement the main security arm of a government they believe is illegitimate. "Traitors! Traitors! Traitors!" chanted some individuals on the Capitol steps on January 6. "The blue does not back you," read a message from a pro-Proud Boys group on the social networking service Parler, "They back the men who pay them."[54]

While this analysis does not conduct a comprehensive analysis of *why* there was a rise in the number and percentage of active-duty and reserve personnel involved in domestic terrorist attacks and plots, there are several hypotheses worth considering. For example, it would be worth examining whether the deployment of soldiers to controversial battlefields such as Iraq and Afghanistan triggered a backlash against U.S. society and the government (much like with the Vietnam War); whether military personnel have been increasingly influenced by the political polarization prevalent in the United States; or whether military personnel have been more active on the internet and social media platforms, which has contributed to radicalization. In addition, there may be other social, economic, educational, or cultural variables at play, along with the possible proliferation of charismatic individuals that have spread propaganda in the military.

OTHER FINDINGS

CSIS also examined trends in the number and characteristics of attacks and plots. This section analyzes the data in two parts: number of incidents and fatalities, and perpetrator ideology.

Incidents and Fatalities: In 2020, the number of domestic terrorist attacks and plots increased to its highest level since at least 1994, though fatalities were relatively low. Across all perpetrator ideologies, there were 110 domestic terrorist attacks and plots in 2020—an increase of 45 incidents since 2019 and 40 more incidents than in 2017, the year which previously had the most terrorist attacks and plots since the beginning of the data set. Despite this sharp increase in terrorist activity, the number of fatalities from domestic terrorist attacks was at its lowest level since 2013. Five people were killed in terrorist attacks in 2020—an 86 percent decrease from 2019, when 35 individuals died in terrorist attacks.

There are several possible explanations for this drop in lethality. First, there were 21 terrorist plots recorded in 2020 which were disrupted before an attack could take place. Some decrease in fatalities, then, may be attributed to the effective work of the FBI and other law enforcement agencies in preventing attacks.

Second, there were no mass-casualty terrorist attacks in 2020. All five victims were killed with firearms in five separate attacks. In comparison, there were seven fatal attacks each in 2018 and 2019, resulting in 19 and 35 fatalities, respectively. Though the number of fatal attacks was similar, each of these previous years included a mass-casualty attack that significantly raised the total. In 2018, Robert Bowers murdered 11 people at the Tree of Life synagogue in Pittsburgh, Pennsylvania, and in 2019, Patrick Crusius murdered 22 people at a Walmart in El Paso, Texas. This alone does not explain the reduction, however, because there was ample opportunity for similar mass-casualty events in 2020. As highlighted in Figure 2, soft targets such as demonstrators and private individuals were frequent targets of terrorist attacks and plots. Furthermore, previous CSIS analysis found that vehicles were increasingly common weapons in terrorist attacks in 2020, joining firearms, explosives, and incendiaries as some of the most commonly used weapons—all of which have high potential lethality.[55]

Third, the restraint shown in those attacks may point to perpetrators prioritizing sending a message through fear rather than fatalities. Though there has been substantial rhetoric about bringing about a second civil war—such as from the Boogaloo Bois and some white supremacists—many extremists may wait for their ideological adversaries to act first, whether through violent action or policy change that is perceived as an existential threat. This is consistent with the philosophy put forward by militia leaders such as

Figure 3: Percentage of U.S. Terrorist Attacks Targeting Government, Military, and Police Facilities and Personnel, 1994–2020

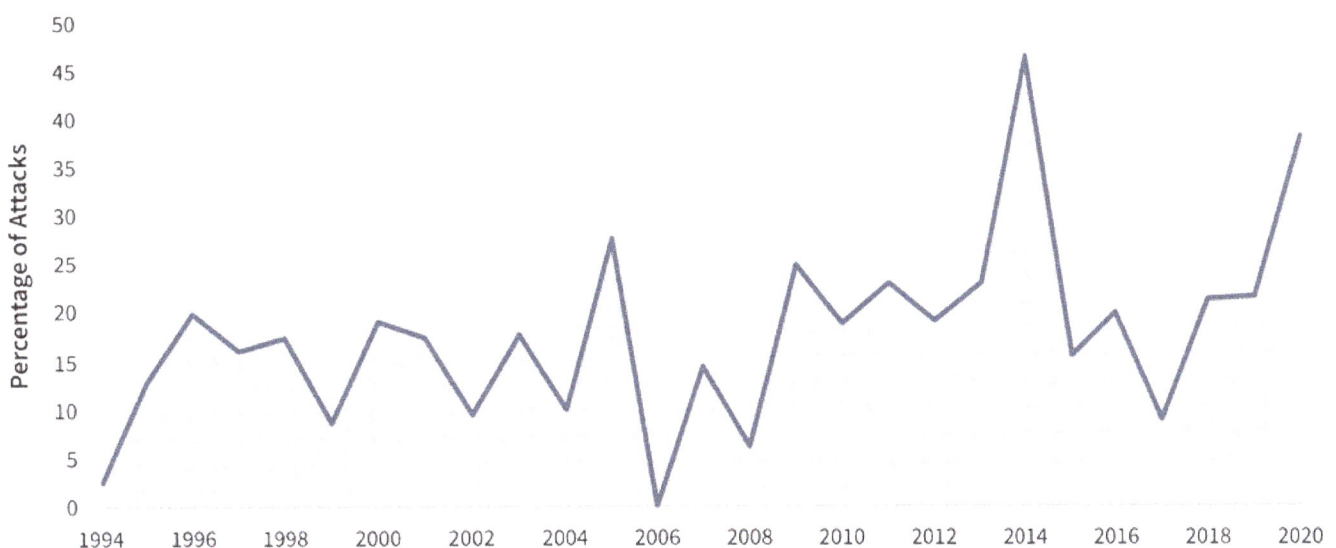

Note: Target data exclude foiled terrorist plots, the targets of which are not always known.

Source: Data compiled by CSIS Transnational Threats Project.

Figure 4: Number of U.S. Terrorist Attacks and Plots and Fatalities, 1994–2020

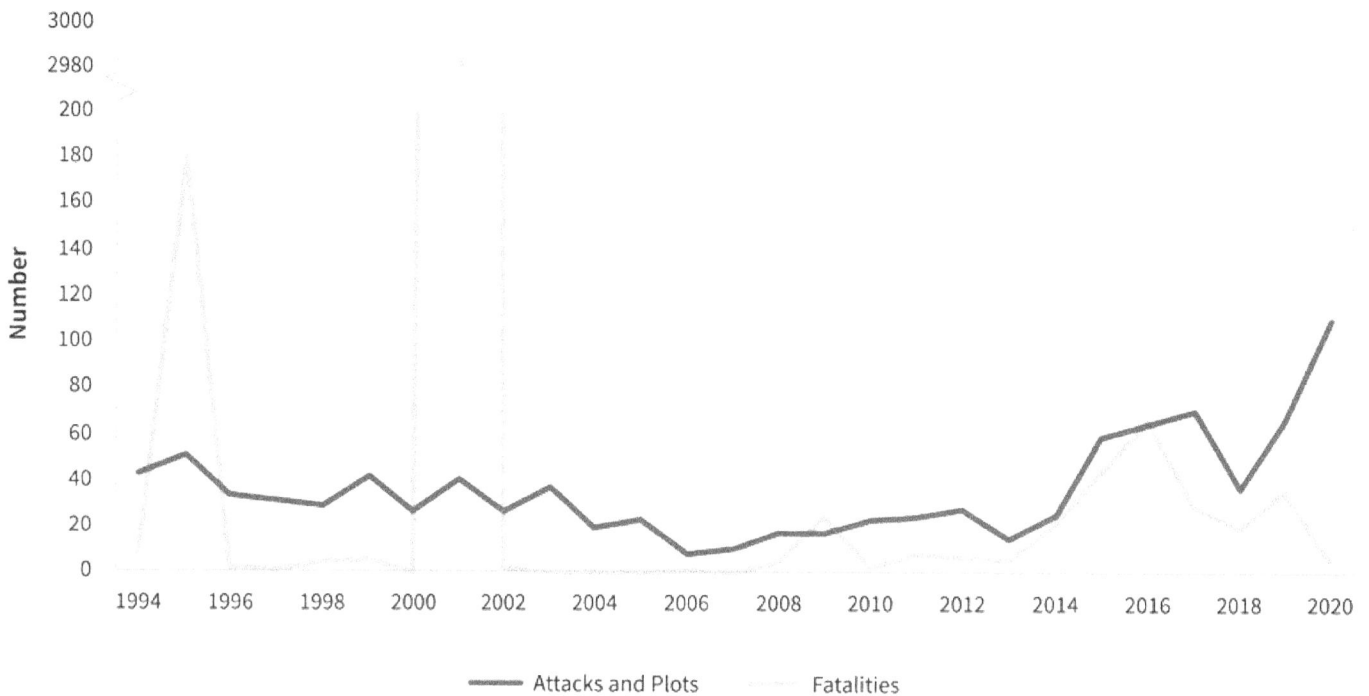

Note: Fatality data exclude perpetrators. Data from 1995 include the Oklahoma City bombing, in which 168 victims died. Data from 2001 include the 9/11 attacks, in which 2,977 victims died.
Source: Data compiled by CSIS Transnational Threats Project.

the Three Percenters' co-founder Mike Vanderboegh, who in 2008 advised his followers not to "fire first" and instead to wait and act under the justification of the common defense so as to "not cede the moral high ground."[56]

Perpetrator Ideology: CSIS also coded the ideology of perpetrators into one of five categories: ethnonationalist, religious, violent far-left, violent far-right, and other. (The link to the methodology, which includes definitions of these categories, can be found at the end of this brief.) All religious attacks and plots in the CSIS data set were committed by terrorists motivated by a Salafi-jihadist ideology.

White supremacists, extremist militia members, and other violent far-right extremists were responsible for 66 percent of domestic terrorist attacks and plots in 2020—roughly consistent with their share in other recent years.[57] For example, on June 7, Harry H. Rogers—a self-proclaimed leader of the Ku Klux Klan—intentionally drove his pick-up truck into a crowd of Black Lives Matter demonstrators in Henrico, Virginia. One protester was injured, and Rogers received a six-year prison sentence.[58] In addition, anarchists, anti-fascists, violent environmentalists, and other violent far-left extremists conducted 23 percent of terrorist attacks and plots in

2020—an increase from the previous three years, in which violent far-left incidents comprised between 5 and 11 percent of all domestic terrorist attacks and plots. For example, on August 29 in Portland, Oregon, Michael Reinoehl—an Antifa extremist—followed two members of the far-right group Patriot Prayer and then shot and killed one of them, Aaron "Jay" Danielson.[59]

Meanwhile, the portion of attacks and plots inspired by a Salafi-jihadist ideology fell to 5 percent in 2020—a sharp decline compared to recent years such as 2019, in which they comprised 29 percent of incidents. For example, on May 21, Adam Aalim Alsahli—a Syrian-born U.S. citizen inspired by jihadist figures such as Ibrahim al-Rabaysh—drove his vehicle into the gate of Naval Air Station Corpus Christi in Texas and then opened fire on a guard.[60] The proportion of attacks and plots by ideology in January 2021 remained roughly consistent with the 2020 data.

POLICY IMPLICATIONS

U.S. military and law enforcement agencies need to better understand the scope of the problem through better data collection and analysis. The U.S. military has already taken steps along these lines in such areas as sexual assault and suicides. At the moment, the number of active-duty military personnel, reservists, and police involved in domestic terrorism is relatively small, though it is rising.[61]

These challenges will persist since extremist networks seek to embed their members in the military and law enforcement agencies and to actively recruit current and retired personnel.[62] The Russian government has also recognized that these groups may be vulnerable to extremist ideologies and has targeted active-duty personnel, reservists, veterans, and police through an aggressive cyber and disinformation campaign on digital platforms.[63] Military and law enforcement personnel have valuable skills that extremist networks want, such as small unit tactics, communications, logistics, reconnaissance, and surveillance. They may also have access to weapons and explosives. In January 2021, for example, several pounds of C-4 explosives went missing from a Marine Corps base in Twentynine Palms, California.[64]

Any effort to disrupt extremism in the military must address all stages of service. In vetting new recruits and renewing existing security clearances, for example, revisions to the SF-86 process should help identify individuals associated with extremist networks. At least one reservist who participated in the January 6 Capitol attack held a security clearance and was well known among his colleagues for harboring extremist views.[65] An FBI database of lone offender terrorism in the United States indicated that 10 percent of offenders between 1972

and 2015 took steps to join the military but were either disqualified during the application process or dropped out after realizing they might not meet the qualifications.[66] Deterrence is critical. The DoD should publicly announce any changes to its vetting processes to deter those with extremist views from even attempting to join the military.

U.S. military and law enforcement agencies need to better understand the scope of the problem through better data collection and analysis.

The military and police should also increase their focus on counterextremism education as well as offer clear reporting and oversight processes for current service members and police officers. This may include training personnel on identity signaling within extremist networks, including symbols displayed in tattoos and on apparel. On the law enforcement side, organizations such as the International Association of Chiefs of Police (IACP) and the Police Executive Research Forum (PERF) should increase efforts to better understand and counter extremism within police forces. Finally, there should be a focus on veterans and individuals exiting the services, who are at an increased risk of recruitment.[67]

Figure 5: Number of U.S. Terrorist Attacks and Plots by Perpetrator Orientation, 1994–2020

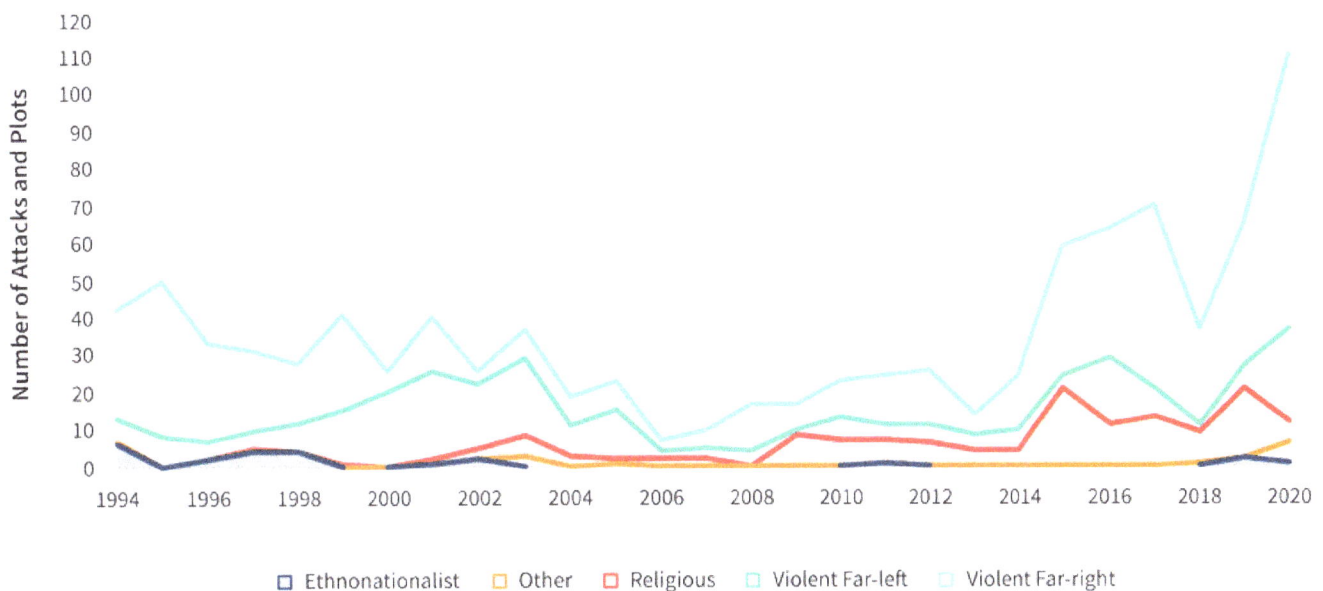

Source: Data compiled by CSIS Transnational Threats Project.

A data-driven understanding of the nature of extremist behavior among military and law enforcement personnel could help inform and prioritize these efforts. For example, CSIS analysis found that while there was an increase in active-duty and reserve personnel involvement in terrorist attacks and plots, the majority of perpetrators affiliated with the military in recent years were veterans. Though the military does not have as much influence over the behavior of veterans once they separate from the military, the DoD could pull service records for all military-affiliated perpetrators and gather information to better understand the causes. Such patterns could inform efforts to disrupt radicalization pathways before individuals leave the military. Congressionally directed or agency-initiated efforts by the Department of Veterans Affairs (VA) could also help identify and counter extremist activity among veterans, and data-sharing agreements between the DoD and VA could strengthen deradicalization efforts.

Simultaneously, the U.S. government should prepare for the military, law enforcement, and other government agencies to continue to be frequent targets of domestic terrorism. Attacks against these institutions are increasing from extremists of diverse ideologies. This risk may be exacerbated by such issues as gun control, immigration, and Covid-19 policies. The DoD and law enforcement agencies should conceptualize efforts to counter domestic extremism as an issue of self-defense and support for their personnel. This concern may shape strategies to eliminate extremist ideology among service members. For example, individual commanders could work to build a trusting environment to report and address these problems framed in terms of unit defense and cohesion, rather than levying blame.

Furthermore, concerns about extremism in the military and law enforcement are not confined to the United States.[68] Germany has faced significant problems, from which the United States may be able to draw some lessons. In November 2020, a German government investigation identified 26 soldiers and 9 police officers who organized and participated in online chat groups that shared far-right, anti-Semitic, and neo-Nazi content.[69] The investigations came on the heels of an October 2020 report by the Federal Office for the Protection of the Constitution (Bundesamt für Verfassungsschutz, or BfV), which documented more than 1,400 cases of far-right extremism in the police and intelligence services over the previous four years.[70] In 2020, Germany's Defense Ministry identified 20 far-right extremists within a company of the country's elite special forces, the Kommando Spezialkräfte. The German military disbanded the 2nd Company, though 48,000 rounds of ammunition and more than 135 pounds of explosives went missing from the unit's stockpiles.[71] More broadly, the European police agency Europol warned in a confidential report that extremist groups in Europe attempted to bolster their "combat skills" by recruiting military and police members.[72]

Of broader concern, the U.S. government does not publicly release data on terrorist attacks and plots, nor on the characteristics of perpetrators. However, if a centralized data collection effort were established, data analysis could offer an objective mechanism for apportioning counterterrorism resources and efforts relative to actual threats. For example, CSIS data show that domestic terrorist attacks and plots from violent far-right and far-left actors are on the rise, while Salafi-jihadist-inspired terrorism is declining. This presents a clear case for continuing to redirect resources away from Salafi-jihadist to other types of extremism.

Despite these challenges, one reason for hope is the low number of deaths from domestic terrorism. Terrorism from violent far-right and far-left extremists has not killed many Americans—at least not recently. This could change, of course, as Timothy McVeigh illustrated in 1995. Terrorism expert Brian Jenkins once wrote that "terrorism is theater" and "terrorists want a lot of people watching, not a lot of people dead."[73] These aphorisms may not have been true of al-Qaeda and Islamic State adherents, as Jenkins recognized.[74] But the data certainly raise questions about how far most domestic terrorists are willing to go today. ■

Seth G. Jones is senior vice president and director of the International Security Program at the Center for Strategic and International Studies (CSIS) in Washington, D.C, and author most recently of Three Dangerous Men: Russia, China, Iran, and the Rise of Irregular Warfare *(W.W. Norton).* **Catrina Doxsee** *is a program manager and research associate with the Transnational Threats Project at CSIS.* **Grace Hwang** *is a research assistant with the Burke Chair in Strategy and Transnational Threats Project at CSIS.* **Jared Thompson** *is a research assistant with the Transnational Threats Project at CSIS.*

The authors give special thanks to Bruce Hoffman, Cynthia Miller-Idriss, Colin Clarke, *and* David Brannan *for their review* *of the document—including the data set—and their helpful critiques. Thanks also to **Jerry Bennett**, **Mark Cancian**, **James Cheney**, **Eric McQueen**, **Joseph Moye**, and **Jacob Ware** for their comments. Finally, thanks to **Nicholas Harrington** for his help in updating the data set.*

For an overview of the methodology used in compiling the data set, please see here.

This brief is made possible by general support to CSIS. No direct sponsorship contributed to this brief.

ENDNOTES

1   See, for example, Cynthia Miller-Idriss, "When the Far Right Penetrates Law Enforcement: America Can Learn from Germany," *Foreign Affairs*, December 15, 2020, https://www.foreignaffairs.com/articles/united-states/2020-12-15/when-far-right-penetrates-law-enforcement; Daniel Koehler, *A Threat From Within: Exploring the Link Between the Extreme Right and the Military* (The Hague, Netherlands: International Centre for Counter-Terrorism, September 2019), https://icct.nl/app/uploads/2019/09/ICCT-Koehler-A-Threat-from-Within-Exploring-the-Link-between-the-Extreme-Right-and-the-Military.pdf; and Heather J. Williams, "How to Root Out Extremism in the U.S. Military," Defense One, February 1, 2021, https://www.defenseone.com/ideas/2021/02/how-root-out-extremism-us-military/171744/.

2   Office of the Under Secretary of Defense for Personnel and Readiness, *Report to Armed Services Committees on Screening Individuals Who Seek to Enlist in the Armed Forces* (Washington, DC: U.S. Department of Defense (DoD), March 2021), https://media.defense.gov/2021/Mar/02/2002592042/-1/-1/0/REPORT-TO-ARMED-SERVICES-COMMITTEES-ON-SCREENING-INDIVIDUALS-WHO-SEEK-TO-ENLIST-IN-THE-ARMED-FORCES.PDF. The referenced report is Andrée E. Rose et al., *Leveraging FBI Resources to Enhance Military Accessions Screening and Personnel Security Vetting*, OPA Report No. 2020-080-0 (Seaside, CA: Defense Personnel and Security Research Center, Office of People Analytics, June 2020).

3   Eric Schmitt, "Lloyd Austin Ramps Up the Fight Against Right-Wing Extremism Within the Military," *New York Times*, February 3, 2021, https://www.nytimes.com/2021/02/03/us/lloyd-austin-extremism-military.html.

4   Examples include Jacob Fracker, Thomas Caldwell, William Chrestman, Donovan Crowl, Christopher Kuehne, Nicholas Ochs, Dominic Pezzola, Jessica Watkins, Graydon Young, Joseph Biggs, Gabriel Garcia, and Barton Shively. See Jennifer Valentino-DeVries, Denise Lu, Eleanor Lutz, and Alex Leeds Matthews, "A Small Group of Militants' Outsize Role in the Capitol Attack," *New York Times*, February 21, 2021, https://www.nytimes.com/interactive/2021/02/21/us/capitol-riot-attack-militants.html; Program on Extremism, *"This is Our House!" A Preliminary Assessment of the Capitol Hill Siege Participants* (Washington, DC: George Washington University, 2021), https://extremism.gwu.edu/sites/g/files/zaxdzs2191/f/This-Is-Our-House.pdf; and Michael Robinson and Kori Schake, "The Military's Extremism Problem Is Our Problem," *New York Times*, March 2, 2021, https://www.nytimes.com/2021/03/02/opinion/veterans-capitol-attack.html.

5   Bart Jensen, "'A Nightmare Scenario': Extremists In Police Ranks Spark Growing Concern After Capitol Riot," *USA Today*, March 22, 2021, https://www.usatoday.com/in-depth/news/politics/elections/2021/03/21/police-charged-capitol-riot-reignite-concerns-racism-extremism/4738348001/.

6   Lloyd J. Austin, "Video: A Message from the Secretary of Defense," Department of Defense, February 19, 2021, https://www.defense.gov/Explore/News/Article/Article/2509632/a-message-from-the-secretary-of-defense-on-extremism/.

7   Lloyd J. Austin, "Memorandum for Senior Pentagon Leadership, Defense Agency and DOD Field Activity Directors, Subject: Stand-Down to Address Extremism in the Ranks," Department of Defense, February 5, 2021, https://media.defense.gov/2021/Feb/05/2002577485/-1/-1/0/STAND-DOWN-TO-ADDRESS-EXTREMISM-IN-THE-RANKS.PDF.

8   Inspector General, "Memorandum for Secretary of Defense, Subject: Evaluation of Department of Defense Efforts to Develop and Implement Policy and Procedures Addressing Ideological Extremism Within the U.S. Armed Forces (Project No. D2021-DEV0PB-0079.000)," Department of Defense, January 14, 2021, https://media.defense.gov/2021/Jan/14/2002565175/-1/-1/1/D2021-DEV0PB-0079.000_REDACTED.PDF.

9   "Transcript: Mayor de Blasio Holds Media Availability," Office of the Mayor, City of New York, January 11, 2021, https://www1.nyc.gov/office-of-the-mayor/news/018-21/transcript-mayor-de-blasio-holds-media-availability.

10 See, for example, Daniel Milton, Andrew Mines, and Angelina Maleska, "The Military Doesn't Even Know How Bad Its Extremism Problem Is," *Washington Post*, March 29, 2021, https://www.washingtonpost.com/outlook/2021/03/29/military-extremism-january-6/.

11 Based on the 2020 data, less than four ten-thousandths of a percent of all active-duty troops and two ten-thousandths of a percent of all reservists were involved in domestic terrorism—though they still represented 6.4 percent of all attacks and plots that year.

12 On definitions of terrorism, see, for example, Bruce Hoffman, *Inside Terrorism*, 2nd ed. (New York: Columbia University Press, 2006), 1–41, https://www.rand.org/pubs/commercial_books/CB386.html; and Global Terrorism Database, *Codebook: Inclusion Criteria and Variables* (College Park, MD: University of Maryland, October 2019), https://www.start.umd.edu/gtd/downloads/Codebook.pdf.

13 Bruce Hoffman, *Inside Terrorism*, 3rd ed. (New York: Columbia University Press, 2017), 44. Also see, for example, Global Terrorism Database, *Codebook: Inclusion Criteria and Variables* (College Park, MD: University of Maryland, October 2019), https://www.start.umd.edu/gtd/downloads/Codebook.pdf.

14 18 U.S. Code § 2331.

15 On similarities and differences between terrorism and hate crimes, see Tore Bjørgo and Jacob Aasland Ravndal, *Extreme-Right Violence and Terrorism: Concepts, Patterns, and Responses* (The Hague: International Centre for Counter-Terrorism, September 2019), https://icct.nl/publication/extreme-right-violence-and-terrorism-concepts-patterns-and-responses/; Daniel Koehler, *Violence and Terrorism from the Far-Right: Policy Options to Counter an Elusive Threat* (The Hague: International Centre for Counter-Terrorism, February 2019), 9, https://icct.nl/wp-content/uploads/2019/02/Koehler-Violence-and-Terrorism-from-the-Far-Right-February-2019.pdf; James B. Jacobs and Kimberly Potter, *Hate Crimes: Criminal Law and Identity Politics* (New York: Oxford University Press, 1998); Kathleen Deloughery, Ryan King, and Victor Asal, "Close Cousins or Distant Relatives? The Relationship Between Terrorism and Hate

"Crime," *Crime & Delinquency* 58, no. 5 (October 2012): 663–88, doi:10.1177/0011128712452956; Randy Blazak, "Isn't Every Crime a Hate Crime? The Case for Hate Crime Laws," *Sociology Compass* 5, no. 4 (April 2011): 244–55, https://www.researchgate.net/publication/260416492_Isn't_Every_Crime_a_Hate_Crime_The_Case_for_Hate_Crime_Laws; and Donald P. Green, Laurence H. McFalls, and Jennifer K. Smith, "Hate Crime: An Emergent Research Agenda," *Annual Review of Sociology* 27 (August 2001): 479–504, doi:10.1146/annurev.soc.27.1.479.

16 Christopher Wray, "Worldwide Threats to the Homeland," Statement before the House Homeland Security Committee, 116th Cong., 2nd sess., September 17, 2020, https://www.fbi.gov/news/testimony/worldwide-threats-to-the-homeland-092420.

17 See, for example, Louis Beam, "Leaderless Resistance," *The Seditionist* 12 (February 1992): 5.

18 For recommendations on countering this decentralized threat through bottom-up intelligence analysis and closer monitoring of digital platforms, see, for example, Seth G. Jones, Catrina Doxsee, and Nicholas Harrington, "The Tactics and Targets of Domestic Terrorists," CSIS, *CSIS Briefs*, July 30, 2020, https://www.csis.org/analysis/tactics-and-targets-domestic-terrorists.

19 "The Threat From Within: Domestic Extremists in the United States Military," Soufan Center, *IntelBrief*, March 10, 2021, https://thesoufancenter.org/intelbrief-2021-march-10/.

20 Kathleen Belew, *Bring the War Home: The White Power Movement and Paramilitary America* (Cambridge, MA: Harvard University Press, 2018), 136–37.

21 Kimberley L. Phillips, *War! What Is It Good For?: Black Freedom Struggles and the U.S. Military from World War II to Iraq* (Chapel Hill, NC: University of North Carolina Press, 2012), 226.

22 Louis Beam's father also served as a soldier and fought in World War I. Christian G. Appy, *Working-Class War: American Combat Soldiers and the Vietnam Wars, 1945-1990* (New York: HarperCollins, 1991).

23 Louis R. Beam, Jr., *Essays of a Klansman* (Hayden Lake, ID: A.K.I.A. Publications, 1983).

24 L.J. Davis, "Ballad of an American Terrorist: A New-Nazi's Dream of Order," *Harper's Magazine*, July 1986.

25 On Weaver's account of Ruby Ridge, see Randy Weaver and Sara Weaver, *The Federal Siege at Ruby Ridge: In Our Own Words* (Marion, MT: Ruby Ridge, Inc., 1998).

26 See, for example, Cynthia Miller-Idriss, *Hate in the Homeland: The New Global Far Right* (Princeton, NJ: Princeton University Press, 2020); Barry J. Balleck, *Modern American Extremism and Domestic Terrorism: An Encyclopedia of Extremists and Extremist Groups* (Santa Barbara, CA: ABC-CLIO, 2018); and Bruce Hoffman and Jacob Ware, "The Challenges of Effective Counterterrorism Intelligence in the 2020s," Lawfare, June 21, 2020, https://www.lawfareblog.com/challenges-effective-counterterrorism-intelligence-2020s.

27 U.S. Congress, *House Un-American Activities Committee Report on the Activities of the Ku Klux Klan* (Washington, DC: Government Printing Office, 1967).

28 Jack McLamb, *Operation Vampire Killer 2000: American Police Action Plan for Stopping World Government Rule* (Phoenix, AZ: PATNWO, 2000).

29 See, for example, Federal Bureau of Investigation, *White Supremacist Infiltration of Law Enforcement* (Washington, DC: Federal Bureau of Investigation, October 17, 2006), https://oversight.house.gov/sites/democrats.oversight.house.gov/files/White_Supremacist_Infiltration_of_Law_Enforcement.pdf.

30 Andrew Macdonald [William Luther Pierce], *Turner Diaries* (Washington, DC: National Alliance, 1980), 98.

31 Federal Bureau of Investigation, *White Supremacist Infiltration of Law Enforcement*, 5.

32 Federal Bureau of Investigation, *Lone Offender: A Study of Lone Offender Terrorism in the United States (1972-2015)* (Washington, DC: U.S. Department of Justice, Federal Bureau of Investigation, November 2019), 17. https://www.fbi.gov/file-repository/lone-offender-terrorism-report-111319.pdf/view.

33 Michael German, *Hidden In Plain Sight: Racism, White Supremacy, and Far-Right Militancy in Law Enforcement* (New York: Brennan Center for Justice, August 27, 2020), https://www.brennancenter.org/our-work/research-reports/hidden-plain-sight-racism-white-supremacy-and-far-right-militancy-law.

34 Maeve Reston, "Ex-Guard Gets 17-1/2 Years for Helping Prison Gang," *Los Angeles Times*, June 27, 2006, https://www.latimes.com/archives/la-xpm-2006-jun-27-me-nazi27-story.html.

35 In at least one case, one perpetrator (Air Force Staff Sergeant Steven Carrillo) was involved in two terrorist incidents. There were also some incidents in the CSIS data set that were perpetrated by multiple individuals who were current or active military or law enforcement personnel. For more details on the coding, please see the methodology linked at the end of this brief.

36 U.S. Department of Justice "U.S. Army Soldier Arrested for Attempting to Assist ISIS to Conduct Deadly Ambush on U.S. Troops," press release, January 19, 2021, https://www.justice.gov/usao-sdny/pr/us-army-soldier-arrested-attempting-assist-isis-conduct-deadly-ambush-us-troops.

37 U.S. Department of Justice, "Federal Grand Jury Indicts Three Men For Seeking To Exploit Protests In Las Vegas And Incite Violence," press release, June 17, 2020, https://www.justice.gov/usao-nv/pr/federal-grand-jury-indicts-three-men-seeking-exploit-protests-las-vegas-and-incite; and Brett Barrouquere, "Three Nevada 'Boogaloo Boys' Arrested by FBI in Firebombing Plot," Southern Poverty Law Center, June 9, 2020, https://www.splcenter.org/hatewatch/2020/06/09/three-nevada-boogaloo-boys-arrested-fbi-firebombing-plot.

38 U.S. Department of Justice "U.S. Army Soldier Charged with Terrorism Offenses for Planning Deadly Ambush on Service Members in His Unit," press release, June 22, 2020, https://www.justice.gov/opa/pr/us-army-soldier-charged-terrorism-offenses-planning-deadly-ambush-service-members-his-unit.

39 United States of America v. Steven Carrillo, Criminal Complaint, United States District Court for the Northern District of California, May 29, 2020, https://www.justice.gov/opa/press-release/file/1285706/download. United States of America vs. Robert Alvin Justus, Jr., Criminal Complaint, United States District Court for the Northern District of California, Case No. 4:20-mj-70771-MAG, May 29, 2020, https://www.justice.gov/opa/press-release/file/1285696/download; and "Two Defendants Charged with Murder and Aiding

and Abetting in Slaying of Federal Protective Service Officer at Oakland Courthouse Building," U.S. Department of Justice, June 16, 2020, https://www.justice.gov/opa/pr/two-defendants-charged-murder-and-aiding-and-abetting-slaying-federal-protective-service.

40 U.S. Department of Justice, "Two Off-Duty Virginia Police Officers Charged in Federal Court Following Events at the U.S. Capitol," press release, January 13, 2021, https://www.justice.gov/usao-dc/pr/two-duty-virginia-police-officers-charged-federal-court-following-events-us-capitol.

41 "Statement of Facts, Description: Complaint w/Arrest Warrant," U.S. Department of Justice, Case 1:21-mj-00036, January 12, 2021, https://www.justice.gov/usao-dc/press-release/file/1353461/download.

42 See, for example, Anthony McCann, *Shadowlands: Fear and Freedom at the Oregon Standoff* (New York: Bloomsbury, 2019).

43 United States of America v. Adam Fox, Barry Croft, Ty Garbin, Kaleb Franks, Daniel Harris, and Brandon Caserta, Criminal Complaint, Case 1:20-mj-00416-SJB, October 6, 2020.

44 Darcie Moran and Joe Guillen, "South Carolina Man Extradited in Whitmer Kidnap Plot," *Detroit Free Press*, October 20, 2020, https://www.freep.com/story/news/local/michigan/2020/10/20/south-carolina-extradited-whitmer-kidnap-plot-paul-bellar/3653588001/.

45 Jennifer Steinhauer, "Veterans Fortify the Ranks of Militias Aligned With Trump's Views," *New York Times*, January 20, 2021, https://www.nytimes.com/2020/09/11/us/politics/veterans-trump-protests-militias.html.

46 For example, the founder and leader of the Oath Keepers, Stewart Rhodes, served in the U.S. Army and was honorably discharged following an injury from a parachute jump.

47 "Joseph Fischer - Complaint and Statement of Facts," United States District Court for the District of Columbia, criminal complaint, February 17, 2021, https://www.justice.gov/usao-dc/case-multi-defendant/file/1369301/download; and Hannah Knowles, "'Front of the Pack': Off-duty Pa. Officer Charged at Police During the Capitol Riot, FBI Says," *Washington Post*, February 21, 2021, https://www.washingtonpost.com/nation/2021/02/21/officer-joseph-fischer-charged-capitol-riots/.

48 Jensen, "A Nightmare Scenario."

49 Office of District Attorney Kim Ogg, Harris County, Texas, "Former Houston Police Captain Charged with Holding Repairman at Gunpoint in Bogus Voter-Fraud Conspiracy," press release, December 15, 2020, https://www.harriscountyda.com/former-houston-police-captain-charged-holding-repairman-gunpoint-bogus-voter-fraud-conspiracy; and Jaclyn Diaz, "Ex-Houston Police Officer Charged In Attack Over Bogus Election Fraud Plot," NPR, December 16, 2020, https://www.npr.org/2020/12/16/946995614/ex-houston-police-officer-charged-in-attack-over-bogus-election-fraud-plot.

50 Target data include only terrorist attacks and not foiled plots, the targets of which are not always known.

51 In one case, Brian Maiorana made terrorist threats against both law enforcement and government targets. This incident is counted in both subcategories.

52 See, for example, *We Are Antifa: Expressions Against Fascism, Racism and Police Violence in the United States and Beyond* (Vancouver, Canada: Into the Void, 2020).

53 Mark Bray, *Antifa: The Anti-fascist Handbook* (Brooklyn, New York: Melville House, August 2017), 130.

54 Marisa J. Lang and Peter Jamison, "Rioters breached the Capitol as they waved pro-police flags. Police support on the right may be eroding, experts warn," *Washington Post*, January 8, 2021, https://www.washingtonpost.com/local/capitol-police-officers-support/2021/01/08/a16e07a2-51da-11eb-83e3-322644d82356_story.html.

55 Seth G. Jones, Catrina Doxsee, Nicholas Harrington, Grace Hwang, and James Suber, "The War Comes Home: The Evolution of Domestic Terrorism in the United States," CSIS, *CSIS Briefs*, October 22, 2020, https://www.csis.org/analysis/war-comes-home-evolution-domestic-terrorism-united-states.

56 Mike Vanderboegh, "Resolve," 2008.

57 On the rise of the violent far-right, see Miller-Idriss, *Hate in the Homeland*.

58 Shannon Taylor, "Henrico community members: Please see my complete statement below regarding an arrest last night by Henrico Police after a man drove a truck into protestors," Facebook, June 8, 2020, https://www.facebook.com/ShannonTaylorVA/photos/a.1351162298359756/1733983986744250; Shannon Taylor, "Henrico community: Please see my complete statement below," Facebook, June 25, 2020, https://www.facebook.com/ShannonTaylorVA/photos/a.1351162298359756/1750676268408355; and Allyson Waller, "Virginia Man Who Drove Into Protesters Gets 6 Years in Prison," *New York Times*, August 11, 2020, https://www.nytimes.com/2020/08/11/us/kkk-harry-rogers-guilty.html.

59 Lewis Kamb and Hal Bernton, "Portland Shooting Suspect Followed Right-wing Activists After Spotting Them Downtown, Unsealed Arrest Warrant Says," *Seattle Times*, September 5, 2020, https://www.seattletimes.com/seattle-news/portland-shooting-suspect-followed-right-wing-activists-after-spotting-them-downtown-unsealed-arrest-warrant-says/; Neil MacFarquhar, Mike Baker, and Adam Goldman, "In His Last Hours, Portland Murder Suspect Said He Feared Arrest," *New York Times*, September 4, 2020, https://www.nytimes.com/2020/09/04/us/portland-shooting-michael-reinoehl.html; and Destiny Johnson and Cassidy Quinn, "Unsealed Documents Shed Light on Moments Before Fatal Downtown Portland Shooting," KGW8, September 4, 2020, https://www.kgw.com/article/news/local/multnomah-county-district-attorney-provides-new-information-in-homicide-case/283-629b983a-620a-469e-bc03-4b365a99a547.

60 Maria Cramer, Michael Levenson, and Katie Benner, "Shooting at Texas Base Was 'Terrorism Related,' F.B.I. Says," *New York Times*, May 21, 2020, https://www.nytimes.com/2020/05/21/us/nas-corpus-christi-shooting.html; Alexandria Rodriguez, "NAS-CC Shooting Suspect Adam Alsahli was a Del Mar College Student," *Corpus Christi Caller Times*, May 23, 2020, https://www.caller.com/story/news/crime/2020/05/23/nas-corpus-christi-terrorist-shooting-adam-alsahli-del-mar-college-student/5249685002/; and Sam LaGrone, "FBI Identifies Man Killed in 'Terrorism-Related' Gun Battle at NAS Corpus Christi," USNI News, May 22, 2020, https://news.usni.org/2020/05/22/nas-corpus-christi-attacker-originally-from-syria-reports-say-fbi-continues-investigation-into-terrorism-related-gun-battle.

61 See, for example, New Jersey Office of Homeland Security and Preparedness, *Supplemental Threat Assessment 2020-2021: The Convergence of COVID-19, Nationwide Civil Unrest, and the Upcoming Presidential Election* (Trenton, NJ: State of New Jersey, New Jersey Office of Homeland Security and Preparedness, September 2020), 5, https://www.njhomelandsecurity.gov/analysis/2020-2021-supplemental-threat-assessment; and Texas Department of Public Safety, *Texas Domestic Terrorism Threat Assessment* (Austin, TX: January 2020), 4, 38, https://www.dps.texas.gov/sites/default/files/documents/director_staff/media_and_communications/2020/txterrorthreatassessment.pdf.

62 Hoffman and Ware, "The Challenges of Effective Counterterrorism Intelligence in the 2020s."

63 Suzanne Spaulding and Devi Nair, *Why the Kremlin Targets Veterans* (Washington, DC: CSIS, November 8, 2019), https://www.csis.org/analysis/why-kremlin-targets-veterans; and Kristofer Goldsmith, *An Investigation Into Foreign Entities Who Are Targeting Servicemembers and Veterans Online* (Silver Spring, MD: Vietnam Veterans of America, September 17, 2019), https://vva.org/trollreport/.

64 Philip Athey, "Several Pounds of C-4 Explosives Allegedly Missing from California Marine Base," *Marine Corps Times*, February 4, 2021, https://www.marinecorpstimes.com/news/your-marine-corps/2021/02/04/several-pounds-of-c-4-explosives-are-missing-from-california-marine-base/.

65 United States of America v. Timothy Louis Hale-Cusanelli, Motion for Emergency Stay and Appeal of Release, United States District Court for the District of Columbia, Case No. 21-cr-37 (TNM), March 12, 2021.

66 Federal Bureau of Investigation, *Lone Offender*, 18.

67 See, for example, Pete Simi, Bryan F. Bubolz, and Ann Hardman, "Military Experience, Identity Discrepancies, and Far Right Terrorism: An Exploratory Analysis," *Studies in Conflict and Terrorism*, 36 (July 2013): 654–71, https://www.tandfonline.com/doi/full/10.1080/1057610X.2013.802976#.UsrEqrTikck.

68 See, for example, Koehler, *A Threat From Within*.

69 "Germany Investigates Soldiers Over Anti-Semitic, Far-Right Group Chat," Deutsche Welle, November 27, 2020, https://www.dw.com/en/germany-investigates-soldiers-over-anti-semitic-far-right-group-chat/a-55755101; and "Germany: 9 Police Officers Probed Over Far-Right Chat Groups," Deutsche Welle, November 24, 2020, https://www.dw.com/en/germany-9-police-officers-probed-over-far-right-chat-groups/a-55708146.

70 Kate Connolly, "Hundreds of Right-Wing Extremist Incidents by Germany Security Services Revealed," *The Guardian*, October 6, 2020, https://www.theguardian.com/world/2020/oct/06/report-reveals-hundreds-of-rightwing-extremist-incidents-by-german-security-services.

71 Nina Werkhäuser, "German Elite Military Force Fights Far-Right Extremism In Its Ranks," Deutsche Welle, November 3, 2020, https://www.dw.com/en/german-armed-forces-bundeswehr-elite-unit/a-55485194; and Cynthia Miller-Idriss, "When the Far Right Penetrates Law Enforcement: America Can Learn from Germany," *Foreign Affairs*, December 15, 2020, https://www.foreignaffairs.com/articles/united-states/2020-12-15/when-far-right-penetrates-law-enforcement.

72 Darko Janjevic, "Europe's Right-Wing Extremists Try Recruiting from Police, Army," Deutsche Welle, September 24, 2019, https://www.dw.com/en/europes-right-wing-extremists-try-recruiting-from-police-army/a-50557142.

73 On "terrorism is theater," see Brian M. Jenkins, *International Terrorism: A New Kind of Warfare* (Santa Monica, CA: RAND, June 1974), 4, https://www.rand.org/pubs/papers/P5261.html. On "terrorists want a lot of people watching, not a lot of people dead," see Brian M. Jenkins, "International Terrorism: A New Model of Conflict," in David Carlton and Carla Schaerf, eds., *International Terrorism and World Security* (London: Croom Helm, 1974).

74 Brian M. Jenkins, Testimony Before the Subcommittee on Emerging Threats and Capabilities, Committee on Armed Services, United States Senate, November 15, 2001, https://www.govinfo.gov/content/pkg/CHRG-107shrg79736/html/CHRG-107shrg79736.htm.

Office of the Attorney General
Washington, D. C. 20530

October 4, 2021

MEMORANDUM FOR DIRECTOR, FEDERAL BUREAU OF INVESTIGATION
                                DIRECTOR, EXECUTIVE OFFICE FOR U.S. ATTORNEYS
                                ASSISTANT ATTORNEY GENERAL, CRIMINAL DIVISION
                                UNITED STATES ATTORNEYS

FROM: THE ATTORNEY GENERAL

SUBJECT: PARTNERSHIP AMONG FEDERAL, STATE, LOCAL, TRIBAL,
                          AND TERRITORIAL LAW ENFORCEMENT TO ADDRESS
                          THREATS AGAINST SCHOOL ADMINISTRATORS, BOARD
                          MEMBERS, TEACHERS, AND STAFF

In recent months, there has been a disturbing spike in harassment, intimidation, and threats of violence against school administrators, board members, teachers, and staff who participate in the vital work of running our nation's public schools. While spirited debate about policy matters is protected under our Constitution, that protection does not extend to threats of violence or efforts to intimidate individuals based on their views.

Threats against public servants are not only illegal, they run counter to our nation's core values. Those who dedicate their time and energy to ensuring that our children receive a proper education in a safe environment deserve to be able to do their work without fear for their safety.

The Department takes these incidents seriously and is committed to using its authority and resources to discourage these threats, identify them when they occur, and prosecute them when appropriate. In the coming days, the Department will announce a series of measures designed to address the rise in criminal conduct directed toward school personnel.

Coordination and partnership with local law enforcement is critical to implementing these measures for the benefit of our nation's nearly 14,000 public school districts. To this end, I am directing the Federal Bureau of Investigation, working with each United States Attorney, to convene meetings with federal, state, local, Tribal, and territorial leaders in each federal judicial district within 30 days of the issuance of this memorandum. These meetings will facilitate the discussion of strategies for addressing threats against school administrators, board members, teachers, and staff, and will open dedicated lines of communication for threat reporting, assessment, and response.

The Department is steadfast in its commitment to protect all people in the United States from violence, threats of violence, and other forms of intimidation and harassment.

ONE HUNDRED SEVENTEENTH CONGRESS

Congress of the United States

House of Representatives

COMMITTEE ON THE JUDICIARY

2138 RAYBURN HOUSE OFFICE BUILDING

WASHINGTON, DC 20515–6216

(202) 225–3951
Judiciary.house.gov

May 11, 2022

The Honorable Merrick B. Garland
Attorney General
Department of Justice
950 Pennsylvania Avenue, N.W.
Washington, DC 20535

Dear Attorney General Garland:

In sworn testimony before this Committee, you denied that the Department of Justice or its components were using counterterrorism statutes and resources to target parents at school board meetings.[1] We now have evidence that contrary to your testimony, the Federal Bureau of Investigation has labeled at least dozens of investigations into parents with a threat tag created by the FBI's Counterterrorism Division to assess and track investigations related to school boards. These cases include investigations into parents upset about mask mandates and state elected officials who publicly voiced opposition to vaccine mandates. These investigations into concerned parents are the direct result of, and would not have occurred but for, your directive to federal law enforcement to target these categories of people.

On October 4, 2021, in response to a request from the National School Boards Association that the federal government use counterterrorism tools, including the Patriot Act, to target parents at school board meetings, you issued a memorandum directing the FBI to address these threats.[2] The press release accompanying your memorandum highlighted the FBI's National Threat Operations Center to serve as a snitch-line for tips about parents at school board meetings.[3] By October 20, the FBI had operationalized your directive. In an FBI-wide email, the FBI's Counterterrorism Division and Criminal Division announced the creation of a new threat tag—EDUOFFICIALS—and directed all FBI personnel to apply it to school board-related threats.[4]

---

[1] *Oversight of the United States Department of Justice: Hearing Before the H. comm. on the Judiciary*, 117th Cong. (2021) (testimony from Hon. Merrick Garland, Atty Gen., U.S. Dep't of Justice).

[2] Memorandum from Atty Gen. Merrick Garland, U.S. Dep't of Justice, Partnership Among Federal, State, Local, Tribal, And Territorial Law Enforcement to Address Threats Against School Administrators, Board Members, Teachers, and Staff (Oct. 4, 2021).

[3] Press Release, U.S. Dep't of Justice, Justice Department Addresses Violent Threats Against School Officials and Teachers (Oct. 4, 2021).

[4] Email from Carlton Peeples, Deputy Assistant Director, Criminal Investigative Div., Fed. Bureau of Investigation, to FBI_SACS (Oct. 20, 2021).

We have learned from brave whistleblowers that the FBI has opened investigations with the EDUOFFICIALS threat tag in almost every region of the country and relating to all types of educational settings. The information we have received shows how, as a direct result of your directive, federal law enforcement is using counterterrorism resources to investigate protected First Amendment activity. For example:

- In one investigation begun following your directive, the FBI's ████ Field Office interviewed a mom for allegedly telling a local school board "we are coming for you." The complaint, which came into the FBI through the National Threat Operations Center snitch-line, alleged that the mom was a threat because she belonged to a "right wing mom's group" known as "Moms for Liberty" and because she "is a gun owner." When an FBI agent interviewed the mom, she told the agent that she was upset about the school board's mask mandates and that her statement was a warning that her organization would seek to replace the school board with new members through the electoral process.

- The FBI's ████ Field Office opened an investigation, subsequent to your directive, into a dad opposed to mask mandates. The complaint came in through the National Threat Operations Center snitch-line and alleged that the dad "fit the profile of an insurrectionist" because he "rails against the government," "believes all conspiracy theories," and "has a lot of guns and threatens to use them." When an FBI agent interviewed the complainant, the complainant admitted they had "no specific information or observations of . . . any crimes or threats," but they contacted the FBI after learning the Justice Department had a website "to submit tips to the FBI in regards to any concerning behavior directed toward school boards."

- In another case initiated after your directive, the FBI's ████ Field Office opened an investigation into Republican state elected officials over allegations from a state Democratic party official that the Republicans "incited violence" by expressing public displeasure with school districts' vaccine mandates. This complaint also came into the FBI through the National Threat Operations Center snitch-line.

This whistleblower information is startling. You have subjected these moms and dads to the opening of an FBI investigation about them, the establishment of an FBI case file that includes their political views, and the application of a "threat tag" to their names as a direct result of their exercise of their fundamental constitutional right to speak and advocate for their children. This information is evidence of how the Biden Administration is using federal law enforcement, including counterterrorism resources, to investigate concerned parents for protected First Amendment activity. Although FBI agents ultimately—and rightly—determined that these cases did not implicate federal criminal statutes, the agents still exerted their limited time and resources investigating these complaints. This valuable law-enforcement time and resources could have been expended on real and pressing threats.

These investigations into concerned parents were the direct result of your October 4 directive to the FBI. Each of the cases was initiated following your directive. Each of the complaints came into the FBI through the same snitch-line—the National Threat Operations Center—highlighted in the press release accompanying your October 4 memorandum. One complainant even told an FBI agent that they reported the tip to the FBI because of the snitch-line, despite having "no specific information" about any actual threat. These facts lead us to conclude that these investigations into concerned parents, and likely many more like them, would not have occurred but for your directive.

Parents have an undisputed right to direct the upbringing and education of their children,[5] which includes voicing their strong opposition to controversial curricula at local schools. This whistleblower information raises serious concerns that your October 4 memorandum will chill protected First Amendment activity as parents will rightfully fear that their passionate advocacy for their children could result in a visit from federal law enforcement. You have refused to rescind your October 4 memorandum and its anti-parent directives. In light of this new whistleblower information, we again call on you to rescind your October 4 memorandum.

Committee Republicans have been investigating the Biden Administration's misuse of law-enforcement resources to target concerned parents since last fall.[6] You have failed to substantively respond to our requests for documents and your sworn testimony to the Committee is now contradicted by whistleblower information. Please be assured that Committee Republicans will not let this matter drop. Accordingly, we request the following information:

1. Produce all documents and materials identified in our letters to Departmental components dated November 1, 2021, November 2, 2021, November 3, 2021, and November 18, 2021, immediately; and

2. Take all reasonable steps immediately to preserve all records responsive to our letters to Department components.

In addition, we remind you that whistleblower disclosures to Congress are protected by law and that we will not tolerate any effort to retaliate against whistleblowers for their disclosures.

Sincerely,

Jim Jordan
Ranking Member

Mike Johnson
Ranking Member
Subcommittee on the Constitution,
Civil Rights and Civil Liberties

---

[5] *Troxel v. Granville*, 530 U.S. 57, 65 (2000) (citing *Meyer v. Nebraska*, 262 U.S. 390, 399 (1923)).
[6] Letter from House Judiciary Committee Republicans to Hon. Christopher A. Wray, Dir., Fed. Bureau of Investigation (Nov. 3, 2021).

The Honorable Merrick B. Garland
May 11, 2022
Page 4

cc: The Honorable Jerrold L. Nadler
       Chairman

A REUTERS SPECIAL REPORT

School boards get death threats amid rage over race, gender, mask policies

Local school officials across the United States are being inundated with threats of violence and other hostile messages from anonymous harassers nationwide, fueled by anger over culture-war issues. Reuters found 220 examples of such intimidation in a sampling of districts.

By GABRIELLA BORTER, JOSEPH AX and JOSEPH TANFANI | Filed Feb. 15, 2022, 11 a.m. GMT

This story contains text, images and audio clips with offensive language.

The letter came to the home of Brenda Sheridan, a Loudoun County, Virginia school board member, addressed to one of her adult children. It threatened to kill them both unless she left the board.

"It is too bad that your mother is an ugly communist whore," said the hand-scrawled note, which the family read just after Christmas. "If she doesn't quit or resign before the end of the year, we will kill her, but first, we will kill you!"

School board members across the United States have endured a rash of terroristic threats and hostile messages ignited by roiling controversies over policies on curtailing the coronavirus, bathroom access for transgender students and the teaching of America's racial history.

Reuters documented the intimidation through contacts and interviews with 33 board members across 15 states and a review of threatening and harassing messages obtained from the officials or through public records requests. The news organization found more than 220 such messages in this sampling of districts. School officials or parents in 15 different counties received or witnessed threats they considered serious enough to report to police.

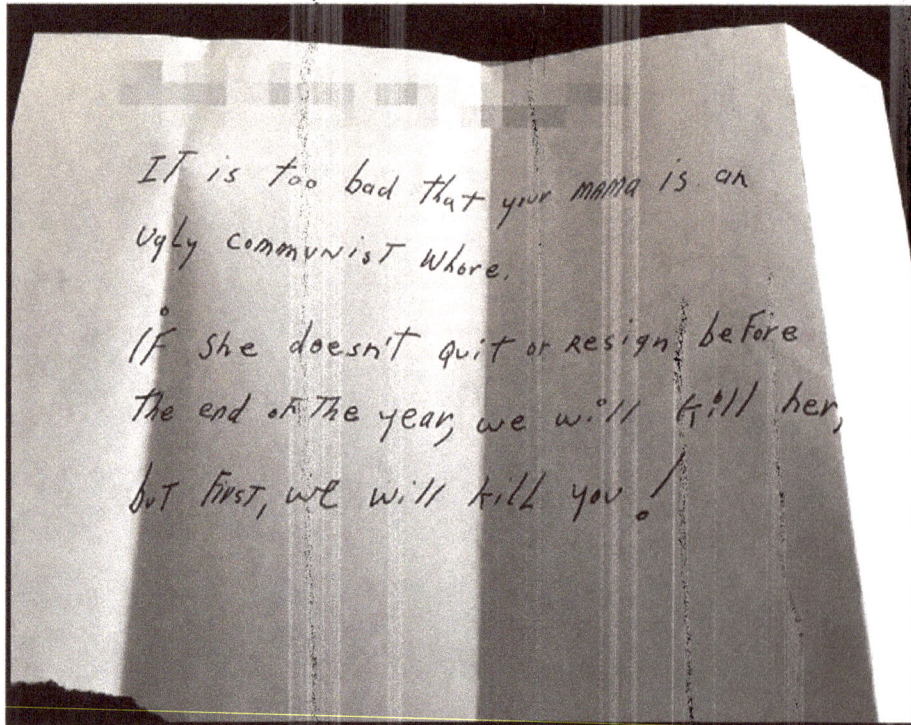

Threatening letter sent to the home of Loudoun County, Virginia, school board member Brenda Sheridan

While school controversies are traditionally local, these threats often come from people out of state with no connection to the districts involved. They are part of a rising national wave of threats to public officials – including election officials and members of Congress – citing an array of grievances, often underpinned by apocalyptic conspiracy theories alleging "treason" or "tyranny."

About half the hostile messages documented by Reuters were sent to Sheridan, former chair of the Loudoun County, Virginia, school board, amid controversies over coronavirus protections, anti-racism efforts and bathroom policy. Twenty-two messages sent to Sheridan or the entire board included death threats or said members should be or would be killed.

In June, she received a threat saying: "Brenda, I am going to gut you like the fat f---ing pig you are when I find you."

The message, like the letter to her home, also threatened her children. Reuters agreed not to publish any personal details about Sheridan's family members, at her request, because of her continuing safety concerns.

Board members in Pennsylvania's Pennsbury school district received racist and anti-Semitic emails from around the country from people angry over the district's diversity efforts. One said: "This why hitler threw you c--ts in a gas chamber."

In Dublin, Ohio, an anonymous letter sent to the board president vowed that officials would "pay dearly" for supporting education programs on race and mask mandates to stop the coronavirus. "You have become our enemies and you will be removed one way or the other," it said.

School officials reported the messages to law enforcement in those three cases, as in many others documented by Reuters. No one has been arrested for sending these threatening messages, though a few people have been arrested for unruly or threatening behavior at board meetings.

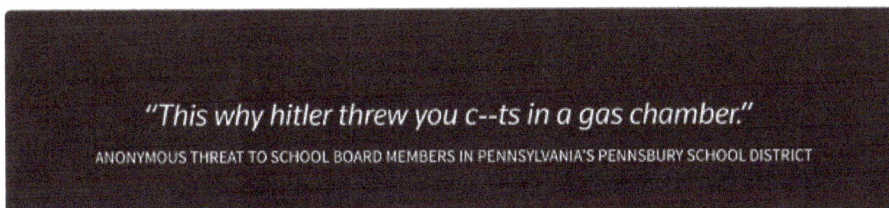

> ## "This why hitler threw you c--ts in a gas chamber."
> ANONYMOUS THREAT TO SCHOOL BOARD MEMBERS IN PENNSYLVANIA'S PENNSBURY SCHOOL DISTRICT

Attorney General Merrick Garland vowed last year to devote federal resources to combating threats to school officials after the National School Boards Association in September sent the White House a request for federal enforcement to stop the "growing number of threats of violence and acts of intimidation occurring across the nation." But the association's plea for help only added to the controversy as Republican politicians argued the administration of President Joe Biden, a Democrat, sought to censor free speech and label dissenting parents as terrorists. Nineteen state school boards withdrew their membership or withheld dues from the national association in protest of its Sept. 29 letter.

The school boards association apologized to its state members for the letter on Oct. 22, saying there was "no justification" for some of its language, without specifying what it regretted. The organization did not respond to requests for comment.

The hostility faced by school officials mirrors the campaign of fear documented by Reuters against U.S. election workers in response to former President Donald Trump's false claims of voting fraud. A federal election-threats task force was announced in June, after a Reuters investigation that month revealed the widespread threats. In January, the task force reported the arrests of two people who had threatened election officials.

RELATED CONTENT

Campaign of Fear: The Trump world's assault on U.S. election workers

Reuters unmasks Trump supporters who terrified U.S. election officials

Biden's Justice Department has also convened a task force on threats to school officials. The department, however, declined to say who serves on it, whether the task force has met or whether it was investigating any threats. In a statement, the department said it had "taken action" to prevent violence and intimidation of "those who are threatened because of the jobs they hold," including school board members, election workers and other public officials.

The Federal Bureau of Investigation, in a statement, characterized Attorney General Garland's commitment to protect school officials as simply highlighting the FBI's "ongoing efforts" to address threats of violence "regardless of the motivation." The agency emphasized it was not "investigating parents who speak out or policing speech at school board meetings."

Nearly half of the 31 school boards contacted by Reuters said they had added extra security at meetings, limited public comment or held virtual meetings when in-person gatherings became too chaotic.

In Luray, Virginia, a woman furious about mask mandates was charged by local police with making a threat after she told school board members at a January meeting that she would "bring every single gun loaded and ready" to school. The woman, Amelia King, emailed an apology to board members before the meeting was over, saying she was speaking figuratively and "in no way" meant to imply she would bring firearms to a school.

King's lawyer declined to comment on the pending charge.

Some board members have quit their posts or decided not to seek reelection. A board member in Gwinnett County, Georgia, said she bought a gun for self-defense after prolonged online harassment. The board chair in Union County, North Carolina, said she installed cameras outside her house at "every angle." Sheridan – the Loudoun County board member – said she rarely goes out in public alone anymore.

Jean Marvin, the board chair in Rochester, Minnesota, said a barrage of threats there last year deeply unsettled her fellow board members and her own children: "They said, 'Mom, they're going to kill you. They know where you live.'"

Jon Tigges is detained following a controversial Loudoun County school board meeting in Ashburn, Virginia that included discussion of critical race theory. REUTERS/Evelyn Hockstein

Living in fear

The wave of mostly anonymous threats has emerged against a backdrop of public protests by a new constellation of local and national activist groups, such as Moms for Liberty, No Left Turn in Education and Parents Defending Education. Parents started some groups. Others have ties to veterans of the conservative movement or Republican political operatives.

Many Republican elected officials have sought to harness the anger over education policy in advance of this November's midterm congressional elections, releasing strident statements or passing laws addressing the issues igniting the school protests.

Much of the anger focuses on critical race theory, a once-obscure academic school of thought frequently targeted by Trump. Rarely taught outside law schools, the theory holds that racial bias – intentional or not – is baked into many U.S. laws and institutions because of the nation's history of slavery and segregation. Many conservative parents and politicians now use the term as an epithet for a wide range of anti-racism efforts and teaching on race relations that they say attempts to indoctrinate students with an anti-white and anti-American worldview.

One group, Fight for Schools, is led by Ian Prior, a former deputy director of public affairs in Trump's Department of Justice. The group took in $10,000 in donations in the past year from 1776 Action, a national group opposing critical race theory that is run by veteran Republican operatives. The organization also accepted $5,000 from the Presidential Coalition, which is overseen by former Trump deputy campaign manager David Bossie.

Neither 1776 Action nor Bossie responded to requests for comment.

Fight for Schools has staged protests at board meetings since early 2021 over pandemic-related closures and teaching on race. The organization is also leading a recall campaign seeking to oust Sheridan from the Loudoun County board before the next school board elections.

Brenda Sheridan, former chair of the Loudoun County school board, stands outside the board's headquarters in Ashburn, Virginia. REUTERS/Evelyn Hockstein

Reuters found no evidence that any of the new advocacy groups are involved in threatening board members with violence. Fight for Schools, in a statement, condemned threats of physical harm, personal attacks and harassment.

The board in Loudoun County, a Washington suburb, first came under fire in 2020 over pandemic school closures. Anger built as the district implemented anti-racism efforts in August of that year, including teacher training.

By June 2021, many parents were also incensed by a proposed policy to allow transgender students to use bathrooms matching their preferred gender identity. The anger grew after the parents of a female student who was sexually assaulted in a school bathroom in May told reporters that her attacker was a "gender fluid" student. Authorities said the student was a male who wore a skirt the day of the attack. Loudoun County's juvenile court declined to comment or release records on the case, citing legal privacy protections for juvenile suspects.

Conservatives seized on the case as evidence of the danger of bathroom policies seeking to accommodate transgender students. But the district's policy did not take effect until August, well after the attack.

Sheridan, the board chair in 2021 and still a member, became a primary target for intimidation. She reported the June threat to "gut" her to authorities. But police investigators failed to identify a suspect, highlighting difficulties in investigating anonymous threats.

The Loudoun County Sheriff's Office submitted a search warrant to Google to collect information on the sender, who had used a Google email address, police reports show. But the warrant turned up multiple IP addresses, leaving investigators with "no viable investigative leads" to find the perpetrator, according to a police report.

"There's no way to know: Did that come from someone from another state, or is it my neighbor down the street who knows my routine?" Sheridan said.

Reports from the county sheriff's office, obtained through a public records request, show law enforcement was notified of more than 50 menacing messages directed toward the school board between April and November. Investigators did not pursue about half the cases after determining the messages did not constitute a criminal threat.

Police did make inquiries in at least 26 cases, including one email saying: "You people need to be arrested, tried and then hung by the neck until you're dead." But investigators either could not identify a suspect in those cases or determined they did not have enough evidence to seek prosecution, a police spokesperson said.

Reuters wrote to dozens of the email addresses used to send hostile or threatening messages to Sheridan and the Loudoun County school board. Six people responded. One self-described "patriot" spoke of rage over "leftist scum" and "Antifa." Another said "LGBTQ is an abomination." A third blasted the district's anti-racism program, saying that telling children "that race will determine their outcomes in life is truly sick."

One had written to Loudoun superintendent Scott Ziegler in June. "Your life is being laid bare on the open and dark web. I don't condone what's gonna be sent to those close to you or the danger they may be in," the email said, "but you personally do deserve it."

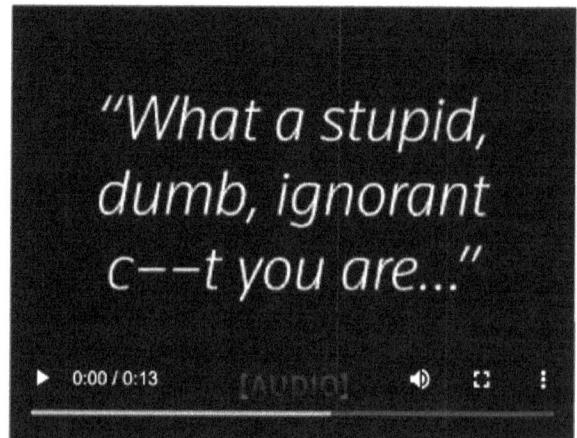

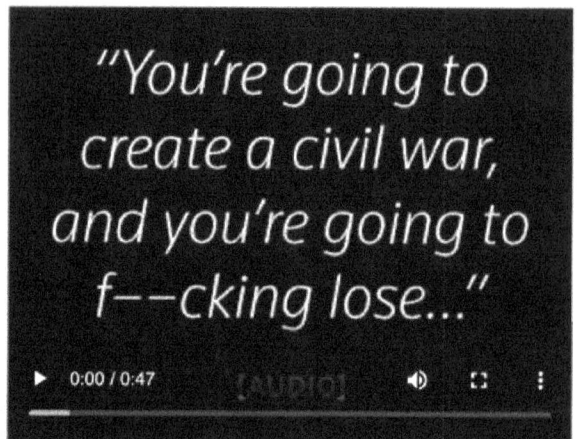

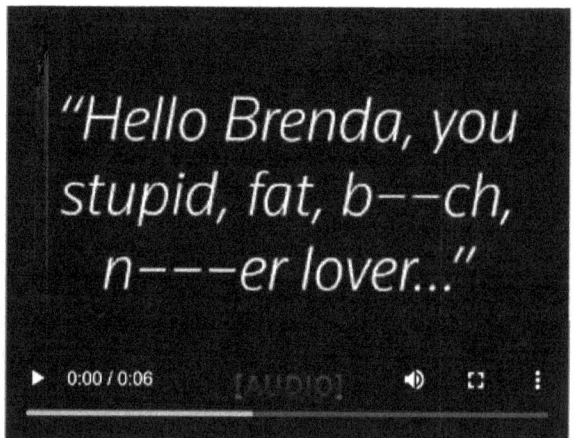

Click to hear hostile voicemails to Loudoun County, Virginia school board member Brenda Sheridan

Contacted by Reuters, the person who sent the message, who did not give a name, said it was prompted by rage over the student sexual-assault incident. "I was warning him, not threatening him," the sender said in an email. "I'm not looking to be labeled as anti trans. I'm just anti rape in schools."

Ziegler declined to comment.

Elicia Brand leads a crowd of angry parents and community members in the singing of the Star Spangled Banner after a Loudoun County school board meeting was halted by the school board because the crowd refused to quiet down, in Ashburn, Virginia. REUTERS/Evelyn Hockstein

'Treason' and 'tyranny'

The people who threaten school board members often cast coronavirus and race-education policies not merely as misguided or offensive, but as part of a larger conspiracy to commit "treason" or impose "tyranny."

The message threatening to remove Dublin, Ohio, board members "one way or the other" came from a man who identified himself as "James Baker" of "Citizens to Remove CRT from America," referring to critical race theory. Reuters was unable to confirm the identity of the sender.

"All Americans know the schools have become Indoctrination Centers for Marxism," read the message, which was also sent to other districts. "WE ARE COMING AFTER ALL OF YOU STINKING TRAITORS OF AMERICA!"

Chris Valentine, the board president at the time, said the threat was the worst example of the hostile messages district officials have endured since the start of the pandemic. Valentine said he started worrying whenever he noticed an unfamiliar car parked outside his home.

"It's easily been the most difficult year-and-a-half of my life," Valentine said.

Dublin police reviewed the letter and "found no safety concerns or credible threats," a police spokesperson said. Still, the department added officers to ensure security at the next school board meeting.

> ## "WE ARE COMING AFTER ALL OF YOU STINKING TRAITORS OF AMERICA!"
> THREAT SENT TO SCHOOL BOARD MEMBERS IN DUBLIN, OHIO

In Rochester, Minnesota, members faced months of threats and outbursts at meetings over mask mandates, critical race theory and other hot-button issues. Marvin, the board president, said her son grew so concerned that he insisted on driving her to board meetings and waiting in the parking lot to ensure her safety.

302 of 315

Northwest Allen County school board meetings in Indiana became so heated last fall that police officers assigned to the district refused to continue providing security unless the board took action to rein in its increasingly unruly meetings, according to an email sent by a school resource officer to the board president.

"I truly am concerned for the safety of everyone at those meetings as are the other officers who have worked them," Sergeant Kevin Neher wrote to the board president at the time, Kent Somers, on Sept. 17, in an email reviewed by Reuters.

In response, the board eliminated public comment for its next meeting. Several board members as well as the schools superintendent, Christopher Himsel, had to be escorted by half a dozen police officers to their cars, Himsel said in an interview.

Neither Neher nor Somers responded to requests for comment.

At least two parents from the district reported a local resident to the FBI, after the man posted menacing messages about school officials on Facebook, according to one of the parents. One threat to Somers warned that someone might "bag and tag your ass in a parking lot." The same man posted a message urging others to get "firearms, ammunition and extensive training" to fight the "tyranny before us," according to a police report documenting the messages. Another parent who helps oversee a Facebook group opposing the district's mask policies posted a video of himself firing a rifle to show he was not merely a "digital soldier," according to a screenshot of the message provided by a parent to Reuters.

A spokesperson for the Indianapolis FBI office declined to confirm or deny any investigations into these threats. Allen County police documented several of the messages but did not take any further action, according to a police report.

The Board of School Directors of the Pennsbury school district listen to members of the public at a meeting at Fallsington Elementary School in Falls Township, Pennsylvania. REUTERS/Hannah Beier

Calls for enforcement

Christine Toy-Dragoni, the then-board president in Pennsylvania's Pennsbury school district, requested FBI involvement after her board received a slew of hateful messages.

As Pennsbury's conflicts gained national attention, board members were deluged with racist, anti-Semitic and threatening messages, nearly two dozen of which Reuters viewed.

"You better grow eyes in the back of your head motherf---er," said a message to board members in July.

Christine Toy-Dragoni, former president of the Board of School Directors of the Pennsbury school district, at Fallsington Elementary School in Falls Township, Pennsylvania. REUTERS/Hannah Beier

The board's Toy-Dragoni responded in October with a public statement calling on the FBI to act. "These threats of violence and sexual assault and these expressions of transphobic, anti-immigrant and anti-Jewish hatred are certainly not protected by the Constitution, and must be investigated by the FBI," she said.

The school district reported the threats to local police and the FBI. Falls Township Police Chief Nelson Whitney said in an interview that his detectives spent several months working with the FBI to investigate threatening emails and other communications received by Pennsbury board members. He said state and federal prosecutors ultimately decided that the messages, "although offensive, did not rise to the level where a charge would be filed."

In the nearby North Penn district, a report that spread on conservative media about a classroom diversity exercise prompted one man to call an elementary school on Feb. 6 and leave a voicemail that threatened the teacher with sexual violence and death.

"Mass of people who know who you are," the man said. "They will fucking see your head swinging from a pole."

Jonathan Kassa, a North Penn board member, said the threat was reported to local police and the FBI. Kassa said the threat is one of many the district has received.

"This isn't some one-off, random event," Kassa said in an interview. "I certainly hope law enforcement and our legislators are paying much closer attention to what seems to be an increasingly serious threat."

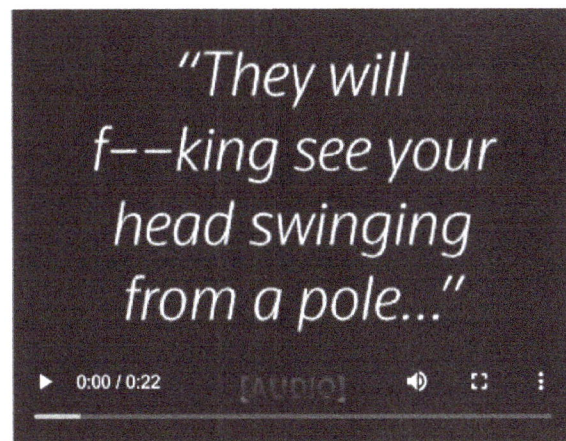

"They will f--king see your head swinging from a pole..."

► 0:00 / 0:22 [AUDIO]

Click to hear a voicemail threat left at a school in Pennsylvania's North Penn school district on Feb. 6

Local police in Hatfield Township said they have opened an investigation. Spokespeople for the FBI declined to comment on whether the bureau was investigating the threats in the Pennsbury and North Penn districts.

In Brevard County, Florida, school board member Jennifer Jenkins faced threats and intimidation after supporting a district mask mandate. Then someone filed a false claim against her with the Florida Department of Children and Families, alleging she abused her daughter. Police in Satellite Beach, Florida, determined the claim to be unfounded and tried, unsuccessfully, to determine the identity of the person who made the false report.

Jenkins told Reuters she has installed security cameras at her home, where anti-mask demonstrators staged multiple protests. She still feels unsafe at times, worried that the threats will escalate to violence.

"All it takes," she said, "is one psychotic fringe loony toon."

Schools Under Siege
By Gabriella Borter, Joseph Ax and Joseph Tanfani
Photo editing: Corinne Perkins
Art direction: John Emerson
Edited by Colleen Jenkins and Brian Thevenot

f 🐦 in ⊙ ✉ 🖨

Follow Reuters Investigates f 🐦

OTHER REUTERS INVESTIGATIONS

Brain Teaser

Elon Musk says his brain-chip company will make the paralyzed walk and the blind see. But Neuralink still struggles to secure clinical-trial approval.

Lost Soles

A Reuters investigation found some shoes meant for recycling in Singapore ended up in shops in Indonesia, where it is illegal to import second-hand clothing.

Narcos Inc

Scandal has dogged ex-soccer great Cuauhtémoc Blanco, a rising political star in Mexico. He has a key backer: Mexico's president.

A Russian graveyard reveals Wagner's prisoner army

A rapidly expanding cemetery in a southern Russian village offers insight into the convicts who are fighting - and dying - for the secretive mercenary army of Wagner Group.

ONE HUNDRED SEVENTEENTH CONGRESS

Congress of the United States
House of Representatives

COMMITTEE ON THE JUDICIARY

2138 RAYBURN HOUSE OFFICE BUILDING

WASHINGTON, DC 20515–6216

(202) 225–3951
judiciary.house.gov

August 10, 2022

Ms. Jill Sanborn
Senior Director Geopolitical Strategy & Risk Analysis
Roku Inc.
1701 Junction Court, Suite 100
San Jose, CA 95112

Dear Ms. Sanborn:

On July 27, 2022, we wrote to FBI Director Christopher Wray about whistleblower disclosures that FBI officials were pressuring agents to reclassify cases as "domestic violent extremism" (DVEs) even if the cases do not meet the criteria for such a classification.[1] Between January 2020 and April 2021, according to public information, you served as the Assistant Director of the FBI Counterterrorism Division, and then as Executive Assistant Director of the National Security Branch until you left federal service.[2] Accordingly, we believe that you may possess information relating to this matter and we request your assistance with our inquiry.

Whistleblower disclosures made by multiple FBI employees from different field offices suggest that FBI agents are bolstering the number of cases of DVEs to satisfy their supervisors. For example, one whistleblower explained that because agents are not finding enough DVE cases, they are encouraged and incentivized to reclassify cases as DVE cases even though there is minimal, circumstantial evidence to support the reclassification. Another whistleblower stated that a field office Counterterrorism Assistant Special Agent in Charge and the FBI's then-Assistant Director of the Counterterrorism Division pressured agents to move cases into the DVE category to hit self-created performance metrics. This whistleblower identified you as one official who exerted pressure on agents to reclassify cases as DVE matters.

The Committee on the Judiciary has legislative and oversight jurisdiction over the Department of Justice and the FBI pursuant to Rule X of the Rules of the House of Representatives. We are investigating several allegations concerning the politicization of the FBI, including allegations that the FBI is padding its DVE data. Your testimony is necessary to

---

[1] Letter from Jim Jordan, Ranking Member, H. Comm. on the Judiciary, to Christopher A. Wray, Dir. Fed. Bureau of Investigation (July 27, 2022).

[2] @Jill Sanborn, LINKEDIN, https://www.linkedin.com/in/jill-sanborn-74a402190; Press Release, Fed. Bureau of Investigation, *Jill Sanborn Named Assistant Director of the Counterterrorism Division* (Jan. 8, 2020); Press Release, Fed. Bureau of Investigation, *Jill Sanborn Named Executive Assistant Director of the National Security Branch*, (May 7, 2021).

advance our oversight. We therefore ask that you please contact Committee staff to schedule a transcribed interview as soon as possible, but no later than 5:00 p.m. on August 24, 2022. You may contact Committee staff at (202) 225-6906.

Thank you for your attention to this matter.

Sincerely,

Jim Jordan
Ranking Member

Mike Johnson
Ranking Member
Subcommittee on the Constitution,
Civil Rights and Civil Liberties

Department of the Treasury
Internal Revenue Service
Tax Exempt and Government Entities
P.O. Box 2508
Cincinnati, OH 45201

Date:
07/26/2022

Employer ID number:
88-1807315

Person to contact:
Name: Customer Service
ID number: 31954
Telephone: (877) 829-5500

Accounting period ending:
December 31

Public charity status:
170(b)(1)(A)(vi)

Form 990 / 990-EZ / 990-N required:
Yes

Effective date of exemption:
April 8, 2022

Contribution deductibility:
Yes

Addendum applies:
No

DLN:
26053586005532

KASH FOUNDATION INC
717 KING STREET SUITE 200
ALEXANDRIA, VA 22314

Dear Applicant:

We're pleased to tell you we determined you're exempt from federal income tax under Internal Revenue Code (IRC) Section 501(c)(3). Donors can deduct contributions they make to you under IRC Section 170. You're also qualified to receive tax deductible bequests, devises, transfers or gifts under Section 2055, 2106, or 2522. This letter could help resolve questions on your exempt status. Please keep it for your records.

Organizations exempt under IRC Section 501(c)(3) are further classified as either public charities or private foundations. We determined you're a public charity under the IRC Section listed at the top of this letter.

If we indicated at the top of this letter that you're required to file Form 990/990-EZ/990-N, our records show you're required to file an annual information return (Form 990 or Form 990-EZ) or electronic notice (Form 990-N, the e-Postcard). If you don't file a required return or notice for three consecutive years, your exempt status will be automatically revoked.

If we indicated at the top of this letter that an addendum applies, the enclosed addendum is an integral part of this letter.

Letter 947 (Rev. 2-2020)
Catalog Number 35152P

For important information about your responsibilities as a tax-exempt organization, go to www.irs.gov/charities. Enter "4221-PC" in the search bar to view Publication 4221-PC, Compliance Guide for 501(c)(3) Public Charities, which describes your recordkeeping, reporting, and disclosure requirements.

We sent a copy of this letter to your representative as indicated in your power of attorney.

Sincerely,

Stephen A. Martin
Director, Exempt Organizations
Rulings and Agreements

Letter 947 (Rev. 2-2020)
Catalog Number 35152P

DONALD J. TRUMP

June 19, 2022

The Honorable Debra Steidel Wall
Acting Archivist of the United States
U.S. National Archives and Records Administration
Washington, D.C.

Dear Ms. Wall,

I write to designate two individuals – Kash Patel and John Solomon – as my representatives for
access to Presidential records of my administration, pursuant to the Presidential Records Act, 44
U.S.C. §§ 2201 – 2207, and 36 C.F.R. § 1270.44(a)(4).

Kashyap Pramod "Kash" Patel can be reached at patelkpp@gmail.com and (516) 330-628. John
Solomon can be reached at Jsolomon@justthenews.com and (202) 236-5606. Both individuals
meet the requirements for access to records under 36 C.F.R. § 1270.44(a)(4).

Thank you for your attention to this request.

Sincerely,

cc: Mr. Gary M. Stern
       Mr. John Laster

Return of Organization Exempt From Income Tax

Form **990**

Under section 501(c), 527, or 4947(a)(1) of the Internal Revenue Code (except private foundations)

Department of the Treasury
Internal Revenue Service

▶ Do not enter social security numbers on this form as it may be made public.
▶ Go to www.irs.gov/Form990 for instructions and the latest information.

OMB No. 1545-0047

2021

Open to Public Inspection

A For the 2021 calendar year, or tax year beginning _____ and ending _____

B Check if applicable:	**C** Name of organization							**D** Employer identification number
☐ Address change	Center for Renewing America, Inc.							
☒ Name change	Doing business as							85-4307005
☒ Initial return	Number and street (or P.O. box if mail is not delivered to street address)					Room/suite	**E** Telephone number	
☐ Final return/terminated	300 Independence Avenue SE						202-656-8825	
☐ Amended return	City or town, state or province, country, and ZIP or foreign postal code						**G** Gross receipts $	1,042,274.
☐ Application pending	Washington, DC 20003							
	F Name and address of principal officer: Russell Vought						**H(a)** Is this a group return for subordinates?	☐ Yes ☒ No
	same as C above						**H(b)** Are all subordinates included? ☐ Yes ☐ No	

I Tax-exempt status: ☒ 501(c)(3) ☐ 501(c) ( ) ◀ (insert no.) ☐ 4947(a)(1) or ☐ 527   If "No," attach a list. See instructions

J Website: ▶ www.americarenewing.com   **H(c)** Group exemption number ▶

K Form of organization: ☒ Corporation ☐ Trust ☐ Association ☐ Other ▶ _____   **L** Year of formation: 2020   **M** State of legal domicile: DE

Part I   Summary

1	Briefly describe the organization's mission or most significant activities: Conduct original research and analysis of public polic to advance a renewing of America.		
2	Check this box ▶ ☐ if the organization discontinued its operations or disposed of more than 25% of its net assets.		
3	Number of voting members of the governing body (Part VI, line 1a)	**3**	5
4	Number of independent voting members of the governing body (Part VI, line 1b)	**4**	4
5	Total number of individuals employed in calendar year 2021 (Part V, line 2a)	**5**	7
6	Total number of volunteers (estimate if necessary)	**6**	9
7 a	Total unrelated business revenue from Part VIII, column (C), line 12	**7a**	0.
b	Net unrelated business taxable income from Form 990-T, Part I, line 11	**7b**	0.

		Prior Year	Current Year
8	Contributions and grants (Part VIII, line 1h)		1,042,274.
9	Program service revenue (Part VIII, line 2g)		0.
10	Investment income (Part VIII, column (A), lines 3, 4, and 7d)		0.
11	Other revenue (Part VIII, column (A), lines 5, 6d, 8c, 9c, 10c, and 11e)		0.
12	Total revenue - add lines 8 through 11 (must equal Part VIII, column (A), line 12)		1,042,274.
13	Grants and similar amounts paid (Part IX, column (A), lines 1-3)		0.
14	Benefits paid to or for members (Part IX, column (A), line 4)		0.
15	Salaries, other compensation, employee benefits (Part IX, column (A), lines 5-10)		403,658.
16a	Professional fundraising fees (Part IX, column (A), line 11e)		0.
b	Total fundraising expenses (Part IX, column (D), line 25) ▶ 57,544.		
17	Other expenses (Part IX, column (A), lines 11a-11d, 11f-24e)		333,074.
18	Total expenses. Add lines 13-17 (must equal Part IX, column (A), line 25)		736,732.
19	Revenue less expenses. Subtract line 18 from line 12		305,542.

		Beginning of Current Year	End of Year
20	Total assets (Part X, line 16)		354,539.
21	Total liabilities (Part X, line 26)		48,997.
22	Net assets or fund balances. Subtract line 21 from line 20		305,542.

Part II   Signature Block

Under penalties of perjury, I declare that I have examined this return, including accompanying schedules and statements, and to the best of my knowledge and belief, it is true, correct, and complete. Declaration of preparer (other than officer) is based on all information of which preparer has any knowledge.

Sign Here	▶ Signature of officer		Date
	▶ Russell Vought, President		
	Type or print name and title		

	Print/Type preparer's name	Preparer's signature	Date	Check ☐ if self-employed	PTIN
Paid Preparer Use Only	Daren Daiga	Daren Daiga	11/15/2022		P01074795
	Firm's name ▶ Capin Crouse, LLP			Firm's EIN ▶	36-3990892
	Firm's address ▶ 1330 Avenue of the Americas, Suite 23A New York, NY 10019			Phone no. 505-502-2746	

May the IRS discuss this return with the preparer shown above? See instructions   ☒ Yes ☐ No

132001 12-09-21   LHA **For Paperwork Reduction Act Notice, see the separate instructions.**   Form **990** (2021)

Extended to November 15, 2022

Form 990
Return of Organization Exempt From Income Tax
Under section 501(c), 527, or 4947(a)(1) of the Internal Revenue Code (except private foundations)

▶ Do not enter social security numbers on this form as it may be made public.
▶ Go to www.irs.gov/Form990 for instructions and the latest information.

2021

Open to Public Inspection

Department of the Treasury
Internal Revenue Service

A For the 2021 calendar year, or tax year beginning _____ and ending _____

B Check if applicable:	**C** Name of organization	**D** Employer identification number
[ ] Address change	Conservative Partnership Institute	82-1470217
[ ] Name change	Doing business as	
[ ] Initial return	Number and street (or P.O. box if mail is not delivered to street address) · Room/suite · **E** Telephone number	
[ ] Final return/terminated	300 Independence Ave SE · (202)742-8988	
[ ] Amended return	City or town, state or province, country, and ZIP or foreign postal code · **G** Gross receipts $ 45,707,730.	
[ ] Application pending	Washington, DC 20003	
	F Name and address of principal officer: Edward Corrigan	**H(a)** Is this a group return for subordinates? [ ] Yes [X] No
	same as C above	**H(b)** Are all subordinates included? [ ] Yes [ ] No

I Tax-exempt status: [X] 501(c)(3) [ ] 501(c)( ) ◀ (insert no.) [ ] 4947(a)(1) or [ ] 527

If "No," attach a list. See instructions

J Website: ▶ www.cpi.org

H(c) Group exemption number ▶

K Form of organization: [X] Corporation [ ] Trust [ ] Association [ ] Other ▶ **L** Year of formation: 2017 **M** State of legal domicile: DE

Part I | Summary

Activities & Governance

1 Briefly describe the organization's mission or most significant activities: **See Schedule O for complete mission statement.**

2 Check this box ▶ [ ] if the organization discontinued its operations or disposed of more than 25% of its net assets.

3	Number of voting members of the governing body (Part VI, line 1a)	3	7
4	Number of independent voting members of the governing body (Part VI, line 1b)	4	4
5	Total number of individuals employed in calendar year 2021 (Part V, line 2a)	5	31
6	Total number of volunteers (estimate if necessary)	6	4
7a	Total unrelated business revenue from Part VIII, column (C), line 12	7a	0.
b	Net unrelated business taxable income from Form 990-T, Part I, line 11	7b	0.

		Prior Year	Current Year
Revenue	8 Contributions and grants (Part VIII, line 1h)	7,106,027.	45,027,954.
	9 Program service revenue (Part VIII, line 2g)	15,485.	653,505.
	10 Investment income (Part VIII, column (A), lines 3, 4, and 7d)	3,776.	2,892.
	11 Other revenue (Part VIII, column (A), lines 5, 6d, 8c, 9c, 10c, and 11e)	-922,881.	23,379.
	12 Total revenue - add lines 8 through 11 (must equal Part VIII, column (A), line 12)	6,202,407.	45,707,730.
Expenses	13 Grants and similar amounts paid (Part IX, column (A), lines 1-3)	0.	3,907,356.
	14 Benefits paid to or for members (Part IX, column (A), line 4)	0.	0.
	15 Salaries, other compensation, employee benefits (Part IX, column (A), lines 5-10)	3,133,402.	4,654,508.
	16a Professional fundraising fees (Part IX, column (A), line 11e)	0.	0.
	b Total fundraising expenses (Part IX, column (D), line 25) ▶ 3,010,594.		
	17 Other expenses (Part IX, column (A), lines 11a-11d, 11f-24e)	2,815,192.	8,598,558.
	18 Total expenses. Add lines 13-17 (must equal Part IX, column (A), line 25)	5,948,594.	17,160,422.
	19 Revenue less expenses. Subtract line 18 from line 12	253,813.	28,547,308.

		Beginning of Current Year	End of Year
Net Assets or Fund Balances	20 Total assets (Part X, line 16)	2,629,044.	31,688,292.
	21 Total liabilities (Part X, line 26)	1,231,616.	1,611,496.
	22 Net assets or fund balances. Subtract line 21 from line 20	1,397,428.	30,076,796.

Part II | Signature Block

Under penalties of perjury, I declare that I have examined this return, including accompanying schedules and statements, and to the best of my knowledge and belief, it is true, correct, and complete. Declaration of preparer (other than officer) is based on all information of which preparer has any knowledge.

Sign Here	▶ *Ed Corrigan* Signature of officer	November 15, 2022 Date
	▶ Edward Corrigan, President and CEO Type or print name and title	

	Print/Type preparer's name	Preparer's signature	Date	Check [ ] if self-employed	PTIN
Paid Preparer Use Only	Hemali Kane, EA	HKane	11/15/22		P01337292
	Firm's name ▶ Rogers & Company PLLC			Firm's EIN ▶ 58-2676261	
	Firm's address ▶ 8300 Boone Boulevard, Suite 600 Vienna, VA 22182			Phone no. (703) 893-0300	

May the IRS discuss this return with the preparer shown above? See instructions [X] Yes [ ] No

132001 12-09-21 LHA **For Paperwork Reduction Act Notice, see the separate instructions.** Form **990** (2021)

See Schedule O for Organization Mission Statement Continuation

SCHEDULE I
(Form 990)

Department of the Treasury
Internal Revenue Service

OMB No 1545-0047

2021

Open to Public
Inspection

Grants and Other Assistance to Organizations, Governments, and Individuals in the United States

Complete if the organization answered "Yes" on Form 990, Part IV, line 21 or 22.

▶ Attach to Form 990.

▶ Go to www.irs.gov/Form990 for the latest information.

Name of the organization: Conservative Partnership Institute

Employer identification number: 82-1470217

Part I General Information on Grants and Assistance

1 Does the organization maintain records to substantiate the amount of the grants or assistance, the grantees' eligibility for the grants or assistance, and the selection criteria used to award the grants or assistance? .... [X] Yes [ ] No

2 Describe in Part IV the organization's procedures for monitoring the use of grant funds in the United States.

Part II Grants and Other Assistance to Domestic Organizations and Domestic Governments. Complete if the organization answered "Yes" on Form 990, Part IV, line 21, for any recipient that received more than $5,000. Part II can be duplicated if additional space is needed.

1 (a) Name and address of organization or government	(b) EIN	(c) IRC section (if applicable)	(d) Amount of cash grant	(e) Amount of noncash assistance	(f) Method of valuation (book, FMV, appraisal, other)	(g) Description of noncash assistance	(h) Purpose of grant or assistance
American Cornerstone Institute Inc 300 Independence Ave SE Washington, DC 20001	86-1545903	501(c)3	160,950.	0.			Mission and program support
American Accountability Foundation 300 Independence Ave SE Washington, DC 20003	85-4391204	501(c)3	335,100.	0.			Mission and program support
America First Legal Foundation 300 Independence Ave SE Washington, DC 20006	86-2190372	501(c)3	1,334,105.	0.			Mission and program support
American Moment Inc 300 Independence Ave SE Washington, DC 20003	85-1875789	501(c)3	336,000.	0.			Mission and program support
American Voting Rights Foundation 455 Carriage Lane Hudson, WI 54016	87-1891209	N/A	1,005,000.	0.			Mission and program support
Center for Renewing America 300 Independence Ave SE Washington, DC 20003	85-4307005	501(c)3	583,701.	0.			Mission and program support

2 Enter total number of section 501(c)(3) and government organizations listed in the line 1 table .... ▶ 7.

3 Enter total number of other organizations listed in the line 1 table .... ▶ 1.

LHA For Paperwork Reduction Act Notice, see the Instructions for Form 990.

Schedule I (Form 990) 2021

132101 10-26-21

313 of 315

Part II Continuation of Grants and Other Assistance to Domestic Organizations and Domestic Governments (Schedule I (Form 990), Part II.)

(a) Name and address of organization or government	(b) EIN	(c) IRC section if applicable	(d) Amount of cash grant	(e) Amount of noncash assistance	(f) Method of valuation (book, FMV, appraisal, other)	(g) Description of non-cash assistance	(h) Purpose of grant or assistance
Institute For Citizen Focused Service - PO Box 26141 - Alexandria, VA 22314	86-2967724	501(c)3	100,000.	0.			Mission and program support
Public Interest Legal Foundation Inc - 32 E. Washington St. - Indianapolis, IN 46204	45-4355641	501(c)3	50,000.	0.			Mission and program support

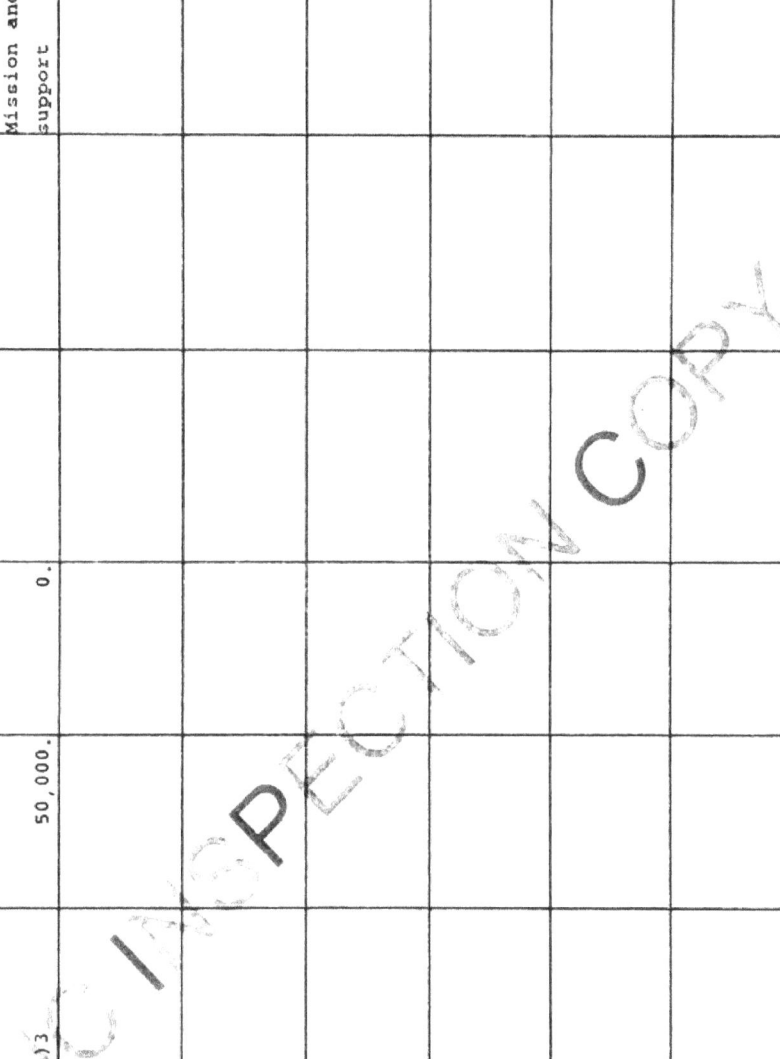

Schedule I (Form 990)

132241
11-18-21

Conservative Partnership Institute 82-1470217 Page 2

Part III | Grants and Other Assistance to Domestic Individuals. Complete if the organization answered "Yes" on Form 990, Part IV, line 22.
Part III can be duplicated if additional space is needed.

(a) Type of grant or assistance	(b) Number of recipients	(c) Amount of cash grant	(d) Amount of non-cash assistance	(e) Method of valuation (book, FMV, appraisal, other)	(f) Description of noncash assistance

Part IV | Supplemental Information. Provide the information required in Part I, line 2; Part III, column (b); and any other additional information.

Part I, Line 2:

Periodic reports of the use of grant awards are required of the grantee

organization's leadership to the management at Conservative Partnership

Institute.

315 of 315

32

132102 10-26-21

www.ingramcontent.com/pod-product-compliance
Lightning Source LLC
Chambersburg PA
CBHW080412270326
41929CB00018B/3000